Labour and the Political Economy in Israel

THE LIBRARY OF POLITICAL ECONOMY

POLITICAL ECONOMY is the old name for economics. In the hands of the great classical economists, particularly Smith, Ricardo and Marx, economics was the study of the working and development of the economic system in which men and women lived. Its practitioners were driven by a desire to describe, to explain and to evaluate what they saw around them. No sharp distinction was drawn between economic analysis and economic policy nor between economic behaviour and its interaction with the technical, social and political framework.

The Library of Political Economy has been established to provide widely based explanations of economic behaviour in contemporary society.

In examining the way in which new patterns of social organization and behaviour influence the economic system and policies for combating problems associated with growth, inflation, poverty and the distribution of wealth, contributors stress the link between politics and economics and the importance of institutions in policy formulation.

This 'open-ended' approach to economics implies that there are few laws that can be held to with certainty and, by the same token, there is no generally established body of theory to be applied in all circumstances. Instead economics as presented in this library provides a way of ordering events which has constantly to be updated and modified as new situations develop. This, we believe, is its interest and its challenge.

Volumes in the Library

Division of Labor and Welfare: An Introduction to Economic Systems—Louis Putterman
Dangerous Currents: The State of Economics—Lester Thurow
The Political Economy of Nationalism—Dudly Seers
Women's Claims: A Study in Political Economy—Lisa Peattie and Martin Rein
Urban Inequalities under State Socialism—Ivan Szelenyi
Social Innovation and the Division of Labour—Johnathan Gershuny
The Structuring of Labour Markets: A Comparative Analysis of the Steel and Construction Industries in Italy—Paola Villa
Monetarism and the Labour Market—Derek Robinson
Agrarian Impasse in Bengal: Institutional Constraints to Technological Change—James K. Boyce
Does Aid Work?—Robert Cassen and Associates

Labour and the Political Economy in Israel

Michael Shalev

OXFORD UNIVERSITY PRESS
1992

Oxford University Press. Walton Street. Oxford OX2 6DP
Oxford New York Toronto
Delhi Bombay Calcutta Madras Karachi
Petaling Jaya Singapore Hong Kong Tokyo
Nairobi Dar es Salaam Cape Town
Melbourne Auckland
and associated companies in
Berlin Ibadan

Oxford is a trade mark of Oxford University Press

Published in the United States
by Oxford University Press. New York

British Library Cataloguing in Publication Data
Data available

Library of Congress Cataloging-in-Publication Data
Shalev, Michael.
Labour and the political economy in Israel/Michael Shalev.
p. cm. — (The Library of political economy)
Includes bibliographical references and index.
1. Histadrut ha-kelalit shel ha' ovdim be-Erets-Yiśre 'el—History.
2. Trade-unions—Israel—History. 3. Industrial relations—Israel—History.
4. Israel—Economic policy. I. Title. II. Series.
HD8660.A5H584 1992 338.95694—dc20 91–25159
ISBN 0–19–828513–2

Typeset by Graphicraft Typesetters Ltd., Hong Kong
Printed in Great Britain by Bookcraft (Bath) Ltd, Midsomer Norton, Avon

Contents

Preface

My firsthand acquaintance with the subject-matter of this book dates back twenty years, to my immigration from New Zealand to Israel. After an interlude in Britain to complete a second degree, I began teaching courses at the Hebrew University on the labour market, the labour movement, and industrial relations. At the time I had but a limited capacity to read Hebrew sources, but by combing everything I could find in English I succeeded in presenting myself (in retrospect, not too convincingly) as an expert on the Israeli scene. Meanwhile, especially after moving to the University of Wisconsin to pursue a Ph.D. and an exciting collaboration with Walter Korpi, my interests became increasingly focused on comparative labour issues within the OECD bloc. Nevertheless, on returning to Israel in 1979, teaching responsibilities again made it imperative that I learn more about the Israeli scene. The more I did so, the more perplexed I became by the similarities and differences between Israel and the western nations.

While continuing in Israel the work I began abroad on comparative studies of strikes and public policy, I came increasingly to ask why it was that the success of the 'new political economy' in comprehending national variation between other rich capitalist democracies could not be replicated in Israel. In particular, although the political position and institutional structure of the labour movement were highly reminiscent of European social democracy, Israel's working class was deeply divided along national and ethnic lines, large parts of its labour relations system were rent by turbulence, and it was far from replicating the universalistic welfare states and relative economic stability attributed to social-democratic corporatism in Scandinavia and Austria. I began to see that this was a puzzle which could do more than challenge the assumptions and empirical findings of colleagues in Europe and North America about the correlates of social democracy and neo-corporatism. It could also help me, and other students of Israeli society, to grasp the nature of Israel's 'exceptionalism', and to better understand why its labour movement has so disappointed the hopes and expectations of intellectuals on the left.

My first forays into empirical research were aimed at assessing the labour market implications of the unseating of the long-entrenched Labour Party in the late 1970s.[1] The initial assumption of this research was that such a dramatic rightward swing in the composition of government as Israel's 'political upheaval' would likely result in a major increase in unemployment and place considerable strain on corporatist mechanisms of labour quiescence. Actual developments turned out to be far more complicated and interesting than this—although I would never have realized it without the hard work and inspired analyses of three graduate students with whom it was my privilege to work during this period: Yoni Reshef, Sara Leventhal (Shartal), and above all, Lev Grinberg. I also continued to pursue more informally the distinctiveness of the Israeli case by ferreting out and reinterpreting previous research. These efforts produced mountains of notes and several working papers, this time evaluating social policy, class voting, and industrial conflict.

In the autumn of 1983 my family and I left Israel for a sabbatical year in North America, where it was my intention to start bringing together the material I had by then accumulated into a critical, comparatively-oriented volume on the labour movement and industrial relations in Israel. I spent a lot of time during that sabbatical in mastering my first personal computer and other compelling pursuits which were only tangential to the book. One of the barriers to making more substantial headway was the feeling that I still had much to learn from untapped Israeli sources, especially so far as history (economic and political, as well as social) was concerned. Eventually this disquiet led me (and most of my contemporaries) to take the plunge into original archival research, a fascinating window on to Israel's pre-sovereignty era. This done, prodded by well-wishers and formal obligations alike, I made great efforts to bring the book to completion; but genuine progress awaited further opportunities to link Israeli questions to theoretical and comparative issues of a broader kind.

Happily, these opportunities were afforded by my participation in three stimulating collective endeavours—one a volume edited by Baruch Kimmerling, which encouraged me to take up more systematically the relations between Jewish and Palestinian labour; another an international study led by T. J. Pempel, which placed the Israeli case within the intriguing *problématique* of single-party dominance; and the third, a collection of macroscopic case studies of national domestic policy which was the brainchild of Frank Castles.[2] It was in writing the last of these essays that I became convinced that my study of the political economy of labour must inevitably lead to a concern with the growing power of capital in Israel's political economy. The work of another graduate student, Shimshon Bichler, was very helpful in developing this line of analysis.

By the summer of 1988 it was possible to lay out a first draft of the bulk of the book, but the tasks of integrating and sharpening the individual essays and adding introductory and concluding chapters remained daunting enough to appear insurmountable. Thanks to the perceptive suggestions and willing emotional and moral support of my wife, Debby Shalev, and my friend Gershon Shafir, and with the help of the astute editorial skills of Jon Simons, the book finally began the transition to a finished product. This product is a different one, in my view a better one, than what it was in my power to achieve five years ago. The freedom to improve (and the liberty to agonize!) would not have been mine without the support both of my publishers (specifically, Andrew Schuller of OUP) and my colleagues. The latter deserve an especially honourable mention, for I have consistently enjoyed their backing despite not only broken deadlines, but also my unabashedly critical stance towards some of their work.

In addition to those individuals already mentioned by name, in the course of my research and writing I have also had the benefit of the counsel of a great many other colleagues in Israel and abroad. Limitations of both space and memory prohibit a full accounting, but I would like to take this opportunity of expressing my gratitude to Leah Baider, Mike Barnett, Joel Beinin, Debbie Bernstein, Bob Brym, Naomi Chazan, Colin Crouch, Shmuel Eisenstadt, John Goldthorpe, Nachum Gross, Shmuel Hadar, Niamh Hardiman, Shlomo Hasson, Joan Hooper, Peter Katzenstein, Walter Korpi, Ralph Kramer, Peter Lange, Moshe Lissak, Peter Medding, Frances Piven, Jonas Pontusson, Ada Poraz, Marino Regini, Martin Rein, Andy Rosenhek, Dietrich Rueschemeyer, Zvi Schuldiner, Adam Seligman, Yonathan Shapiro, Ira Sharkansky, Arie Shirom, David Soskice, George Strauss, Sid Tarrow, Goran Therborn, Lloyd Ulman, Samuel Valenzuela, Avraham Zloczower, and Elia Zureik.

I dedicate this book to my parents, Eve and Syd Silver, and my children, Daniel, Inbal, and Avinoam. Their fate has to a very large extent been shaped by my original decision to make Israel my home. The Shalev and Silver families have experienced many joyful occasions in this country, but we have also found much in its social and political landscape which is ugly and painful. This book is in a sense a personal attempt to come to terms with these disappointments by better understanding them. I will be much encouraged if it also succeeds in shedding some revelatory light for those who are close to me.

Michael Shalev

Jerusalem,
November 1990

Notes

1. I gratefully acknowledge the financial support made available to these studies by the Ford Foundation (through its Israel Trustees), the Institute for the Study of Labour and Society (Tel Aviv University), and the Levi Eshkol Institute (Hebrew University). The major findings of these research projects appear in Chapter 5, much of which is based on an article originally published in Hebrew in a journal of critical sociology edited by Deborah Bernstein and Shlomo Swirski (Shalev, 1984). Subsequently, an abbreviated English version of this study appeared under the title 'Labour, State and Crisis: An Israeli Case Study' in *Industrial Relations*, 23(3), Fall 1984, 362–86.
2. I wish to acknowledge the kind co-operation of both the editors and publishers of the papers which developed out of these three projects in allowing me to draw freely upon them in this book. Specifically, I would like to thank Baruch Kimmerling and the State University of New York Press for the use in Chapter 2 of material from Shalev (1989*a*); T. J. Pempel and Cornell University Press for permission to base Chapter 3 on Shalev (1990*b*); and Francis G. Castles and Polity Press for allowing major portions of Shalev (1989*b*) to be introduced into Chapters 6 and 7.

A Note on Language

All translations from Hebrew were made by the author. Bibliographical references to publications in Hebrew have been handled in the usual way. Titles are translated into English and marked parenthetically as 'in Hebrew', whereas the names of journals and publishing houses are transliterated. In the body of the text Hebrew terms (except for the proper names of some institutions) have been translated into English, in order to minimize the burden on readers without a knowledge of Hebrew. For instance, *va'ad ovdim* in Hebrew is referred to as workers' committee, whereas we preserve the Hebrew title of the central labour organization (the *Histadrut*).

Where it was necessary to make transliterations the guiding principle was that they should be intuitively meaningful to the non-specialized reader. In this spirit the guttural Hebrew letter 'chet' is represented, in the Germanic style, by 'ch'. An illustration is our spelling of the name of the *Cherut* (Freedom) Party, often misleadingly rendered as Herut. Our conventions were, however, suspended in instances where there was a conflict with the customary Latin spelling adopted by authors and other persons referred to by name. Finally, while some foreign terms in other languages have been italicized, in order to avoid excessive use of emphasis Hebrew transliterations—except for their very first occurrence in the text—have not been italicized, with the exception of the index. Hebrew terms are capitalized, however, with the exception of 'kibbutz', a word which has become incorporated into standard English usage.

List of Figures

List of Tables

Introduction

From the vantage point of 1990, the labour movement of Israel is a story of success turned to failure. The Labour Party, unseated in 1977 after more than four decades of hegemony, has been condemned to choosing between uneasy partnership with the right or abdication from government. The Party long ago exhausted the immense prestige it once enjoyed as the result of its responsibility for the achievement of Jewish statehood and the state's successful defence against both external attack and the internal strains of mass immigration and economic development. Even Labour's control of the national workers' organization, the *Histadrut*, is no longer secure. And the Histadrut itself has been immeasurably weakened by grass-roots alienation and a decade and a half of right-wing or coalition governments. The membership of the labour organization is stagnant or dwindling and large sections of the vast economic empire which was once a cornerstone of the Histadrut's power are currently in a state of collapse. Finally, the labour movement's ideological programme, a moderate synthesis of labourism and nationalism, has become increasingly remote from the centre of political discourse. Neither Labour, now predominantly a middle-class party, nor the Histadrut, which excludes from its ranks Israel's Palestinian proletariat, can credibly claim the mantle of socialism. Worse still for its political fortunes, the Labour Party's nationalist credentials and its authority on issues of peace and security have been compromised by its own contradictions and indecisiveness and the rise of fundamentalist Zionism.

It is not the purpose of this book to recount the story of these ongoing processes of institutional breakdown and political decline. Instead, we seek to provide sufficient historical breadth, and analytical depth, to make possible a more persuasive understanding of these failures than offered by previous scholarship. The essential historical context, for our purposes, is the period between the turn of the twentieth century and Israel's attainment of sovereignty in 1948. In these years some half-a-million Jewish settlers reached the shores of Palestine.[1] Some of them immigrated solely out of Zionist conviction, but most were in flight from rising nationalism, anti-

Semitism, and shrinking economic opportunities and turned to Palestine because other destinations were closed to them. The ranks of the first wave of Jewish immigrants in this century (the Second *Aliyah*) included the architects and many of the future leaders of the labour movement. These newcomers were self-styled pioneers who saw their move both in terms of personal redemption and as part of an ambitious political project, to defend and 'normalize' the Jews as a nation by resettling them in their historic homeland, ultimately as a politically autonomous community. Most regarded themselves as socialists, but they rejected the predominant view in Jewish-socialist circles that the 'Jewish problem' would be solved in Russia and Europe, in the universalistic context of class struggle. Rather, it was up to the Jews themselves to create a just and socially balanced society, and this they could achieve only in their own land.[2]

In addition to this ideological common ground, the newcomers of the pioneering era shared a number of economic traits. They had little or no financial means (even though the parents they left behind were typically *petit bourgeois*) and such human capital as they possessed was of nugatory economic value in Ottoman Palestine. The lands of Zion were too expensive for independent settlement, while even the limited market for manual labour among Jewish employers was fully supplied, in most cases by Arabs whose labour was considerably cheaper than that of the immigrants. The colonists thus faced problems of sheer survival which were initially so devastating that all but a small minority either returned home or sought alternative destinations. Those who remained embarked upon experiments in institution-building which have lent the labour movement in Israel an enduring specificity.[3] One of these innovations, which in many respects crystallized the accumulated experience of the Second Aliyah, was the umbrella organization of Jewish workers called the Histadrut—in full, the General Organization of Workers in the Land of Israel. The founding of the Histadrut represented a marriage between organized Zionism—a settlement movement without settlers, and the propertyless pioneers—a workers' movement without work.

Many of the social scientists who have studied the labour movement in Israel have been preoccupied by its affiliated rural settlements, both collectives (kibbutzim) and co-operative villages (*moshavim*). This study, however, is solely concerned with the

Histadrut and the associated Labour Party historically known as *Mapai*. Our focus on the organizational and political activity of Israeli labour reflects not only a desire to redress the present imbalance in the literature; it is also a *theoretical choice*. For, from the perspective of the 'new political economy'—which studies working-class mobilization and its links to politics and the economy in the capitalist democracies of the West—labour unions and parties are the actors of central concern.

In the words of one of its leading practitioners (Goldthorpe, 1984: 1, 3–4), the ultimate motivation of the new political economy has been a timely interest in examining 'the effect on the performance of modern economies of the political systems with which they are enmeshed and, in turn, of the larger social structures and processes which comprehend economy and polity alike'. Lying at the forefront of these broader structures and processes are 'the divisions and conflicts between groups and classes (and their organizations, movements and parties) which are inseparable from the workings of a capitalist economy'. On the basis of these theoretical assumptions, a growing body of conceptual and empirical work has argued that strong national labour organizations, working in tandem with governing socialist parties, generate distinctive state policies and structures—with two noteworthy consequences: (*a*) a viable class compromise which serves workers' interests and simultaneously reinforces the power and solidarity of the labour movement; and (*b*) a framework for concerted action among the state and 'peak associations' of labour and capital which provides a societal cushion against disruptive forces, including the strains of global economic crisis.

From the standpoint of the Israeli case, the political economy of labour raises a series of questions which have thus far been absent from research agendas yet hold great promise of clarifying and explaining the distinctiveness of the labour movement of Israel and making it more accessible to international scholarship. This book endeavours to take up this task and, in the process, to develop a fresh perspective for students of Israeli society and its contemporary dilemmas and contradictions. The specific concerns considered in this study are motivated both by a substantive interest in telling untold stories about Israel and by theoretical issues drawn from the political–economic analysis of labour movements and industrial relations. In principle, the book could have been structured in terms of either one of these agendas, but only to the disadvantage of one or the other of its intended audiences. We therefore chose a framework which is partly chronological, but primarily issue-based. Because most chapters are self-contained essays dealing with discrete puzzles, those who wish to track the course of a specific phenomenon over the entire span of the study will sometimes find it necessary to locate their topic anew in several different chapters. But most of these loose threads are tied together by cross-references and, more explicitly, in the concluding chapter of the book.

In the remainder of this introduction we will do two things. One is to elucidate more specifically the theoretical and comparative issues—drawn from the study of *social-democratic corporatism*—framing the six chapters which form the core of the volume. The other is to explain why the analytical perspective and specific universe of comparison adopted in this study are especially well suited to analysis of the Israeli case. These discussions will not exhaust the ambitions of the book or the full complement of the theoretical building blocks with which it has been constructed. Rather, the latter will be introduced in the context of individual chapters, and reviewed in the conclusions.

In the 1970s, in the context of significant and largely unanticipated developments in politics and industrial relations in the capitalist democracies of the West, interest in both social democracy and 'neo-corporatism'[4] mushroomed. During roughly the first two post-war decades macro-social trends, which included rapid economic growth, the political incorporation or quiescence of labour parties, and what appeared to some as a 'withering away' of industrial conflict, gave rise to a conception of class conflict as being increasingly isolated from both economic and political forces. In the pluralistic-industrialism or convergence perspective which came to predominate in American social science, industrial relations were viewed as a distinguishable subsystem of society relatively detached from the political economy at large. Leading scholars in the field were preoccupied with designing more effective institutional arrangements for collective bargaining and the settlement of disputes between workers and employers. The political aspirations and struggles of workers as a class were widely regarded as having been dulled by their integration as citizens and fragmented through the prism of pluralistic politics—having thus become largely irrelevant to trade unions and the practice of industrial relations.[5]

With the undermining of established forms of class accommodation in the Western nations during the third post-war decade, labour movements and labour relations once again became a central concern of scholarship and policy debate. The simultaneous strike and wage explosions of the late 1960s revived class and related distributional struggles as a major economic and political issue.[6] In the 1970s this problem was confounded by the added economic strains introduced by intensified global competition and sharp energy and commodity price rises. The growing economic and political strength of organized labour during the post-war period and the accompanying entrenchment of the full-employment welfare state, were now seen as carrying the capacity to destabilize societies organized around capitalist market economies and liberal-democratic politics. Observers of widely differing ideological persuasions argued that labour's enhanced position had generated a structural potential for inflationary wage pressure, political disorder, and fiscal crisis. It followed that the striking cross-country variations in the extent to which different nations proved vulnerable to crisis were linked to the characteristics of labour movements and their position in the political economy.[7]

This is the context in which the synthetic model that we call 'social-democratic corporatism' (hereafter, SDC) came to prominence. The social-democratic parties of the West may be identified simply enough by their ideological commitment to nonrevolutionary parliamentary socialism and their institutional affiliation to the Socialist International.[8] However, in this book we use the term social democracy more narrowly, as a shorthand for its most 'advanced' carriers—those reformist socialist parties which are virtually unchallenged on the left of the political spectrum, enjoy a large electoral following, more or less continuously participate as leading or coequal members of the political executive, and are closely linked to a trade union movement which embraces a majority of the wage earners. Although individual components of this syndrome are present in a fair number of the Western nations, the only ones which embodied *all* of them through most of the post-war period are Sweden, Norway, Austria—and Israel.[9]

'Corporatism' is a far more complex and contested concept. Indeed, much of the vast literature on the subject which has emerged since the pioneering work of Philippe Schmitter and his associates has been devoted to debating just what corporatism means. For the majority of theorists, it is a metaphor for a particular style of interest-group organization and/or public policy-making which characterizes the polities of Continental Europe and Scandinavia, particularly the smaller ones.[10] In this study, however, we are more narrowly interested in applications of the corporatist model to the bi- and trilateral relations between labour movements, organized business interests, and the state. The literature is also divided on the issue of whether the defining characteristics of corporatism are to be sought in behavioural outcomes, cultural and ideological characteristics, or institutional structures.[11] Our preference is to treat these criteria as empirically contingent corollaries. The essence of corporatist industrial relations, in our view, is that national trade union élites undertake to co-ordinate and limit worker demands on the basis of understandings or agreements with the state and organized employers.[12] By these criteria, it is apparent that within the nations of the OECD bloc, corporatism overlaps only partially with social democracy. The mature social democracies of Western Europe and Israel are in fact but one subset of the corporatist universe. The other is to be found in Germany, the Low Countries, and those of the Scandinavian nations in which social democracy has fallen short of hegemony, but corporatist tendencies are nevertheless evident.

Now that the intellectual context and terms of reference of social-democratic corporatism have been defined, we shall introduce a range of propositions which enjoy widespread currency in the literature on SDC and which this book employs as provocative starting-points for analysis of the Israeli case. In all, six 'stylized facts' are considered, each of which presents a striking contrast to the Israeli experience.

1. *In the beginning, there was class solidarity.* Social-democratic theory holds that neither of the institutional pillars of SDC—a single, major left-wing party which garners most of the working-class vote and a single or dominating labour organization with a high degree of internal authority—are possible without a solidaristic tradition of trade unionism.[13] Only what have been called 'class-oriented' union movements are likely to achieve organizational centralization of authority at the peak and a high level of

mass political identification at the base. The establishment of the Histadrut indeed signified the early emergence of a class-oriented and highly corporate (unitary and centralized) form of worker organization. But the Zionist labour movement was permeated by the ambition of achieving economic, political, and organizational isolation of Jews from Arabs—especially the Arab working class. This conjunction of external segregation with internal solidarity presents a puzzle, particularly since many of the principals of the Zionist labour movement claimed to be acting in the name of socialist values.

The obvious solution to this puzzle is that in Palestine, working-class unity was simply swept aside by the 'cross-cutting' effect of the Arab–Jewish conflict. Yet, despite the persistence of the national conflict after the creation of a sovereign state of Israel, the Histadrut chose to incorporate partially the Arab citizens of Israel—only to subsequently close its doors to the Palestinians of the West Bank and Gaza after their territories were occupied by Israel in 1967. In Chapter 2 we explore how these shifting positions in the stance of organized Jewish labour towards the Palestinians can be interpreted in the context of changing political and economic circumstances. In doing so we aim to show that the strategic choices made by the Zionist labour movement can be analysed in terms of generic theories which go beyond the specific *problématique* of class and nationality in Palestine and Israel.

2. *Out of solidarity came hegemony*. Socialist parties have become entrenched in government only when workers overwhelmingly vote for them. At the same time because the workers' ballots are never sufficient to win an electoral majority, labour parties with a will to govern are compelled to seek allies from outside the working class. Accordingly, the success of a labour party that aspires to political hegemony depends not on sacrificing appeals to the working class and its solidarity, but on the continued viability of these appeals in the face of political co-operation with outsiders. Solidaristic labour organizations play a crucial role in this context by mobilizing voters and resources behind socialist parties and immunizing their followers against dilution of working-class consciousness. In all, this is a recipe for political dominance which stands in pointed contrast to the typical underpinnings of right-wing hegemony. Successful parties of the right emphasize interests and allegiances which run inside or across class lines; and they rely heavily on

particularistic and nakedly instrumental incentives to mobilize popular support.[14]

Despite its electoral dependence on the loyalty of voters affiliated to a central labour organization, the Labour Party of Israel came to rest on a strikingly multi-class base. In its earlier years the labour movement indeed adopted the social-democratic political strategy of enfolding workers within a class-oriented community. But it combined this strategy with reliance on material incentives and appeals to supra-class (national) loyalties. These additional strings to Mapai's bow became especially prominent after statehood was achieved, when the party became increasingly detached from its labouristic past—but none the less remained entrenched in a position of dominance. Chapter 3 is an attempt to interpret the evolving bases of Labour Party hegemony, both before and after sovereignty. Our purpose is not only to place some central features of Israel's political history in historical context, but also to show how they may be fruitfully analysed from a political-economy perspective which takes off from key insights of the social-democratic model.

3. *Out of incumbency came class compromise*. One of the theoretically and politically most important implications of social-democratic corporatism refutes a key prediction made by both Marx and Engels and the post-war advocates of liberal pluralism. Where it occurred, the political ascendancy of workers' parties brought with it not an intensification or revolutionary culmination of labour militancy, but a distinctly peaceful truce in the class war. Once the state apparatus was firmly in the hands of a labour-movement party, social democracy became wedded to corporatism and fiercely combative class relations were eclipsed by what has been termed a 'historic compromise' between organized labour and capital.[15]

By the 1930s the Jewish labour movement in Palestine met the accepted theoretical prerequisites for such a compact between the class representatives of labour and capital. Yet despite repeated initiatives by the Zionist authorities throughout the inter-war period, no formal class compromise was achieved and industrial relations continued to be conducted in a highly decentralized framework. Chapter 4 sets out to resolve this paradox by means of an analysis of the political economy which goes beyond the conventional stress on the strength of labour unions and parties. This analysis is intended not only to sharpen our understanding of the conditions for corporatist compromises. It also provides an overall portrait of capitalism, the labour market, and the state in the Jewish community of Palestine.

4. *Social-democratic corporatism and the crisis of full employment.* Sustained full employment has been the core economic-policy priority of stable left-wing governments. Partisans of SDC interpret this as an effective response to both the economic pre-conditions for corporatism and the political requirements of social democracy. On the one hand, full employment constitutes an essential quid pro quo for union restraint and on the other, a means of minimizing divisions among workers and encouraging their loyalty to 'the party of full employment'. Sceptics have argued, however, that without the discipline of unemployment, worker assertiveness might reach the point of undermining profitability and challenging the authority of employers, unions, and labour parties alike.[16]

Chapter 5 is a case study of precisely such a 'crisis of full employment'. This crisis precipitated a deep recession which was, in part, a thinly veiled attempt to reinstate labour discipline by the whip of joblessness. This raises the question of why an entrenched Labour government and a corporatist peak association of labour would resort to a policy which is seemingly incompatible with the logic of SDC. As in the previous chapter, we find that resolving the paradox calls for a wide-ranging analysis of the political economy and its evolution.

5. *Consequences of social-democratic corporatism for social policy and economic performance.* Although its critics have justly disputed the socialist potential of social democracy, two important claims on its behalf are empirically unimpeachable. One is that the full-employment welfare state has achieved its fullest elaboration under long-standing social-democratic governments. The other is that this is a pattern of domestic policy which significantly curtails (while very far from abolishing) the economic insecurities and inequalities which are the burden of wage-earners in a capitalist economy. In turn, favourable public policies encourage workers to respect class compromise and contribute thereby to the governability of capitalist economies by working-class parties. This has been especially important at times when the chips are down—most notably in the 1970s when SDC provided unusually effective insulation against economic destabilization. Moreover, by reinforcing

working-class solidarity the social and economic policies characteristic of successful Labour governments also help to reproduce their own political hegemony.[17]

A number of the policy preferences and outcomes characteristic of other social-democratic and corporatist settings are missing from the Israeli variant of SDC. This is true of the size and character of the welfare state, the level of distributive conflict, and, above all, of Israel's record concerning economic growth and price stability in the wake of the economic 'shocks' of the 1970s. We argue in Chapter 6 that in many respects these divergences are symptoms of the historical and institutional peculiarities of the Israeli setting discussed in previous chapters. We also explain how the exhaustion of earlier sources of strength in Israel's political economy can account for the state's disastrous management of the economic crisis.

6. *Social-democratic corporatism and the structural power of capital.* Socialist movements historically aspired to eliminate altogether the uniquely privileged role of capitalists in private-property market economies. One of the hallmarks of social democracy is its strategic premise of coexistence with capital on the basis of 'political control of the economy'. The assumption is that governing left parties can shape patterns of capital accumulation and income distribution so as to defend workers' material interests without either economic or political disruption. To enjoy such steering capacities, however, the state must attain some measure of autonomy from business interests.[18]

In Chapter 7 we propose the thesis that the decline of this autonomy lay at the very heart of the crises which shook Israel's political economy in the 1970s and beyond—the Labour Party's eviction from office and the peaking, not long thereafter, of a hyper-inflationary spiral which could have had a tragic ending for democracy as well as economic stability in Israel. Paradoxically, in the early years of Israel's existence the economic autonomy of the state had been remarkably pronounced as a result of its almost exclusive control of the major sources of accumulation. Chapter 7 traces what happened in the intervening years to reverse the balance of power between capital and the state, and why it was so consequential for the state's ability to steer processes of economic adjustment.

A comparative perspective is essential for meeting the concerns of the two audiences at whom this book is targeted. Those who wish to comprehend national uniqueness cannot afford to fall victim to insularity. Accordingly, we believe that readers, for whom an understanding of the Israeli case is intrinsically important, will find that viewing it on a broader cross-national canvas facilitates both the formulation of new puzzles and the development of new understandings of familiar concerns. At the same time, parochialism must also be transcended in order to situate the Israeli case in terms which will permit its more informed inclusion in the research efforts of comparative political economists.

Students of Israeli society seeking to locate it in a wider context often fall victim to the temptation either to over-emphasize Israel's uniqueness or to exaggerate its equivalence to more familiar settings. In the first of these categories, sympathetic observers of the Zionist labour movement have frequently attributed a kind of 'Israeli exceptionalism' to their subject. This is true for instance of the argument that because the Jewish worker-pioneers were committed to socialist values and Jewish national revival, it would be inappropriate to look for parallels with other circumstances in which settlers have displaced natives or 'cheap' labour has been forcibly excluded from high-wage jobs.[19] By employing adjectives like 'social-democratic' and 'corporatist' without sufficient qualification, other scholars make the reverse error of implying an unfounded affinity between the labour movements and state/society relations of Israel and Europe.[20] But however inconvenient, it is unfortunately true that in discussing labour unions and parties in Israel, when we say union we don't exactly mean union, when we say left we do not mean left, and even when we say labour we may not really mean labour.

Whether because they recognize the limitations of analogies between Israel and other developed capitalist democracies or as the result simply of a paucity of information, comparative researchers have typically excluded Israel from their studies. This is unfortunate for the very reason that providing their contextual peculiarities are recognized, 'deviant' cases can be a source of great insight in cross-national research. This should certainly be true of Israel where the power, scope, and politicization of the labour movement in its heyday are exemplary from the perspective of SDC, yet at the same time there is a far from neat conformity to many of the model's expectations. In such an instance the meeting between case and model is a source of paradoxes with the potential to enrich general theory. It is our expectation, therefore, that as well as offering empirical grist for others' mills, this book will furnish some modest theoretical lessons for the comparative analysis of labour and the political economy in OECD countries. It should be made clear, however, that the present study is not an analytical exercise in the strictly deductive tradition of aspiring to 'confirm' or 'disprove' an a priori model. We rarely compare Israel directly with other nations, relying instead on comparative scholarship primarily as a resource for posing questions.[21]

It may legitimately be asked, however, whether the rich democracies of the West are the most appropriate frame of reference for a comparatively informed study of the labour movement and industrial relations in Israel. One obvious point of disparity is that politics in Israel are preoccupied by acute existential issues of national identity, security, and boundary-drawing. Israel is also less advanced in economic terms, and its prosperity has always depended heavily on capital accumulated beyond the country's borders. These and other characteristics potentially invite comparison to quite different contexts to that chosen for this study. For example, the labour movement's emergence prior to either the formation of a democratic regime or the growth of an industrial capitalist economy and the primacy it afforded to national revival and state-building goals in working-class mobilization are reminiscent of the experience of 'new nations' in the Third World. Alternatively, Beverly Silver (1990) has recently argued that at least two hallmarks of Israel's political economy—the primacy of the state *vis-à-vis* 'both dominant and subordinate classes and groups' and its success in controlling resource inflows and outflows by 'non-market mechanisms'—are typical of nations located on the semi-periphery of the world economy.

Perspectives such as these may well prove to be fruitful alternatives to our own—although we suspect that just as Israel itself cannot be neatly pigeonholed, so no single universe should monopolize the project of advancing understanding through comparison. Certainly, Israel's political institutions, its economic system, and international orientation, as well as its labour movement, evince a marked family resemblance to the nations of the OECD bloc. But in the final analysis, our decision to formulate the puzzles of the Israeli case in relation to the historical experience and intellectual traditions of those nations must be judged by the relevance of the questions asked and the plausibility of the answers offered.

This book has been conceived as a contribution to an ongoing process of intellectual renewal in Israeli social science. The main lines of our approach—which may be termed 'critical political economy'—are well established in the scholarly community at large, but for the most part have only recently emerged in Israel. We label the approach 'critical' because it is committed to challenging the interpretations and conceptual categories of conventional scholarship (while reserving the right to build upon its undeniable contribution to the accumulation of knowledge). By 'political economy' we mean the study of how political and economic forces interact to shape social processes. Critical political economy may no doubt seek justification on its own merits, but it provides a perspective which is *especially* well suited to a study of Israel and its labour movement.

One reason why this is so is the complacency of the mainstream literature. If one can point to a single, overriding impression left by what was once the dominant school of Israeli sociology, it is the idea of a difficult job having been well done—an accolade awarded above all to the vanguard of Israeli nation- and state-building, the labour movement.[22] According to this image, the seeds of Israeli society were planted by the vision of the Second Aliyah pioneers and their translation of this vision into both individual sacrifice and collective action. After sovereignty was achieved, the leaders of the labour movement were transformed into a state-building élite which successfully met new external and domestic challenges. As could only be expected, however, over time both the *élan* of the leaders and the solidarity of the mass of Israelis were sapped by what Eisenstadt (1985: 564) has called 'the routinization and demystification of the original revolutionary vision'. According to Horowitz and Lissak (1989: 241, 238), a further toll was exacted by the growth of internal 'primordial cleavages' rooted in conflicting beliefs and identities, and the strains of adapting to wars and other 'external historical events'.

This account is profoundly conservative. It echoes the official version of history and the self-image of the founding fathers. It presents an evolutionary view of history that resonates well with the functionalist theoretical perspective of its proponents. It erects a firm dividing line between the 'utopian' or 'revolutionary' prehistory of Israeli society and the mundane and disappointing realities of more recent times. It places enormous weight on ideology and leadership as sources of social transformation, leaving little room for economic conflicts and constraints. It conceives of ethnic tensions as reflecting cultural divisions rather than distributive struggles and views the national conflict between Arabs and Jews as a challenge to Israeli society from beyond its walls, rather than as an endogenous dynamic deeply implicated in the very constitution of that society.

The mainstream view of Israeli society is not the only one represented in Israeli social science, and in the last two decades its hegemony has been seriously challenged. In the 1970s, in the face of painful evidence of social inequality, political turmoil, and military and economic vulnerability several strands of intellectual insurgency arose to challenge accepted thinking. Much of this work produced revisionist histories which cast the labour movement élite in a quite unflattering light. Critical scholarship was also driven by the search for theoretical alternatives to a sociological orthodoxy which had plainly failed to reckon with the conflicts and inequalities accompanying nation- and state-building and capitalist economic development.[23] Israel's invasion of Lebanon, its continuing occupation of the West Bank and Gaza, and the intense political polarization surrounding these issues lent a further impetus to critical social science in the 1980s. Not surprisingly, the major new focus of concern was the national conflict and its manifold ramifications for the formation and development of Israeli society.[24] In a related development, Jewish scholars expressed growing interest in the position of the Palestinians in Israel and the occupied territories, traditionally the 'invisible men' of Israeli social science.[25]

This book has been influenced by these critical projects in at least three ways. The first of these is our decision to *focus on the limits and contradictions* of the familiar achievements of the labour movement and the state-building élite in Israel. That is why we have chosen to underscore the national exclusivism of the Zionist labour movement rather than its role in national reconstruction, the weaknesses rather than the strengths of consensus-building in the pre-state Jewish community, the inadequacies of corporatist labour restraint rather than its contributions to growth and stability, and the puzzles posed by contemporary economic crises rather than those connected to the accomplishments of an earlier era. Second, the task of *rewriting and reinterpreting history* seems to us to be particularly pressing in relation to the labour movement—not least because many earlier works on its origins and formative development are tainted by their authors' internalization of the movement's own myths.[26] In defining the questions which require a return to history we have sought to break with the prevailing retrospective view of the past and concentrate instead on roads that were not taken[27]—why no 'historic compromise', why the failure of the socialist left, why did Labour governments choose to nurture big business and to discipline the working class by unemployment? Third, in this study *the national conflict is crucial, as both dependent and independent variable.* That is, the conflict is seen as the source of much that is distinctive about the Israeli case and, at the same time, as a factor so closely imbricated with the political and economic dynamics of Israeli society that it is in part explicable *by* them.

Beyond these general similarities to the overall thrust of critical social science in Israel, what singles out this work is its embrace of *political economy* as an analytical starting-point.[28] This has called for a determined effort to break down the brittle disciplinary boundary isolating the study of politics and the economy. Scholarship in Israel has respected this division of labour for too long, failing to recognize—or if recognizing, failing to theorize—interconnections between the two spheres.[29] No less regrettably, the study of labour relations has developed as yet another seemingly autonomous terrain, heavily influenced by the applied orientation and absorption in institutional detail characteristic of the Anglo-American tradition.

This book adopts the alternative of a macroscopic perspective on labour organization and industrial relations, turning for inspiration to some of the central questions animating the Marxist tradition: what are the forces which advance and retard the solidarity of the working class; under what circumstances can labour movements succeed in wielding state power by democratic means; if they do succeed, what are the consequences for class conflict and the rule of capital? To pose such questions dispassionately is necessarily to take issue with the voluntaristic conception of social change which is a legacy of both Zionist ideology in general, and the Labour Zionist variant of socialism.[30] The inevitable result of equating politics with ideology and acts with intentions is that analysis of conflicts and contradictions becomes imprisoned within the theoretically barren *problématique* of why 'reality' fails to conform to the ideals held by the founding fathers. But ideologies are themselves an integral element of the social reality that it is the task of social science to explain. At this stage in the development of our understanding of Israeli society, realist analyses of the kind offered by political economy offer the greatest potential for enlightenment.

Notes

1. Information on Jewish immigration, Arab displacement and other features of Israel's 'political demography' may be found in Appendix 1.
2. For standard introductions to Zionist history and ideology see Laqueur (1972) and Hertzberg (1966). On Jewish labour politics in Europe and Russia, see Peled (1989*b*); Frankel (1981); and Brym (1978).
3. The most insightful discussions of these historical experiments are those of Kimmerling (1983*b*) and Shafir (1989).
4. The prefix 'neo' is one of several (others are 'liberal' or 'democratic') intended to convey that the revival of the corporatist model refers to its contemporary manifestations in the liberal-democratic societies of the West.
5. See, among others, Kerr *et al.* (1960); Dunlop (1958); Lipset (1981 [1960]); Kornhauser, Dubin, and Ross (1959). The thesis of a 'withering away of the strike' was proposed by Ross and Hartman (1960).
6. Barkin (1975); Crouch and Pizzorno (1978).
7. Many of the leading cross-national studies in this vein appeared in the following edited volumes: Lindberg, Crouch, and Offe (1975); Hirsch and Goldthorpe (1978); Castles (1982); Goldthorpe (1984); Lindberg and Maier (1985); Keman, Paloheimo and Whiteley (1987); and Castles, Lehner, and Schmidt (1988).
8. Paterson and Thomas (1977).
9. See Korpi and Shalev (1980: 317) for a summary of these characteristics of labour movements in the OECD countries. In subsequent discussion of the advanced social democracies of Western Europe,

we follow the convention of implicitly casting Sweden as their leading exemplar. We are, however, aware that in many respects the Austrian case (like Israel, although less dramatically) reveals the limitations of a 'Swedo-centric' view.

10. Schmitter (1974); Schmitter and Lehmbruch (1979); Lehmbruch and Schmitter (1982); Katzenstein (1985).
11. For some representative interventions in this debate see Martin (1983); Crouch (1983); and Cox (1988).
12. Among the most influential applications of corporatism to industrial relations and class conflict are those of Crouch (1977;1982*b*;1985); Panitch (1986); Regini (1982; 1984); and Streeck (1981;1984). The economic trade-off under corporatism has been articulated in a variety of theorizations, including Przeworksi's (1985) concept of 'class compromise' and Flanagan, Soskice, and Ulman's (1983) notion of 'variable bargaining intensity'. The classic analysis of 'political exchange' between organized labour and the state is that of Pizzorno (1978). Marks (1986) is among those who have emphasized the variety of institutional arrangements consistent with corporatist industrial relations.
13. For discussions of the conditions for working-class solidarity see Rokkan (1970); Griffin, O'Connell, and McCammon (1989); and Shalev and Korpi (1980).
14. On the conditions for social-democratic hegemony see Przeworksi (1985); Korpi (1978); Castles (1978); and Pontusson (1990). A variety of case studies of one-party dominance, both left and right, are collected in Pempel (1989).
15. See Korpi (1983) and Korpi and Shalev (1980); and for dissenting interpretations of the Swedish compromise, Therborn (1985: 587–9) and Fulcher (1987: 237–41). Korpi himself rejects the use of 'corporatism' to describe what he prefers to call 'societal bargaining'.
16. For a succinct summary of the link between full employment and SDC see Castles (1978, esp. 124). The close relationship between full employment and social democracy has been widely discussed, for instance by Martin (1973) and Korpi and Shalev (1980). Flanagan, Soskice, and Ulman (1983), among others, have demonstrated its equally close tie to corporatist wage restraint. On the destabilizing potential of full employment see Kalecki (1943) and Panitch (1976).
17. On links between social democracy, social policy, and inequality see Esping-Andersen (1985*a*; 1990*b*) and Shalev (1983*a*; 1983*b*). Some of the best of the many cross-national studies of the correlates of social democracy and/or corporatism in the period of economic crisis are those of Schmitter (1981); Schmidt (1988); and Hicks (1988).

18. The phrase 'political control of the economy' was the title of a pioneering work by Tufte (1978), who was one of the first scholars to marshal systematic empirical evidence showing that government composition has a significant impact on macro-economic outcomes. Optimism among social-democratic theorists regarding the scope for state autonomy from capital has waned substantially in recent years (e.g. Esping-Andersen, 1987; Fulcher, 1987). See Przeworski and Wallerstein (1982*a*; 1988) for elaborate attempts to verify that there is nevertheless significant scope for effecting the pro-labour distributive interventions favoured by SDC.
19. See, for example, Horowitz and Lissak (1978: 26) and Carmi and Rosenfeld (1989: 10–11).
20. Asher Arian (1989: 82) has spoken of the moderate left (Mapai) in Israel as 'a brand of Western European social democracy', which is also the implicit assumption made by the minority of comparativists who have included Israel in their studies of the OECD nations (Wilensky, 1981; Schmidt, 1982). The work of Bahat (1979), which is discussed in Chapter 1, not only assumes comparability between the Histadrut and union peak organizations in Europe, but specifically asserts that the two are functionally (even if not structurally) extremely similar. In Ishai's authoritative study of interest groups, Israel has been described as 'a greenhouse for the growth of corporatism' (1987: 114), and there is no hint of the distinctive characteristics of Israeli corporatism discussed in this book (see also Grinberg, 1991*a*).
21. In a penetrating overview of historical sociology, Skocpol (1984) contrasts what we have here termed a 'strictly deductive' approach to two other intellectual traditions, both of which are represented in this book. The individual chapters of the volume embody what Skocpol calls *analytic* historical sociology, in which questions about specific contexts are defined in terms of issues raised by general theory. But the volume as a whole is closer to what she labels *interpretive* work, in which a case study is elaborated using theoretically 'pregiven concepts or themes'.
22. This is a characterization which applies mainly to works written in the pre-1973 period. See especially Eisenstadt (1967); Horowitz and Lissak (1971; 1978); Medding (1972). These authors' analyses of contemporary Israel have a far more pessimistic flavour, but at the same time no revision is suggested of their interpretation of earlier periods. See Eisenstadt (1985) and Horowitz and Lissak (1989).
23. Key contributions to the critical sociology of the 1970s include Bernstein (1976); Bober (1972); Ehrlich (1978); Farjoun (1980) [1978]; Rosenfeld and Carmi (1976); Shapiro (1976); Smooha (1978); Yago (1977); and Yatziv (1979). An important role was

also played by the Haifa University journal *Machbarot Lemechkar Ulebikoret*, founded in 1978.

24. For discussions of trends in the approach of Israeli historians and sociologists (respectively) to the national conflict see Morris (1988) and Ehrlich (1987). Works which have placed the conflict at the centre of analysis of Israeli society include Kimmerling (1985); Peled (1989*a*); Peri (1983); Portugali (1986); and Shafir and Peled (1986).
25. See especially Rosenfeld (1978); Semyonov and Lewin-Epstein (1987); and Smooha (1980). This scholarship was stimulated or paralleled by the work of Palestinians (e.g. Jiryis, 1976; Zureik, 1979) and non-Israeli Jews (e.g. Lustick, 1980; Greenberg, 1980: ch. 16).
26. A notable example is a volume by Preuss (1965) entitled *The Labour Movement in Israel*, which remains almost the sole recourse of English-language readers interested in the history of the Histadrut. For detailed evidence of the distortions characteristic of the traditional historiography of the labour movement see Sussman (1969*a*); Shapiro (1976); and Shafir (1989).
27. Compare Swirski (1979).
28. This is also true of two recent related works by Shafir (1989) and Grinberg (1991*a*).
29. In a welcome development which can be attributed to the delayed impact of international trends in the discipline, in the 1980s some Israeli political scientists began to pay more attention to the economic role of the state (e.g. Shimshoni, 1982: ch. 5; Sharkansky, 1987; and Arian, 1989 [1985]: ch. 3). However, with the exception of Reuveni (1980; 1985), all stopped short of embracing political economy as a theoretical paradigm. Almost the sole exception to our characterization in the case of academic economists is Yoram Ben-Porath, whose work includes studies of the impact of elections and government composition on economic policies in Israel (1975; 1983). The same author's introduction to a seminal collection of economists' studies of Israel's economic crisis even refers explicitly to the rise of formerly dependent big capital to a position of 'considerable influence' over the government (1986*b*: 15). Nevertheless, there was no further comment on the topic elsewhere in the volume concerned and, to the best of our knowledge, it has not been subjected to empirical consideration by any professional economist in Israel.
30. Although the mainstream of modern Zionist activity from the beginning rested on struggles at the peak to gain the protection of Palestine's masters and struggles at the base to extend and deepen the Jewish presence there, Herzl's slogan 'if you will it, it is no

dream' has been one of the movement's key emblems. After an initial 'orthodox' phase, even self-styled Marxist socialists within the Zionist camp adopted the view that a transition to socialism was dependent not on capitalist development and class struggle, but rather on the political commitment of the labour movement and the vanguard of the working class to egalitarian economic values and institutional frameworks. Central to this framework was the idea that the creation and mobilization of a Jewish working class in Palestine were a matter of choice rather than the consequence of structural economic and political forces. Similarly voluntaristic conceptions have reappeared in several recent *Marxisant* works on the history of the Zionist labour movement (Cohen, 1987; A. Ben-Porat, 1986).

Part I
The Labour Movement

1

The Histadrut

The Histadrut, the General Organization of Workers in the Land of Israel,[1] was founded in Palestine in December 1920 by the representatives of fewer than 5,000 Jewish settlers. By the late 1980s its membership had grown to 1.6 million. For most of its existence the Histadrut has been universally acknowledged as the most important organization in the country, a critical component of the 'state in the making', and, after sovereignty, considered a partner equivalent in standing with the state itself. This chapter provides a brief introduction to the Histadrut, which is targeted primarily at readers lacking prior familiarity with Israel's peak labour organization.[2] The chapter has two parts. The first offers a concise overview of the labour organization's most prominent institutional features. A subsequent section pinpoints a handful of distinctive characteristics which present particularly noteworthy contrasts to the Western labour movements that constitute the frame of reference for this study. One of these, the Histadrut's internalization of the Israeli–Palestinian conflict and its translation into nationally segmented labour representation, is the subject of the chapter which follows.

Descriptive overview

Activities. The Histadrut is not only a trade union peak organization, but also an economic instrument and a provider of social services on a massive scale. Economic collectives affiliated to the Histadrut and the business corporations which it owns together account for a fifth or more of Israel's national product and employment. Its Sick Fund and Provident Funds dominate the fields of primary health care and supplementary pensions respectively. It also supports a ramified network of services in education, sports, day care, and other public-interest spheres. Prior to Israeli sovereignty, the Histadrut was also responsible for paramilitary defence forces (the *Haganah*), a 'workers' stream' in the education system, and the Jewish community's principal labour exchanges.

Scope. As a trade union, the Histadrut claims some three-quarters of all wage-earners as members and represents even more (about 85 per cent) in negotiating collective agreements, which are often legally binding on the entire relevant labour force. Palestinians living in the occupied West Bank and Gaza are not eligible for Histadrut membership. But approximately three-quarters of all Israeli citizens—men, women, and children, Jews and non-Jews—belong to the 'Histadrut population' in the broadest sense; meaning that their medical care is provided by the Histadrut's Sick Fund (*Kupat Cholim*). This represents a much larger constituency than that of Histadrut trade union members for two reasons. First, the Fund offers its services to various groups of non-dues-paying members (including students, pensioners, housewives, and children). Second, there are several groups of dues-payers who are not wage-earners. They include the members of kibbutzim and other co-operatives, and even privately self-employed persons (including small-scale employers). Overall, the 'unionate' segment of its membership is thus only a minority (no more than 30 per cent) of the wider Histadrut population.[3]

Governance. The internal structure of the Histadrut is centralized, hierarchical, and permeated by political parties. All Histadrut institutions, except shop-level workers' committees, are intended to be governed by party nominees. (This includes middle- and upper-level functionaries as well as executive officers). With the exception of individual Histadrut-owned businesses, governance is constitutionally based on periodic general elections (every three to four years in the case of the national executive and local labour councils, more irregularly and less uniformly in the case of national unions). These elections are identical to those for Israel's *Knesset* (parliament) in that the entire relevant membership group votes as one constituency for party slates. Moreover, since the 1960s nearly all national political parties (other than the religiously-oriented ones) which field candidates in Knesset elections, also participate in Histadrut elections.

Following elections, each party, in proportion to its vote share, nominates delegates to a quasi-parliamentary forum which in turn elects several higher-level governing bodies. The highest of these (the Central Committee, in the case of the Histadrut's national executive) is a cabinet-like body comprised only of the delegates of the governing coalition. Constitutionally, the Histadrut's functional subunits (trade unions, health care, economic enterprises, etc.) are expected to play little if any role in the centre's system of governance. They are, in principle, subject to the overall direction of the central executive and of their own politically-constituted executives. Only the workers' committees deviate from this model, being formed on the basis of frequent (usually annual or biennial) elections in which all employees of an enterprise, department, or broad occupational group (whether or not they are Histadrut members) may cast a ballot for a candidate, rather than a party.

Trade unions. The Histadrut is not a roof-organization of federated trade unions, but (like the ÖGB, its Austrian counterpart) a unitary direct-membership organization. Where relevant, the Histadrut assigns its members to national trade unions, most of which it created. Today there are approximately 40 such bodies, generally either industry-based unions catering to private sector blue-collar workers, or occupationally-based organizations of professional workers. Control over union finances, collective bargaining, and even executive appointments is highly centralized within the Histadrut Executive's Trade Union Division, although in practice professional workers' unions in particular enjoy significant autonomy. Like workers' committees, some of which are virtual national unions, organizations of professional workers are generally exempt from the party-list electoral system.

Industrial relations. Collective bargaining takes place both nationally and locally. Economy-wide 'framework agreements' (typically concluded every two years for each sector) and the cost-of-living-allowance, periodically renegotiated between the Histadrut and the peak association of private employers, constitute the highest level of the system. The government plays a major role at this level, not only as a negotiator but also in steering the outcomes of negotiation. This steering role has taken different forms over the years, including informal intra-party co-ordination (during the long period in which Labour ruled both Histadrut and state), statutory wage freezes, and tripartite 'package deals'. There are also national-level collective agreements for specific industries, occupations, or large firms. Workers' committees, traditionally the bearers only of an ill-defined constitutional mission to act as the labour organization's shop-floor arm, are primarily responsible for negotiating wage supplements at the lowest level, within individual enterprises and plants. It is in the various subnational bargaining units that most strikes occur (they are concentrated in the public sector and often unauthorized by the competent national or local Histadrut bodies) and that wage supplements are negotiated (resulting in considerable 'drift' over the levels established in economy-wide agreements).

Member attachment. Given the Histadrut's multiple functions and the fact that a large bloc of members (those who work for the Histadrut or enterprises owned by it) are not free to choose whether to join, it is hardly surprising that most members do not regard the organization's trade union function as its principal attraction. Opinion polls have consistently shown that the health care programme, the inertia of an affiliation which began automatically in childhood or upon immigration, and automatic employer deduction of dues motivate the affiliation of the vast majority of members. While the Histadrut suffers little from free-riders (indeed, by law many non-members are required to contribute an 'organization fee'), its membership thus includes a sizeable bloc of reluctant followers. Not surprisingly, those who are least free to choose—notably Arab-Israelis, who frequently lack access to non-Histadrut medical services—are also the most likely to belong to the Histadrut; whereas many second-generation '*Sabras*' (Israeli-born Jews) have deserted the labour organization. This does not mean that workers necessarily disapprove of the Histadrut's representation of their interests—in fact, approval in general terms has been surprisingly widespread. But in periods of full employment and among groups with strong labour-market positions, many workers feel that the Histadrut stands in the way of fuller realization of their material interests.[4]

The Histadrut in comparative perspective

Historically, the evolution of the Histadrut deviated quite fundamentally from the European model of labour organization. It did not emerge out of the class struggles contingent upon capitalist industrialization and political democratization; it was primarily concerned with the realization of national interests in the rural sector rather than with the class interests of urban wage-earners; and it was founded from the top down rather than crystallizing and aggregating spontaneous processes of working-class formation. On the basis of our description of the contemporary institutional characteristics of the labour organization, it will be clear that the Histadrut is extraordinarily comprehensive in the scope of both its membership and functions, and remarkably centralized and politicized in its structure and mode of operation. But which of its characteristics differ in kind and which only in degree, in comparison with the labour movements of the West?

In its class-wide boundaries and multiple foci of activity, the Histadrut is clearly reminiscent of early twentieth-century European labour movements, with their tightly linked amalgam of party, unions, and co-operatives and their provision of services catering to the entire range of workers' needs (Kassalow, 1969). These movements, however, were forged in struggles connected with the growth of industrial capitalism and the wresting of political rights from the state, and expressed the alienation of the working class from its political, social, and economic milieu. In contrast, the Histadrut's establishment chronologically preceded both industrialization and the formation of a democratic sovereign state. Indeed, its most important aspiration was to concentrate and direct the energies of its constituency towards the attainment of economic development and statehood. Like other socialist movements of the period, the labour-Zionist élite aspired to achieve labour hegemony in politics and the economy. But rather than pursuing these transformational goals through the medium of class struggle, the labour movement was committed to non-revolutionary 'constructive' activity (land settlement, economic development, immigrant absorption) directed to the realization of supra-class national objectives, as well as to the creation of a labouristic 'workers' society' (*Chevrat Ovdim*).

The Histadrut is notable for more than the unusual goals and circumstances which attended its foundation. The evolution of European labour movements typically followed a developmental path running from particularistic to class mobilization, and from action in the labour market to political activity. The founding of the Histadrut, on the other hand, signified the determination of the

Zionist labour movement to pre-empt particularistic organization in favour of class organization; and the labour parties of the Jewish community of Palestine preceded the trade union sphere of organization and action.

It is true that there are, today, marked similarities between the Histadrut and its counterparts in Scandinavia, Austria, and Germany. This holds for most of the institutional dimensions which distinguish social-democratic labour movements from those in other Western nations: high membership coverage or 'density', organizational unity and centralization, and an intimate relationship with a socialist party with long experience of government. Yet it is also possible to identify three fundamental differences.

Fusion of labour with capital and the state. Israel's 'union confederation' performs functions which are elsewhere the province of either the state or business. This in itself does not render the Histadrut unique. For example, Germany has a (diminishing) sector of union-owned enterprises, the USA has its union-administered pension funds, and unemployment insurance in Sweden remains to this day in trade union hands. But in the Israeli setting the scope of similar activities is incomparably greater. Moreover, far more than in other countries, the Histadrut traditionally relied on its social and economic functions, not only its trade union role as the workers' representative, in order to attract and retain rank-and-file members.

No less significantly, the expansion of several of the Histadrut's non-union functions following Israeli sovereignty did not emerge, so to speak, outside the state. On the contrary, this expansion was expressly intended to serve concrete interests of the government and the ruling party. The Histadrut's health care system was effectively utilized to draw citizens into the labour organization and its political sphere of influence. The labour organization's pension funds, which, under agreements with employers, automatically enroll by far the majority of all wage-earners outside the public sector, developed in a vacuum deliberately created by modest provision for the aged under Israel's national social security scheme. By special official permit much of the vast accumulation of the Histadrut scheme was rolled back into investments in the labour-movement economy. This economic complex was rationalized in terms of working-class interests, yet employees of the large corporations owned by the Histadrut enjoyed no legal rights of ownership or management beyond those accorded to workers in privately owned enterprises. The real significance of the Histadrut's economic empire was that it equipped the Labour Party with an extraordinary means of mobilizing rank-and-file support, dispensing political patronage, financing party activity, and managing the macro- and micro-economy.[5]

A further important facet of the overlapping of social policy, economic and trade-union roles in the Histadrut is manifested in the collective bargaining sphere. The labour organization's wage demands are palpably constrained by its interests as an employer and, equally, by the prospect of gaining (or losing) the state concessions and subsidies on which the successful operation of its entrepreneurial and social service activities is dependent.[6]

Intimacy of party and peak association. The 'primacy of party' (Medding, 1972) in the internal affairs of Israel's labour movement is (or was, for most of its history) without parallel in the Western nations. A detailed comparative portrait of linkages between labour parties and peak labour organizations in Israel and two West European countries is presented in tabular form in Appendix 3. The author of the study on which our table is based (Bahat, 1979) contends that centralized union movements and ruling social-democratic parties in all three countries have developed similar structural and behavioural ties. Where there is dissimilarity, Bahat believes that it primarily reflects the kind of public image which the labour movement wishes to project, because in practice different structures end up serving common functions with similar effects.

While this is indeed true of such features as the party's financial dependence on union support and the close working relationship between union and party leaders, it is nevertheless the case that only in Israel has the party directly and openly controlled the selection of candidates for Histadrut posts, formally requiring its 'emissaries' to operate as a party faction and accept party discipline. In practice, the party's authority and its mediating role between Histadrut and state were seriously challenged in several periods and have weakened considerably over the last several decades. It is nevertheless clear that in its heyday, Mapai (Labour Party) influence over the Histadrut was qualitatively greater than in any of the non-Communist labour movements of the West. It is also apparent that the weight of political parties in the governance of the Histadrut has stifled internal democracy and that it seriously undermines the legitimacy of the labour organization's representational role in the eyes of rank-and-file workers.[7]

Labourism and nationalism. The Histadrut, in the words of an official document, 'was the framework devised by the pioneers to pave the way for independent statehood' (Malkosh, 1961: 3). Its historic mission as a settlement movement, dedicated to building up an economic, political, and territorial infrastructure for a future Jewish 'national home', sets the Histadrut apart from the main thrust of working-class mobilization in other settings. One of the most important facets of its role in nation- and state-building were the struggles of the Histadrut, prior to sovereignty, to exclude Arabs from 'Jewish-only' labour markets. The labour organization has played a continuing although less overt role since sovereignty in the political and economic subordination of the Palestinians, both the Arab citizens of Israel and (since 1967) the residents of the Occupied Territories. It must be added, however, that unlike the 'racially-bounded' labour movements of South Africa and the American South (Greenberg, 1980), the Histadrut has never accepted this interpretation of its national role. Our own analysis of the exclusivism and discrimination practised by the Histadrut towards Palestinian labour seeks to develop an analytical rather than normative interpretation of this controversial issue. It is to this analysis, and the evolving historical context of the Histadrut's intermingling of labourism and nationalism, that we now turn.

Notes

1. While it is customary to follow the Histadrut's own practice in translating its full Hebrew title as The General *Federation* of Labour [in Israel], the literal translation preferred here is a more accurate rendering. For simplicity and following accepted convention, the abbreviated Hebrew title 'Histadrut' (which means organization) is used throughout this book.
2. For English-language readers, it should be pointed out that no comprehensive treatment of the Histadrut is available and existing work is often outdated. The only book-length studies, none of which are

easily accessible, are an anthology edited by Avrech and Giladi (1973) and several unpublished dissertations (Lucatz, 1961; Glatt, 1973). Other useful introductory material may be found in the numerous articles by local experts and visitors to Israel which have appeared over the years in the major British and North American journals of industrial relations. (For a bibliography see Mironi and Flagler, 1975.) Zweig (1959); Shirom (1975); and Reshef (1986) are good examples of this genre. For Hebrew-language readers, there are now several full-length works on industrial relations in Israel, for example, Galin and Harel (1978) and Shirom (1983). The latter is particularly comprehensive, both in time-span and the range of topics covered. In preparing the present chapter we have also drawn on official Histadrut publications, especially Bartal (1989).

3. Most of the cited calculations were based on data appearing in the Histadrut's *Statistical Yearbooks* for 1969–73, or in Bartal (1989). The Histadrut furnishes no differentiated statistics of membership of the self-employed, but a 1985 Dahaf Institute sample survey made available to the author indicated that half of the self-employed—compared with two-thirds of urban Jewish adults as a whole—were affiliated to the Histadrut. Another survey, based on a large sample of employed adult men in the early 1980s, found a membership rate of 54% of the self-employed compared with 77% among wage-earners (Nahon, 1989: table 23). Indeed, more than 40% of *employers* (with at least five employees) belonged to the labour organization!
4. For various opinion-poll findings on membership attitudes, see Friedman *et al.* (1966); Reshef (1981: 85–7); and Galin and Harel (1978). Regarding membership densities, the Dahaf survey mentioned in the previous note indicated that overall nearly 80% of Arabs, two-thirds of Jews, and barely more than half of the second-generation 'Sabras', were Histadrut members. (For confirmatory findings see also Nahon, 1989: table 23.) Not surprisingly, among wage-earners coverage was highest among workers employed in Histadrut enterprises—nearly 90%, compared with just over 60% in the private sector.
5. Details concerning the scope, content, and structure of the labour-movement economy are provided in Appendix 2. We refer to the significance of the Histadrut's business activity at several subsequent points in the body of the volume, especially Chapters 3 and 7.
6. This issue is more fully discussed in Chapter 6.
7. Mapai's influence on the Histadrut has been chronicled by Medding (1972) and Tokatli (1979); see also Yanai (1981). On the issue of internal democracy in the Histadrut see Shirom (1980). For a classic and more recent treatment of leader–member relations in the trade union domain see respectively Friedman (1963; 1976) and Grinberg (1985).

2

Accounting for Exclusivism

The Histadrut and the Palestinians

The Israeli labour movement's far-reaching internalization of the Israeli–Palestinian conflict and, specifically, the national exclusivism which historically characterized the mobilization of the Jewish working class in Palestine, fundamentally distinguish the Israeli case from its social-democratic counterparts. This distinctiveness arises from what has correctly come to be understood as the hallmark of successful social-democratic labour movements, namely, their ability to organize workers solidaristically *as a class*.

Working-class solidarity, as is well known, has in some societal and historical contexts been hampered by cleavages which cut across class lines. Indeed, such cleavages have at times been so deep as to have 'pillarized' the labour movement itself. Typically, the literature on social democracy has regarded such phenomena as no more than unfortunate remnants of processes of nation-state formation which pre-dated working-class formation.[1] While one leading theorist (Esping-Andersen, 1989: 17) has recently conceded that 'we cannot assume that socialism is the natural basis for wage-earner mobilization', he too appears to regard *pre-capitalist* solidarities as the most important alternative force framing worker organization. The case of Palestine/Israel suggests an additional possibility in societies where workers are deeply divided along ethnic or other primordial lines—namely, that the economic dynamics of the meeting *in the labour market* between such groups sets in train *both* separatist forms of worker organization and ethnic tension.

Our inspiration for this hypothesis derives from the variant of labour market segmentation theory elaborated by Edna Bonacich.[2] Bonacich's is a 'supply-side' theory which traces ethnically based segmentation of employment to the fact that ethnic differences frequently correspond to a split between 'cheap' and 'expensive' labour. Processes such as colonization or migration cause ethnically distinct communities to enter the labour market with lesser social and political power and lower 'reservation wages' (economists' parlance for the minimum compensation for which people are willing to work). Typically, members of these groups are accustomed to a lower level of living; suffer from ignorance of prevailing standards and political weakness; and enter the market with limited aspirations, as temporary sojourners or to supplement other sources of income. Given the inherent tendency of capitalist employers to drive down the price of labour, the higher-paid group of workers—if unable to force cheap labour out of the market altogether—will often seek protection by subordinating their competitors to caste-like niches in the job structure.

This is evidently a quite different dynamic to that suggested by the better-known 'demand-side' perspective on segmentation. According to the latter, the technological and product-market conditions facing employers on the economic periphery give rise to unstable demand for labour and extreme sensitivity to labour costs in this sector. In their search for cheap and fluid pools of labour, peripheral firms naturally gravitate towards the members of weak social groups. It follows that the creation of a caste-like identity between 'bad' jobs and 'marginal' workers does not result from the specific characteristics of the labour pool available to the secondary market—in effect, if this pool didn't exist, it would have to be created.[3] For Bonacich, however, it is relations of competition between more and less exploitable labour which are at the heart of ethnically-based segmentation of the labour market. To put the point more bluntly, it is her view that the rationale for deep-seated 'ethnic' conflicts is in the first instance economic. In this vein Gershon Shafir (1989) has argued that the initial encounter between Jewish settlers and the indigenous Arab population of late Ottoman Palestine constituted precisely the kind of split between cheap and higher-paid labour to which Bonacich referred. Shafir has carefully documented the diverse responses of Jewish labour (which were by no means limited to the dualist/caste solution) in the years prior to the First World War.

The dynamic of labour-market conflict theorized by Bonacich is especially suited to addressing the two tasks occupying this chapter. First, it offers an explanation for the Jewish settlers' embrace of national exclusivism as a cardinal principle of labour organization, and the consequent blending of nationalism and labourism which became institutionalized in the Histadrut. Second, the emphasis in Bonacich's model on the potential variety of strategies and outcomes in a split labour-market situation is particularly appropriate to a dynamic analysis of the Israeli case, which constitutes something of a natural laboratory in this respect. The reason is that Jews and Palestinians have met in the labour market in three quite different historical contexts: at the onset of modern Zionist settlement, when the Jews were a small and relatively powerless minority; after Israel's establishment and the Palestinians' dispersion, under conditions of Jewish political and demographic supremacy; and finally, since the 1967 war, with the added ingredient of a sizeable influx of non-citizen Arab labour working inside Israel's *de jure* borders, but living alongside them under military occupation.

Our explanation of the continuities and modifications in Jewish labour's national exclusivism in these three periods accepts Bonacich's insight into the economic logic of ethnic conflicts, but intentionally stops short of advocating a purely economistic analysis. Conflicts of interest between Jews and Arabs over the distribution of employment (and even more profoundly, the distribution of land) were indeed the inevitable consequence of Zionist settlement in Palestine. Arab reactions to Jewish colonization and Jewish responses to Arab hostility in turn did fuel the evolving separatist nationalism on both sides. Yet, some of the protagonists sought to harness the developing national cleavage in the service of their class and political interests. On the Zionist side, it was the labour movement which played this role. By becoming the standard-bearer of Jewish exclusivity the organized workers sought to enforce their claims to the material and political resources of the Zionist community.[4] The politics of nationalism thus became intertwined with, and in part detached from, the economic mainsprings of nationalism. In this context, as we shall demonstrate, the Arab-Jewish cleavage became a potentially important component of exchange relations between the Histadrut, the labour movement's political wing and the state.[5]

The formative era of national separatism

The idea of Zionist colonization of Palestine was one response (primarily of the *Ashkenazi* Jewry of Russia and Poland) to the push of anti-semitism and the pull of modern nationalism. It was in fact the choice of only a small minority, and most of the *Ashkenazim* either immigrated to the New World or remained in Europe only to perish in the Holocaust. 'Labour Zionism' was a particular branch of European Zionist thought and activity, which arose out of the polarization of Jewish socialists (against the background of the rise of communism) between an internationalist majority and those who believed that socialism could only be realized within an autonomous Jewish 'national home'. The first Jewish settlers inspired by labour Zionism, the members of the Second *Aliyah* (literally, ascension to Zion), reached Palestine in the early 1900s. There they encountered a problem of 'undercutting' by Arab labour which was virtually impossible to solve—whether by co-operation or by aggression—in the framework of the labour market. We argue below that the worker-pioneers found a way out of the deadlock by contracting an alliance with organized Zionism, which was at bottom a marriage of convenience. Jewish labour got the benefit of political sympathy and, more importantly, of economic subsidy to workers and their collective institutions. In return, their leaders undertook to manage the labour movement by Zionist criteria—which included keeping Arabs out of both jobs and workers' organizations in the Jewish sector.

In the closing years of the Ottoman period, prior to the First World War, the economy of Palestine was composed essentially of an Arab sector centred around the farming family; a 'traditional' Jewish urban sector which survived on charity and a primitive market economy of trade, services, and small-scale craft production; and Jewish rural colonies (*moshavot*) based mainly on plantation agriculture, along the lines of the vineyards established by Rothschild money and initiative in Rishon Letsiyon and elsewhere. The labour Zionist pioneers sought to establish themselves in this third sector, which was heavily dependent on the utilization of Arab wage labour.[6] But it was the only one of the three which could offer paid employment (essential since the pioneers had no capital of their own to purchase or work the land) and which was consistent with their strategic objectives: manual labour, 'return' to the land and to agricultural pursuits, and building a Jewish territorial and economic presence in Palestine.

The planter-capitalists were not opposed to these objectives, but faced powerful economic incentives not to participate in their realization by hiring Jewish workers. First, the cost of 'reproducing' (feeding, housing, educating) Jewish labour was high in comparison with Arab labour. This was due not only to a difference in minimally acceptable living standards, but also to the fact that many Arab labourers enjoyed the actual or potential support of village agriculture and extended kinship networks. Second, the Jews' initial productivity was lower than the Arabs, because of their inexperience in manual labour generally and agricultural labour specifically. Third, Jewish workers' class consciousness, politicization, and organization hampered employers' efforts to exert control over the labour process, a threat to both power and productivity. Moreover, while constituting at first only an ideological rather than a practical challenge to the existing political economy in the plantations, the Jewish labourers were perceived as a potentially destabilizing force in the long run.

From exclusion to collectivism

Building on the work of Bonacich, four possible theoretical outcomes may be anticipated in a labour market which, on the supply side, is characterized by a split between high-cost and low-cost workers (where 'cost' encompasses all four of the dimensions just referred to—reproduction, productivity, control, and stability). If the higher costs of 'expensive' workers are to be preserved, this can be done in one of two ways: they must succeed either in raising 'cheap' labour to their own level or in developing institutional mechanisms for eliminating competition between the two groups. Failure of 'expensive' labour to preserve its differential arises also under two basically differing circumstances: either by exit (unemployment or movement to markets in other sectors or locations); or equalization with the costs of 'cheap' labour. These four possibilities are summarized in Table 2.1.

The dilemma of unskilled Jewish labour was real enough. Not only was its economic and political attractiveness to Jewish employers inferior to that of Arab workers, but the latter were available in almost 'unlimited' supply. Zvi Sussman has demonstrated the existence of three substantial pools of Arab labour: semi-proletarian farmers, the unemployed, and migrants from elsewhere in the region. Moreover, on the basis of over-time and cross-sectional variation in comparative wage rates for Jews and Arabs

TABLE 2.1. *Potential outcomes of competition between high- and low-cost labour*

	Victory of high-cost labour	Defeat of high-cost labour
Integration of the competing groups	Upward cost equalization	Downward cost equalization
Differentiation of the competing groups	Exclusion or segmentation of low-cost labour	Exclusion of high-cost labour

and in skilled versus unskilled pay, Sussman shows quite convincingly that Arab competition genuinely constrained the wages of (unskilled) Jewish workers during the pre-state period.[7]

In the early years of the Second Aliyah, the new settlers responded to these circumstances by pursuing a radical strategy of *excluding* low-cost labour. The 'Hebrew labour only' struggle in this period involved a direct confrontation with both Jewish employers and their Arab employees, with the intention of transferring most or all of the jobs held by Arabs to unemployed Jewish workers. But at various times and with limited success, the Jewish labourers complemented their largely futile efforts to coerce the farmers to accept this wholesale substitution by experimenting with means of *compensating them* for the accompanying cost burden. Some of the proffered compensations were symbolic. Thus, Jewish labour leaders tried to appeal to shared feelings of national solidarity by advocating the importance of Hebrew labour for the absorption of Jewish settlers and the development of an autonomous Jewish infrastructure. They also stressed the injustice of depressing the living standards of Jews to the 'primitive' Arab level, and the danger that an Arab proletariat in Jewish employment would develop both class and national hostility towards the Zionist enterprise. Some of the workers more palpably contributed to the appeal to national solidarity by hiring themselves out to the farmers as their defenders against Arab attacks on Jewish life and property—attacks which critics argued were in part triggered by the Jewish workers' efforts to acquire Arab jobs.

Until both the farmers' security and their supply of hired labour were threatened by mass Arab rebellions—the first of which broke out in 1921 and the most intense in 1936—the purely national comparative advantage of Jewish labour was limited. A second compensatory strategy took the form of efforts to bridge the gap between Jewish and Arab *labour costs* without insisting on higher Jewish *wages*. In this vein, the WZO (World Zionist Organization) organized training farms designed to acclimate Jewish labour to agricultural work even before immigration, thus raising their productivity to Arab levels. The workers established regional 'trade unions' which helped lower their reproduction costs by pooling resources in a mutual-aid framework, for which subsidy from the international Zionist movement was sought. Finally, some respite from the cost problem was provided by subsidies allocated directly to farmers employing Jewish labour. The common denominator of all of these attempts at compensation was a hybrid strategy unforeseen in Table 2.1—lowering the cost of expensive labour, but without defeating its interests or forcing it to share the labour market with cheaper rivals.

A more theoretically predictable tack for Jewish labour was to attempt to segment the labour market by drawing national boundaries between low-paid and high-paid jobs. There were indeed periods prior to World War I in which Jewish farmers consented to reserve higher-paid skilled jobs for Jewish workers, partly in the expectation that keeping Arabs out of sensitive jobs would deny them leverage for raising the wages of their unskilled compatriots. But on the whole, in the pre-war period compensation and segmentation proved to be equally limited solutions to the labour-market problem of Jewish workers, and no more effective than the campaign to exclude Arabs by confrontational means. Jewish labour responded instead with what may be called an economic-collectivist strategy.[8] This strategy embraced a variety of experiments. Partial collectivization, such as group contracting, implied merely a more cost-efficient way of competing for jobs held by Arabs. Producer co-operatives sought to transfer this competition from the labour market to product markets, where it began to be supplemented by collective modes of distribution to further cut costs and facilitate market penetration. A sprinkling of fully socialized communes (forerunners of the *kibbutzim*) strove to some extent for total autarky.

The alliance between labour and Zionism

While collectivism offered the advantages of scale, pooling of reproduction costs, and a share of the surplus hitherto appropriated solely by the farmers, it was still insufficient to make economic autonomy viable. A further essential ingredient was the participation of 'national capital' (the funds of organized world Zionism), both to provide the initial infrastructure and to subsidize the workers' losses. Indeed, it is hardly accidental that the transformation of the *avant-garde* of pioneers, from wage-earners struggling with Arabs in the labour-market arena to settlers struggling to acquire territory, coincided with the opening of the world Zionist movement's Palestine Office in 1908. From the subsequent establishment of the first tiny agricultural commune, collectivism went hand in hand with partnership between organized workers and the Zionist movement. This partnership initially rested primarily on material rather than political or ideological grounds. This was a period in which the workers (and even the labour movements in the Diaspora with which they were affiliated) were only weakly represented in the institutions of world Zionism. Indeed, the most influential of the workers' parties regarded the Zionist movement's largely *petit bourgeois* rank and file, and particularly its élite (composed in part of Jewish magnates and closely tied to them as financiers) as the class enemies of labour Zionism.[9]

The most important basis for collaboration was *exchange*.[10] The workers, unlike other Diaspora Zionists, were willing to make the move to Palestine. They were ready to compete actively with or help circumscribe Arab labour, rather than reinforcing the Arabs' presence by employing them. And unlike the independent farmers, they sought to develop economic frameworks which would enhance Jewish autonomy and provide the basis for absorbing propertyless Jewish immigrants. Finally, it was only the labourers who, out of both inclination and necessity, were willing to take on the most arduous and financially least rewarding roles in the settlement process. The labour movement's options were similarly confined. By this time the problem of Arab competition in the plantations had been resolved in the worst possible way—by the exclusion of high-priced Jewish labour. Most of the pre-war pioneers had deserted Palestine and the minority that remained had deserted wage labour in agriculture. The emergent alternative of communitarian rural settlement was unrealistic without outside financing. For organized labour to hold on to its remaining base and provide jobs and other essentials to newcomers, external aid was an equally urgent prerequisite.[11] Given the apparently dim prospects for development-spurring private investment in Palestine, the extension of economic collectivism[12] in partnership with Zionist funds was clearly the most promising strategic response.[13] Indeed, only in this light is it possible to comprehend both the timing of the Histadrut's foundation and its distinctive agenda.[14]

In 1920, when the Histadrut was established, urban labour organizations committed to conventional trade union activity (i.e. struggles with employers over employment security, job rewards, and control of the labour process) were still in their infancy. But by the middle of the decade the vast majority of Histadrut members were wage-earners in the towns and expectations regarding economic collectivism had been drastically scaled down in view of a dearth of finance for new settlement and the emergence of a vigorous (if still primitive) urban economy in the wake of substantial *petit bourgeois* immigration (the Fourth Aliyah). Nevertheless, trade unionism remained only a secondary concern for the Histadrut centre, and its leadership was inclined to restrain the workers' pursuit of their immediate interests in the context of the employment relation.[15] 'Pure-and-simple' trade unionism was essentially at odds with the labour movement's national role. The labour élite believed that trade union pressure ought to be directed solely towards reserving jobs in the Jewish sector for Histadrut members and safeguarding the 'Jewish minimum wage'—but without discouraging investment and harming the country's 'absorptive capacity'. Another consideration—although one which was not made explicit—was the fear that the logic of collective action in the market arena might lead Jewish workers to join forces with their Arab counterparts in struggles against Jewish employers. This would have contradicted the core commitment of the labour movement (in the context of its alliance with Zionism) to place the Jewish working class at the head of the nation-building struggle.

So long as Jewish workers constituted a minority of the labour force, and one lacking the political power to impose limits on Arab labour supply, they also had no compelling incentive from a self-interested labour market perspective to act in solidarity with Arab labour. The result of these vectors of economic and political forces was a policy of excluding Arabs from the ranks of the Histadrut and discouraging sporadic rank-and-file initiatives which implied *de facto* Jewish solidarity with Arab labour.[16] Jewish radicals continued to strive for 'joint organization', but for the Zionist left (by far the most influential opposition) this support was primarily at the level of principle rather than practice. By 1927, when the issue was formally resolved, the Histadrut's leaders were ready to endorse concrete proposals for united Jewish-Arab trade union activity only within the sphere of public and foreign employers—that is, in work-places where there was no hope of excluding Arabs and the best prospects for Jewish employment lay in raising Arab wages to Jewish levels. To preserve the Histadrut's character as the instrument of the national interest of Jewish workers, even this limited unionization of Arab labour would not be actively encouraged. It would proceed in a separate Arab-only framework which, in conjunction with the Histadrut, would officially constitute the 'Palestine Labour League'.

As Chaim Arlosoroff, a leading labour politician and an economist by training, pointed out to the supporters of joint organization, no matter how many Arabs were organized alongside Jewish workers, Jewish employers would always be able to find other Arabs willing to undercut their wage standards. Yet it is difficult to escape the impression that rather than seeking to dull this tension, the leaders of Jewish organized labour acted to exacerbate it. The most conspicuous example of this covert policy occurred when the economy was in the throes of an economic crisis (1926–7) and the Histadrut initiated the deliberate transfer of thousands of unemployed workers from the towns to the agricultural colonies, where they would inevitably be thrown into competition with Arabs over the distribution of employment. As it was, the difficult conditions faced by those workers who remained in the towns had the effect of dampening the interest in binational trade unionism which had earlier surfaced in the mixed cities of Haifa and Jaffa. But in the rural Moshavot many of the embittered urbanites, together with leftist newcomers to the country and veteran pioneers who realized that the Zionist movement lacked the means to realize their dream of communal settlement, threw their support behind the Arab–Jewish trade union struggle. They rejected outright the official strategy of an alliance between Jewish workers and farmers against Arab labour. In response, and fortified by fears aroused by the 1929 Arab 'disturbances', Ben-Gurion and his colleagues heightened their rhetoric against the Arab worker as the Jews' national rival. They warned their supporters that solidarity with the non-Jewish proletariat would not provide them with insurance against Arab opposition to Jewish immigration or violence against Jewish life and property.

Towards Jewish segregation and insulation

With economic recovery at the end of the 1920s, the stimulus of mutual desperation was removed from the campaign for 'workers' brotherhood' (as the movement for joint organization was called). The Histadrut had officially set up the rudiments of a segregated structure for activity among Arab labour—a central Arab Department; special 'clubs' and other local activities to foster Arab sympathy; and separate unions for Arab workers in mixed localities (mainly Haifa) and branches (notably the railways). In the same year (1930) the two major labour movement parties combined to form Mapai (the Palestine Workers' Party), which rapidly became the most powerful political force in both the *Yishuv* (Jewish community of Palestine) and the world Zionist movement. Concurrently, as a result of rapid economic growth associated with the 'German Aliyah' (*c.*1933–6), the immanent conflict between high-cost (Jewish) and low-cost (Arab) labour was for the most part resolved by the expanding opportunities for Jewish workers within urban Jewish localities.

Precisely at this point, when the material basis for the national struggle had weakened, the Mapai leadership stepped up its commitment to the sanctity of all-Jewish labour and supported violent efforts to force Arabs out of their jobs—efforts impregnated with racist and nationalist rhetoric which parts of the labour élite believed possessed considerable 'educational' value.[17] The targets of this 'education' were, on the one hand, the rank and file of the Jewish labour movement and, on the other, the members of non-labour strata which Mapai's leaders had come to regard as essential allies in their political struggle against both left- and right-wing challengers within the Zionist community. In response to calls from the left for more militant class struggle, these leaders turned to Jewish workers with an appeal—couched in the lexicon of class struggle—to direct their aggression towards Arab labour; and they endowed this aggression with a higher national purpose. To potential sympathizers outside the organized working class, the labour movement successfully portrayed itself as locked in a struggle (against both Arab workers and unpatriotic Jewish employers) on which the very viability of the national home hinged—thereby enhancing its reputation for Zionist achievement and blunting the critique mounted by Zionism's militant right wing.

Some elements in the Jewish labour movement were deeply troubled by the contradiction between their self-professed socialist principles and the movement's praxis of aggression towards Arab labour, and the issue of principle continued to be heatedly debated among various factions.[18] But there was no retreat from the cornerstone of Histadrut policy: to play, at most, a reactive role in relation to organizing Arab labour which would prevent Arabs from acquiring the capacity to influence Histadrut policy-making from within; to zealously guard against any separation of the Histadrut's labouristic and Zionist functions; and to pre-empt spontaneous co-operation between Jewish and Arab trade unionists. In the event, political and economic developments in the late 1930s worked very much in favour of the realization of these restrictive principles. The Arab general strike of 1936, and the subsequent reluctance of some Jewish employers to rehire Arab strikers, marked the beginning of the end of Arab employment in the Jewish sector. The process was completed by the dramatic decline of the citrus branch (the principal employer of Arabs) before and during World War II. The urban Jewish economy was characterized during the war itself by boom conditions generated by the requirements of the British forces stationed in the Middle East. The consequent labour shortage provided Jewish workers with sufficient leverage to prevent potential Arab penetration.

The conjunction of ascendancy of the national conflict with dramatic shifts in the economic structure and conjuncture, thus finally made it possible for Jewish labour to achieve relative insulation from Arab competition through the device of near-total exclusion. This was a far cry from the abysmal failure of the pioneers at the turn of the century to evict Arabs from the work force of Jewish farmers. Yet it was this very failure which had taught the pioneers' leaders a historic lesson: that unless the Arabs could be defined as the national adversaries of all Jews, bourgeois as well as proletariat, there was little hope of 'conquering' jobs for which the Jews were over-priced. The alternative to keeping Arabs out was to allow them into inferior jobs and reserve the better work for Jews; but this required that Jewish wages be subsidized. In the absence of a state apparatus responsive to Jewish labour's interests, the only possible source of subsidy was the Zionist movement. The priorities of the latter (Jewish settlement and economic self-sufficiency) were clearly inconsistent with a strategy of segmentation, which would have implied dividing the jobs offered by the Jewish sector of the economy between Jewish and Arab 'castes'. This taught the Jewish labour movement in Palestine a second historic lesson, the one which underpinned the creation of a roof organization of Jewish labour deeply committed to the fulfilment of Zionist tasks: it demonstrated the advantages of an alliance with organized Zionism over the alternative of class-wide solidarity.

After 1948: Why not equalization?

Our earlier theoretical discussion suggested that where high- and low-cost workers share the same labour market, the former are likely to face a choice among three strategies for preventing the loss of their wage advantage: upward equalization; the exclusion of low-cost labour, or the segmentation of jobs on the basis of a rigid boundary between the jobs open to otherwise competing groups of workers. We have seen that the predominant response of the Jewish labour movement in Mandatory Palestine was advocacy of exclusion. But following the creation of the State of Israel in 1948, exclusion began to be overtaken by a strategy of segmentation—specifically, Arabs' confinement to inferior positions and conditions in the labour market, coupled with their partial incorporation into the Histadrut along segregated lines. That a policy of protecting Jewish employment by denying jobs to Arabs gradually became outmoded after 1948 is not surprising, if only for the reason that Jewish labour was no longer outnumbered by a potentially open-ended supply of Arab competitors. The interesting question is why did the segmentation solution win out over the alternative of upward equalization? What was it that prevented the full integration of Arab citizens into both the Histadrut and the labour market?

During 1948–9 the Jewish sector of Palestine succeeded in

erecting and defending a sovereign state to which the new Arab Israelis—a frightened and humiliated minority—posed little objective danger. In Rosenfeld's words (1978: 387), in the post-sovereignty context 'The barriers that the Jewish workers' movement had interposed between it and the Arab masses were now down'. Not only were the Jews now the politically dominant and expanding majority, but also those Arabs who remained within Israel's borders were less of a threat to Jewish national interests. The mass flight of most of their compatriots had distanced those Arabs who remained from the influence of their former economic and religious leaders, who had vigorously opposed both Zionism and socialism. And too, an argument which had in the past often been voiced by labour Zionists—that the Arabs were 'unorganizable' because of their internal divisions and continued ties to village agriculture[19]—was outmoded by the nature of the Arab labour force after 1948. Most Arabs were already (or would soon become) fully proletarianized, and internal religious and other cleavages within the emergent Palestinian working class were substantially weaker than in the past.

The failure of the inclusion option was partly the product of the broader context characterizing the immediate post-sovereignty period, which featured a variety of forces antithetical to the labour movement fulfilling the potential for truly class-wide solidarity. At the organizational level, as Lustick (1980:168) has pointed out, all the nation-building instruments of the Yishuv (including the Histadrut) were alike in 'projecting and institutionalizing' pro-Jewish and anti-Arab behaviour into the post-sovereignty era. At the subjective level, the long legacy of national and economic struggle with the Arabs, now joined by fresh memories of a bloody war, had hardened the hearts of most Jews against the Palestinian Arabs. Fears that Arab citizens would act as a fifth column to undermine Israel's security further intensified these biases. In the early years, there were those—not only on the nationalist right, but also within Mapai—who hoped that the Arabs of Israel would literally disappear, and the government was accused of systematic harassment in pursuit of this eventuality. Subsequently, while both Jews and Arabs largely came to perceive the existence of an Arab minority as permanent, Jewish suspicions persisted, feeding upon the continuing external conflict with the Arab states and the threat of terrorist incursions into Israel. But independent of genuine security considerations, all policy-makers shared the view that territorial concentration of Arabs in strategic areas, or the emergence of political and economic independence in the 'Arab sector', would constitute tangible threats to Israel's character as a Jewish state.[20]

The politics and economics of exclusion

That the broader geopolitical context of Arab–Jewish relations profoundly affected the Histadrut's post-sovereignty policy towards Arab labour is pointedly demonstrated by the 'deviant' turn that this policy took during the interim period between the UN resolution in favour of partition (November 1947) and Israel's declaration of independence (and the subsequent Arab invasion) in May 1948.[21] An internal Mapai committee on 'Problems of the Histadrut in the (Future) State', headed by the labour organization's next Secretary-General, Pinhas Lavon, recommended early in 1948 that the Histadrut should:(*a*) open up its labour exchanges to Arabs; (*b*) support 'very-close-to' wage equalization; and (*c*) move in the direction of full organizational integration of non-Jewish workers.

From a narrow labour-market perspective these were surprisingly generous recommendations. For although the Jewish state envisaged by the UN would have excluded the major loci of Arab settlement in Palestine, the anticipated arrival following statehood of masses of Jewish immigrants, combined with the expectation of an open economic border between the two new states, was bound to revive Jewish–Arab competition for scarce jobs in the short term. It can only be concluded that the political calculus of the Histadrut élite had retained its 'functional autonomy' from purely economic interests. The most important consideration at work was presumably the need, from a state-building perspective, to ease the problems of governing relations between the future Jewish state (with extremely vulnerable borders) and its Arab neighbour. Harmony would be promoted, on the one hand, by refraining from discriminating against Arabs in the labour market and, on the other, by trying to persuade Arab workers (initially in the framework of the Palestine Labour League) to award political allegiance to the state and the party, as well as to the Histadrut.

Viewed this way, the actual course of events during 1948–9—an amalgam of Arab attacks from within and across the borders and

Jewish response and belligerence, which ended up expanding and strengthening Israel's initial borders—had a double significance. Not only were hearts hardened, but there was now no basis for the expectations of geopolitical vulnerability and economic integration which had earlier encouraged Mapai to support an equalization strategy for the Jewish labour movement. The leaders of a relatively well-secured state with demonstrated military superiority, with economically and politically closed borders, and in which Jews outnumbered Arabs by more than six to one, saw little incentive to adopt a conciliatory stance. Arab citizens were literally sealed off under a military government which was more than capable of combating any danger they posed to either the authority of the state or Mapai's standing at the polls. Indeed, largely due to the regime of politicized military rule, Mapai succeeded in early Knesset elections in winning proportionately far more Arab than Jewish support.[22]

The shift in the political climate for collaboration between Jewish and Arab labour after 1948 was not only the consequence of geopolitical developments, but also reflected important strategic choices made by Mapai's leaders in the government of the new state. The dominant centrist wing of the labour movement found more reason than ever to pursue the political strategy embodied in their earlier struggle for Hebrew labour—one which sought power in a cross-class Zionist coalition, rather than a cross-national socialist coalition. The search for alliances with the states and Jewish communities of the West, a belief in the necessity of appealing to the new Eastern Jewish electorate[23] on nationalist rather than socialist grounds, and above all, the wish to construct a strong party/state at the centre of the political economy all led Mapai's government leaders further to the right.[24]

The labour movement parties to Mapai's left (now merged into *Mapam*, the United Workers' Party) opposed this drift. They argued that the labour movement's pre-state institutions should retain their pre-eminence and should bear primary responsibility for the political mobilization of both Arabs and Eastern Jews along class lines; and they opposed any alliance with the West or abandonment of socialist aspirations. While Mapam was at the peak of its political strength in the immediate post-1948 period, this strength only heightened Mapai's determination to oppose a programme which it regarded as utopian and antithetical to the national interest. Representatives of Mapam did not enter the Cabinet until the mid-1950s. Even in the Histadrut, where the left functioned simultaneously as an extra-parliamentary opposition and a major partner in the ruling coalition, Mapai enjoyed majority standing and with it the ability to determine the main thrust of policy.

Not only was the political constellation at élite level in support of binational class solidarity rather feeble; but on the ground, in the labour-market arena, there were powerful forces in the first decade of sovereignty favouring continuity with the pre-state Histadrut strategy of Arab exclusion. By 1951 immigration had doubled the Jewish population, in an economy which had only recently begun to enter the modern industrial age and which sorely lacked the wherewithal to finance imports even of food and other necessities. Though large sections of the new-immigrant population were effectively eliminated as a competitive threat—by their confinement in transit camps, employment on public works, and dispersal to outlying areas and also by stiff disincentives to employers to lay off veterans—there remained a substantial pool of immigrant unemployed, especially among the 'Eastern' newcomers.[25] While the Histadrut welcomed these newcomers into its ranks organizationally and politically, its labour-market policies in practice encouraged their channelling into unskilled manual labour and the widening of wage differentials in favour of Ashkenazi veterans.[26]

Under these circumstances, it would have taken a great deal of political and ideological commitment to binational class solidarity to counteract the temptation for Jewish workers to try to bar Arabs from the labour market. Moreover, this temptation was enhanced by the chances of effectively implementing closure, immeasurably greater now than they had been prior to 1948. A strong state apparatus with the overriding goal of realizing Jewish national interests was now in place, and it was controlled by representatives of the Jewish labour movement. Military rule in the Arab localities, where most Arab citizens lived, made it technically straightforward to deny them the capacity to commute to jobs in Jewish localities. Jewish employers were in a relatively weak position to advocate the hiring of cheap Arab labour, since the public and Histadrut sectors (where there could be no question of harming Jewish workers) dominated the economy, and even private business depended heavily on the state.

Steps towards partial incorporation

The result of these conditions was that until the late 1950s, when the labour market experienced a transition from substantial unemployment to excess demand, the Histadrut's local institutions actively took steps to limit Arab employment; while at the national level, the labour organization embraced only a very limited programme for the Arabs' organizational integration. In this period, access to manual work with Jewish employers was formally controlled by labour exchanges still linked to the Histadrut, which refused their services to the residents of Arab localities and openly discriminated against non-Jews resident in mixed areas. A limited number of special state employment offices were set up especially to serve Arab areas, but their activities were confined to the distribution of relief work. This is not to say that no Arabs found work in the Jewish sector. In the first place, there were employers—especially those relying on low-paid seasonal labour, notably in agriculture—who actively sought out the services of Palestinian workers. In order to reap the political benefits of military rule, the authorities responded to this demand (and the willingness of the economically strained Arab population to meet it) by issuing travel permits via influential local figures capable of delivering Arab acquiescence and votes. Nevertheless, the number of permits made available and the stringency with which the permit system was enforced were distinctly sensitive to the depth of unemployment among Jewish workers. And to the extent that Arabs succeeded in getting jobs despite such unemployment, local Histadrut labour councils responded with demonstrations, and the Histadrut exchanges (or vigilante rank-and-filers) revived the pre-state practice of forcibly 'lowering' non-Jews from their jobs.[27]

During the same period the national policy of the Histadrut, grappling with the concrete issue of whether to accept non-Jews as members, made only gradual and limited departures from the traditional principles of excluding Arabs from 'Jewish jobs' and sponsoring no more than dual labour organization. Immediately after sovereignty was attained an internal debate broke out between Mapam, which demanded 'absolute class equality' (equal pay and a nationally unified Histadrut), and most of Mapai, which believed that the national interests of Arab and Jewish workers were too opposed to sustain anything more than Histadrut patronage of a 'fraternal' Arab workers' organization (Kantor, 1977: 42–7).[28] The conservative approach won out, and for roughly the first five years after Israel's establishment the Histadrut concentrated its organizing efforts on reviving the Palestine Labour League. Then in 1953 it permitted Arabs to affiliate to Histadrut 'mutual aid' programmes, and to participate in segregated local trade unions. But they were barred from participating in internal governance; and the Histadrut's labour exchanges, local branches, and (to a great extent) health service remained officially or effectively closed to Arabs. Accordingly, these tentative steps towards incorporation were met by an equally tentative response.[29]

Implications of the transition to full employment

During the 1950s, then, Histadrut policy could be described as essentially a continuation of the pre-sovereignty pattern. Despite *de facto* tolerance of a limited Palestinian presence on the payroll of Jewish employers and tentative organizational steps to incorporate Arabs as members, the overriding strategic premise continued to be one of exclusion. The turning-point arrived at the end of the decade, beginning with the admission of those Arabs accepted for military service (a small minority, principally Druze) in 1958; and then, in the following year, with an official decision to accept all 'loyal' non-Jewish citizens as full members. Changing labour-market conditions provided a major stimulus. The emergence of labour shortages, against a background of rapid expansion in the construction and manufacturing branches, drew substantial numbers of commuters from Arab localities into wage work for Jewish employers.[30] Given the relaxation of the competitive threat to Jews as a result of the aggregate shift towards full employment, and given also that Palestinians were confined to insecure and unattractive job slots (from which underprivileged Jews were correspondingly enabled to escape), exclusion had become an anachronism.

Three responses followed, almost simultaneously: the opening of the Histadrut's doors to Palestinian members; relaxation of the military government's restrictions on their freedom of movement; and the inclusion of non-Jews in the scope of a new law which nationalized the labour exchanges. As in the preceding period, policies towards Palestinian labour reflected not only the interests of the Jewish work-force, but also the fact that with sovereignty

Jewish labour had come to enjoy a powerful voice within the state. The new Employment Exchange Law embodied this transition in its institutionalization of the practice of local preference, as a result of which Arabs are not offered work in Jewish areas unless the job cannot be filled locally.[31]

The acceptance of Arabs into the Histadrut was also effected on terms which safeguard the interests of Jewish workers. Incorporation takes place in the framework of an institutional dualism which severely limits the capacity of the Histadrut's Palestinian members to engage in effective trade union action. There was no departure from the standard Histadrut practice that local union officers attached to labour councils serve only workers who are resident in the council's area of jurisdiction. This system makes it very difficult for commuter labourers (at least half of Arab wage-earners) to address grievances to labour councils in the (Jewish) localities where they are employed. Instead, their complaints are filtered by various official or unofficial intermediaries, and are often 'kicked upstairs' to the Histadrut's central Arab Department after receiving an unenthusiastic local response.[32] At a different level, the Arab Department's traditional preference for institutional segregation of the Histadrut's contacts with its Palestinian members, on the basis of clientelism and patronage, intentionally left little room for these members to become an effective power bloc capable of changing their status within the Histadrut. On the contrary, over the long period during which Arabs were formally barred from full participation in the Histadrut polity, patterns of co-optation and patronage were developed which continue to constrain the propensity of Arab Histadrut activists to militantly press Palestinian interests.[33]

The declining risk of joblessness, and the strong grounds for Jewish workers to expect that Arab permeation of the labour market would be regulated in accordance with their interests, explain why the Jews did not oppose the demise of blatantly exclusionary policies towards Arab labour. The supply-side conflict between Jewish and Palestinian labour had become sufficiently benign to permit a strategic shift in favour of 'caste' segmentation.[34] But there were also other reasons why radical exclusion had become outmoded by the second decade of statehood. The transition to rapid economic growth and full employment stimulated employer interest in new pools of cheap and flexible labour. Israel's

Arab citizens were eager to meet this demand on account of the state's policies of appropriating Arab land, denying development infrastructure or subsidies to Arab localities, and offering far less generous social welfare (public housing, education, and income maintenance) to the Arab population (see Chapter 6). Since the Histadrut continued to espouse its pre-state policy of flexibility towards marginal employers (any Jewish economic footholds were regarded as better than none), it was inclined to take a tolerant view of the existence of cheap labour.

Another important factor at odds with indefinite Arab exclusion from employment by Jews was the economic burden which it would impose on the state. As a result of gifts from foreign governments and Jewish communities the Israeli state enjoyed a remarkable capacity to meet the business sector's extensive requirements for capital subsidy. Nevertheless, its resources were by no means unlimited. Furthermore, capital subsidy was concentrated in the public and Histadrut sectors of the economy (to an extent which indeed allowed them the luxury of an all-Jewish work-force) and the largest private-sector concerns. The perpetuation of a more generalized Arab exclusion would have required not only compensating private employers directly for the inaccessibility of Arab labour, but also offsetting the absence from the labour market of a low-cost labour pool capable of limiting the leverage of high-cost labour.[35] With Arabs barred entirely from the Jewish sector, the government would also have needed to find ways to provide alternative jobs within segregated Palestinian 'homelands'. This would not have been easy. Either the jobs would have had to be publicly funded (again running into resource constraints); or the government would have had to allow Jewish investments to flow into Arab areas (taking jobs away from Jewish workers); or it would have had to permit and even foster the development of an independent Arab economy. This last course of action was absolutely opposed to the policy-makers' strategy of preventing Palestinian citizens from acquiring an autonomous economic infrastructure and, on the contrary, fostering their dependence on state-regulated access to the Jewish economy as a mechanism of political control.[36]

Arab segregation as political exchange

The interests and priorities of the state and the ruling party not only shaped the Histadrut's role *vis-à-vis* Palestinian citizens by favouring a particular pattern of Arab incorporation into the labour market. They also became internalized into the Histadrut's relationship with the Arab minority as part of a *de facto* compact (a 'political exchange' in Pizzorno's (1978) terms) which provided the labour organization with distinct incentives for 'patriotism'. Recall that our question is why, once the labour market conflict between Jews and Arabs was dulled by the approach of full employment, the Jewish labour movement adopted a policy of segmentation rather than equalization towards the Arab minority. Although the forces which have been identified thus far were consistent with the move to segmentation, political exchange was an additional and probably decisive pre-condition. The Histadrut's partial and dualistic incorporation of non-Jewish citizens was part and parcel of *the political role delegated to it by the party/state*, a role for which, it will be argued, the Histadrut has always been amply rewarded.

What was it about the Histadrut that attracted this political role? Essentially the answer is that in order to persuade Israeli Arabs to vote Mapai and to reconcile themselves to living in a Jewish-dominated society, it was not enough simply to make them dependent on the Jewish economy and to operate mechanisms of direct repression. Because of the partial inclusion of Arab citizens within the democratic framework (that is, their right to vote), it was also necessary to develop instrumentalities capable of mobilizing Arab leadership cadres and voters, propagandizing on behalf of the state and the party, and co-opting dissenters. In view of its *partial* distancing from the state and the party, the Histadrut constituted just such an instrumentality. Moreover, it was important to the state that implementation of the Histadrut's economic and social service functions in the Arab sector be carried out in line with the goals of Arab economic and political subordination; and important to the party that they be employed to help mobilize voters.

With this logic of exchange in mind, let us now consider the important issue of *timing*. The Histadrut's shift towards incorporation of Arab members at the end of the 1950s was closely related to changes in the political climate among the Palestinian citizenry. The secondary effects of their growing penetration of Jewish workplaces (they could no longer be literally sealed off, and the permit system was becoming unworkable) together with the beginnings of economic and social consolidation of the Arab communities, the rise of the Communist Party as a vehicle for Arab political opposition, and the weakening of the Jewish consensus in support of military rule, had the combined effect of undermining the effectiveness of coercive methods of regulating the Arab population and mobilizing its votes. Under these conditions there was a clear need for an intermediary less sullied by the stain of the military government era than the agencies of the state itself. It is true that the Histadrut has never succeeded among Israeli Arabs in casting off 'the negative image of a body serving as an "arm of the authorities and the majority party"' (Reches, 1976: 2). Still, from the outset the Histadrut was at least formally detached from the state; it was in a position to provide a wide range of services otherwise unavailable to Arab communities (not only trade union representation but also health insurance, agricultural marketing, and vocational education[37]); and it fitted comfortably into the network of state and party bureaux engaged in exchange of information and administrative co-ordination *vis-à-vis* the Arab minority. It was therefore only natural that the Histadrut should simultaneously take on the tasks of playing an intermediary role for the party and at the same time 'reducing the reservations of the Arabs towards the State of Israel' (Landau, 1976: 4).

This interlocking of Histadrut, party, and state has received a wide variety of concrete expressions.[38] Much of the labour organization's activity has been directed towards the co-optation of power-brokers within Arab communities. In the past, such efforts focused on traditional clan leaders and notables, but more recently the Histadrut has striven 'to fashion a loyal new generation which will identify *politically* with the state' (Reches, 1976: 7, emphasis in original). Thus, the Histadrut has co-operated with the authorities in regulating the allocation of privileges (for example, the issuance of travel permits when the military government was in place); it has acted as a front organization for the distribution of selective benefits (such as university scholarships) financed by the state; and it has directed the vast pool of patronage jobs at its disposal to young Arab 'key men' on the rise in their communities. The Histadrut has also been directly responsible for activities designed to foster Arab loyalty to Israel. It has been active among university students, not only in sponsoring informational activities but also in offering positive inducements (paid positions) to 'hostile' activists. It has used the withdrawal of services (for example, sporting and cultural facilities) to put pressure on communities where Communist influence is on the rise. And for many years the Histadrut operated the only Arabic-language daily newspaper (heavily self-censored) available to many Israeli Arabs.

The Histadrut's efforts at co-optation and persuasion have not only been directed to serving the interests of the state, but are also intended to strengthen the position of the Labour Party in Arab communities. It has exercised this responsibility so heavy-handedly, that the head of the Party's 'minorities division' has publicly urged local Histadrut officials to act with 'genuine comradeship' towards Arab members and to 'no longer see them only as electoral objects' (Cohen, 1983). The Histadrut's party-political role is evident not only at election time, but also is subtly expressed in the institutional design under which Arab citizens have been incorporated into the Histadrut. From the outset there arose a pattern of separate offices within various divisions of the Histadrut Executive, with the major role played by a central Arab Department charged with administering the local matters which for Jewish citizens (and some Arabs) are delegated to labour councils.

The model of segregated and highly centralized bureaucratic control is used by state agencies as well, and has the effect of isolating Arabs from standard practices and entitlements and keeping control over their affairs firmly in the hands of Jewish officials. It has made it easier for the Histadrut to operate 'side by side with . . . and at times complementary to the activities undertaken by the authorities' (Landau, 1976:10). But the absence of labour councils, which went along with the institution of the Arab Department, also indicates a fear that the councils would furnish Palestinian nationalists with an arena for political mobilization and hurt the Labour vote. Beginning in 1980, a series of reforms were initiated under the Labour Party's new slogan of 'integration of minorities', which culminated at the end of 1986 in the formal closure of the current successor to the Arab Department. Simultaneously, the majority of Arab localities were placed within the jurisdiction of labour councils in neighbouring Jewish areas where, judging by previous experience, it could be expected that official or unofficial 'mini Arab Departments' would handle their affairs. The political motive for this reform was made explicit by an internal Labour Party review which concluded that where the Histadrut had established branches in Arab communities in the past, this had provided a generous electoral opening for the Communists and was also associated with a weakening of commitment among the party's local activists. 'Integration', on the other hand, makes it possible not only to avoid this scenario in areas previously under the jurisdiction of the Arab Department, but also to dismantle the local political activity which had sprung up around existing Arab labour councils.[39]

It remains to specify just why the Histadrut agreed to become an arm of state and party policies towards Arab Israelis. In the early years, Histadrut compliance was due in part to its instinctive internalization of party/state objectives and considerable susceptibility to their authority. But it is also clear that the Histadrut has received tangible direct and indirect benefits. These have included gaining access to a captive membership at low cost, in part the result of substandard services but also due to unadvertised state subsidy of Histadrut programmes in the Arab sector. More diffusely, to the extent that the Histadrut successfully serves the vital interests of party and state *vis-à-vis* Arab citizens, this furnishes it with 'credits' which may be assumed to come into play when concessions from the state or the party are sought in seemingly unrelated spheres. In short, the Histadrut's relationship with Palestinians in Israel is part and parcel, however implicitly or invisibly, of the overall context of its relations of political exchange. Beyond this, the labour organization has of course been motivated by the benefits flowing to its core constituency, the Jewish working class, as a result of state support of a nationally segmented labour market.[40]

The relevant interventions of the state have encompassed a wide spectrum of discriminatory practices, some of which have already been alluded to. On the supply side, severe constraints on the economic base of Arab communities, denial of full welfare state protection, and the provision of inferior educational opportunities have 'pushed' the majority of Israel's Palestinian citizens into the secondary labour market.[41] Meanwhile, on the demand side Arabs are prevented from being 'pulled' into the primary labour market by widespread (and in many cases questionable) 'security' requirements, the practices of the public labour exchanges, and (in an earlier period) limitations on freedom of movement. The signal contributions of the state to Arab inferiority in the labour market are, however, not solely the result of a trade-off of state sponsorship of segmentation in return for the Histadrut's political assistance in the Arab sector. The Israeli state's in-built bias in favour of the interests of Jewish citizens and the autonomous weight of many sections of the Jewish work-force would quite possibly have constituted sufficient conditions in themselves for the emergence of a lowly stratum of jobs designated as 'Arab work'. On the other side of the equation, even without the quid pro quo of segmentation, the Histadrut and the state have had sufficient complementary interests to motivate the political exchange which has in turn sustained the organizational and political pattern of relations between the Histadrut and Palestinian citizens.

One final note of reservation concerns the long-term viability of the exchange calculus of Histadrut activity in Israel's Arab sector. Increasing political self-assertiveness on the part of Arab-Israelis and the Labour Party's loss of control over the political executive since 1977, have undoubtedly diminished the relevance of the division of labour between Histadrut, party, and state which developed in the 1950s. Nevertheless, the Histadrut's internalization of 'state responsibility' remains essentially intact, while reforms of its apparatus in the Arab sector during the 1980s clearly reveal that the labour organization continues to strive to serve Labour Party interests. The continuing significance of these political foundations of Histadrut practice is rendered all the more salient by the absence of a comparable rationale in the third historical phase of the labour organization's relationship with Palestinian labour. This new context, brought about by Israel's conquest of former Jordanian and Egyptian territory in June 1967, is our next concern.

After 1967: Economic integration and organizational exclusion

The occupation of the West Bank and Gaza Strip which followed the third Arab–Israeli war raised anew the spectre of conflict between low- and high-priced labour. Jewish labour potentially confronted a new Arab minority which was both numerically large and in acute economic straits. But in sharp contrast to the pre-sovereignty context, the Jews could realistically expect the state to protect their interests. Indeed, the authorities were in a position to exert near-absolute control over the participation of non-citizen

Palestinians in the labour market of Israel proper. The response which emerged in the early years, when the future of the occupation was in doubt, subsequently remained unaltered by the economic and territorial 'creeping annexation' of the occupied territories. It represented a repetition (and actual deepening) of the kind of labour market segmentation already practised *vis-à-vis* Arab citizens, coupled with a policy of exclusion of Palestinians in the territories from the Histadrut. This new mutation constitutes in effect a hybrid of the Jewish labour movement's pre-1948 *organizational* praxis and its *labour market* praxis during the period since sovereignty. This suggests two interesting questions. Why did the Histadrut choose not to oppose the employment of non-citizens, given the harm it could potentially cause to the interests of citizen labour? And why, on the other hand, did it end up reproducing only the economic and not the organizational dimension of its existing relations with Arab labour? For, unlike the trade unions of the West, when they were confronted with a similar phenomenon in the framework of migrant labour (the 'guest worker' system),[42] the Histadrut has neither gradually opened its doors to the Palestinians of the territories, nor mounted forceful campaigns to drive them from the labour market in periods of economic crisis.

Before turning directly to a consideration of the Histadrut's role, it is necessary to introduce the principal features of the participation of non-citizen Palestinians in the labour market inside Israel's pre-1967 borders.[43] The entry of workers from the occupied territories began immediately following the war even though, with the exception of residents of East Jerusalem, their employment in Israel was initially forbidden. This prohibition reflected the danger that the labour market (which was still in the throes of the severe economic recession which had begun late in 1965) would be swamped by masses of unemployed workers from Gaza and the West Bank. In the summer of 1968 it was officially decided to allow workers from the territories to accept jobs in Israel, but based on approval of individual applications and within the limits of an overall quota to be set in consultation with the Histadrut. The take off began in the spring of 1969, when the estimated number of non-citizen Palestinians employed in Israel reached 15,000, of whom only a third had been processed legally by the Employment Service. During the early 1970s, a period of rapid economic growth in Israel with unemployment at a historic low, the phenomenon of commuter labour from the territories expanded rapidly to a level of 65,000 by 1973. In the wake of the economic crisis following the Yom Kippur War and the first oil price shock this expansion was halted—but not reversed. From the late 1970s the numbers crept up again and, prior to the Palestinian uprising which broke out at the end of 1987, had passed the 100,000 mark—a very sizeable bloc of the total work-force in the territories (roughly one-third for the West Bank and a half for Gaza).[44]

While non-citizen Palestinians constitute only a small proportion of Israel's global labour force of 1.5 million, they represent a prominent or dominant element in several branches (notably agriculture and construction) and numerous menial/unstable occupations. In effect, workers from the territories have replaced citizen Palestinians as the stable core at the bottom of Israel's occupational structure. From an employer perspective, these workers have played an important role in several respects. They have sheltered some industries (notably construction) from the need to make costly technological innovations; filled unstable and poorly paid jobs which are spurned by citizens 'buffered' by public education and income maintenance; and, during economic downturns, have been far more willing than Israeli workers to accept wage cuts. Finally, a variety of evidence suggests that the presence of non-citizen Palestinian labour has had the effect of depressing the overall wage gains of citizen labour (at least during the initial influx), as well as weakening specific vulnerable groups within the Israeli working class. Still, state intervention (or failure to intervene) has to some extent had the effect of shielding the citizen work-force. In particular, non-enforcement of equal pay laws, referral of only undesirable work through the Employment Service, and the military government's repression of Palestinian trade unions have significantly facilitated the confinement of non-citizen workers to the secondary labour market.

The Histadrut's contribution to Palestinian segmentation[45]

Clearly, none of this could have happened without the sanction of the Histadrut. Yet the most conspicuous feature of the Histadrut's response to the employment of workers from Gaza and the West Bank and their emergent role within the labour market has been its posture of non-decision and non-involvement. Since the onset of the occupation, the Histadrut has on a few occasions only raised the issue for debate and decision-making in its highest executive body, the Central Committee. No concrete steps have been taken to enrol non-citizen Palestinians as members or even to bring them under the umbrella of the labour organization's social services on a non-membership basis. The Histadrut supports the principle of equal wages and benefits and is formally committed to providing workers from the territories with the protection of local unions and work-place committees. But in practice almost the sole contact between these workers and the Histadrut is an 'organization tax' deducted from the wages of those who are under the care of the Employment Service.

The records of Histadrut policy discussions during the early years of the occupation reveal that its governing bodies supported the establishment of mechanisms for preventing cheap labour from flooding into the Israeli labour market. But beyond this, the Histadrut was content to allow the pace and conditions of the Palestinians' employment in Israel to be determined by the combined effects of market forces and the government's interpretation of Israel's geopolitical requirements. In the latter realm members of the Histadrut élite, like other politicians in Israel, were deeply divided over the 'hawkish' strategy which actually took hold, of foreclosing territorial compromise by tightly linking the economy of the occupied territories to employment in and trade with Israel. But all Israeli leaders, in the government and the Histadrut alike, accepted the premise that so long as Israel ruled the territories it was necessary to raise economic standards and provide employment in order to prevent violent unrest among the occupied population. In principle these economic targets could have been achieved in a variety of ways. Development of the territories themselves was an obvious possibility but an unattractive one, since it would have drained resources (whether public or private) from the Israeli economy. Moreover, there was a danger in this case of the territories becoming an economic competitor, as well as acquiring the economic infrastructure necessary for political independence.

In the final analysis the option of employment in Israel was compelling, even to most 'doves', because of the pressure of unsatisfied employer demand for cheap unskilled labour. War-related employment growth after the Six Day War—in construction, in expanding military industries, and in the army proper—gave rise to severe labour shortages in the civilian building industry, in agriculture, and (in time) lower-level service and production jobs in the private sector. In addition, the state's economic ministers and bureaucrats were anxious that rapid growth and labour-market bottlenecks not give rise to a general wage explosion. Hence, they viewed the entry of labour from the territories as a desirable antidote. The Histadrut itself had clear interests in the same direction. In its role as a corporatist labour organization with responsibilities for economic stabilization and wage restraint, the Histadrut could hardly have relished the prospects of a return to the conditions experienced under full employment earlier in the decade—inflation, wildcat strikes, and difficult-to-manage conflicts among rival groups of workers (Chapter 5). And, as the owner of the largest industrial and construction firms in the country, it was bound to be receptive to non-citizen workers, either for filling job vacancies or for moderating general wage rises. Consequently, when in November 1968 an ageing labour-movement figure from the pre-state era pleaded for a return to the movement's historic principles by seeking out *Jewish* workers and volunteers to combat labour shortages, he received short shrift from the Histadrut's Secretary-General, who stated: 'I'm not talking about "Hebrew Labour". There are branches of the economy thirsty for manpower' (cited by Slutsky, 1985: 37).

The economic rationale for the entry of workers from the territories could not have earned the labour organization's blessing, had these workers posed a serious threat to the interests of Histadrut members. But it soon became clear that this was not the case. The combination of rapid growth in aggregate employment, new opportunities for upward job mobility by citizens, and extensions of the welfare state safety net covering many of those unable to benefit from these trends made direct competition for jobs an unlikely prospect—at least, not unless the state had encouraged an unlimited flow of non-citizen labour.[46] Whatever the benefits of an 'open' labour market from the perspective of the military government or nationalist politicians, or its economic justification, no Israeli government would be willing to preside over Jewish citizens and Arab non-citizens fighting over the same jobs or to risk the popular support of those voters (mainly Eastern Jews) most vulnerable to displacement. On the other hand, the sectors of Israeli organized labour that count most for the Histadrut—namely, professional employees and workers in 'essential' public services and the large corporations owned by the Histadrut and the state—had ample market and/or organizational strength to prevent the entry of non-citizen labour into their work-place (except in jobs they wanted to leave), and sufficient political clout to oblige the state to cover the resultant economic cost.

The determinants of organizational exclusion

If we return to the theory of cost-split labour markets, it will now be apparent that there is little reason for surprise at the Histadrut's preference for a segmentation strategy over the alternatives of exclusion or integration. The possible benefits of this strategy far outweighed its attendant risks, especially as the issue was considered following several decades of successful experience with the segmentation of Israel's Palestinian citizens. Something more of a puzzle is posed by the Histadrut's organizational and political relationship with Palestinian labourers from the territories, since here there was a substantial departure from the model adopted in relation to Arab citizens. Instead of a process of gradual and segregated organizational incorporation and a relationship of political tutelage, we find a definite pattern of exclusion. It was argued earlier that the reasons for the peculiar pattern of inclusion of non-Jewish citizens had to be sought in the realm of political exchange between the Histadrut and the party/state. It is necessary to turn in this same direction in order to grasp why this pattern was *not* adopted *vis-à-vis* workers from the occupied territories.

The fundamental difference between the two contexts is that under conditions of occupation, the regime's need for popular legitimation and the ways in which it can be achieved are quite different to the requirements of a liberal democracy, however illiberally it may act in relation to national minorities. The government of Israel does not need to stand for re-election in Gaza, and neither does it expect the residents of the West Bank to approve of its rule. Moreover, during the first two decades of military government, the regime had at its disposal sufficient positive and coercive instruments to maintain the occupation without having to resort to intermediary instruments of persuasion. Moshe Dayan, who designed and directed the occupation in its formative years, was at one point receptive to overtures from the Histadrut's Arab Department to re-enact its political bridge-building role on the other side of the green line, since he believed that this would further the cause of *de facto* annexation.[47] But nothing came of this, because of the opposition of doves and others in the government who feared the diplomatic repercussions, and resistance by the military government and the Ministry of Labour which opposed losing important functions to the Histadrut.

No less significant for understanding the non-emergence of political exchange as a basis for Histadrut activity among non-citizen Palestinians, has been the state's reluctance to meet the labour organization's demands for material incentives. Instead of 15 per cent of the wages of workers from the territories which it had initially hoped to obtain, after two decades of bickering with the authorities the Histadrut is entitled to only the same one per cent tax which is levied on citizen non-members. Moreover, it has been unable to enforce its claim to the customary worker and employer contributions to Histadrut Provident Funds. During the first few years following the Six Day War, when the system of commuter labour was being set up, the principle was established that in order to prevent unfair competition not only wage rates but also the deductions applicable to workers from the territories should be harmonized with Israeli standards. The Histadrut's enthusiasm for this principle derived in part from the expectation that it would receive deductions normally earmarked for its own pension, sickness, and other social insurance programmes; but instead the money was passed to the Treasury. The Ministry of Labour, the Treasury, and the military government all have an interest in the perpetuation of this system, which has deprived the Histadrut of revenues believed to run into hundreds of millions of dollars.[48] The Histadrut has periodically tried to call attention to the issue by publicly accusing the Ministry of Labour of failure to implement the policy of equal pay and benefits, and by threatening to embarrass Israel internationally. Countercharges of Histadrut neglect by public officials, as well as the Histadrut's own international sensitivities, have generated a series of largely empty commitments to furnishing trade union protection to the Palestinian workers from the territories.[49]

Conclusions

The Histadrut has never practised binational class solidarity between Jewish and Palestinian workers. But within this essential continuity, both the nature of Arab–Jewish conflict in the labour market and the Histadrut's response have exhibited distinctive characteristics in different historical periods. Prior to sovereignty Jewish labour constituted an expensive enclave within a sea of cheap labour, and it lacked the political capacities to establish the right to privileged treatment. The Jewish labour movement responded with aggressive attempts to bar Arabs from holding jobs. After 1948 Arab workers in Israel became a labour-market minority under conditions of pronounced political subordination, and Jewish labour consented to permitting the utilization of Palestinians' labour—conditional, however, on Jews choosing not to exercise their preferential right to employment. Since the Six Day War an even cheaper and weaker pool of non-citizen Arab labour emerged as a result of the occupation, a development which reinforced the construction of a quite rigid nationality-based segmentation of the job structure.

The common denominator of each of these historical contexts has been the coexistence of 'cheap' and 'expensive' labour in a potentially undifferentiated market. The settlers' initial encounter with this split labour market was the most important factor leading Jewish organized labour into its historic alliance with the Zionist movement and along the path of militant nationalism. At a later stage there occurred a transition from an exclusionary to a 'caste' strategy, in the course of which the splitting of the labour market (the differential reservation wage of Arabs and Jews) was itself transformed. From its beginnings as a historical accident predetermined by the transplantation of European settlers into a traditional economy, the Palestinians' role as a cheap labour force became far more a consequence of policies pursued by the Histadrut and the state, independently of labour market considerations.

The threefold periodization which highlights the evolution of the Histadrut's labour-market strategy also captures the major turning-points in its organizational relationship with the Palestinians. In the Yishuv era, the labour organization was committed to playing at most a reactive role in organizing Arabs. Its leaders were determined to prevent any separation of the Histadrut's labourist and Zionist functions or any possibility of Palestinian trade unionists acquiring the capacity to influence policy-making from within. In the dramatically changed political and labour-market conditions associated with Israeli sovereignty, there was no longer a contradiction between adherence to these priorities and the organization of Arab labour, especially since their inclusion was effected within institutional arrangements based on segregation and control. Following the territorial expansion of 1967, organizational policy came full circle with the exclusion of workers from the West Bank and Gaza from Histadrut membership and most of its services.

While the Histadrut has always exhibited an awareness of the economic dilemmas posed by a cost-split labour market, its relationship with the Palestinians has also been a function of political dynamics, partly growing out of the logic of the labour market nexus and partly independent of it. In the formative encounter at the close of the Ottoman period, the damaging consequences of Arab competition convinced most of the political leaders of Jewish labour that insulation from this competition could only be achieved in the context of a more general polarization of Arabs and Jews. Later, while the practical struggle to bar Palestinians from employment in the Jewish economy yielded limited instrumental benefits, the labour élite retained its enthusiasm for this struggle because it provided potent support for the labour movement's claim to hegemony over the entire Zionist Yishuv. The campaign for 'Hebrew labour' not only presented the movement as having taken on one of the most difficult challenges of the Zionist project. It also assisted labour leaders in preventing their rank and file from drifting beyond their control by providing a focus for solidarity and, at times, by deflecting workers' attention away from labour Zionism's limited success in defending their economic interests.

The state and party-building strategies which the labour movement embraced following sovereignty encouraged the Histadrut to opt for continuation of Jewish labour-market exclusivism, despite the markedly diminished economic threat posed by Arab labour. When with the transition to full employment the remaining labour-market rationale for exclusion dwindled, the Histadrut continued to shun the path of binationalism. In this it was guided not only by the material benefits which Jewish workers and employers could obtain from institutionalizing the economic disadvantages of

Palestinian citizens in a segmented labour market; but also by the willingness of the state and the ruling party to reward the labour organization for using its segregated and clientelistic relationship with Arab members as an effective means of mobilizing their political allegiance.

The entry of commuter labourers from the occupied territories signalled a new era in the relationship between the Histadrut and the Palestinians. On the one hand, this has been a phase of continuity: extension of the trend towards a nationally divided labour market and the virtual eclipse of 'Jewish-only' rhetoric. Yet there has also been a sharp break with the tradition of treating Arab workers as objects of exchange between the Histadrut and political élites. The barring of Palestinians from the Histadrut prior to sovereignty, and their bounded 'integration' afterwards, are contrasting manifestations of essentially the same dynamic of political exchange. But in relation to non-citizen Palestinians from the occupied territories, neither the authorities nor the Labour Party have required the Histadrut's legitimizing and controlling activities; and the price which the Histadrut wished to exact for its services was unacceptably high. This shift to a relationship of competition for the right to mediate and profit from the labour-market encounter between Jews and Palestinians joined other trends antithetical to the Histadrut's political role. By now the national conflict has progressed far beyond the formative stage when the labour organization performed yeoman service in directing Arab–Jewish relations into an adversarial matrix. Even the task which the Histadrut took on after sovereignty, of assisting in the mobilization and control of Arab citizens, has become increasingly ineffective and incongruous.

In presenting the Israeli–Palestinian conflict as a product of the dynamic interaction between Arabs and Jews on the soil of Palestine, and in insisting on the role of material interests in elevating the national cleavage to predominance, we have consciously parted ways with prevailing Jewish understandings of Israeli society.[50] The relevant scholarship concerning the labour-market conflict which arose in the formative period of Zionist colonization, has generally embraced one of two alternative views. The 'official' position, traditionally adopted by historians close to the labour movement, is that as a matter of a priori Zionist and socialist principle, the worker-pioneers were opposed from the outset to the employment of Arab labour by Jewish employers. The rationale for this exclusionary attitude is self-evident from a Zionist perspective, while the socialist argument was that by hiring Arabs the Jews would be setting themselves up as the economic overlords of a non-Jewish proletariat.

An alternative, 'revisionist' interpretation, is that the impulse for labour-market separatism was essentially economic—Jewish and Arab competition for jobs. In time, however, as labour Zionism's socialist fervour weakened, as Arab opposition to Jewish nationalism became more violent, and as the labour movement élite recognized the intra-communal political benefits of championing exclusively Jewish employment, then the labour-market conflict became almost indistinguishable from the national struggle between Arabs and Jews.[51] Without rejecting this interpretation we have gone one step further to argue that the national conflict itself was to an important extent the product of how Jewish labour pursued its labour-market interests. In other words, neither Arab animosity to Zionism, nor Zionist labour's national hostility towards the Arabs, were purely exogenous forces superimposed upon the market nexus. Rather, they were shaped by conflicts taking place within that nexus.

A second point on which this chapter is at odds with mainstream writings about Israel is the relative weight of ideology versus interests in explaining the labour movement's internalization of national (and later also state) interests. It is once again possible to distinguish a quasi-official view, which attributes a great deal of altruistic commitment to the pioneers, or, alternatively, a debunking revisionism, which presents ideology as a smoke-screen for self-serving interests.[52] We have here taken for granted the primacy of rational–economic motivations for the members of labour organizations, especially under conditions in which compelling material interests are at stake. It does not follow, however, that collective *political* action belongs to a different world, the world of ideology rather than interest. The major differences between the regulation of labour markets by individual bargaining, collective bargaining, and political forms of exchange concern the institutional framework and the criteria by which power is mobilized, rather than labour's intent in entering into exchange.[53] There is thus a good deal of theoretical plausibility (as well as historical evidence) for the view that the Histadrut's internalization of the conflict between Israeli and Palestinian nationalism has, from its very beginning, been rooted in an instrumental calculus. The Zionism in 'labour Zionism' cannot be separated from the pressing need of the original propertyless settlers to combat their economic vulnerability and, at a subsequent stage, from the labour movement's desire to advance its organizational and political interests. The ideology which the pioneers brought with them is therefore most appropriately viewed as a repertoire which predisposed rather than predetermined action. In Portugali's words (1986: 335), '"Proletarianization" was transformed into "the conquest of labour" [from Arab labourers], "ruralization" into the "conquest of land" [from the Arabs].' Jewish labour's nationalism, like its economic collectivism, was primarily forged in Palestine, on the anvil of political exchange.

The Jewish workers of Palestine organized broadly and centrally, and they loudly and eloquently spoke the language of class politics—except that in a binational community theirs was, by and large, a 'socialism in one nation'. We pointed out at the beginning of this chapter that, in view of the Israeli labour movement's institutional resemblance to working-class organizations in social-democratic corporatist settings, its tradition of national exclusivism constitutes something of a theoretical puzzle. Many studies of working-class mobilization have assumed that comprehensive and concentrated labour organization can only develop on the basis of an encompassing class solidarity. In turn, in the tradition of political sociology pioneered by Rokkan (1970) and others, 'cross-cutting cleavages', like race and religion, have been viewed as antithetical to the class organization of labour. Applied to the Jewish–Arab case, this model would surmise that the national cleavage constituted a pre-existing political mould into which working-class mobilization, when it came, was poured. On the contrary, however, in Palestine the mobilization of Jewish workers and the emergence of the national conflict were chronologically and causally interlaced as the labour movement sought and acquired the vanguard role in a more general struggle for Jewish separatism.

Our discussion has tried to transcend the limitations of theories which assume a simple polarity between worker solidarity and static social, economic, or political 'cleavages'. It has been suggested instead that Jewish labour organization in Palestine/Israel has been driven by an economic and a political logic, which are distinguishable although closely connected. Theoretically, this constitutes an argument for a political-economy analysis which more effectively integrates the economic and the political. Specifically, our case study points to the error of treating rifts among workers generated by the competitive logic of labour markets, and politicized organizational splits linked to primordial distinctions like race or religion, as two different sources of working-class fragmentation. In Palestine the labour-market conflict between workers of two nationalities was, to a significant degree, the source of the developing national enmity between them. Jewish–Arab economic competition propelled Jewish labour into the arms of organized Zionism, a partnership which both enabled and required the Jewish working class to organize under the roof of a comprehensive peak organization. In Palestine at least, economic frictions thus did not atomize the working class, as Marx and Engels might have feared. Instead, as Bonacich anticipated, they drove its most 'advanced' section to organize along highly solidaristic yet exclusionary lines.

Notes

1. See, for example, Shalev and Korpi (1980).
2. While the idea of 'non-competing labour' or 'balkanized labour markets' has a long history in economics, modern theories of dual or segmented markets arose out of attempts to trace the origins of racial inequality to labour market structures and dynamics. For samplings and overviews of the literature on segmentation see Edwards, Reich, and Gordon (1973); Kalleberg and Sorensen (1979); Lever-Tracy (1984); and Rosenberg (1989). For a lucid exposition of Bonacich's theory see her original (1972) statement of the theory; and also Bonacich (1976; 1979). An especially insightful treatment is offered by Peled and Shafir (1987).
3. Gordon (1972); Harrison (1974); and Doeringer and Piore (1971) are classic 'demand-side' texts. Gordon, Edwards, and Reich (1982) is a more recent vintage, which departs from the deterministic flavour of some earlier work. However, these authors, too, stress primarily the role of 'peripheral' employers' demand for low-wage labour, adding, however, that 'core' and service-industry employers also contribute to ethnic job segregation by exploiting race as a means of marking off labour market segments within the firm.

4. This argument is more fully elaborated in Chapter 3.
5. In this and other chapters we make frequent use of the term 'the state'. Contemporary social science has experienced a highly publicized resurrection of the concept of the state, and for good reasons (see, for example, Evans, Rueschemeyer, and Skocpol, 1985; Carnoy (1984); Panitch (1986); Block (1987). At one level, we speak of the state merely as a convenient form of shorthand which, at its grandest, represents the totality of the public institutions that collectively monopolize sovereignty and the legitimate right to exercise coercion within given territorial boundaries. Particularly in Israel, where what Sharkansky (1979) has called the 'margins' of the Israeli state are inordinately broad, it is not easy to identify a uniquely public sphere which is distinguishable from 'civil society'. In most of this book when we speak of the state as an actor, we refer in practice to the critical loci of public authority in Israel regarding social, economic, and labour policy: the Cabinet (particularly the Minister of Finance), the relevant bureaucracies (mainly the Treasury and the Bank of Israel), and the most influential parliamentary committees (especially the Finance Committee).

   But there is also a more abstract meaning of the state, which views it—like other social institutions—as possessing a logic and an internal dynamic which, for example, transcend particular governments. Because we think it is analytically fruitful to do so (for reasons to be discussed in the Conclusions to this book), we often speak of the state in this abstract fashion, *as if* it were a single coherent actor. In these instances we find it legitimate to take a macroscopic view of the state, largely relying on broad circumstantial evidence to infer the motives and actions of the individuals and subunits which 'really' make up the state.
6. The following discussion of the background to the Histadrut's establishment relies upon evidence assembled in Shafir's (1989) innovative study, as well as another recent work on the Second Aliyah period (Ben-Porat, 1986) which revives the conventional interpretation. For information on the labour-market conditions faced by Jewish workers and their responses, we have drawn upon the survey of the 'Hebrew labour struggle' prior to 1929 which appears in the Introduction to Anita Shapira's (1977) authoritative work.
7. See Sussman (1969*a*: ch. 3).
8. There is a consensus among virtually all writers on the emergence of economic collectivism in labour Zionism that the initial impetus was instrumental/pragmatic rather than programmatic. Standard sources in English on the labour-movement collectives include Viteles (1966); Daniel (1976); and Preuss (1965).
9. See Shapiro (1976: 79).

10. Insistence on the calculative foundation of the labour movement's embrace of what he terms 'mutual dependence' with organized Zionism was one of the signal contributions of the now classic study by Yonathan Shapiro (1976) of the *Achdut Avodah* Party cited in n. 9. For a survey of the philosophy of the Palestine Office of the WZO, which reveals much about the practical calculus on which co-operation with organized labour first developed see Reichman and Hasson (1984). Arthur Ruppin, the head of the Palestine Office and the architect of its colonization policy, was quite clear about the nature of the exchange between Zionism and the working-class pioneers. For a succinct statement, see his article in *The New Judea*, 26 Sept. 1924.
11. The importance of Zionist subsidy for economic collectivism (which from 1920 came under the direction of the Histadrut) and even for the labour organization's day-to-day operating costs, has been documented by Tsachor (1979: 132–9); Gross (1979: 47–50); and Shapiro (1976: 71–82). An analysis of financial reports by Lucatz (1961: 214–17) reveals that throughout the Mandatory period the Histadrut's supporters in the USA supplied the majority of the revenues of the Histadrut Executive (whose budget financed the operation of the central bureaucracy, aid to co-operatives, and 'educational' activity).
12. As it developed in the immediate post-war period, 'economic collectivism' implied the following practical steps: (*a*) extension of the various forms of producer co-operation, outside as well as within agriculture, to eliminate worker dependence on wage labour; (*b*) mechanisms intended to facilitate access to new jobs coming into existence as the labour market expanded—notably, collective self-employment and labour-controlled employment offices; and (*c*) the labour movement's contribution (through subsidized 'mutual aid') to meeting the costs of workers' participation in both the private and socialized economies.
13. We have over-simplified the discussion of the partnership between the labour and Zionist movements by presenting it not only as a logical but also an uncontested development. In fact, however, opposition did emerge on both sides of the alliance. Pro-bourgeois forces within the Zionist movement launched several major battles against earmarking the bulk of its funds for the Histadrut and its various instrumentalities, and advocated alternative forms of settlement intended to attract the middle classes. Metzer (1979) is a comprehensive study of 'national capital' and the conflicting claims over it. Shapiro (1976: ch. 8) has analysed the pivotal struggle which developed in the late 1920s, showing how it contributed to the merger of the two main workers' parties and their decision to try

to conquer the Zionist movement electorally. Within the labour movement, communists and proto-communist elements consistently opposed co-operation between the working class in Palestine and the bourgeoisie in the Zionist movement. For further details see Margalit (1976) and our own discussion of the left opposition to Mapai, in Chapter 3.

14. Since our primary concern in this section of the chapter is to explain the origins of the Histadrut's internalization of the conflict between Zionism and the Palestinians, this is not the place to engage in extended debate regarding the historical forces which gave birth to the Histadrut. For readers with an interest in this issue, some additional remarks are, however, appropriate. First, for the sake of clarity it should be acknowledged that the Histadrut was not a radical innovation for the Jewish labour movement in Palestine. Rather, it represented the culmination of earlier experiments (the agricultural unions and Achdut Avodah)—the result of 'institutional learning' and the new conditions brought about by British rule.

A second and more important caveat—or actually, refusal to enter a caveat—concerns a major discrepancy between our account and conventional renderings of the background to the Histadrut's establishment. The latter (e.g. Preuss, 1965; Lucatz, 1961; Kolatt, 1973) typically stress the role of the post-war wave of pioneer immigrants (the Third Aliyah). These idealistic youngsters, influenced by their experiences in Russia following the 1917 revolution, doubtless contributed to the demand for Jewish 'class unity'. It is also true that the disdain of the newcomers towards partisan appeals made it clear that a continued contest between the two workers' parties of the time in providing services to the still tiny community of labour colonists would be politically ruinous. Yet in our view these trends were of less significance than the fact that a unified framework which could unite the labour movement functionally and politically, was the essential practical pre-condition for implementing a programme of economic collectivism in partnership with the Zionist Organization.

This emerges clearly from the establishment of the Workers' Bank (*Bank Hapoalim*), a key instrument by which Zionist funds were channelled to the labour movement's economic collectives (Greenberg, 1983; esp. 39–41). After the war the most important new opportunities for collectivism lay in group contracting for construction and roadbuilding. When the two main labour parties responded by setting up rival contracting offices, it became apparent that competition was a barrier both to winning contracts and to acquiring the Zionist financial aid necessary even to purchase basic equipment. These problems could not be overcome until after the establishment of the Histadrut, which took upon itself the tasks of unifying the existing contracting offices and formally adopting the Workers' Bank. Only then did the Zionist Organization release the bank's founding capital, which it had promised a bipartisan delegation of labour leaders a year earlier.

15. The strains in relations between the Histadrut leadership and rank and file to which this gave rise are discussed in Chapter 4.
16. The fate of Jewish proposals for 'joint organization' during the 1920s and 1930s has been documented by Shapira (1977). See ch. 2 in each of the major sections of her volume.
Several significant exceptions to the Jewish policy of Arab exclusion are worth citing because they rather clearly prove the rule:

1. Not long after the Histadrut was established, Ben-Gurion (who was the labour organization's Secretary-General until 1935) proposed that the Jews seek out 'economic, political and cultural concerted action' with the 'toiling Arab masses'—including the establishment of binational trade unions. But soon after, the labour leader and his Achdut Avodah Party revived the demand to reserve 'Jewish jobs' for Jewish workers and proposed an alternative conception of 'joint organization' on a separate-but-equal basis (Shapira, 1977: 64–9). This about-face occurred because it had rapidly become clear that, contrary to initial expectations: (*a*) the Jews were not about to become a majority ruling an autonomous 'national home'; (*b*) most Jews would now be dependent on paid labour for economic survival; and (*c*) it was unrealistic to expect that if offered Jewish–Arab working-class co-operation, Arab workers would be willing to side with the Zionist cause in opposition to their own leaders.

2. A second exceptional case has been documented by Grinberg (1986). This was a ten-day joint strike by Jewish and Arab truck drivers during 1931. The key to the Jewish labour movement's support of this strike was that it was launched in an industry split down the middle between Jews and Arabs and that the target of the strike was the Mandatory authorities, whose tax and fuel-price policies had been hurting the drivers. Ben-Gurion tried to put an early end to the strike, and when it was over rejected overtures from some Arab and Jewish elements to use it as a springboard for deepening binational co-operation. Instead, the Jewish drivers (who like the Arabs were largely self-employed) were persuaded to form a Jewish-only co-operative under the Histadrut's auspices.

3. Finally, the 1925 strike at the Nesher cement works (on which see a report by one of the participants; Studni, 1974) is a reveal-

ing instance of opposition by the labour élite to spontaneous, binational trade union activity. This was a case in which Jewish strikers enlisted the solidarity of 80 contract labourers who had been brought from Egypt to perform construction work at the quarries. After the dispute was resolved, the Haifa labour council—clearly disturbed by the initiative taken by its rank and file—overruled the Jewish workers' request that the settlement make provision for the Arabs who had stopped work at their request.

17. This is not to say that there was no labour-market rationale at all for Jewish hostility towards Arab labour during the boom years. Shapira (1977: 229) points out that while the so-called 'purification' of 'Jewish' work-places (from the impurity of non-Jewish labour) was out of place in the context of labour shortages, the sponsors of the campaign against Arab labour were able to appeal to the anxiety among some Jewish workers that Arabs might beat them in the race for the high-paying jobs proliferating in some industries, particularly construction. Despite this, Shapira's account indicates that the urban revival of the Hebrew labour campaign was not a response to grass-roots concerns, but a deliberate attempt by the leadership to compensate for the natural death of the struggle against Arab workers in the Moshavot.
18. For a survey of opinions and ideological positions in the Zionist labour movement *vis-à-vis* 'the Arab problem' see Lucatz (1961: 218–39).
19. The argument about 'unorganizability' had two components. The economic (the genuine problem of virtually unlimited supply and the fact that many Arab workers were only semi-proletarianized) was discussed earlier in this chapter. The other hypothesis is a cultural one. The view that problems of language and 'mentality' severely hampered co-operation between Jewish and Arab workers was echoed by Shapira (1977), although her own evidence and that of other studies cited earlier clearly belie such assumptions.
20. For general background material on the social, political, and economic position of Israel's Arab minority see Jiryis (1976); Lustick (1980); Smooha (1982); and Zureik (1979).
21. This section relies on documentary evidence brought to light by Segev (1986: 44–6). See Segev's book in general, and in greater detail the work of Kamen (1987) on Jewish policy towards the Palestinians at the time independence was proclaimed and regarding the experiences of the Israeli-Arab community in the aftermath of statehood.
22. Mapai's success in the Arab sector is analysed in greater detail in Chapter 3.

23. By 'Easterners' we refer to the *Mizrachim*, those Jews who immigrated to Israel from North Africa and the Middle East, as distinct from 'Westerners' (Ashkenazim), those of European origin.
24. On Mapai's swing to the right see in particular Rosenfeld and Carmi (1976). We further discuss the implications of sovereignty for Mapai's political strategy and for its programmatic priorities in Chapters 3 and 6.
25. The Central Bureau of Statistics conducted its first sample survey of the labour force in 1954, a year in which the aggregate level of unemployment was probably already falling due to the onset of substantial economic growth. Comparative unemployment rates for the major Jewish population groups were: Western veterans = 3%, Western newcomers (immigrated since 1948) = 8%, and Eastern newcomers = 15% (CBS Special Publications No. 56, Table 7).
26. Among the Histadrut's contributions to ethnic segmentation among Jews were the major role played by Histadrut-linked industry and agriculture as an employer of new immigrants in unskilled jobs; the labour organization's consent to large-scale public works paying below-market wages; and its conspicuous failure to press for universal social insurance against unemployment and other risks in a context where veterans enjoyed 'permanent' status and were eligible for generous seniority-linked compensation in the event of dismissal. For an authoritative analysis of the ethnic division of labour see Bernstein and Swirski (1982). We place this issue in a wider political–economic context in subsequent chapters.
27. The conditions of Arab employment in the Jewish sector during the 1950s are reviewed by Ben-Porath (1966; see also 1984) and by Jiryis (1976: 219–24). Ben-Porath (1966: 51–2) explicitly notes that the military government co-operated with the Ministry of Labour in regulating the issuance of travel permits in accordance with fluctuations in Jewish unemployment, while Lustick (1980: 204–7) indicates the partisan–political aspect of the system.
28. The polarization of positions in the Histadrut on the issue of Arab incorporation should, however, not be exaggerated. Even the supporters of organizational unity accepted, in Mapam's own words, 'the supremacy of Zionist realization and of the task of ingathering the exiles' (Kantor, 1977: 98). In so far as declarations such as this constituted more than ritualistic deference to the hegemonic ideology of the period, it is hard to see how the 'supremacy of Zionism' etc. could have been implemented without sacrificing 'complete class equality'.
29. We have reconstructed the process of Histadrut incorporation of Arab citizens from a number of sources including Kantor (1977); Regev (1985); and Landau (1976). Note that in addition to the

creation of local Arab unions cited in the text, Arabs were also supposed to be offered representation in several of the Histadrut's existing national unions operating in branches with sizeable concentrations of Palestinian employment. However, this did not eventuate in either of the branches—agriculture and personal services—in which Palestinian wage-earners were concentrated at this stage.

30. Ben-Porath's analysis (1966: ch. 2) of the position of non-Jews in the employment structure indicates that during the 1958–64 period the major developments were Arab entry into construction and their persistence in agriculture while Eastern Jews were departing.
31. According to Watad (1966: 31) the legislation also entitles the exchanges to remove workers from outside the area in order to free jobs for unemployed local residents. It should be pointed out that the establishment of exchanges in non-Jewish localities is to this day grossly incomplete, particularly in the Galilee.
32. The impression that the Histadrut's trade union services to Arab members continue to be limited and ineffectual is suggested both by university-sponsored research (Regev, 1985; Leventhal-Shartal, 1985) and by friendly critics of Histadrut policy (Reches, 1976; Cohen, 1983). Some Arab workers have access to a labour council or a similar body in their area of residence which may try to intervene on the worker's behalf; although because of the jurisdictional set-up, this has to be done (in Reches' words) 'almost covertly'. Even this option is lacking in the majority of Arab localities where there is no Histadrut branch. It is doubtful whether the Histadrut's more recent policy of having Arab areas without councils 'adopted' by those in adjacent Jewish localities has improved Arab access to trade union protection.
33. In the context of a comparative analysis of South Africa, Israel and Alabama, Stanley Greenberg (1980: ch. 16) offers some useful information regarding the barriers to Arab political participation inside the Histadrut. For additional discussion see Chapter 3, n. 36.
34. A growing body of scholarly work affirms the existence of a caste-like polarization of Arab and Jewish (citizens) jobs. We say 'caste-like' because the nationality division is not so rigid as to be *literally* a caste boundary. Moreover, as a result of the windows of opportunity opened by general economic expansion and the efforts and ingenuity of many Israeli Arabs, they have come to share in part in processes of occupational mobility. Nevertheless, persistent Jewish–Arab income and status differentials and the limited avenues for investment open to those Arabs who have accumulated wealth are testament to continued relations of economic subordination. For relevant empirical evidence see, among others, Matras and Weintraub (1977);

Rosenfeld (1978); Haidar (1985); Semyonov and Lewin-Epstein (1987: ch. 2–4); and Shavit (1988).

35. It may seem questionable to assume that a fairly small Arab minority in the labour force, concentrated in a narrow stratum of jobs within the private sector, was capable of affecting the general level of labour militancy. However, even if the segments of a dual labour market are non-competitive in the sense that workers are unlikely to experience mobility between them, wage levels in the lower-paid segment may still constitute a floor level for wages elsewhere. As opponents of a legal minimum wage in Israel and elsewhere never fail to point out, if the floor level of wages is raised then more advantaged workers may also insist on increases.
36. This thesis has been explicitly articulated by Lustick (1980: ch. 5).
37. For vocational education, Regev (1985) offers an instructive analysis of the activities and curricula of the Histadrut network of *Amal* schools. Regev documents not only the scope of Histadrut activity in this sphere, but also the labour organization's direct role in preparing non-Jewish citizens for jobs in the secondary labour market.
38. Most of the observations in this and the following paragraph are based on specific events and practices noted by Lustick (1980: 138, 184, 205, 212, 220, and 226–9). We also drew upon statements by Reches (1976: 10) and Halabi (1981: 14).
39. The political and trade union significance of the labour councils has been discussed by Reches (1976) and Regev (1985) respectively. See Israel Labour Party (1983) for the internal review cited in the text, and Goell (1987) on the practical implementation of 'integration'. A year after the 'closure' of the then current incarnation of the old Arab Department, a senior Histadrut official confided in the present author that this was essentially a public relations measure with little substantive content.
40. A further possibility, which cannot, however, be indicated with any certainty due to an unsurprising dearth of reliable evidence, is that Arab confinement to the secondary labour market is fostered by the economic interests of the Histadrut in its entrepreneurial role. These interests are, however, not necessarily direct. It is true that the agricultural settlements and construction companies associated with the Histadrut are heavily dependent on the labour of Palestinians (citizens and non-citizens alike). But at the same time, and to a markedly greater extent than private firms, the Histadrut's industrial enterprises give preference to the employment of Jewish workers. This is the result of several objective factors, the relative weight of which is unclear. In any event, it is not unreasonable to suppose that the captains of Histadrut industry have viewed with equanimity the greater reliance of private manufacturers on 'cheap

Arab labour', since this has gone hand in hand with a structural division between the 'competitive' (and disproportionately private) and 'monopoly' (and disproportionately Histadrut) sectors of the economy. This division, predicated on the traditionally more favourable access of Histadrut enterprises to investment funding and monopolistic privileges, gave the labour-movement economy a distinct edge in occupying the more capital-intensive and strategically important niches of industry.

41. A significant exception to this generalization should be noted, namely, the existence of a sizeable public-sector labour market in local Arab communities which has been the principal destination for Palestinians with higher education and has allowed them almost unique access to the upper reaches of the occupational structure. Nevertheless, the range of opportunities available in this labour market (which are heavily confined to the teaching profession) is far more restricted than in the 'Jewish' public sector. And, as a recent study demonstrates (Semyonov, 1988: table 4), it yields incomes which are substantially lower than those received by comparably situated Jewish employees.
42. The parallel between non-citizen Palestinians and European guest workers should not be taken too literally, despite the close points of resemblance in the location and status of these groups in the host labour market (Semyonov and Lewin-Epstein, 1987: ch. 6). One obvious difference is that Israel has major non-economic aspirations at stake. But also, Israel directly controls economic and political conditions in the guest-workers' home economy.
43. The published version of the article on which the present chapter is based (Shalev, 1989*a*) includes a fuller discussion and bibliography regarding the labour-market position of Palestinians from the occupied territories and its effects on Israeli workers. The most comprehensive work on this subject is a volume by Semyonov and Lewin-Epstein (1987). The important issue of how state agencies regulate the entry of Palestinians from the territories is addressed by Greenberg (1985) and Shalev (1986). For discussions of broader aspects of the political economy of the occupation see the numerous publications of the 'West Bank Database Project' and its founder, Meron Benvenisti.
44. The 1973 and subsequent data cited here are published estimates from household surveys conducted by the Central Bureau of Statistics. The account of earlier developments is based on newspaper reports. Note that from 1973 a stable majority of about two-thirds of the non-citizen Palestinians employed in Israel obtained their jobs through, and were paid by, the Employment Service. In the 1980s this proportion fell to roughly one-half.
45. The following discussion of Histadrut policies and practice is based

partly on independent research (utilizing documentary sources, newspaper accounts, and interviews with officials of the Histadrut, Palestinian unions, and the Ministry of Labour). We have also drawn heavily on source materials collected by Slutsky (1985).

46. Different elements within the state did not always take the same positions on the issue. A year after the war the military government wanted to deal with unemployment in the territories by allowing the residents unhampered access to the Israeli labour market, whereas the Ministry of Labour advocated phased and supervised entry. The forces represented by the Ministry of Labour prevailed.

47. The Arab Department's ambitious plans for the territories (codified in the 'Meshel Programme' of 1972) unsuccessfully tried to market the Histadrut as 'a barrier against the growth of hostile organizations' in the territories. To this end, the same step-by-step incorporation practised in relation to Arab Israelis was advocated, except that to minimize Palestinian hostility and international criticism it would stop short of actual membership. The Histadrut would field a full range of social services and economic enterprises in the territories, with particular stress placed on social and cultural good will and propaganda activities (including adult education courses on 'Democracy in Israel'!). The Histadrut stressed its readiness to work in close co-ordination with the military government and the relevant Israeli ministries. The Meshel Programme must also be understood as the Arab Department's answer to the 'Harel Plan', sponsored by another division of the Histadrut Executive, which had advocated normalization of the Palestinians' relationship with the Histadrut including full membership. Due partly to shifts in the internal political constellation in the Histadrut, Harel's plan emerged stillborn and the Arab Department conception was embraced in its stead.

48. This issue has figured prominently in the annual investigations and reports on labour conditions in the occupied territories by the International Labour Organization. Credible official information on the magnitude and disposal of the deductions involved is non-existent, but see newspaper investigations by Amir Shapiro (*Davar*, 13 July 1978) and Yehudit Winkler (*Ha'aretz*, 17 July 1983).

49. As early as 1974 the Histadrut Executive instructed work-place workers' committees to accept responsibility for the implementation of prevailing wage and benefit standards *vis-à-vis* workers from the territories. This policy was largely unimplemented (see e.g. opinion-poll evidence reported by Bar, 1983). After many years of refusing to grant Palestinian commuters trade union protection, many local labour councils agreed to designate one of their officers as responsible for handling these workers' grievances. However, this system does not bind the local union officers attached to the councils, who

are not inclined to regard workers from the territories as part of their constituency. The Histadrut Executive has a special watch-dog committee entrusted with the protection of these workers. Employing only one part-time official, this committee has functioned mainly to disseminate information to workers and occasionally to put pressure on individual employers guilty of practices which, if made public, would cause (or have already caused) embarrassment to the Histadrut. Perhaps the Histadrut's most important policy measure has been its assent to the suppression of Palestinian labour unions in the West Bank. Despite initial expressions of 'class solidarity' by the Histadrut leadership, the organization's officials have supported the military government view that these unions are no more than fronts for Palestinian nationalism and terror activity. The Histadrut has remained silent in the face of harassment of the Palestinian unions and the imprisonment or deportation of their leaders, thereby contributing to the inability of these unions to provide union representation for members (the vast majority) who are employed in Israel—a scenario clearly distasteful to the Histadrut.

50. This author, however, is not alone in embracing the critical perspective described here. Other Israeli Jewish writers, including Swirski (1979); Kimmerling (1983*b*); and Portugali (1986) have developed a similar critique. We have been particularly inspired by Gershon Shafir's (1989) recent study. He develops an analysis of Jewish–Arab relations in the labour market in the initial period of colonization which is very close to the interpretation presented here of the background to the Histadrut's establishment. A similar explanation was also offered by Flapan (1979).
51. Preuss (1965) is a good example of the 'official' view. The 'revisionist' approach is represented by Kimmerling's remarks (1983*a*: 50) and by the general tenor of the seminal studies by Sussman (1969*a*) and Shapira (1977).
52. Shapiro (1976) is the leading 'debunker'. In the course of a long-standing debate with mainstream thinkers, particularly Eisenstadt (e.g. 1967) and Horowitz and Lissak (e.g. 1978), he has accused them of failing to transcend interpretations promoted by and for the founding fathers of Israeli society.
53. In Israeli literature the linkage of political exchange to ideological/political motives has been explicitly proposed in Friedman's influential model of political versus economic trade unionism (1974). This may be compared with Pizzorno's (1978) pioneering formulation of political exchange in contrast to other forms of labour activity. On the scope for and limits of politicization of the trade union agenda under political exchange see Crouch (1982*a*: ch. 6).

3

Accounting for Hegemony

The Sources of Mapai's Supremacy

Mapai—a dominant party

Mapai (the Hebrew acronym for Palestine Workers' Party) is one of the few political parties in the Western democracies which succeeded in attaining the status of a 'dominant party'.[1] The formation of Mapai in January 1930 was the result of a merger of the two leading labour-movement parties of the *Yishuv*. (It will be recalled that Yishuv is the Hebrew term for the Jewish 'settlement' in Palestine prior to Israel's attainment of sovereignty in 1948). In two major electoral contests only a year after its foundation, Mapai signalled the growing political strength of organized Jewish labour. The party received 40 per cent of votes for the 'Elected Assembly' of the Yishuv, and 60 per cent of the Palestinian ballots cast for delegates to the international Zionist Congress.[2] By 1933 Mapai had won a substantial electoral edge over the other camps in the world Zionist movement and from 1935 its leader, David Ben-Gurion, served as chairman of the Jewish Agency Executive. Ben-Gurion subsequently became Prime Minister of Israel, and his successors remained at the head of every government formed until the late 1970s.

Prior to the 1969 elections Mapai was reconstituted as the Israel Labour Party, which is the principal partner in the 'Labour Alignment' (*Ma'arach*). Ignoring these name changes, then as Figure 3.1 shows, Mapai's share of the ballot remained extraordinarily stable for 25 years, in spite of the profound changes in the size and composition of Israel's electorate which occurred soon after the creation of the state. While garnering typically only about one-third of the popular vote (more if satellite Arab electoral slates are incorporated with the Mapai vote, as in Figure 3.1), until the mid-

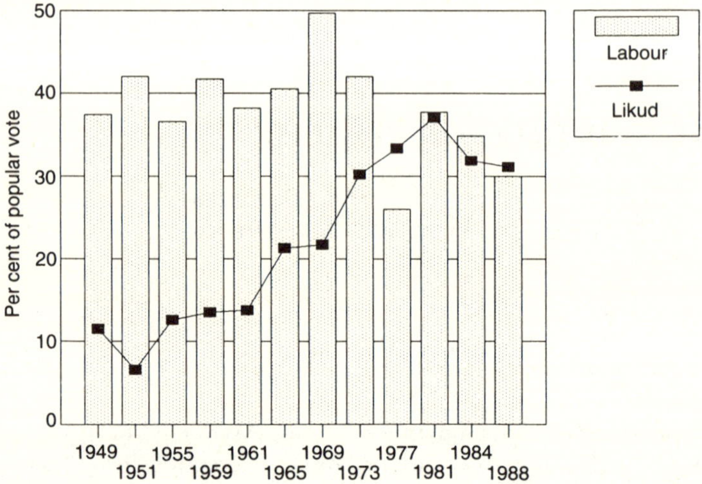

FIG. 3.1. The Labour and Likud vote: 1949–88

Source: *Statistical Abstract of Israel.*

Note: 'Labour' is the Labour Alignment and, before 1965, Mapai with the addition of their satellite 'Arab lists'. 'Likud' is Cherut prior to 1965 and Gachal between 1965 and 1973.

1960s the party consistently commanded at least twice the voter support enjoyed by any one of its opponents on the left or right. Given, in addition, the wide political gulf between these adversaries, no other party could feasibly contemplate forming a government without Mapai, while Mapai on the other hand could play off a variety of alternative coalition scenarios.

In the decade or so prior to what is known in Israel as the political 'upheaval', which unseated Mapai/Labour, the Party's electoral standing deteriorated; but it succeeded in partially redressing these losses by forming alliances with the labour-movement parties to its left. Nevertheless, since the major parties of the right also entered into a series of electoral partnerships, from the mid-1960s there was a progressive narrowing of the distance separating the rival blocs (the Alignment and the *Likud* or 'Unity Party'). And in the historic elections of May 1977, with the addition of a 'flash' centrist party (the Democratic Movement for Change) which siphoned off nearly a third of the Alignment's supporters, the traditional balance of parliamentary forces was overturned—terminating more than four decades of continuous governance by Mapai-led coalitions.[3]

The remarkable length and continuity of Mapai's political dominance was, it should be stressed, not merely a matter of its ability to sustain a clear plurality of the popular vote in the face of relatively weak and divided competitors. Mapai could also be described as a hegemonic party in other, deeper senses. The party's positions on key issues represented the centre of a far-flung consensus; it enjoyed the power to direct and co-ordinate a highly ramified institutional complex; and its pre-eminence encompassed the entire spectrum of political action.

1. Ideologically, Mapai's interpretation of Israel's national mission, its military and geopolitical strategy, and its principal domestic policy commitments were internalized by the vast majority of Jewish citizens. It is true that during the first few decades after sovereignty, political debate on *domestic* issues was formally conducted in contested terms (such as 'capitalism' versus 'socialism') on which Mapai's official position was well in advance of the electorate at large and even of the views of its own supporters. Nevertheless, the principal lines of the social and economic policies actually pursued by Mapai—full employment, generous state subsidy of both consumers and producers, and the mixed private-public economy—were widely regarded (in Jewish eyes) as appropriate to the country's foremost tasks. These were: to attract and absorb immigrants, to promote economic infrastructure and growth, and to encourage national solidarity. In practice, the debate between the political blocs on domestic issues revolved around the political consequences of the role of the state, not the nature of that role *per se*.

2. Institutionally, Mapai's capacity to govern was greatly enhanced by the fact that the party's sphere of influence was not limited to the political executive. It also controlled the other major arms of the state (the army and the bureaucracy), and the great centres of quasi-state power inherited from the Yishuv era (the Jewish Agency and the Histadrut).

3. Beyond the ideological and institutional realms of dominance, there lies the arena of the extra-parliamentary politics of protest and pressure groups. Here, too, Mapai enjoyed noteworthy success. At its peak, the party successfully installed itself as mediator

among the most important organized interests and between them and the state. Simultaneously, it managed to prevent the emergence of 'disorganized' interests as credible political challengers.[4]

Mapai and social democracy

Mapai quite clearly embraces, indeed epitomizes, all the *functional* hallmarks of one-party dominance[5]: a routinized monopoly over the formation of governments, the ability to pre-empt or control non-party forms of political action, and a high degree of legitimacy in the eyes of most of the mass public. But the particular structures of dominance and the historical trajectory of its emergence and reproduction are, if anything, even more nationally distinctive in Israel than in each of the handful of other Western polities in which a single party has enjoyed long-term supremacy. On the face of it, the most striking points of resemblance between Israel under Mapai/Labour and other one-party dominant regimes are those with Sweden under social democracy. While Sweden's Social Democratic Party (SAP) has consistently acquired a larger share of the popular vote than Israel's Labour Party, in both instances decades of unbroken governance rested on successful coalition-building and a fragmented opposition. Like Mapai, the Social Democrats were the 'natural party of government' in more than just electoral terms. Above all, both Sweden and Israel were dominated by *labour-movement* parties—not only in the weak sense of parties belonging to the Socialist International, but more importantly, in their heavy reliance on a broadly based and highly centralized peak labour organization for financial backing, voter mobilization, and the legitimation of government policy.[6]

The difficulty in analysing the Israeli case through the prism of social democracy is that the defining characteristics and underlying ethos of Israel's labour movement depart quite strikingly from the European experience in a number of central respects. First, as the preceding chapters have shown, the historic mobilization of the Jewish working class in Palestine was based on a preference for national exclusivism over class solidarity. The labour movement treated class struggle objectives as secondary to the Zionist project of national revival and political sovereignty. Second, as we shall argue more fully at the close of this chapter, the labour movement's dominance in Israel was, in many respects, founded on elements (nationalism, 'opportunism', machine politics) more appropriately identified with strong parties of the *right*. Third, and most striking of all, unlike other successful parliamentary socialist parties, for at least three decades Mapai's mass base has depended more on the middle strata than on the loyalty of working-class voters.

The 'inverted' class composition of Mapai/Labour is particularly incongruous in view of the consensus among students of social democracy, that socialist parties can only become entrenched in government if the workers overwhelmingly vote for them. This pattern of working-class political mobilization is, in turn, generally assumed to depend on the labour movement's success in mobilizing workers for collective action in the market arena. Solidaristic labour organizations like Sweden's LO (blue-collar peak association) possess a unique capacity for organizing workers along class lines, inculcating a highly politicized sense of class identity, and committing their human and financial resources to political struggle.[7] In Israel, however, the organized working class *in strictu sensu* has been one component only, and an increasingly marginal one, of the labour movement's electoral following. Blue-collar wage-earners constitute only a minority of the Histadrut's constituency, which includes all grades of white-collar and professional workers, and even many of the self-employed. Consequently, except for the labour organization's early years, working-class mobilization is by itself an inadequate explanation of the roots of Mapai's historic success. Such an explanation would be altogether incongruous for the mature Mapai/Labour—a hegemonic labour party bereft of a distinctively working-class following.

Our approach to unravelling the sources of Mapai dominance rests on both a contextual analysis, which emphasizes the specific historical setting in which it took root; and on an analytical perspective, which draws particular inspiration from the 'new political economy' of labour movements and class relations. Certainly, there is no escaping the fact—emphasized to a greater or lesser degree by all students of Mapai—that the politics of nation-building and, specifically, the labour movement's essential role in promoting the Jewish interest in colonization and state-making, were central to its paramountcy, especially prior to Israeli sovereignty. Nevertheless (and this is our first general theoretical point), it is also reasonable to assume that the parties and voter alignments of Israel (and earlier, the Jewish Yishuv) were structured—just as they have been in other societies—by class and other economy-based interests and cleavages. Second, nation-building, however dramatic, does not signal the disappearance of political economy. Wherever democracy organizes politics and capitalism organizes the economy, a critical prerequisite for dominance by any party—but especially one without a natural affinity to the capitalist class—is its capacity when governing to manage class and other distributional conflicts, and to steer economic development and performance in directions which strengthen the bases of its power. Our third starting point is the importance of asking not only why Mapai succeeded, but also why its rivals failed. A convincing historical analysis is obliged to explain counter-factual as well as actual outcomes; otherwise it is too easy to slip into the conservatism of assuming in hindsight that what happened, had to happen. Fourth and finally, our interest in Mapai's competitors has also been inspired by scholarship on stratification generally, which has argued that class power is most appropriately studied in *relational* terms. In the context of the present analysis, this makes it necessary to address the puzzles of Mapai's ascendancy over the right, on the one hand, and the more radical left of the political spectrum on the other.

A notable feature of the extensive literature on Mapai/Labour is that, despite a certain amount of theoretical and methodological pluralism, most of this work has in common a quite pronounced evasion of precisely the theoretical assumptions which we have just outlined.[8] Typically, political processes have been treated in voluntaristic terms, as a function solely of the will of political élites. Consequently, debate has focused on the subsidiary question of why these élites were so successful—was it because of ideological commitment, inspired consensus-building, or skilful manipulation? Cultural and institutional explanations have dominated the literature, with the economy viewed as exogenous to political processes rather than as a motivating force for political action and an integral parameter of governance. Finally, the limited *manifest* role of class and class conflict in Israeli politics has been interpreted by most scholars as tantamount to their *actual* irrelevance, especially in comparison with national and ethnic conflict and solidarity—which have themselves been viewed as largely autonomous from economic forces.

The substantive analysis developed in this chapter distinguishes between two different historical eras and associated regimes of dominance. The first of these regimes, established virtually at the moment of Mapai's creation, was responsible for the party's pre-eminence in the polities of the Yishuv and the Zionist movement at large prior to Israeli sovereignty. The second was born during the 1940s, in the midst of radical changes in the political and economic conditions for Mapai dominance which emerged in the wake of the Second World War and then statehood. It was this renegotiated version of Mapai's historic hegemony on which the party and its successors based their unchallenged position as governing party during the first two decades of Israel's existence. The decline and apparent demise of Labour dominance, manifest since the 1970s, is analysed in the final chapter of this book as part of the wider crisis which engulfed Israel's political economy during this period.

The era of ascendancy

During the 1920s the parties that established the Histadrut found it necessary—if they were to secure the political exchange with Zionism on which the labour movement was premised—to expand their electoral appeal sufficiently to become the leading political force within the domestic and international Zionist communities. This was a definitive motive, in 1930, for the amalgamation into Mapai of the two rival labour Zionist parties founded soon after the turn of the century. At the twelfth Zionist Congress in 1921, labour parties had collectively polled a mere 8 per cent of the world-wide vote. Ten years later united Mapai's share was close to 30 per cent, and thereafter it rapidly overtook the parties of the centre and right.

The first two chapters of this volume discuss in some detail a number of formative attributes of the Israeli labour movement which are of particular relevance to Mapai's rise to political dominance in the pre-sovereignty period. The Jewish worker-pioneers who began colonizing Palestine in the early 1900s sought to redress their difficult economic plight by contracting an alliance with the Zionist movement. This alliance was responsible for the labour movement's distinctive national exclusivism and preference for colonization and economic collectivism over class-wide solidarity and trade union struggle. Under the conditions prevailing in

Mandatory Palestine this was a model with compelling substantive attractions for propertyless Jewish immigrants, while it also (for reasons we shall explain) aroused the loyalty of large sections of the middle strata of the Yishuv.

A second noteworthy aspect of the praxis of labour Zionism in Palestine was its concentration in a single organizational framework—the Histadrut. In addition to the potency of the political power resources implied by the breadth of the Histadrut's mass membership and its extraordinary range of functions, this remarkable labour organization was, by design, thoroughly impregnated with the interests of the party élites responsible for its initial establishment and subsequent management. The fact that the Histadrut was created from the top down, at the behest of political parties and with a system of governance designed to maximize their influence, evoked powerful incentives for the labour organization to serve partisan interests. In accordance with this design, the Histadrut never developed the capacity to lead and innovate strategically for both wings of the labour movement. In effect, it was expected to function as the executive arm of a settlement/state-building project on the one hand, and as a clientelistic party machine on the other.

The political impotence of the right

The labour movement's rise to political supremacy reflected not only the unique opportunities which it faced, and their skilful exploitation, but also the barriers facing political mobilization of the right. Many of these difficulties were *structural* in character, as suggested by the results of elections for the Jewish 'national institutions', which from very early on awarded a pivotal position to the labour parties.[9] They reflected a number of profound biases in the political economy of the Yishuv which favoured the labour movement and impeded its political opponents.

1. The class structure of Jewish Palestine featured a broad middle layer of landlords, artisans, shopkeepers, and small-scale contractors and manufacturers. Satisfaction of key existential needs of these middle strata depended more critically upon organized labour than on the bourgeoisie.
2. While it proved virtually essential for the propertyless followers of the workers' movement to mobilize politically in order to find

solutions to problems of basic economic survival, no such impetus prevailed among business interests.

3. Both labour and capital confronted acute internal cleavages. But whereas on the workers' side the principal division—that between Jews and Arabs—*contributed* to organization and solidarity, divisions within the capitalist class hampered the emergence of collective action and consciousness.

The middle strata. The 'Fourth Aliyah' in the mid-1920s was by far the largest wave of Jewish immigration to Palestine to date. In its unplanned and involuntary nature and predominantly *petit bourgeois* composition, it was prototypical of the immigrations of the Mandatory period. Notably absent from the ranks of the newcomers were the upper-middle classes and the wealthy. Instead, most arrivals had only enough means to become small *rentiers* or businessmen. Many others were occupied in petty trading or self-employed in small workshops, finding themselves on the margin of proletarianization. Under these circumstances, the attraction of the labour movement's nation-building *élan* was joined by overlapping economic interests.[10] For these middle strata, either heavily dependent on the working class as clientele or, alternatively, vulnerable to joining its ranks during depressions, what was good for the workers was in a tangible sense good for the Yishuv as a whole. On the other hand, the same economic logic of mutual support and access to Zionist subsidies that drove the propertyless workers to organize, might conceivably also have inspired the *petite bourgeoisie*. But like the old middle classes everywhere, they were endowed with a limited predisposition for collective action—the result of their individualistic outlook, spatial and economic dispersion, and contradictory class position between capital and labour. In good times they did not need to organize, and in bad times labour-controlled communal organizations could conceivably do more than the capitalists to relieve them from hardship. Still, they might have become a major counter-force to labour's political dominance had they become the target for political entrepreneurship of any substance. However, the political and cultural leaders of the Jewish middle classes of Eastern Europe largely stayed away from Palestine.

In the late 1920s a major challenge from the right emerged with the intention of filling this vacuum. The 'Revisionist' Party, under the leadership of Vladimir Jabotinsky (the forebears of the *Likud* and Menahem Begin), was founded in 1923 as a protest against what was perceived as a lack of militance in the Zionist movement against British restrictions on Jewish immigration to Palestine and periodic Arab violence directed against the Yishuv. Subsequently, the Fourth Aliyah wave of non-socialist immigration emboldened the Revisionists to embrace a programme which would appeal to the economic interests of the middle strata, demanding that they receive a larger share of the WZO (World Zionist Organization) budget.[11]

A fundamental barrier facing the Revisionists' (or any other) attempt to draw the *petite bourgeoisie* into an effective anti-labour political movement was the indispensability of organized labour for addressing crucial existential issues. The labour movement, not the Revisionists, set the outer limits of the Jews' territorial presence in Palestine, organized their defence against Arab attack, and channelled subsidies to the financially stricken among them. None of this prevented the Revisionists from accusing the labour movement of fulfilling these responsibilities with insufficient vigour—an appeal which in the early 1930s helped raise their political stock. Indeed, Revisionism became a serious threat to the left, its followers serving to undercut Histadrut members in the labour market and its leaders beginning to attract organized farmers, manufacturers, and others to the idea of a united right-wing coalition.

Complementing the domestic threat posed by the Revisionists, in the late 1920s the labour movement was also obliged to confront the hostility of prominent Jewish businessmen and other procapitalist figures outside Palestine who were acquiring considerable influence on the Zionist movement and demanding an end to its special relationship with organized labour. Mapai's leaders responded to these ominous developments at home and abroad by a strategic reorientation intended to emphasize their commitment to the nation as a whole and to build political bridges beyond the labour movement. At the world congresses of the WZO, beginning in 1929 (even before Mapai's creation) the labour parties appeared on a joint ticket and began to participate in governing coalitions. In the early 1930s these coalitions became explicitly oriented towards excluding the Revisionists, who in 1935 affirmed their own marginalization by establishing a rival Zionist organization. In the domestic arena, Mapai's mass base was consciously widened by attempts to attract *petit bourgeois* votes, in part by a new ideological readiness to legitimate the contributions of the middle classes to the nation-building project. Meanwhile, in the labour relations sphere Mapai did its best to appease employers and their allies by reining in union militancy. Attempts to commit the Histadrut to an explicit peace treaty in industry failed, but the labour-movement élite communicated its conciliatory stance in other ways—in its handling of labour relations issues at enterprise level; in its informal contacts with top employer representatives; and in its willingness to sanction joint business ventures with private capital.[12]

Alongside its express determination to keep the peace between the classes within the Yishuv, the labour movement embraced an unwritten commitment to go to war with *outsiders*. As we pointed out in the previous chapter, despite the fact that the 1932–6 period was one of economic prosperity and declining unemployment, a demonstrative struggle was launched against the employment of Arab labour by Jewish employers. The effect was to cement the popular identification of the labour movement as the spearhead of the Jewish national struggle, while at the same time branding the most significant right-wing sectors (the Revisionists and the citrus farmers) as anti-Zionist because of their practical opposition to Histadrut demands.[13] In 1936 the Arabs of Palestine launched a general strike-cum-insurrection which seemingly vindicated both the labour movement's policy of promoting Jewish economic self-sufficiency, and its leaders' publicly voiced opinion that the conflict between the two national movements was intractable. The Arab revolt was exploited by Mapai to reinforce its nationalist appeal to non-labour groups. Underlying this success was the fact that a policy of national separatism was complementary to the economic interests of the great majority of Jews, including the non-labour strata, most of whom neither employed Arabs nor were tied to them commercially.[14]

The bourgeoisie. Business opposition to the policy of Jewish economic separatism espoused by the labour movement was limited to only a few capitalist sectors which, despite their economic strength, were obliged to pay a penalty of political isolation.[15] This was particularly true of citrus farming, the leading branch of private agriculture. The orange growers' need for unskilled seasonal labour, coupled with their proximity to rural Arab society, prompted many to circumvent the Histadrut and to defy openly the 'Jewish-only labour' norm prevailing in most urban branches. Considering the status of citrus as a profit centre and Palestine's only significant export branch, the citrus growers might, in principle, have taken the political initiative on behalf of business. But precisely because they were exporters, these farmers were isolated from other sections of the bourgeoisie, whose dependence on the domestic market (and on various forms of Zionist subsidy) encouraged assent to the policies of the leadership of the labour movement and the Zionist institutions.

As we show in some detail in the next chapter, also within the urban Jewish economy different sections of capital had distinct economic interests, often as a result of conflicting labour requirements and policies. The lack of a common labour-market incentive to organize the capitalists, as well as the limited gains which could be hoped for from collective pressure for economic concessions from the Mandatory authorities, further reinforced their weak propensity for solidarity. But the leadership vacuum among the bourgeoisie was not only the result of the diverse interests of its major factions. It also reflected the fundamental weakness of the Yishuv economy, which lacked virtually any comparative advantage and, for the most part, failed abysmally to attract *big* capital. The country's dearth of natural resources together with its limited domestic market, relatively expensive labour for the region, and constricted credit facilities inevitably deterred large private investors (either immigrant or absentee).

In the circumstances of the Yishuv, therefore, capital was weak in every respect that theoretically might have provided a counterweight to the *political* standing of the labour movement: it lacked either coherent common interests or a leading sector strong enough to impose its own project, was fragmented in terms of ownership, and faced only weak inducements to organize or engage in formal political action. On the other hand, capital enjoyed a definite edge over most of the working class in *market* relations. Nevertheless, the role of the bourgeoisie in the political economy at large was less consequential than is normal in capitalist societies. The privileged position of the capitalist class in market economies results from the decisive impact of profitability on investment, and thereby on the prosperity of the society as a whole. It is true that the flow of private Jewish funds into Palestine far exceeded the sums transferred by the Zionist movement. Despite this, as in other settler societies, much of the money was sunk into land purchases and construction rather than capital accumulation, and most productive investment was small-scale. The prosperity of Palestine was dependent mainly on Jewish immigration and capital inflow, and thus on factors exogenous to the Yishuv economy—the intensity of anti-Semitism in Europe, the feasibility of alternative destinations for immigrants, the wealth which the newcomers brought with them, and the extent of Jewish and Zionist philanthropy emanating from the Diaspora.[16]

To sum up then, in the Jewish community of Mandatory Palestine the political balance between the labour movement and the right was tipped in Mapai's favour by a combination of economic and political forces. In the economic realm the modest qualitative role of private capital accumulation, the relatively broad overlap between the interests of the working class and the middle strata, and the contrasting urgency for capital and labour of material incentives for collective action, all had the effect of limiting the potential for right-wing political mobilization in comparison with the working class and widening the scope for labour-movement appeals to the non-labour strata. These appeals were consciously intensified during the 1930s as Mapai responded assertively to the rise of middle-class influence in both the Yishuv and world Zionism, in effect by pre-empting the core of the Revisionists' platform—their proposals for class co-operation and their more militant stance *vis-à-vis* the Arabs of Palestine. Also in the realm of the political, Mapai benefited immensely from the labour movement's dedication to what were earlier termed the 'existential' needs of all classes. These were not only economic but also included the Jews' immediate personal and collective security and their future in Palestine.

In this respect, the significance of the labour movement's historic alliance with Zionism went beyond the opportunity to attract material support for the movement and its followers. The commitment of organized labour to Jewish nationalism, settlement, and self-defence also provided the basis for the 'spiritual' hegemony which is the true emblem of one-party dominance (Shapiro, 1976: 238–9). Fortunately for Mapai, the political arena in which the labour movement's nation- and state-building role was most salient to voters—the international Zionist movement—also controlled the material resources on which the labour movement's strength was dependent. The party's political success was noticeably less impressive in local government and the political institutions of the Yishuv. But the limited authority and other resources at stake in this arena meant that little harm was done thereby to Mapai's overall supremacy.[17]

The weakness of the left opposition

Mapai's simultaneous ideological and instrumental strength also helps to illuminate its success in dominating the labour movement camp *internally*. Not only could the party provide workers with an uplifting role in national rebirth, but it did so alongside many eminently practical activities addressed to their present and future security in Palestine and their immediate material interests. Through the Histadrut, Mapai was able to offer Jewish wage-earners access to employment and vital social services. These weighty assets notwithstanding, the party was hardly immune to threats from the left—any more than it was spared the Revisionist challenge. In fact throughout the pre-state period, the contradictions of the Histadrut/Mapai model of working-class mobilization gave rise to heated debate and, at times, also to substantial opposition movements.[18] Three sources of tension (often overlapping in their effects) were particularly significant in this context.

1. The contradiction between Mapai's socialist rhetoric and a praxis which increasingly emphasized national separatism on the one hand, and class co-operation on the other.
2. The Histadrut's extreme centralization of authority and power in the hands of the party élite and the party machine.
3. The secondary status of the urban working class, expressed both in the subordination of the trade union function to the labour movement's national tasks, and in Mapai's growing political interest in 'peace in the Yishuv'.

By the 1930s the most important dissenters to the left of Mapai were kibbutz-based groups, who regarded themselves as the socialist conscience of the labour movement, and urban rank-and-filers, who mobilized sporadically in opposition to central Histadrut/ Mapai authority. These two groups eventually joined forces in the

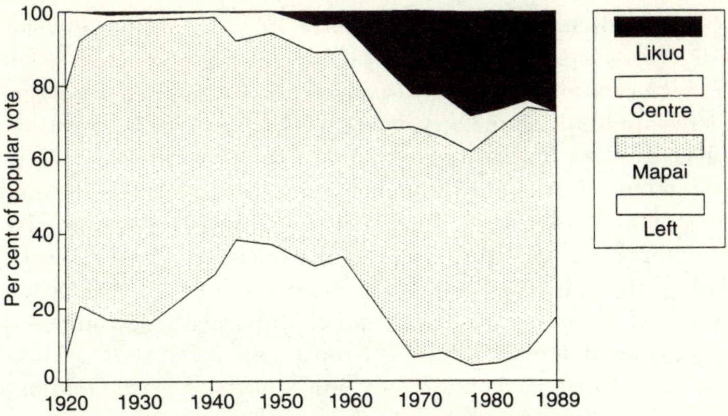

FIG. 3.2. The voting in Histadrut elections: 1920–89

Sources: Tokatli (1979: 181), corroborated and supplemented by information in Perlmutter (1957), Lucatz (1961), Galin and Harel (1978), Ben-Meir (1980) and reports of the Histadrut's Organization Division.

Note: 'Left' indicates parties to the left of Mapai. 'Mapai' includes its two constituent parties prior to 1930 and the successor 'Alignments' from 1965. 'Likud' includes earlier representations of its constituent parties within the Histadrut framework. All remaining parties are classified as 'Centre'.

1940s to form a united opposition within the Zionist camp. There were also a number of communist or proto-communist fringe groups opposed in principle to the reigning synthesis of socialism and Zionism. Between the first and sixth Histadrut conventions (1920–44) the collective standing of the opposition labour parties grew from 7 per cent to 38 per cent of the ballot (see Figure 3.2). At the end of the period Mapai found itself with only a bare majority with which to rule the labour organization.

This impressive showing should not conceal the fact that it was only in the wake of two historic changes—the transition to a full-employment economy and the approach of sovereignty—that the left emerged as an autonomous and relatively broad-based political actor. The more characteristic conditions of the Yishuv era severely hampered the labour movement opposition. The juxtaposition of propertyless colonists confronting cheap local labour, which gave birth to the Histadrut, points to the compelling attraction of the Histadrut model to its followers. A concrete symptom was the ambiguity expressed by most of the Zionist radicals towards class solidarity with Arab labour and their failure (except in periods of economic collapse) to effectively rouse Jewish workers to the cause of joint labour organization. On the other hand, Mapai's privileged access to 'national capital' and the control exercised by party activists over the labour exchanges and other Histadrut services placed the party apparatus in a powerful position *vis-à-vis* the vulnerable unskilled majority of the Jewish working class. In its relationship with more advantaged sections of the working class, Mapai and its predecessors sanctioned a markedly accommodative policy in the Histadrut to prevent the alienation of skilled workers.

Political dexterity played an important part in reinforcing Mapai's inherent advantages. Embarrassing inequalities within the working class were masked by what Lissak (1985: 246) describes as the labour movement's earnest cultivation of 'the status symbols of a "socialist workers culture"'. Internally, while Mapai made very effective use of the substantial material resources in its control, the radicals sometimes had difficulty keeping their top leaders fed, let alone supporting lower-level cadres. In critical struggles for hegemony over urban wage-earners soon after the Histadrut's establishment, Mapai's principal ancestor (Achdut Avodah) had acted with extreme ruthlessness towards rivals and challengers. Later, when the party took control of the WZO and the quasi-governmental Jewish Agency, its powers expanded to include the rationing of entry visas to Palestine in favour of potential Mapai supporters. Finally, within the Histadrut polity the party élite exploited its controlling position to set the constitutional rules of the game in internal affairs, or to ignore them altogether.[19]

Beyond the advantages enjoyed by Mapai as a result of the structural position of Jewish labour and the party's political skill, a good part of the dissidents' weakness was internal. The three major oppositional elements (kibbutzim, urban workers, and left radicals) had partially conflicting interests and objectives. Kibbutz socialism was communitarian and the kibbutzim were the élitist vanguard of the labour movement's Zionist project. Urban militants were essentially trade unionists and intellectuals committed to a populist struggle against the labour bureaucracy. The left-wing radicals, those who rejected the Histadrut model of Zionist collectivism and in some cases Zionism itself, suffered from special handicaps. Unlike the urban or kibbutz oppositions, they lacked an inbuilt organizational infrastructure on which to build their movements. The

Communists, whose challenge was met by harsh acts of repression by the authorities, failed after an early and short-lived blooming to gain any significant mass following among Jewish workers. Communism also encountered opposition from within the Yishuv, in which the Histadrut played an active role.[20] In addition, the intensifying national conflict and pressures from the Soviet Union strained the basis for binational co-operation, and in the early 1940s pro- and anti-Zionist Communist Party factions openly split. Another party of Jewish radicals, Left *Poalei Tsiyon*, was more sympathetic to Zionism but still out of touch with the sentiments of the Jewish working class. As Margalit (1976) has argued, the latter were alienated by the party's internationalism, its opposition to collaboration between the labour movement and the bourgeoisie in the world Zionist movement, and its continued cultural and organizational ties with Diaspora Jewry. Each of these orientations flagrantly contradicted the premises on which the ability of the Zionist labour movement to serve both individuals' instrumental needs and more lofty national goals depended.

The question remains of why it was that Mapai's success in the 1930s, predicated as it was on the party's retreat from its labourist orientation, failed to spawn more effective opposition from within the labour-movement camp. As Przeworksi (1985) and other students of labour-movement parties insist, there is usually a price to be paid—in the alienation of core supporters and erosion of the class consciousness on which labour solidarity feeds—when leftist parties seek an electoral majority by embracing cross-class appeals. Yet *realpolitik* propelled Mapai towards just such a dilution of its working-class character. We have already noted Mapai's sensitivity to the political challenges posed by Revisionism and by economic liberals within world Zionism. But the political problem facing the labour movement was also social-structural. From the mid-1920s onwards, both immigration and the economy altered in ways which enlarged the middle classes and strengthened the market at the expense of labour movement-sponsored economic collectivism. Moreover, Palestine's economic development and the rise of the Jewish 'national institutions' altered the composition of the working class itself, increasing white-collar employment at the expense of the unskilled proletariat.[21] Mapai moved towards the middle ground in order to forestall the possibility, immanent in these social-structural trends, that the right would be strengthened.

On joining the Zionist Executive in 1933 David Ben-Gurion,

Mapai's leader, embraced a consciously supra-class appeal, advocating that the labour movement should follow his example and subordinate itself (and the class interests of the workers, if necessary) to the good of the nation. As could be expected, this strategic shift to the right indeed incited backlash from the left, but not enough to catapult the left to hegemony within the labour movement or to force Mapai's leaders to forego its transition to a 'catch-all party'. An important reason is that, as Yonathan Shapiro (1976) has documented, the leadership's delegation of the party's day-to-day management to a clandestine 'apparatus' lodged in the Histadrut bureaucracy had the effect of infusing Mapai's most important cadres with a vested interest in preserving the Histadrut's labourist functions. This became most dramatically manifest in 1935, when an attempt by Ben-Gurion to blunt the Revisionists' challenge (by secretly concluding a formal truce with Jabotinsky, their leader) was overturned by the efforts of the party apparatus, which refused to accept concessions that would have qualified the right to strike and have ended the Histadrut's exclusive control over its labour exchanges. Ironically, therefore, for all the tension it introduced within Mapai, the coexistence between a centrist party élite and party cadres committed to labourism permitted the party to have the best of both worlds—to defuse the right and gain middle-class votes without sacrificing the labour movement's contribution to the political mobilization of the working class. In this sense Mapai resembled the Scandinavian social democratic parties which, as Przeworksi and Sprague (1986: 78–9) have shown, also relied on strong central labour organizations to preserve their core working-class constituency in the face of diversification of the party's class base.

In managing this hazardous internal dialectic, Mapai was aided considerably by specific conjunctural forces. After 1934 the Palestinian economy entered a prolonged recession which gravely weakened the capacity of workers to independently pursue their class interests. At the same time, the party's control of the Jewish Agency enabled it to trim the power of the Histadrut by shifting a number of the labour organization's public functions into the Agency's domain. The net effect was to narrow the capacity of Histadrut members and officials to challenge the new strategic drift. Most important of all, the Arab strike/revolt, which broke out in 1936, and the rise of European anti-semitism, which heightened tensions with the British over immigration quotas, gave Mapai ample opportunity to shift the centre of political debate to the national plane. Most of the left opposition was obliged to follow suit. The party capitalized on these developments by formally escalating Zionism's political demands to encompass territorial independence. Just as it had done in the preceding period by reviving the Hebrew labour struggle, Mapai was able once again to shape and exploit the politics of nationalism in order to defend its hegemony.[22]

The transition to and from sovereignty

In spite of cataclysmic historical transitions during the course of four decades of Mapai rule—the Jews' transformation from an unwelcome minority to the majority in a sovereign state, a succession of wars, mass immigration, and rapid economic development and growth—the party's structure, ideology, and even office-holders exhibited a remarkable degree of continuity. Nevertheless, Israel's creation in 1948 blunted several of Mapai's traditional assets and created major new challenges and opportunities. Less obviously, the party's hegemony had already faced challenges generated by new socio-economic and political developments during World War II. Indeed, several of the most compelling issues which Mapai faced after 1948 originated in wartime—in particular, the delayed formation of a modern working class and the growth of a modern economy in which the labour movement itself was the largest investor and employer. With this in mind, we shall preface our discussion of Mapai dominance in the first decade of Israeli sovereignty with a survey of developments during the preceding decade.

Wartime transformations

In Palestine, as in many other countries, the war ushered in a number of far-reaching changes in the structure and functioning of the political economy. These changes were linked to industrial advance and the shift from a depressed to a full-employment economy. The growth of a Middle Eastern market closed off from traditional sources of imports and, more importantly, the emergence of a vigorous British demand for Palestinian goods and services to meet wartime needs had, by 1941, begun to pull the economy out of a six-year period of stagnation. Industry was transformed into the leading sector and by the end of the war it employed close to a third of the labour force (about 10 percentage points more than previously).[23]

The struggle for working-class loyalty. Not only did the number of industrial workers soar during the war, but they became more concentrated and more militant. The Histadrut and its political leaders responded to rank-and-file activism by beefing up the traditionally negligible involvement and authority of central Histadrut organs in the field of wage bargaining. With the help of the government—now Jewish industry's most important client—the Histadrut and the Manufacturers' Association, for the first time, began to engage in economy-wide pay negotiations.[24]

The emergence of a substantial new proletariat—often with no prior partisan commitment but with considerable self-confidence due to prosperity and full employment—seriously threatened Mapai's standing among the mass public. The factions and parties of the left were much more supportive of labour militancy than Mapai, and their following among urban trade unionists spread. The kibbutz-based opposition was also strengthened politically by its custodianship of an élite strike force (the *Palmach*) which, during the war, became the leading arm of the Yishuv's expanding paramilitary activity. Against the background of continuing friction over long-standing issues—class co-operation, the internal governance of the labour movement, and Palestine's political future—these developments prompted the leftist 'Faction B' to secede formally from Mapai in 1944. Four years later, it became the major partner in a short-lived experiment in left unity, the Mapam Party.[25]

Since the late 1930s Mapai had been active in exploiting the Histadrut as a means of attracting the growing number of politically uncommitted workers: by stepped-up social provision (benefits dependent directly upon Histadrut membership and indirectly on political loyalty); by attempts to centralize Histadrut trade union activity; and by vigorous political competition with the left for control of workers' committees. Beyond the labour-market arena, Mapai chose to endorse partition as its immediate political objective in the national struggle. The party's commitment to statehood, even at the cost of territorial sacrifice, gained far broader appeal than the argument of the left-wing kibbutzim that partition would be premature, because the settlements had not yet completed their mission of establishing a territorial and socialist infrastructure for the future Jewish state. Faction B and other left-wing groups did enjoy considerable success in mobilizing those Histadrut members who had not yet been drawn into Mapai's net—but their numbers were insufficient to upset Mapai's majority in the labour organization. Outside of the Histadrut, with the exception of the kibbutzim, the left opposition made only weak electoral headway. In any case, its gains were offset by Mapai's stepped-up efforts to attract members of the middle strata, such as artisans and small merchants.[26]

The labour-movement economy. Another wartime innovation which proved to be a harbinger of Mapai's future success was the Histadrut's widening entrepreneurial role in a rapidly modernizing and growing economy. At the time of the labour organization's foundation, Ben-Gurion had envisioned it as the epicentre of a tightly centralized network of co-operative enterprises on which both economic development and the settlement programme of the Yishuv would rest. Instead, the labour-movement economy developed along two main axes, both relatively independent of central direction. One of these is a congeries of frameworks for collective self-employment (like the kibbutzim and Israel's bus and truck co-operatives) which, in terms of both ownership and control, are only loosely tied to the Histadrut. The other consists of corporations owned by the Histadrut but managed by salaried executives who, while subject in some respects to political selection and guidance, from the outset behaved similarly to their private-sector counterparts. The one major difference was that profits, if any, were ploughed back in their entirety rather than distributed to shareholders—nominally the entire Histadrut rank and file.

Even during the inter-war period, there were sections of the labour-movement economy (notably in transportation and mixed farming) that dominated their respective branches; and during the construction booms of the 1920s, the Histadrut's contracting company was by far the largest employer in the industry. But prior to the war, the Palestine economy's most consistently expanding productive branches—manufacturing and citrus growing—had been almost exclusively in private hands. As a result of the hostilities, however, citrus exports were halted while manufacturing and large-scale construction each received a tremendous boost. *Solel Boneh*, the Histadrut building company, expanded rapidly and began to diversify into industry. Consequently, the Histadrut, for the first time, controlled an enterprise which was simultaneously: (*a*) a large-scale employer; (*b*) a big profit-maker, and (*c*) a leading power in the most dynamic sector of the economy.[27]

Important new political-economic opportunities followed. First, a major bloc of wage-earners directly dependent on the Histadrut for employment constituted fertile ground for the recruitment of party activists and the instilling of mass loyalty. Second, a thriving enterprise could furnish the party with a generous fund of well-paid patronage jobs, as well as covert financial subventions. Third, ownership of a large, rapidly growing concern situated on the cutting edge of the country's economic development implied a significant political capacity to steer the economy in general. Of course, each of these potential advantages for Mapai depended on its ability to exert political control over the managers of Solel Boneh. Not surprisingly, the latter, although party appointees, were able to exploit the potency of the resources under their control as a lever for gaining autonomy. But in return for the freedom to build up their economic power, Histadrut entrepreneurs were willing to yield at least partial access to the potential political benefits.

Sovereignty and the reconstruction of the Histadrut

Our earlier analysis of the inter-war period made it clear that the Histadrut was always a critical component of Mapai's political hegemony, particularly in mediating the bonds between individual workers and the party. The wartime developments just reviewed indicate that the centrality of the Histadrut became even more pronounced. On the one hand, the labour organization itself was home to an important new challenge to Mapai's dominance: the rise of rank-and-file mobilization, which threatened to split the Jewish working class into autonomous fragments unattached to the party or, worse still, under the sway of the left. At the same time, part of the Histadrut élite—the managers of its business enterprises—was presiding over the rise of a Mapai-affiliated economic sector with weighty implications for political recruitment of the mass public and political management of the economy. The dilemmas associated with control of the workers and the labour-movement entrepreneurs alike intensified after 1948. But, in addition, the first decade of sovereignty introduced several new challenges to Mapai dominance for which the party also sought solutions via the Histadrut.

First, after 1948 the electorate grew enormously and, more importantly, altered in composition. Mass immigration of 'Eastern' (or *Sephardi*) Jews from North Africa and the Middle East and the enfranchisement of those Palestinian Arabs who remained within Israel's borders generated sizeable blocs of voters lacking any a priori basis for identification with Mapai.[28] They were viewed by party leaders as unlikely to develop loyalty to its traditional values and institutions. A second, even more fundamental, innovation derived directly from the attainment of sovereignty itself. On the one hand, Mapai and its leaders were well positioned to harvest the political prestige attendant on their role in constructing and defending the newly founded Jewish state. But paradoxically, the party's very success in state-building implied that the labour movement's unique role in colonization and self-defence, and thus its indispensability for catering to the perceived long-term interests of all social strata, was at an end. The role of the Histadrut in the post-1948 political economy is the key to the persistence of Mapai's dominance under these dramatically altered conditions.

Strengthening the Histadrut. After 1948 state authority was harnessed along a broad front in order to remedy the Histadrut's long-standing institutional lacunae as a would-be corporate peak association. During the Yishuv era, rival minority labour organizations and competition from Arab and unorganized Jewish labour had made it impossible for the Histadrut to achieve a representational monopoly. These obstacles were definitively removed by a mix of informal and statutory interventions. The state also proved to be a potent ally of Mapai's Histadrut chiefs in their struggles to foster worker loyalty and to prevent trade union autonomy.[29]

The functions as well as the structure of the Histadrut were revised following the attainment of sovereignty. The major issue at stake was the division of labour between the Histadrut and the authorities *vis-à-vis* public responsibilities previously in the domain of the labour organization. The motives and manoeuvring involved in this process were complex, but as Arian (1978) has shown, the overriding political logic is clear. Mapai forcibly 'nationalized' those Histadrut functions which had become important power bases for the left opposition (the Palmach military force and the labour school system). The state also took control of resources (like the labour exchanges), which would generate no less political pay off in a state than a 'movement' framework. On the other hand, the labour organization's social services and its affiliated economic enterprises were permitted to remain in the movement sphere and came to enjoy substantial informal privileges, on the understanding that they would continue to serve the needs of the party. Thus, the Histadrut's Sick Fund was largely shielded from competition with either public health authorities or competing private organizations. Its ranks were swollen by the granting of automatic trial memberships to new immigrants, paid for by the Jewish Agency. The Histadrut's pension and provident funds were given free rein to expand by the social policy of the state, which deliberately circumscribed potentially competitive public income maintenance programmes. Special exemptions from standard tax and investment requirements later turned these funds into a vast source of cheap finance for the expansion of Histadrut-owned enterprises.[30]

Complementary to these interventions by the state, the party itself played an active role in subordinating a strengthened Histadrut to political ends. At rank-and-file level, an aggressive and successful campaign was launched to undermine the standing of the left opposition among veteran rank-and-file workers and to preempt control of workers' committees formed to represent new immigrants. Workers' committees played their part in supporting the party's hegemony by assisting it to distribute patronage, create bonds of material dependence, recruit activists, disseminate propaganda, and punish or co-opt dissenters. At the Histadrut centre, the party supported reforms extending the centralization of the trade union function which had begun during the war. Mapai also acquired a major role in mediating, and in some cases arbitrating, between Histadrut and state élites on matters of national wages policy. The fact that Histadrut leaders were appointed by the party, and that the state was in a position to manipulate its regulation and subsidization of the labour organization's non-union functions (economic enterprises, health care, etc.), encouraged the Histadrut to co-operate in endorsing and policing wage restraint.[31]

Politicization and 'corporatization' of the Histadrut fostered some important pre-conditions for the perpetuation of Mapai's rule. On the one hand, the Histadrut was encouraged to perform a *mobilizing* function by bringing the mass public into the labour movement's sphere of influence and furnishing instrumental dependencies and a political milieu in which their loyalty could be cultivated. On the other hand, it was encouraged to act in its capacity as the country's premier organized interest association to *legitimate* Mapai's policies in government (especially those with distributive implications), at times actively reining in worker militancy in accordance with government stabilization policies.

The role of Histadrut enterprises. The labour-movement economy was also called upon to contribute to the objectives of mobilization, legitimation, and political management of the economy. Its role was accentuated by dramatic expansion of Histadrut-affiliated corporations and collectives after 1948. By the late 1950s the Solel Boneh concern alone generated 8 per cent of Israel's national income, and overall the labour-movement sector of the economy encompassed a quarter of the labour force. As a result, fully half of all economically active Histadrut members were, to some extent, associated with the labour organization in earning their livelihood. The Histadrut's economic activity had also experienced a number of quiet but far-reaching internal changes which further concentrated economic power among the managers of large enterprises. The result was a bitter struggle, which climaxed in 1959 when the party decreed that Solel Boneh be split up into three subunits and removed its chief executive from office.

Within the shifting limits of party control over the Histadrut-owned business sector, the Histadrut became enormously important to the post-sovereignty regime of Mapai dominance.[32] First, the political loyalties of thousands of newcomers, mostly Easterners, were tied to the fact that they found jobs (initially at a time of high unemployment) in Histadrut construction and industrial firms. Second, as in the past, these enterprises also enriched the party with jobs and money. Third, the Histadrut's synthesis of labour representation and capital accumulation contributed to Mapai's capacities for governance in the area of labour relations. It is true that the Histadrut's dual role as both union and boss has at times generated severe problems of internal co-ordination and external credibility. But another consequence of this unorthodox arrangement is that the labour organization has internalized the capitalist logic that profitability is the essential pre-condition for worker gains. With this innate 'taste' for labour restraint, as well as its excellent contacts (through the executives of the labour-movement economy) with big business in other sectors, the Histadrut constituted an attractive partner for the state when public policy went in search of wage moderation.

Mapai, the state, and capital

The contributions of the labour movement economy to Mapai's post-sovereignty regime of dominance were not confined to providing the ruling party with voters and resources and promoting labour peace. The ramified economic empire linked to Mapai also provided it with a realistic mechanism for politically managed economic development—one which had the effect of simultaneously dividing and compensating the bourgeoisie proper. As an instrument for promoting growth, the labour-movement economy was bound to be assigned substantial responsibilities in view of the continued paucity of private entrepreneurial capital at home and Israel's unattractiveness to investors from abroad. The alternative possibility, to entrust all public economic initiative to state-owned enterprises, was barely contemplated. Both considerations of accountability (public corporations had inevitably to be subject to public scrutiny) and Mapai's unchallengeable authority in the Histadrut (which it controlled outright, being spared the power-sharing imperatives which the party faced in the parliamentary sphere) meant that it was easier to steer this form of public sector by political criteria and for partisan gain.

The fact that Mapai had acquired the instruments of sovereignty raised a more far-reaching possibility, namely, that it would finally bring about the transition to socialism of which labour-movement ideologues had long dreamed. In reality, after taking power the party failed even to raise the issue of nationalization—a 'non-decision' which must be understood first and foremost as a political choice. Externally there was the danger of compromising Israel in the eyes of allies it was anxious to court, namely, the government and the Jewish community of the United States. Inside the labour movement, the Mapam opposition was a vociferous champion of extending collective ownership. But in the early years Mapam was a political rival. Mapai preferred to continue its long-standing co-operation with clerical and bourgeois parties rather than yield to Mapam's more far-reaching demands for portfolios and programmatic shifts.

Mapai's key economic policy-makers also seem to have recognized that exclusive nurturing of the Histadrut sector would have upset the internal distribution of power within the party. On the other hand, undue favouritism towards private capitalists would have hampered party direction of the economy and carried palpable political risks. The party had proven in the past that coexistence with private capital helped to perpetuate the weak and fragmented political mobilization of the right. The labour-movement economy's very existence scotched any possibility of capital mobilizing solidaristically behind a single political movement. At the same time, the more significant private entrepreneurs were silenced politically by economic concessions, some of them channelled through the Histadrut itself.

To appreciate the significance of Mapai's policy of support for both private and labour-movement capital, it is necessary to recognize the awesome dimensions of the role of the state apparatus in underwriting economic expansion. This issue, and its long-term significance for Mapai hegemony and the autonomy of the state, will be discussed more fully in Chapter 7 of this book. Here it is sufficient to point out this remarkable consequence of sovereignty, that it furnished the party/state with the power to allocate all of the most important resources for capital accumulation: land, private savings, and most of all, prodigious streams of loans and gifts from abroad. It was on this basis that the political élite chose to provide heavily subsidized finance for the lion's share of the investments made by large enterprises in all sectors of Israel's economy.[33]

Mass politics: The mobilization of new publics

The various state and party interventions designed to strengthen external and internal political direction of the Histadrut, together with the growth of the labour movement economy, bore tangible fruit for Mapai at the polls. As late as the 1969 elections (the first for which appropriate published data are available), the vast majority of Histadrut members voted for the Labour Alignment.

They also contributed the vast majority of all Alignment votes. Citizens' personal indebtedness for assets like housing and employment was evidently integral to the Histadrut's success in instilling political loyalty.[34]

The Histadrut's activities in mobilizing the mass public were complementary to those of the party machine at the neighbourhood level. In both cases Mapai's pull was greatest among newcomers of Eastern origin. There was a glaring discrepancy between Israel's official ideology of welcoming the Jews of North Africa and the Middle East after their centuries of 'exile' from the Holy Land, and the harsh reality of cultural prejudice and economic discrimination against Eastern Jews and their subjection to crude political manipulation for partisan gain. Yet despite their disappointments, most of the immigrants who poured into Israel from Morocco, the Yemen, and other countries of the region during the first decade of statehood were relatively easily drawn into Mapai's sphere of influence. Sentiments of Messianism associated with Israel's establishment, and the Easterners' admiration for Ben-Gurion, the party's charismatic leader, played a part in forging this unlikely alliance. But more important was the extreme vulnerability of most Eastern-origin newcomers, who arrived in Israel without independent means and had great difficulty in utilizing either personal connections or collective action to influence the terms of their entry into Israel's economy and society.[35]

The Easterners formed the largest but not the only bloc of new voters on which Mapai's continuing electoral plurality depended after 1948. Arabs and the new Jewish middle classes also afforded Mapai with badly needed support. But the party's pull—both its instrumental attractions and the mediating role played by the Histadrut—were very different in these two instances.

Palestinian citizens. The Arab population remaining within Israel's borders after 1949 had experienced a trauma of vast proportion. Panic, expulsion, and new boundary lines reduced the non-Jewish population of the new state of Israel to barely over 10 per cent of the Arab community in Mandatory Palestine at the time of the British withdrawal. Moreover, the losses included the Palestinian Arabs' most prominent strata and leadership figures, in both the political and economic spheres. At the material level the disaster was compounded by Israel's large-scale confiscation of land and water resources together with initially strict regulation of Arab entry to the labour markets of the Jewish economy.

A political regime was established for the Arab sector which combined local surveillance and administration by a military government with the freedom to vote in national elections. From the outset, Palestinian voters constituted an important segment (close to one-tenth) of the Israeli electorate. Until the late 1950s, when economic and political pressures joined to undermine the viability of military rule, Mapai was well placed to capture the lion's share of these ballots. In the 1955 elections, for example, the party received only one-third of the Jewish vote. Yet in conjunction with nominally independent but actually subsidiary Arab slates, it garnered two-thirds of the votes cast in Arab localities. The source of this discrepancy was clearly attested by repeated calls from both the left- and right-wing parliamentary opposition for the end of military rule over Arab citizens.

In the 1960s Labour retained its Arab majority by a combination of co-optation, repression, and barter. But the policy of all Israeli governments has been to deny either a Palestinian or a pan-Arab national identity to the Arab minority, and to impose restrictive, particularistic criteria on the distribution of public goods and services to Arab citizens and communities in order to sustain their political and economic subordination. The major vehicle for (largely symbolic) Arab opposition to these policies, aside from the option of non-voting, has been the Communist Party. Beginning in 1961, both the Communist share of the Arab vote and the proportion of abstainers rose for five successive elections. Nevertheless, Mapai/Labour and its associated Arab slates clung to their majority until the 1970s.

Typically, Arab loyalty to Mapai rested on the shoulders of local leaders armed with the power to allocate privileges nominally controlled by the military government. The system was most effective in small villages and other traditional, hierarchical communities. It was, however, supplemented by more 'modern' forms of co-optation and exchange administered by the 'Arab Departments' of government ministries and the Histadrut. In the background there were (and to an extent still are) powerful constraints on Arab-sector politics. For many years Palestinian citizens were obliged to work through Jewish intermediaries within the labour movement due to their exclusion from elementary participation rights.[36] A majority of Arabs are dependent on Jews (or Jewish-controlled public institutions) to earn a living. And Israel's security forces are responsible for extensive vetting, surveillance, and, at times, outright repression of Arab political activity.[37]

The state-made middle class. Mapai's success among Jewish voters in the middle strata and the bourgeoisie rested partly on positive incentives and partly on a continuing political vacuum on the right. From the first systematic political opinion polls, it was evident that the higher strata were no different from all others in awarding Mapai a plurality of their vote. In fact, support for Mapai seemingly tended to *rise* with position in the class hierarchy. This was due, in part, to the success of rival parties in capturing elements of the working class: veteran Ashkenazim (Westerners) who supported the labour-movement left; traditional-minded workers among the new immigrants who favoured religious parties; and Easterners who voted for the right-wing *Cherut* Party in protest against their treatment by the Mapai establishment. Nevertheless, Mapai's relative success among the middle and upper strata was not simply an artifact of its incomplete capture of lower-class voters. The willingness of many professionals, managers, and businessmen to vote Mapai was quite striking, especially given their antipathy towards the labour movement's professed economic ideology.

To some extent this paradox is attributable to the ruling party's generosity towards what Rosenfeld and Carmi (1976) have aptly described as the 'state-made middle class'—entrepreneurs and middlemen who made their fortunes through government concessions and subsidies, as well as the considerable salariat of managerial and professional workers in public employ. Most of this upward mobility affected veterans of the pre-state era, many of whom retained an emotional attachment to the labour movement and expressed appreciation for their good fortune by remaining loyal to Mapai.[38] The traditional middle class, on the other hand, and notably the self-employed, tended to favour the General Zionists (later, Liberals) or Cherut—the two parties which began running together in the 1965 elections and which later formed the Likud alliance.[39]

The constraints on opposition parties

In earlier discussion of Mapai's hegemonic reign over the Yishuv, we noted the inability of the party's opponents (on both left and right) to seriously challenge its hegemony. These failures persisted after 1948, and for essentially the same reasons.

The parties of the right endured profound disabilities during the first two decades of Israeli sovereignty. In part these difficulties were no more than the mirror-image of the labour movement's success in claiming credit for the transition to statehood. The new Cherut (Freedom) Party, a synthesis of older Revisionist political elements and one of the terrorist undergrounds of the pre-sovereignty period, was portrayed by Mapai as a radical movement which had jeopardized the struggle for national liberation and now endangered Israeli democracy. Indeed, some observers regard Mapai's delegitimation of Cherut and its leader, Menahem Begin, as the exclusive determinant of right-wing defeat. This is an exaggerated view and, moreover, does not account for an equally significant cause of right-wing weakness—the failure of the more respectable (and electorally more significant) 'liberal' parties to challenge Mapai's political hegemony.[40]

Developments in the political economy appear to be of greater relevance in this connection. Before 1948, notwithstanding its internal divisions and only partial role in fulfilling the vital interests of other classes, private capital had generated most of the output and employment of the Yishuv economy. But after Israel's creation capitalist immigration dried up, and almost the whole of the inflow of foreign capital—which continued to be indispensable both for bridging the trade deficit and bankrolling economic development— acquired the form of gifts to the Israeli government from foreign states and Jewish communities. In addition, private agriculture—a pivotal branch of the economy for most of the inter-war period—was now dwarfed by state-supported collective and co-operative farming. Theoretically, private industrialists and the not insignificant *petite bourgeoisie* might nevertheless have mobilized as a serious counter-force to Mapai in either pressure-group or party politics. In practice, however, the Manufacturers' Association remained organizationally weak and tangential to public policy making. The Association and major individual businessmen were content to advance their economic interests informally within the political status quo, working in co-operation with Mapai politicians, bureaucrats, and the executives of the labour-movement economy. In the party arena, both the voters and leaders of the Liberals and (to a lesser extent) Cherut were indeed closely identified with business interests and the *petite bourgeoisie*. But Mapai nurtured the division between Cherut and the Liberals by pursuing opposite strategies towards them, of exclusion and inclusion respectively. The Liberals were offered Cabinet portfolios, and major businessmen active in the party or close to it were granted generous state aid, while Cherut (like the Communist Party) was treated as a political pariah.

On a related front, Mapai successfully combined a proven talent for political organization with its unique capacity to direct distributional flows through the state in order to co-opt each of the interest groups which might have turned into economic bases of right-wing political mobilization: farmers, the self-employed, and the new middle class. In a classic case, Mapai captured the national organization of self-employed artisans by granting them favourable access to the politicians and officials whose decisions determined the artisans' economic fate. The party's strength in agriculture had deeper roots. The very creation of the rapidly proliferating collective sector was presided over by party officials (usually from Mapai), and it was heavily dependent on party-regulated access to land, water, credit, and marketing.

Both the mediation of vital economic interests and exposure to an intensely partisan milieu were more difficult to achieve in relation to a third potential constituency of the right, the rapidly growing salaried managerial and professional class. The professionals—most of them state employees—were particularly troublesome to Mapai because their jobs were less politicized and their labour-market position was stronger than any other section of the work-force. Nevertheless, despite a series of celebrated revolts against Histadrut wage policies, university-educated workers were unable to erect an independent associational structure on which political opposition to Mapai might have rested. Soon after sovereignty, with the support of the government, the Histadrut waged a successful campaign to stymie autonomous professional organization. To this day nearly all of the relevant associations remain within the Histadrut fold.[41]

On the left, sovereignty and its aftermath failed to eliminate—

and indeed actually reinforced—the suffusion of left-opposition politics by the logic of the national conflict. Mapai's immediate rivals on the left were gradually absorbed into today's Labour Alignment, while the radicals fractured into an insignificant Jewish wing and a large but isolated Arab wing. In parliamentary terms Mapai's major challenger was Mapam, which, in the first elections after statehood, received 15 per cent to Mapai's 36 per cent for the Knesset, and a massive 34 per cent to Mapai's 57 per cent for the Histadrut. However, this peak was short-lived and in 1954 the left split again when Achdut Avodah reclaimed its independence. Mapam and Achdut Avodah combined typically gained only one-third as many Knesset seats as Mapai and, consequently, were unable to participate in government except on terms acceptable to Mapai. The Histadrut arena was more favourable to these parties, but their role was ambiguous—on the one hand, organizing rank-and-file militancy and, on the other, serving as junior partners in the Histadrut 'cabinet'.

Thus, instead of realizing its aspiration to take over the labour movement and thereby the state, the ultimate fate of the Zionist left was co-optation and marginalization within both spheres. Part of the problem was that the labour-movement opposition faced a formidable opponent. Mapai, and particularly its forceful long-time leader, Ben-Gurion, did not hesitate to exercise the prerogatives of the state to undermine the power bases of the left. The 'nationalization' of former Histadrut functions and Mapai's successful struggle to regain control of renegade trade unions and work-place shop committees have already been discussed. In the same vein, during a period of intense ideological dispute in the kibbutz movement in the early post-state years, Mapai helped spur a crisis which split the movement along party lines. In national politics the retreat of the left was signalled when intense struggle and co-operation with Mapai gave way to participation in government, electoral collaboration, and ultimately actual or virtual mergers.[42]

Certainly, the left suffered from its own liabilities as well. The perennial tension between moderates and radicals was brought to almost unbearable heights by the Cold War, in combination with growing ambiguities in the Soviet Union's stance towards Israel, and revelations of anti-Semitic treatment of Jews throughout the Communist bloc. In addition, the contradictions of the alliance between their urban and kibbutz components continued to haunt both Mapam and Achdut Avodah. The hawkish sentiments, which the Achdut Avodah kibbutzim had inherited from the era of settlement and state-making, conflicted with the urban left's commitment to Arab–Jewish coexistence. Dovishness suffered not only from contradictory ideologies but also from the status of the kibbutzim as major recipients of abandoned or confiscated Arab land. And at times urban and kibbutz activists took conflicting positions which reflected their differing material objectives—high wages and high agricultural subsidies, respectively.

After a promising start, the Communists fared even worse than Mapai's immediate rivals within the labour-Zionist camp. In Israel's first three Knesset elections the Communist Party of Israel (*Maki*), with two-thirds Jewish voters and the other third Arab, enjoyed an expanding share of the vote, approaching 5 per cent in 1955. Subsequently, however, Jewish support fell off and by 1965 separate Jewish and Arab parties were officially constituted. In an innovative study, historian Joel Beinin (1990) reports evidence for the early post-sovereignty years of Maki's significant appeal among Jewish voters, as well as the readiness of the Arab party leadership to come to terms with Israel's existence. Nevertheless, the nationalist sentiment aroused (to some extent deliberately, by Mapai leaders) before and following the 1956 Sinai campaign tarred Maki with a rabidly anti-Zionist appearance in the eyes of the Jewish public, and provoked disenchantment among many of the party's Jewish activists. Growing disparity between Jewish and Arab feeling towards the Soviet Union further reinforced this divide. Disappointment in the early 1960s with the failure of the new and increasingly militant Jewish working class (the Eastern immigrants) to respond to Communist appeals sapped most of the remaining Arab interest in binational activity. Since the mid-1970s radical politics in the Jewish sector (radical in relation to both national and class questions) have been confined to highly splintered fringe groups.

Meanwhile, the Communist Party (in various incarnations) has continued to function primarily as an expression of protest by Palestinian citizens of Israel against institutionalized discrimination and a sense of frustrated national identity. Its appeal is virtually the mirror-image of Mapai/Labour's, rising in Arab communities which are relatively free from the bonds of either traditional clan-based politics or dependence on Jewish-controlled political and bureaucratic apparatuses.[43] Supported by the Jewish consensus—which holds that despite its legality and Knesset representation, the Communist Party is by definition anti-Zionist and bordering on treasonous—the authorities and most Zionist parties actively oppose its influence. An important consequence of this delegitimation is that the Communists are unable to offer their supporters access to state-controlled budgets, permits, and public services vital to the well-being of Arab communities, which have thus far been mediated exclusively by Mapai and other governing parties.[44]

Conclusions: Interpreting Mapai's hegemony

From a comparative perspective, it is by no means obvious to which family of one-party-dominant regimes the Israeli case belongs. Over thirty years ago Amitai Etzioni (1959) argued that while Mapai was programmatically closest to the moderate left in Britain and Europe, from a substantive viewpoint it could best be compared with successful parties of the right in France and Germany, parties which were similarly reliant on the aggregation of diverse interests under the sway of an influential leader. More recently both Arian and Barnes (1974), who sought to rationalize the Israeli Labour Party's success, and Levite and Tarrow (1983), who proposed an explanation for its fall from power, followed a similar logic in choosing Christian-Democratic Italy as their referent for comparison.

Mapai's affinity to some contemporary instances of right-wing hegemony is indeed striking. For, unlike the successful labour-movement parties of Sweden and Austria, dominant parties of the right like those in Italy or Japan combine the support of a diverse variety of publics, such as farmers, the old and new middle classes, and 'traditional' workers. Similarly, while successful left parties draw their primary strength from a distinctively working-class organizational and ideological milieu, popular support for the right is more dependent on particularistic and calculative incentives, whether the vote-buying and patronage of political machines, 'pork barrel' alliances, or pre-electoral pump-priming.[45] Finally, all would-be governing parties are in a fundamental sense conservative. But reliance on supra-class appeals (nationalism, religion, traditionalism) is far more typical of right- than left-wing parties.[46]

The abundant literature on Israeli politics confirms that nominally social-democratic Mapai encapsulates every one of these hallmarks of right-wing dominance. Scholars continue to disagree about the extent to which the labour movement of Israel historically took its socialist pretensions seriously; but they are virtually unanimous concerning three conspicuous features of Mapai dominance. One is the all-important role played by Mapai's judicious use of *material incentives* to individuals and communities via the Histadrut, the urban party machine, and (after statehood) the electoral business cycle. A second is the fact that, following sovereignty, the party managed to mobilize a plurality of voters within *all* classes and exercised a determinate influence over *all* major organized economic interests. Third is Mapai's conscious identification with the interests of the (Jewish) nation as a whole, built upon its paramount role in the struggle for sovereignty and construction of the state.[47]

The fact that Mapai has been at one and the same time a settlement-cum-national-liberation movement and an opportunistic catch-all party and yet, like other dominant parties of the left, relies on a peak labour organization as its principal power base, is confusing although fundamental to the complexity and peculiarity of the Israeli case. But while locating one-party dominance in Israel in comparative terms by means of a simple left-right dichotomy is clearly unsatisfactory, this does not mean that the social-democratic model of one-party hegemony and the Israeli case are mutually irrelevant. Early in this chapter we pointed to Sweden's SAP as a social-democratic party which enjoyed similar political longevity to Mapai. Recently Gøsta Esping-Andersen, one of the foremost theorists of social democracy, has concluded in a re-examination of the sources of SAP supremacy that the role of worker mobilization in trade unions may have been exaggerated as the historic source of social-democratic dominance. He contends that the critical—and remarkable—development in the Swedish case was the SAP's transformation in the 1930s to 'a party of the people, not of a class' (Esping-Andersen, 1990*a*: 49). The resemblance to Ben-Gurion's famous slogan (also coined in the 1930s), 'from class to nation', is unmistakable. And as we have seen, actions followed words as Mapai, under Ben-Gurion, opted for broadly based coalitions in the Zionist movement and the Yishuv's institutions of self-government, sought a negotiated form of co-operation even with arch-enemies like the Revisionists, did its best to defuse industrial conflict, and projected an overarching commitment to 'peace in the Yishuv'.

The rise of the Zionist version of social democracy thus appears to confirm Esping-Andersen's hypothesis that comprehensive and concentrated labour organization is an insufficient condition for labour-movement political hegemony unless, and until, it combines with the active consent of other classes. On the other hand, evident differences in the *content* of the supra-class political appeals of the labour movements of Sweden and the Yishuv are worth noting, because they clearly reveal the distinctiveness of the Israeli case. The SAP's legitimacy was acquired in a struggle for democracy, not for settlement and sovereignty. It tangibly demonstrated the societal benefits of labour-movement rule by engineering a historic compromise between labour and capital, not by turning the working class into the spearhead of national reconstruction. By embracing a Keynesian formula for economic recovery from the 1930s depression, the SAP and other social-democratic parties made the particularistic interest of the working-class in higher wages synonymous with the general interest of all classes in stimulating production.[48] In contrast, the material basis for the status of Jewish labour in Palestine as a *universal class* did not rest solely on the positive implications of working-class prosperity for other classes. It also relied on the shared interest of workers, the middle strata, and much of the bourgeoisie in the economic separation of Arabs and Jews; and on the crucial role of the labour movement in guaranteeing the present security and future political status of the entire Zionist community in Palestine.

This last role could, in principle, have been performed even more assiduously by Mapai's principal challenger on the right, the Revisionists; while for its part the left opposition within the labour movement could, in principle, have overcome Mapai by opposing the compromises on labourism necessitated by 'from class to nation'. But in the special conditions of the Yishuv, the right was unable to pin its fortunes to a hegemonic capitalist class in the economic realm; nor, in the realm of the national conflict, could it invoke the involuntary power of a state apparatus to realize its programme. Adding to their handicaps, neither right nor left oppositions could go very far in winning Mapai's core constituency, the working class. No opposition movement could offer an alternative solution to the practical difficulties inherent in being a newly arrived and/or unskilled Jewish immigrant without independent means. Its near-monopoly over the 'national capital' of the Zionist movement and other forms of Jewish philanthropy provided the labour movement, and thereby Mapai, with the exclusive wherewithal for offering workers direly needed help to acclimatize and sustain themselves in an alien and hostile environment. If we add to this the limited economic basis for right-wing appeals to the Yishuv's large *petite bourgeoisie*, on the one hand, and Mapai's carefully nurtured image as the vanguard of a universal class, on the other, it is possible to see how political economy and the politics of nationalism and state-making blended in the construction of Mapai's hegemony.

A new regime of dominance developed out of the requirements and opportunities of the post-sovereignty era, already foreshadowed to some extent during World War II. Our account of this renegotiated hegemony emphasized the Histadrut's roles as handmaiden to the Mapai party/state—in managing distributional conflicts, stimulating economic growth, attracting new constituencies, and denying footholds to the opposition. This leads to the conclusion that Mapai's success was contingent, above all, on its remarkable ability to exert political direction of economic processes. This is equally true of the party's capacity to harvest the political fruits of the labour-movement economy; its co-optation of middle-class organizations and business leaders; and its effective utilization of instrumental incentives to attract individual voters.

In proposing a political-economy interpretation of the reproduction of Mapai's pre-eminence after Israeli sovereignty, we depart from traditional approaches to single-party dominance in general, and the case of Mapai specifically, which have taken for granted that 'politics is king' (Arian and Barnes, 1974: 599). Certainly, the scope of the tasks and resources embraced by Israel's newly created state apparatus furnished the political élite responsible for its creation with remarkable freedom to fix the contours of Israel's political map. Not surprisingly, this freedom was greatest in the realm of the national conflict, now transformed from an intercommunal to an interstate dispute. In the course of our discussion of Mapai's dominance in the post-sovereignty era we had occasion to note a number of specific illustrations: the dissolution of the military forces, Mapam's most important source of political charisma;

Mapai's indirect exploitation of the conflict as a pretext for capturing the Arab vote; and the benefits which the dominant party enjoyed (and fostered) because the conflict discredited the Communist left in Jewish eyes.

The political consequences of the national conflict, at both the ideological and institutional levels, are explored more extensively in other critical scholarship of recent vintage.[49] There is persuasive evidence that Mapai's top leadership *chose* to base the party's appeal on territorial and military expansionism, in the process nullifying the political options espoused by the left. Mapai also fostered the defence establishment as the core of the new state apparatus and covertly turned it into a key arena of party activity.[50] Consequently, in time, the old-guard leadership, close to the Histadrut and the party machine, was challenged by pretenders who had made their name in the military sphere and represented the new power base developing in the bureaucracies and industries attached to this sphere. This internal tension within Mapai became painfully intense during the early 1960s and provoked a major political regrouping in 1965, in which Ben-Gurion and a coterie of younger men formed a break-away party, while simultaneously Mapai established its first 'alignment' with a left-wing opposition party.

These regroupings have generally been seen as reflecting conflicts within Mapai between a hawkish and a dovish defence strategy, between 'statism' versus the continued primacy of the labour movement, and between the conflicting career aspirations of military men and veteran party *apparatchiks*.[51] Yet the political turmoil inside the party during the 1960s also represented a struggle between politics and political economy—a struggle which political economy won. The alternative to basing party power within the bounds of the state and its military function was to continue to root Mapai's supremacy in its domination of the great centres of economic power—the state's economic ministries, the Histadrut, and the Jewish fund-raising institutions. The ideological struggle was thus not only over statism and militarism but also the economic role of the state, which the challengers were anxious to diminish. Specifically, as a revealing new study by Shapiro and Grinberg (1988) shows, the split in Mapai was the culmination of a series of long-standing disputes concerning the role of the Histadrut in the political economy: whether to 'nationalize' its productive and distributive functions, how far to exert political supervision over the executives of the labour movement economy, and how to respond to the threats to trade union and managerial authority which emerged as full employment freed workers from dependence on the Histadrut/Mapai apparatus. This is not the place to elaborate on these issues, which are discussed more fully in later chapters. Our point in raising them here is to provide grist for the argument that even so notable an instance of the power of 'purely political' factors as the party split, which threatened to put a premature end to Mapai hegemony, cannot be adequately interpreted without an appreciation of political–economic interactions.

This brings us back to the factor, which has been central to the discussion in this chapter, of the reproduction of Mapai dominance following sovereignty—and which may be denoted, following Tufte (1978), as 'political control of the economy'. This need not mean replacing crude political explanations with equally crude economic ones. The literature on Israeli politics in the era of labour-movement dominance has widely recognized the importance of, in effect, vote-buying among citizens who had few alternatives. But there has been far less appreciation of the political significance of Mapai's ability to use its economic leverage in order to structure immediate distributional flows and longer-term patterns of social stratification. The scope of the state as an employer and its effective command over profitability in the business sector, laid the foundations both for Mapai's success among the new middle class and for the support it enjoyed from privately owned big business. Among new immigrants, Mapai succeeded in building up relations of dependency which went far beyond the mere purchase of votes. Party-directed public bureaucracies kept newcomers out of the labour market at the initial stages, directed them into employment in Mapai-controlled public and Histadrut enterprises, and created immigrant agricultural and urban settlements from the ground up with built-in party mediation of life chances. What made it all possible was the Zionist legitimacy enveloping the enormous reach of the labour movement and the state, the unrequited funds made available by friendly governments and supporters abroad, and the unfeasibility of powering economic development primarily by means of private capital accumulation. However, the resulting pattern of state-economy relations was not merely a historical accident, but must also be recognized as a strategy for maintaining one-party dominance. It follows that, as we shall argue in Chapter 7, the erosion of political control of the economy provides a powerful explanation for Mapai/Labour's eventual fall from power.

Notes

1. Maurice Duverger pioneered the notion of one-party dominance (1964: 307–15, 417–18). See Pempel (1990) for a recent comparative analysis.
2. This and subsequent chapters will refer, singly and collectively, to what were known as the 'national institutions' of the Jewish community in Palestine. This term embraced not only the political institutions of the Yishuv itself, but also bodies connected with the international Zionist movement. In functional terms, the domestic institutions focused on local government and the provision of education and social services, while the international bodies bore responsibility for colonization, defence, and other distinctively state-like duties. The system of community-wide representation within the Yishuv, although recognized by the Mandatory government, was voluntary in character and enjoyed limited powers. This system comprised the Elected Assembly (*Asefat Nivcharim*) and its executive, the *Va'ad Leumi* or 'National Committee'. Internationally, the most significant bodies were the World Zionist Organization (WZO) and the Jewish Agency. The WZO held periodic international congresses, which constituted its executive arms. In the 1930s and 1940s the Jewish Agency, which had been provided for in Britain's original League of Nations Mandate, was the officially recognized spokesman for World Jewry's interest in Palestine and the most important vehicle of Jewish self-government in the Yishuv. It partly replaced and partly supplemented the Palestine Zionist Executive, with the important difference that from 1929 onwards the Agency was governed by the leaders of the Zionist movement in collaboration with non-Zionist Diaspora representatives.
3. Election results for the Yishuv period are furnished by Horowitz and Lissak (1978: 90–1, 101–3). For a summary of trends since 1948, see Yanai (1981: ch. 1). Obviously, our statement that Mapai governed for more than four decades is based on inclusion of the 1935–48 period during which Mapai controlled the Jewish Agency while the British ruled Palestine.
4. The gap between Mapai's positions and the attitudes of its supporters was studied by Arian (1968). For discussions of Mapai's control of the army and of government bureaucracies see respectively Peri (1983) and Reuveni (1974). Medding (1972) reviews Mapai's role *vis-à-vis* organized interests around the 1960s, and

Etzioni-Halevy (1975*a*; 1975*b*) has analysed the state's 'absorption of protest' under Labour.

5. The 'dominant-party system' was for many years a leading paradigm of Israeli political sociology. In particular, see the work of Yonathan Shapiro (especially Shapiro, 1978) and Asher (Alan) Arian (e.g. Arian and Barnes, 1974). The acceptance of this paradigm by other observers is illustrated in a more recent analysis by Reuveni (1985).
6. See Korpi (1978) and Castles (1978) for, by now, classic accounts of Swedish social democracy; and Esping-Andersen (1985*a*) and Therborn (1985) for other authoritative contributions. The formal similarity between the Histadrut/Mapai relationship and the pattern characteristic of European social democracy in general was discussed in Chapter 1.
7. The importance of trade union mobilization for labour party success was a theme of earlier work by Walter Korpi and the present author (Shalev and Korpi, 1980). On the Swedish case specifically see Korpi (1978) and Pontusson (1990).
8. Significant and representative studies are those of Eisenstadt (1967); Medding (1972); Shapiro (1978); and Horowitz and Lissak (1978).
9. We refer here to the pattern of voting in the Yishuv itself, rather than (in the case of the Zionist Organization's international congresses) the overall distribution of the ballot, which was influenced mainly by the votes of adherents in the Diaspora. In the elections to the two Zionist congresses convened prior to Mapai's creation (1927 and 1929), the labour parties received the same share of the ballots cast in Palestine (more than 60%) which Mapai garnered at the time of its first participation (1931) in congress elections. In all four 'Elected Assemblies' (the first constituted in 1920) of the Yishuv, Mapai or its predecessors enjoyed a plurality of the delegates. These figures are derived from Ben-Avram (1978: appendices 1 and 3).
10. Aharon Rabinowitz, a senior figure in the labour movement who later assumed responsibility for the Histadrut's trade union functions, was one of those who urged Mapai (and earlier, Achdut Avodah) to exploit the shared economic fate of the workers and the *petite bourgeoisie* and respond to the latter's growing numerical weight in the Yishuv. Rabinowitz (1962: 199) urged 'placing ourselves at the head of their [the *petit bourgeois*'] camp'. Mapai's self-conscious approach to marketing its 'nation-building *élan*' to the middle strata is apparent in the common platform drafted by its two constituent parties on the eve of their unification. This manifesto defined the new Palestine *Workers'* Party as 'the vanguard of the general national struggle' and, partly (but by no means solely) out of deference to the non-socialist partner to the merger, made no mention of class or class struggle. (See Margalit, 1976: 256)

11. Our characterization of the *petit bourgeois* immigrants of the 1920s is based on Carmi and Rosenfeld (1971). The discussion here of the sources of their political weakness draws in part upon Shapiro (1984: 28–32). The Revisionists' deliberate adoption of an economic plank targeted at the middle strata has been documented by Weissbrod (e.g. 1983: 333–4). Scholarly work on the Revisionists' failure is thin. Yonathan Shapiro has stressed Mapai's superior organizational capacities and, eventually, its powers of co-optation (Shapiro, 1978: 155–6). Weissbrod (1984 and 1983, respectively) emphasizes the Revisionist movement's lack of 'positive' and burden of 'negative' ideological weight. Weissbrod's articles provide useful documentation of the Revisionists' rise and fall, and although disagreeing with their central thrust the present discussion borrows several of her specific arguments.
12. Avizohar (1988) has surveyed the strategic and programmatic changes in labour-movement politics which began with Mapai's establishment in 1930. The trend towards crystallization of the right was noted by Shapira (1977: 252–7) and Weissbrod (1983: 335). Shapiro (1976: ch. 8) has analysed the political threat from outside of Palestine and the labour movement's response. See the same source and Shapira (1977: 264, 311) respectively, on the ideological transitions summed up in the slogans 'from class to nation' and 'peace in the Yishuv'. Dedi Tsucker reviews joint ventures between private and Histadrut capital in a dissertation in progress at Tel Aviv University. Evidence of class co-operation is noted in Chapter 4 below, which is devoted to the non-emergence of 'peace agreements' between labour and capital in the Mandatory period.
13. A balanced assessment of the 'positive functions' of the Histadrut's role in sharpening the national conflict in the labour market should note that the political benefits for Mapai were not altogether costless. There was a point at which worker militancy on behalf of 'Hebrew labour' took on its own momentum (Shapira, 1977). The fact that violence was directed against Jewish farmers and unorganized Jewish workers as well as Arabs, alienated some middle-class opinion. Moreover, when the moment for accommodation with the farmers was finally ripe, the rank and file rejected their leaders' authority.
14. Flapan (1979: 227–9) unearthed fascinating evidence of these aspects of the Yishuv's response to the 1936 Arab revolt. He showed that the heads of Mapai and the Jewish Agency sought to perpetuate and even deepen the Arab-Jewish economic separation caused by the strike, on the assumption that it was a necessary precondition for future political separation. In response, a committee of five prominent figures in the Yishuv formulated concrete proposals for Arab–Jewish coexistence (which included an obligation on

private Jewish employers to employ 25% Arab labour). We find it striking that the majority of this 'Committee of Five' directly represented the principal Jewish employers of 'mixed' labour (they were the heads of the electricity and potash companies and the leader of the citrus farmers' association).

15. It should be stressed that this evaluation refers to the period in which the labour movement had already crystallized and become the leading political force in the Yishuv. Shafir (1989) has shown that prior to the era of British rule and its accompanying economic and political transformations, there was significant opposition between the two major classes (labourers and independent farmers) within the Zionist community over the future of Jewish nationalism. Consistent with their economic interests, the farmers opposed the workers' militant, segregationist position.
16. Data for the inter-war period relevant to our characterization of the political economy of the Yishuv include the following estimates. First, during the period 1922–39 'unilateral transfers' (mainly funds brought in by immigrants, together with institutional gifts to the Yishuv) accounted for 56% of Palestine's foreign income. Less than one-third (31%) derived from export earnings. Only 13% took the form of private foreign investment (Michaely, 1963: Table 1). Second, more than three-quarters of total Jewish capital import was private (Jewish Agency, 1947: 375). Third, land purchases and construction together accounted for more than half (53%) of all fixed capital investment in the Jewish sector. Only 12% of the total was devoted to the purchase of manufacturing equipment (Szereszewski, 1968: 74). See Giladi (1965) for discussion of the paradox that although private capital inflow was quantitatively predominant, the right suffered from chronic political inferiority.
17. During 1931, on the heels of Mapai's foundation, elections were held for both the world Zionist Congress and the Yishuv's own Elected Assembly. Mapai's vote in these elections won it 65% of the Palestinian delegates to the Zionist Congress, but only 42% of those for the Assembly (Ben-Avram, 1978). Even more significantly, in Tel Aviv and other all-Jewish areas, local government was routinely dominated by so-called 'civilian' parties representing the middle strata and their organizations (Horowitz and Lissak, 1978: 78).
18. Two valuable sources in English on internal conflicts within the labour movement are Perlmutter (1957) and Shapiro (1976). Ishai's (1978) is the only detailed study of the most far-reaching pre-state split, the breakaway of the so-called 'Faction B' from Mapai in 1944. In the present discussion (and elsewhere) we refrain as far as possible from burdening the reader with the details of names, programmatic nuances, and the complex chain of splits and mergers

characterizing labour politics in the Yishuv (and later, in Israel). A condensed summary is, however, available in Appendix 4. For background material in English see Merhav (1980); Lucas (1974); and Yanai (1981).

19. Goldberg (1975) has studied the definitive case (the labour exchanges) of Mapai control of a resource materially crucial for workers. Yonathan Shapiro (1976; esp. 118–19) provides specifics on the implications of Mapai's monopoly over patronage jobs for the radical opposition. See Chapter 2 of the present volume on the issue of solidarity with Arab labour. The Histadrut's relationship with skilled workers is described by Sussman (1969*a*) and discussed further in Chapter 4, which also expands on Mapai's (Achdut Avodah's) repression of opposition groups. Mapai's control over entry visas has been noted by Lucatz (1961: 265), among others.
20. On the Histadrut's harassment and eviction of communist activists see Miller-Rubinstein (1985).
21. The challenge of assembling comprehensive data on the class structure of the Yishuv (not to mention trends in the class basis of Mapai's vote) still awaits a scholarly response. Juxtaposing data from the government census of 1931 and the joint Histadrut–Jewish Agency census of Jewish wage-earners the previous year, indicates that at the time Mapai was founded the wage-earners constituted well short of half (43%) of the total Jewish labour force. Comparison of the censuses of Jewish wage-earners carried out in 1926 and 1937 shows a precipitous decline in the proportion classified as unskilled labourers (from 25% to 3%). Moreover according to the Histadrut–Jewish Agency survey, in 1930 close to a quarter of the Jewish working class in Palestine was employed in white-collar branches (defined as 'employees in shops and offices, professions, etc.'). By the late 1930s a senior Mapai official reported to an inner-party council that in the Tel-Aviv branch 'dozens of members have in the meantime become employers, shopkeepers, lawyers with large offices . . . ' (Ishai, 1978: 29). Ofer's (1967: 85–95) examination of census data on the branch composition of the labour force shows that in 1931 the social services' share (13%) was not much smaller than thirty years later in the State of Israel. Finally, by 1947, 26% of the Histadrut's employed membership (outside of the collective settlements) was classified by it as clerical or professional workers. The 1930 Histadrut–Jewish Agency findings are as reported by Preuss and Namirovsky (1931); the 1947 Histadrut figures are from a commemorative volume in Hebrew entitled 'In the Thirtieth Year'; and the remaining figures are from Jewish Agency (1947: 66 and 291).
22. The beginnings of 'nationalization' of quasi-state Histadrut

functions are noted by Horowitz and Lissak (1978: 82). Margalit's (1976) study of the most radical of the left-Zionist opposition groups documents how the Arab revolt and the rise of Nazism (and subsequently, the world war) forced the radicals on to the middle ground—and into the institutions—already dominated by Mapai.

23. On wartime industrialization see Jewish Agency (1946). Data collected by Cohen (1980) demonstrate the potential of Jewish versus Arab industry to benefit from wartime demand. See Danelius (1944) and Jewish Agency (1947: 291) for data on changes in industrial workers' share of the labour force.
24. See Chapter 4 for a fuller discussion of wartime developments in industrial relations.
25. It will be recalled that when Faction B left Mapai in 1944 it formed a new Achdut Avodah Party. This party subsequently joined *Hashomer Hatsair* in forming Mapam (Appendix 4).
26. Perlmutter (1957, esp. ch. 7) is the primary source for this discussion of the political history of the 1940s. Mapai's tilt towards the middle classes is noted by Horowitz and Lissak (1978: 88–9).
27. Kleiman (1964*a*) and Greenberg (1983) trace the historical development of the labour economy; Horowitz (1948: 30–4, 157–60) furnishes indications of its relative significance in various branches of the economy. For further details and sources see Appendix 2.
28. Just how large were these new groups? Data from the first Labour Force Survey, in June 1954, indicate that of the one million voting-age persons in the country, 22% were new immigrants from Eastern countries ('Asia and Africa'), and another 8% were non-Jews. Thirty years later the comparable proportions had roughly doubled for Easterners (immigrants and their children) and had risen by over half for non-Jews. On the timing and composition of the Jewish influx and Arab exodus following sovereignty see Appendix 1.
29. The legal framework is reviewed by Shirom (1983). See Chapter 2 regarding the treatment of Arab labour. The role of the state in internal labour-movement conflict reached a peak in 1952 when police and strike-breakers were used to end a bitter struggle for trade union autonomy by merchant seamen, some of whom were associated with left-wing parties (Segal, 1976).
30. On the politics of the Histadrut Sick Fund and the relationship between Histadrut and state social services see respectively, Zalmanovitch (1981) and Doron (1967). On the Histadrut's pension funds see Sarnat (1966).
31. Sources on the politicization of workers' committees and wages policy include Medding (1972) and Sussman (1973*a*). Shirom (1980) has assembled evidence of the Histadrut's oligarchic internal regime. For further discussion of the role of the Histadrut in the

labour market and its relationship with Mapai in this context see Chapter 5.

32. This thesis was argued by a prominent Israeli journalist in the early 1960s (Ben-Porat, 1963–4). Data cited previously on the growing scope of the labour economy are drawn from Sherman (1958) and Plunkett (1958).
33. Schecter (1972) has discussed the non-emergence of a debate over nationalization after 1948. We have relied on Bichler's (1985) study of the 'austerity period' in Israel's early years regarding the post-sovereignty 'shareout' and Mapai's role in the formation of Israel's capitalist class. Patinkin's (1960) survey of the first decade of the Israeli economy includes an assessment of the massive role of the state in investment. For later trends, see Mayshar (1984).
34. Data compiled by Arian (1973: tables 5.1 and 5.2), referring to urban Jewish voters, indicated that just short of four-fifths of Histadrut members voted Alignment in 1969. The same proportion of all Alignment voters were Histadrut members. However, Arian's calculation excluded non-voters and the small non-religious parties, and his survey suffered from a very high rate of non-response on the voting question. A study by Burstein of the same elections, which overcame these problems but used a less representative sample (drawn mainly in Haifa), indicated that only two-thirds of Histadrut members supported the Alignment and that membership gave only a modest boost to the probability of a Labour vote (Burstein, 1973: table 4.10). Burstein (1973: tables 5.10 and 4.8) also found that receipt of Histadrut aid in obtaining jobs or housing raised individuals' likelihood of voting Alignment by about one-third; and that employment in Histadrut enterprises raised it by nearly half in comparison with private-sector employees. Ecological data also support these inferences (Gonen and Hasson, 1983; Gonen, 1984).
35. For a good overview of Mapai's incorporation of the Easterners, see Bernstein (1984). The evolution of local party bosses is traced by Azmon (1985). Israel's reception of the Eastern newcomers and its consequences is the subject of a large literature. For a historian's reconstruction see Segev (1986). For the conventional view and a stringent critique see respectively Eisenstadt (1967) and Bernstein (1980).
36. Arab members were ineligible to vote in Histadrut elections until the 1965 convention. Until 1976 they were also barred from Labour Party membership, and hence technically excluded from submitting their candidacy for the senior elective positions in the labour organization (virtually all of which are filled by the Labour Party). See Greenberg (1980: 375–7) and Cohen (1985: 79).
37. The changed position of the Arab minority after 1948 has recently

been documented by Kamen (1987). Jiryis (1976) and Lustick (1980) provide comprehensive treatments of the politics of the Arabs in Israel. On the politics of the military government see also Cohen (1976: esp. 330). The Histadrut's role in Arab political mobilization is discussed at length in Chapter 2.

38. For the first scholarly survey to demonstrate the 'upside down' class basis of Mapai's mass support see Antonovsky (1966). A series of polls carried out under labour-movement auspices by Lotan (1966) demonstrated that Mapai was perceived by the electorate as relatively neutral towards all of the major strata, *except* 'state employees'. Matras (1965: 132) used ecological correlations for the 1961 elections to show that high-school education or better and white-collar employment both substantially increased the Mapai vote. The continued attachment of upwardly mobile veterans to Mapai was studied by Zloczower (1972).

39. We have already noted the line of succession from Jabotinsky's Revisionist Party (founded in 1925) to Begin's Cherut Party (founded in 1948). The 'General Zionists' were the dominant group in the World Zionist Organization prior to the rise of Mapai, encompassing the mainstream of Zionists (under the leadership of Chaim Weizmann) who were neither left-wing nor religious. The General Zionist *Party* was founded soon after Mapai, as a moderately right-wing alternative to it. In 1935 the party split between a pro-labour 'A' faction (the Progressives) and a pro-middle class and generally more hawkish 'B' group which retained the General Zionist name. In the Palestinian voting for Zionist Congress elections in the 1930s, and the first decade of Knesset elections, the two parties jointly received no more than 15% of the ballot (except in 1951). In 1961 they merged again to constitute the Liberal Party. But the former Progressives broke away (as the Independent Liberal Party) when the joint 'Cherut-Liberal bloc' (*Gachal*) was formed in 1965. In 1973 Gachal presented a joint slate with some smaller right-wing groups, forming the main components of what was officially launched in the following elections as the Likud (Unity) list.

40. On the thesis of Cherut's 'delegitimation' see the divergent views of Levite and Tarrow (1983) and Medding (1990). Regarding the 'liberal' right, note that in the first four Knesset elections (1949–61) the pro-business General Zionists gained an average of 12 seats (out of a total of 120)—compared with 14 for Cherut, 17 for Mapam (including Achdut Avodah), and 17 for the religious parties. The Progressive Party won an average of five seats. Had there been a combined liberal bloc, it would thus have been larger than any of the three other opposition groupings. (See the previous note above for further details regarding the parties of the right.)

41. For evidence of the direct role of the right-wing parties in representing the business sector see Czudnowski (1970 and 1972). On the development of the Manufacturers' Association consult Shirom (1984). Mapai's relationship with the three non-worker strata mentioned in the text, as of the 1960s, is well documented by Medding (1972). Ben-David (1965) reviewed the Histadrut's incorporation of professional unions after sovereignty.
42. On the ambiguities of the left's relationship with Mapai in the Histadrut, see the 'confessions' of a former leftwing activist (Kantor, 1977). Beinin (1990) documents the deradicalization of Mapam and places it within the wider context of Marxist politics in Israel.
43. For a compilation of data on electoral politics in Israel's Arab sector see Cohen (1985). The significance of local autonomy for the growth of Communist influence is clear from experience with local labour councils (mini-Histadruts) in Arab localities. Once established, the councils have provided a particularly favourable setting for the Communists, an association which, once it became noticed by the Labour Party, resulted in a policy reversal in favour of annexing Arab localities to existing councils in Jewish areas (see Chapter 2).
44. As Rouhana (1986) surmises, this was an important reason for the emergence in the 1984 elections of a new Arab-oriented party which tried unsuccessfully to build bridges to Jewish-controlled resources while adopting a radical (in Jewish eyes) position on the national conflict.
45. See the essays in Pempel (1990) for illustrations of both the role of the labour movement in social democratic success and the heterogeneous and 'opportunistic' character of the social sectors linked to successful parties of the right. For an empirical demonstration that recourse to 'electoral business cycles' varies systematically between social-democratic and other regimes see Bordogna (1981).
46. It should be emphasized that the distinctions in this paragraph between parties of the left and right represent differences between 'ideal–typical' dominant labour and conservative parties. There are of course substantial internal differences within the more inclusive left and right families in class base, type of appeal, and so forth and Mapai could certainly not be characterized as the sole hybrid case. We merely wish to argue that it is the only mixed case within the limited universe of *dominant* parties.
47. For diverse views concerning the role of Mapai's socialist ideology in the Yishuv period compare, for instance, Sussman (1969*a*) and Yatziv (1979). The party machine and the party's control of economic interest-groups during the epoch of Mapai's post-sovereignty dominance are well documented (among the references previously noted see especially Medding, 1972; and Aronoff, 1977). The multi-

class character of the Mapai constituency has already been discussed. Ben-Porath (1975) and, more recently, Ben-Hanan and Temkin (1986), are among those who have discerned a pronounced 'electoral business cycle' in Israel.

48. Przeworski and Wallerstein (1982*b*) have noted this important political consequence of the Keynesian 'revolution'.
49. See especially works by Beinin (1990) and Carmi and Rosenfeld (1989).
50. Peri (1983).
51. See, for example, Medding (1972) and Yanai (1981).

Part II

Labour Relations

4

Why no 'Historic Compromise'?

The origins of corporatism and the puzzle of the pre-state setting

In Western Europe, between the two world wars, an acute political-economic crisis gave birth to new patterns of working-class incorporation in politics and attempts under both authoritarian and democratic regimes to introduce a corporatist reordering of relations between labour and capital. In many of the smaller nations where democracy remained intact, there were incipient signs of what became a distinctive pattern of class accommodation in the post-war period, based on stable participation of labour-movement representatives in national governance, explicit commitments to union–employer co-operation, and centralized wage negotiations between peak organizations of labour and capital.[1]

In the 1920s and 1930s, the economic and geopolitical vulnerability of the small nations of Western Europe and their history of relative openness to working-class political participation, uniquely predisposed them for these corporatist developments. In the Scandinavian countries, social-democratic parties achieved sufficient electoral strength during the 1930s to form strong coalition governments committed to a Keynesian response to economic crisis. In the wake of this long-term shift in the political balance of class forces and the new opportunities which it opened up for union-government political exchange, peak associations of unions and employers regularized their relationship. In Norway and Sweden they entered into formal pacts which provided for mutual recognition, an agreed division of labour, and avoidance of confrontational relations. In Switzerland, and to a lesser extent the Low Countries, there were similar tendencies towards centralization of industrial relations and a decline in industrial conflict, although the primary motivating force was fear of economic collapse, Fascism, and war, rather than the aftermath of a major political realignment. In those

West European countries (Denmark, Belgium, and the Netherlands) where formal class compromises failed to emerge during the 1930s, their experience of Nazi occupation and shared interest in peacetime economic reconstruction drew worker and employer representatives into corporatist co-operation during and immediately following the war. The common element underlying all of these cases of small-country corporatism was a recognition of the potentially disastrous consequences of unfettered class warfare to both labour and capital. These consequences included the rise of radical forces on both the left and the right of the political spectrum, forcible appropriation of collective bargaining functions by the state, and increased national vulnerability to economic crisis and foreign conquest.[2]

On the face of it, the Yishuv—the Jewish 'settlement' in Palestine prior to Israeli sovereignty—was ripe for just such a historic compromise between labour and capital. The Histadrut was institutionally structured along quintessentially corporate lines: a highly centralized, multi-functional peak organization claiming a monopoly over representation of the Jewish working class. The very establishment of the Histadrut signalled a readiness on the part of the labour movement and the Zionist political centre to enter into relations of political exchange. Several other features of the Yishuv polity might also be assumed to have facilitated a politically mediated class compromise. The first was the labour movement's ascent to long-term political dominance, a development similar in timing and durability to the rise of social democracy in Sweden. Second, the emphasis on coalition and consensus-building—which, in the absence of sovereign political authority, is said to have characterized conflict-resolution within the Jewish community—should have favoured a political settlement of class conflict. Finally, the vulnerability of the Yishuv to external threats—economic crises spurred by downturns in immigration, violent Arab resistance to Zionism, and anti-Zionist swings in British policy—in theory ought to have heightened national solidarity within the Jewish enclave (and is widely thought to have done so).

These facilitating conditions indeed received concrete expression in repeated initiatives aimed at a corporatist 'peace treaty'. Already in the early 1920s the 'national institutions' of the Jewish/Zionist community responded to a wave of class conflict in the urban centres. Efforts were made to mediate a formal pact between the peak organizations of workers and employers, which would settle the fundamental points of dispute between them and establish permanent machinery for the prevention of open conflict. Yet throughout the period, from the establishment of the Histadrut until World War II, each such initiative met with failure. Ironically, they ceased altogether in the second half of the 1930s, precisely when a unified labour party (Mapai) had ascended to political leadership on a conciliatory platform, the economy was in the throes of a deep crisis and national solidarity had been strengthened as a result of Arab hostility to and British disengagement from the Zionist project. In the event, the goal of a master peace agreement between organized labour and capital was never attained in the Mandatory period. During World War II, with the support of the British administration, wage bargaining was finally moved on to a more centralized footing. And, for a time the Histadrut was granted the status of corporate participant in certain areas of public policy-making, with responsibility for endorsing and implementing labour restraint. Even so, the full flowering of Israeli corporatism awaited the economic and political transformations which accompanied the transitions to statehood and rapid economic growth.

Why did formalized class accommodation, centralization of collective bargaining, and concertation of wage determination with state policies elude the Yishuv? This is a question worth asking. An adequate explanation for the failure of corporatist management of class conflict in the Mandatory period can shed light on the political economy of the Yishuv and the general (theoretical) conditions for the emergence of corporatism. We also aim in this chapter to enrich the historical record of class conflict in Israel's pre-sovereignty experience. Previous studies of the labour movement and industrial relations in Jewish Palestine have alluded to attempts by the Jewish national institutions to engineer agreement on a 'labour convention' (*Chukat Avodah*) between the Histadrut and organized employers. But these allusions are confined to discrete episodes and, as in other areas of the historiography of the Yishuv, scholars have tended (with some exceptions) to reiterate the interpretations offered by the labour movement's own contemporary leaders. The latter were inclined to lay the blame on the capitalists (for lacking the workers' talent for collectivism), or on rank-and-file workers (for refusing to shoulder their 'responsibility to the economy').[3]

Guided by scepticism towards the self-serving and voluntaristic flavour of these interpretations, and inclined theoretically to assume rational behaviour in a context of concrete economic and political interests and constraints, we proceed by analysing the resources and motives which characterized each of the three central actors who are at the heart of any potential class accommodation: the state, organized labour, and capital.

The state. A necessary condition for the emergence of corporatist class accommodation is the coexistence of sufficient *interest* and the requisite *capacities* on the part of the state. To investigate the role of the state in the context of the Yishuv requires analysing both the sovereign institutions of the British Mandate and the quasi-state 'political centre' of the Jewish community. Zionist history has tended to dismiss the role of the British authorities in issues of domestic policy. The assumption has been that the British were apathetic or hostile towards the Yishuv on such issues, while, for their part, the Jewish national institutions developed effective capacities for resolving intra-communal conflict. The latter presumption is evidently contradicted by the very failure of corporatist class harmony to eventuate. Moreover, the view of the British, as having been wed to a policy of non-intervention, belies the remarkable about-face in the stance of the authorities which occurred during the Second World War. Examination of the kinds of state interest and state capacities routinely addressed by political economists makes it possible to account for the pattern of British policy and to explain as well why the political centre of the Zionist movement and the Yishuv repeatedly, but ineffectually, pressed for a corporatist resolution of class conflict.

Organized labour. A second issue which needs to be probed more objectively is the role of the Histadrut itself. Corporatist structures of industrial relations are everywhere conditional on the ability of union peak organizations to overcome conflicts between centre and periphery in the trade union movement. In the Yishuv this problem was complicated by the ambiguities of the Histadrut's trade union function, which was organizationally and strategically marginal, but increasingly central to the labour movement's rank and file and its local apparatus. Conflicts and contradictions internal to the labour organization thus helped to dissuade Histadrut leaders from pressing as strongly as they might have for a more centralized system of industrial relations and a formal settlement with organized employers.

Capital. The final focal point for our analysis is the character of capital in the Yishuv context. That Jewish employers developed weak collective solidarity in the Mandatory period is well known; but it cannot be assumed that this reflected simply a dearth of will or prowess. Instead, as in the analysis of capitalist collectivism more generally, we must look to structural factors—such as divisions between the different sectors of capital, which hampered its mobilization on a class-wide basis in imitation of the corporate organization of labour in the Histadrut. In addition, given that corporatist management of labour relations was apparently insufficiently appealing to drive employers to behave more solidaristically, it must be assumed that capital was able to rely on *alternative ways of countering working-class militancy.* It is one of the purposes of our analysis to identify these alternative sources of labour restraint.

Before turning to the analysis of the state, labour, and capital in the context of Jewish Palestine between the wars, it will be helpful to place the discussion on a more substantive footing by providing a chronological sketch of the major initiatives aimed at moving industrial relations in the Yishuv on to a corporatist footing during the period in question. Both this account and the analysis which follows are deliberately limited to the 1920s and 1930s in order to highlight, at the close of the chapter, the dramatic innovations of the early 1940s and their implications for our interpretation of the preceding period.

Corporatist initiatives in the inter-war period[4]

Early attempts by the political institutions of the Jewish community to sponsor a peace agreement between organized labour and capital surfaced soon after the establishment of the Histadrut at the end of 1920. The first years of Britain's occupation of Palestine were marked by economic expansion as a result of public works programmes and the arrival of the Third Aliyah. Especially after the anti-Jewish riots in Jaffa in May 1921, the development of Tel Aviv was hastened, and land sales and construction boomed. In the spring of 1922 the 'Association of Industrialists and Employers of Jaffa and Tel Aviv' was founded, expressing the emergence of a new stratum of employers situated in between the characteristic workshop form of production and the very few large factories in the country. Almost immediately, leaders of the *Va'ad Leumi* (Jewish National Committee) and the Zionist Executive[5] assisted in concluding an interim labour agreement between the Manufacturers' Association and the Histadrut (which had been founded less than 18 months earlier). The two sides agreed temporarily to restrict lay-offs and to submit disputes to arbitration.

Jewish communal bodies had already been engaged quite extensively in *ad hoc* mediation and arbitration of labour disputes. But by the middle of 1922 they turned to a new tack—to persuade organized labour and industrial employers to enter into a formal *entente* which would lay down agreed general principles on the core issues dividing the parties. However, the economic climate shifted before negotiations towards this end made any progress. The same expansionary forces which had fuelled the economic conjuncture in the Mandate's first years were quickly reversed, and by the winter of 1922 unemployment began to rise. The World Zionist Organization was in difficult financial straits and proved unable to ease the workers' plight. This left the Histadrut and its local labour councils little alternative but to support struggles in the labour market against wage cuts, lay-offs, and the employment of non-union labour. These conflicts, most of them involving only small numbers of workers, were centred around contractors and other enterprises connected with the building industry of Tel Aviv, now in the throes of a painful contraction.

One of the resultant conflicts occurred in Tel Aviv at the Goralsky–Krinitsky carpentry works (a member of the Manufacturers' Association), where 45 workers launched a strike at the end of February 1923 in protest against a wage cut. When the employers used Arab porters under police guard to deliver stockpiled doors and windows to construction sites, the dispute spread into the building industry. Six weeks into the strike, Mayor Dizengoff urged the Zionist Executive to make every effort to bring about a settlement, warning that the industrialists were contemplating responding with a general lock-out. The labour side was willing to accept arbitration, but asked that judgement be pronounced not only on the wage dispute but also on other outstanding issues (especially recognition of the workers' committee and its right to intervene in hiring and firing decisions). Instead, the mediators (led by the head of the Zionist Executive) promised that the national institutions would establish a public committee to lay down guidelines on these and other recurrent non-wage issues in labour disputes.

Accordingly, in June 1923 it was announced that a tripartite 'Committee of Inquiry into Relations between Jewish Workers and Employers' would be established, to be composed of representatives of the Histadrut and the Manufacturers' Association together with prominent neutrals. This initiative at tripartism quickly fizzled when difficulties were encountered in persuading appropriate candidates to serve on the committee. Towards the end of the year, however, renewed efforts were made when the government of Palestine put pressure on the Zionist Executive to consent to the appointment of a public conciliation and arbitration board. But by now the atmosphere was hardly propitious for conciliatory steps on the part of employers: 1923 was a disastrous year for Jewish workers, whose untenable position in the labour market was expressed in increased rates of re-emigration.

From the middle of 1924 the economic conjuncture again turned sharply, with the arrival of a wave of Polish *petit bourgeois* immigrants and the construction-led boom to which it gave rise. With expansion, inflation, and rising demand for labour coming on the heels of a period of heavy unemployment and price and wage cuts, it was not surprising that distributional conflicts intensified in the labour market. Histadrut estimates suggest that whereas in 1923 only 600 workers were involved in strikes and lock-outs, the number of involvements rose to 1,600 in 1924 and 2,600 in 1925—a year in which the total number of urban wage-earners affiliated to the labour organization was only around 10,000. Workers in several big factories recently established in Haifa struck for wage increases and recognition. In Tel Aviv/Jaffa the labour council set out early in 1925 to mobilize the expanding labour force in construction and to compel the contractors to work through its labour exchanges and enter into collective agreements. The employers responded with a lock-out at 60 construction sites. Attempts by the government and the Tel Aviv municipality to end the lock-out failed and the national institutions intervened, appointing a mediation committee. Some of the contractors continued to operate using strike-breakers under police protection, while others signed agreements individually with the labour council. After five weeks the lock-out was finally ended by a provisional agreement (which later broke down) under which all labour would be recruited through the Histadrut, but the contractors would be represented on the management of the labour exchange.

Midway through the lock-out, and in response to a renewed threat from the government that it would act if the Jewish community was unable to, the Va'ad Leumi and Zionist Executive discussed the industrial relations crisis at a special joint session. They decided to invite representatives of labour and capital to tripartite talks on how to bring the strike wave to an end and introduce permanent arrangements to stabilize labour relations. This emergency 'Council on Labour' (*Moetzet Avodah*) convened only a few days later, on 17 February. Participants included the large industrialists, officials of the manufacturers' and contractors' associations in Tel Aviv, Histadrut leaders, and token representatives of other labour organizations (the Yemenites, the religious-Zionist *Mizrachi* movement) and the Artisans' Association. Ben-Gurion, the leader of the Histadrut, argued that arbitration alone was not a solution and that a consensus was required on all the basic issues giving rise to conflicts, to be enshrined in a voluntary labour convention for the Yishuv. Class conflict was inevitable under 'a regime of property', but disputes could be avoided by mutual consent. This would require employers to recognize the Histadrut's monopoly over worker representation, to hire labour solely through its exchanges, to consult with its work-place committees, and to offer basic economic security to its members (Ben-Gurion, 1964: 432–6).

The Council on Labour concluded its deliberations by establishing a trilateral 'Committee of Fifteen' headed by Arthur Ruppin, the Zionist Organization's most prominent local emissary. The new committee convened immediately, resolving to bring all outstanding disputes to a speedy conclusion and to work towards the charter envisaged by Ben-Gurion. Despite objections from the smaller labour organizations, the worker side was represented solely by the Histadrut. The employer delegation was initially more heterogeneous, but in time the contractors (whose association broke up after the lock-out) and the big industrialists (who preferred to operate independently in labour relations) fell out. This left only medium-sized industry, led by the Manufacturers' Association of Tel Aviv, active in the negotiations. After meeting again in March and May, the committee reached agreement on a temporary wage freeze until the autumn, to be followed by adjustment of pay to rises in the cost of living. Consensus was also reached on the establishment of tripartite mediation committees to operate along lines similar to the government's proposal, and on other outstanding issues of principle. But the two sides remained divided on the critical issues of hiring and firing—recognition of Histadrut labour exchanges, the right of workers' committees to veto lay-offs, and compensation for laid-off workers.

The Zionist Executive remained outwardly optimistic that a consensus would be reached, and in June 1925 persuaded the government to drop its dispute-settlement proposal. But in mid-July the negotiations finally broke down, because of the Histadrut's insistence that skilled as well as unskilled labour be allocated solely by its exchanges—a demand which was anathema to employers in a period when craftsmen were in short supply. Another impediment to agreement was the disarray on the manufacturers' side. By mid-year their three regional associations had adopted independent and contradictory positions towards the Committee of Fifteen. Even within the dominant Tel Aviv group, internal differences of opinion on hiring and firing issues effectively paralysed the Association.

In the second half of 1925 a decline in Jewish immigration and capital inflow began to hurt the construction industry. During 1926–7 the Yishuv experienced a period of severe economic crisis which confronted the Histadrut with mass unemployment and the bankruptcy of its building company (Solel Boneh). Berl Katznelson, labour's most respected leader, responded by advocating a more conciliatory line to private capital, including making concessions to the industrialists in order to achieve a master collective agreement. But the Histadrut's local officials, despite their loyalty to party leaders, were unwilling to sacrifice crucial levers on which their mobilization of rank-and-file loyalty was based—the right to strike and Histadrut control of labour exchanges. Moreover, under the depressed economic conditions prevailing in 1927, the manufacturers had little incentive to participate seriously in the revived negotiations in the framework of the Committee of Fifteen.

For the remainder of the decade the Zionist Executive continued unsuccessfully to offer its services as midwife to a peak agreement. The Arab riots of 1929 and their economic consequences further hardened the manufacturers' resistance to a labour convention; but in any case, they had no reason to seek out a class-wide solution to labour problems. After 1927 there was a renewal of economic growth, but immigration remained insignificant and prices fell, and at the beginning of the 1930s the demand for labour slackened. Under these circumstances the scope of labour conflicts in industry remained limited. Outside of the workshop sector accommodation began to flower at the enterprise level, as indicated by growth in informal collective bargaining on non wage questions.[6]

It took new political developments to revive the prospects for a master settlement. At the end of 1932, Revisionism had surfaced as a significant threat to the labour movement, both in undermining the Histadrut's aspiration to control the supply of labour (particularly in agriculture) and as the catalyst for a political challenge from the right, which could potentially carry with it elements of the organized farmers and manufacturers. The general interest of Histadrut leaders in trying to take control of labour relations away from the local level pointed in the same direction as the specific interest of Mapai leaders in trying to shore up the party's position by reaching an understanding with labour's political opponents (who included both employers and non-Histadrut labour). Accordingly, at the Histadrut convention in February 1933, Eliezer Kaplan officially proposed to 'unify and centralize' collective bargaining and again advocated compromises with the industrialists in order to facilitate a framework agreement. But the left opposition outside Mapai and the party's own emissaries in the Histadrut apparatus successfully pressured against making concessions.

Ben-Gurion, whose political field of vision had by now moved beyond the labour movement, responded to this internal stalemate by attempts to mobilize the Mapai-controlled national institutions. At the Zionist Congress in Lucerne in the summer of 1935, the labour movement successfully implemented its new political strategy of 'peace in the Yishuv'. A broad spectrum of parties was included in the new executive and invited to participate in the key Jewish institutions (including the *Haganah* defence force). In the field of industrial relations, after failing to engineer a corporatist class accommodation through negotiations between functional interest-groups, Ben-Gurion turned to the alternative of forging a consensus on labour issues among the leaders of the major parties. Discussions along these lines at the congress were only partially successful, and for the next year they continued in Palestine in the framework of a special labour committee. Subsequently, the head of the Jewish Agency's Labour Department persuaded the committee that its search for a master framework agreement was misplaced for three reasons. First, the incomplete authority of both the Histadrut and the Manufacturers' Association. Second, the national institutions' lack of powers of enforcement. And third, in agriculture, the economic pressures on farmers to prefer Arab over Jewish labour. The 'consociational' format of bargaining among political élites thus proved no more conducive to consensus-building than earlier bipartite and tripartite negotiations. The non-labour political parties involved were only weakly representative of employer interests and could hardly make commitments on their behalf; while the small religious labour organizations operating outside of the Histadrut made it known via their allied parties that they would be unwilling to sacrifice their autonomy.[7]

By late 1935, the Palestinian economy was entering a depression which persisted into the beginning of the 1940s. Although fears were expressed at the time that the economic downturn would revive industrial conflict and intensify tensions surrounding the labour exchanges, employers again found that the business cycle functioned as an effective antidote to labour militancy. The locus of residual labour strife was not industry but agriculture, where unemployment pushed the conflict between Jewish and Arab labour back onto the agenda. The national institutions offered employers in the citrus branch tempting incentives to settle their labour-market conflicts with the Histadrut but the growers demurred, fortified by the shortage of jobs. The depression also left urban labour little choice but to endure five years of declining real wages and employer retreat from collective bargaining. Only after the unique conditions of wartime turned the economy around and generated labour shortages, did the Yishuv experience a wave of worker militancy reminiscent of 1925. But that is a story belonging to a very different political-economic era, one to which we shall return later as an epilogue to the inter-war experience.

Corporatism and the state in the inter-war period

The Jewish 'national institutions'

Our historical survey has shown that, until the economy sank into depression in the late 1930s, proposals for a formal class compromise between organized industry and labour were a recurrent phenomenon in the Yishuv. For the most part, however, these proposals emanated from the quasi-state institutions of the Zionist movement and the Palestinian Jewish community, rather than from the British authorities in London and Jerusalem. The national institutions, anxious from their establishment to demonstrate to the British that the Yishuv could take care of its own troubles, were decidedly embarrassed when labour disputes attracted active intervention on the part of the authorities. But a demonstrated capacity for self-government was only one of the pre-conditions for Zionist consolidation, which was threatened by unregulated class conflict in the Yishuv. In a confidential letter written in 1923, the head of the Zionist Organization's London office pointed out to his counterpart in Jerusalem that, as the client of an imperial power, Zionism had necessarily to be sensitive to the risks that labour radicalism and class warfare might pose to British rule in Palestine, especially in the event that Jewish labour was to 'drive a wedge between Arab masters and men'. Moreover, in so far as the economic development of the Jewish national home was expected to depend on its ability to attract private foreign investment, the Zionist movement was in no position to ignore the deterrent effect of worker militancy on investor confidence.[8]

The national institutions therefore had powerful *interests* in containing class conflict; the problem was one of inadequate *state capacities*—the inability of the Zionist Executive or Va'ad Leumi to exercise coercion, to finance deficits, to create legal obligations, and to distribute or deny legitimacy with sovereign authority. These bodies functioned principally as peace-brokers. They did not and could not play the same role as the state in those West European nations that moved towards corporatist accommodations in this period—on the one hand, presenting labour and capital with a credible threat of seizing responsibility for regulating industrial relations from the organizations in the labour market; and on the other, offering them the material conditions for a settlement (full employment, economic growth, capital subsidy). The national institutions could offer a kind of 'public status' to the peak organizations of labour and capital and to any consensus which they might reach—but were unable to back it up with mechanisms of enforcement. The mediating role of the Zionist political centre was thus much narrower than the comparable potential of the state in Western Europe, and ultimately any settlement depended on the Histadrut and the industrialists themselves.[9] In addition, there was a problematic imbalance between the mediating capacities of the national institutions in respect to labour and capital. Political exchange and incorporation were highly developed so far as the labour movement was concerned, even in the period when its political hegemony was still a distant prospect. The manufacturers, however, were suspicious from the outset of labour's inside track to the national institutions, and balked at the prospect of the Zionist movement dictating terms to employers.

The British regime

The position of the British authorities in Palestine was, of course, quite different to that of the political institutions of the Jewish community, although it has received inadequate consideration in earlier accounts of labour relations in the Yishuv. Sovereign authority was officially ceded to Great Britain by a League of Nations 'Mandate' granted in 1922. This followed the British conquest of Palestine late in 1917 and its ratification by the San Remo Conference in 1920, which was responsible for dividing the spoils of the Ottoman Empire among the victorious great powers. In 1920 the British instituted a civil administration under which economic and social policy-making was split three ways. Overall policy, even on matters of day-to-day governance, was set by the Colonial Office in London (directed, where relevant, by the Cabinet). Other departments of the metropolitan state also exerted considerable influence within their own sphere of competence. The most prominent example was the Treasury, but the Foreign Office and the Board of Trade also played a role in some issues. Finally, there was the local executive authority in Palestine, appointed from London and manned (at all but the lowest levels) by British officials.

While the somewhat unwieldy nature of this state apparatus sometimes hampered coherent administration, it could, in principle, have entered the terrain of corporatist activity during the inter-war period—but refrained from doing so. To explain why this was so requires an understanding, first, of the nature of British interests concerning Palestine, and second, of the relationship between the British state apparatus and the 'civil society' of the Yishuv.[10] The fundamental reasons for Britain's presence in Palestine were strategic—having to do with the protection of vital air and sea routes and the trans-shipment of oil. Equally external to Palestine itself were geopolitical considerations in the context of Britain's relations with world Jewry and the international Zionist movement, on the one hand, and the Arab world on the other. In noteworthy contrast to other colonial outposts, Palestine offered few economic benefits to the imperial power. The scope for profitable extraction of natural resources was limited, and labour was comparatively too expensive and the domestic market too confined for investment in local industrial production to be attractive. There was some interest in Palestine as a destination for goods from Britain and elsewhere in the Empire, although it constituted a relatively insignificant market in global terms. Britain actually ran a sizeable trade deficit with Palestine despite efforts to afford preferential opportunities to British exporters. The reason for the deficit was that while Britain indeed became Palestine's single most important foreign supplier, dominating imports of manufactured goods, this was more than offset by its purchases of Palestinian citrus. But as a result, Palestine depended on Britain for the sale of some 70 per cent of virtually its only export; and the British exchequer profited handsomely by levying an import tax.

There was some sympathy in Colonial Office circles for pleas from Palestine for an easing of this and related impediments to access to British and imperial markets, but to no avail. The persistent denial of 'imperial preference' to Palestine is indicative of the instrumental calculus which dominated policy. In a period of domestic stagnation and international decline, Britain was unwilling to risk the potential economic and political repercussions from its own trading partners which would have resulted from any far-reaching steps to ease Palestine's trading position. In general, the most important policy priority of the metropolitan power, from an economic perspective, was that Palestine should be self-supporting. Both the Treasury, in order to conserve precious fiscal resources, and the Colonial Office, following its traditional conservative convictions, tried to impose a strictly balanced budget on the Palestine government. Attempts were also made to extract whatever economic benefits were possible. Palestine was compelled to repay a number of pre-Mandatory debts, to contribute to the upkeep of locally based imperial military and logistic facilities, and to invest government savings in England on unattractive terms.

At first sight, the implication of Britain's limited economic engagement in Palestine is that the role of its administration in relation to civil society deviated significantly from the expectations of those theorists who perceive the state in capitalist economies as necessarily concerned with providing conditions favourable to private capital accumulation.[11] This is an important issue for the present enquiry. For a given state to provide the conditions for corporatist class accommodation, it must first have an interest in class accommodation *per se*. The implication of theories, which posit structural dependence of the state on capital, is that since labour militancy is directly harmful to accumulation and threatens the legitimacy of capitalism itself, the authorities necessarily intervene to help restrain class conflict. Did the relationship between the British authorities and the private and public capital associated with the Zionist movement resemble this prototypical condition of structural dependence? We argue that, to an important extent, it did.

In the early stages of the Mandate, the authorities invested great hopes in Jewish capital and capitalists. Herbert Samuel, Palestine's first High Commissioner, sought to bridge British and Zionist interests by assuming that the Zionists would, in effect, fill the shoes of the absent British colonists. This was destined to bring economic and other forms of progress to the peasantry of Palestine and thereby buttress the foundations of British rule. However, in response to the evident contradictions between Britain's obligations to Jews and Arabs, policy quickly developed along dualistic lines. The factor most frequently noted in this connection is the Arab opposition aroused by the privileged position which the national home commitment implied for the Jewish settlers. But an equally important element in the evolution of Britain's support for segmented Arab and Jewish political and economic development was the realization that Jewish economic resources could not automatically be harnessed to British interests. The massive influx of money and people into Palestine, which the Zionists initially anticipated, failed to materialize. At the same time, in so far as Zionist funds (or investments by Jewish business interests channelled by the Zionist movement) were forthcoming, they were only for projects directly and pretty much exclusively beneficial to the Yishuv and its future prospects. If the British wanted to relieve themselves of the economic burden of at least Jewish Palestine's development, they would be obliged to actively cater to the needs of Jewish capital, private and 'national'.[12]

The need to maintain regime legitimacy with both Arabs and Jews, while persuading Zionism to fulfill its developmental role, led to a double segmentation of state activity. In the political realm, plans for any formal scheme of integrated representation of the two communities were abandoned. Encouragement was given to community-based self-rule, and the administration embraced a general posture of *laissez-faire*. In the economic realm it adopted a strategy of furnishing modest public assistance to the Arab rural sector, while providing infrastructural conditions under which Jewish capital would be able to power the self-development of the Jewish sector, hopefully with positive spillover to the Arab population. In addition to the British interest in the role of the Jews in Palestine's economic development, responsiveness to the requirements of Jewish capital also reflected fiscal conditions. Given the determination of economic policy-makers in London not to subsidize Palestine, the local administration faced in-built pressures to encourage Jewish economic development with a view to mobilizing public revenues.[13] Finally, British sensitivity to the interests of the Jewish settlers' private and national capital was reinforced by the effectiveness of Zionist political lobbying in London and Jerusalem and in international diplomatic forums.

The overall effect of these forces was especially evident in relation to Palestinian industry (predominantly Jewish-owned) which, according to economic historian Barbara Smith, benefited from 'a fully fledged protectionist policy' by 1927 (1978: 380).[14] Given the substantial dependence of government revenues on customs duties, the British stood to bear tangible fiscal costs as a result of either lowering duties on imported machinery and raw materials or fixing protective tariffs for local products. Nevertheless, officials went some way towards meeting Zionist demands regarding import duties, and they found it especially hard to resist threats from major industrialists that unless afforded aid they would liquidate their investments. To summarize, therefore, the relationship between the Yishuv and the British authorities in matters of economic policy may best be conceptualized as one of interdependence. In return for the provision of what Churchill called 'a British garrison to support Zionist policy', the Jews were expected to swallow their objections to economic burdens such as Britain's domination of non-food imports to Palestine. On the other hand, the British were wary of violating essential Jewish interests. Thus, as a cabinet document put it in 1939, their policy on immigration recognized that without the personal assets and Zionist capital which accompanied Jewish newcomers 'revenue would drop, unemployment would rise, and much greater public expenditure would have to be envisaged' (Finegold, 1978: 89, 109n.).

We may therefore infer the existence of indirect but significant British interests in defending Jewish employers—and the Zionist movement's longer-term prospects of attracting private investment—by supporting disciplined industrial relations. As noted at the outset, however, the existence of a state interest in regulating labour militancy does not by itself connote a particular state *response*. In the case under discussion, state sponsorship of a corporatist solution was highly unlikely. For the government to lead the Histadrut into a corporatist relationship would have meant undermining British legitimacy in Arab eyes—because the Histadrut was evidently an agent of Zionism and because, in political exchange, it would have demanded state intervention to neutralize the labour-market threat posed by Arab workers. The Histadrut intermittently approached the authorities anyway with requests for labour legislation, public subsidy of the workers' Sick Fund, employment of more Jews in the public services at above-Arab wages, and so forth—but with only limited success. The authorities made a point of refraining as far as possible from setting or enforcing statutory labour standards, except at levels inoffensive to the Arab sector.

No less important, alternatives to corporatist regulation were available which largely rendered it unnecessary. As we shall elaborate in later sections, supply-and-demand forces in the labour market were sufficiently potent that class conflict in the Yishuv was, to a substantial extent, self-regulating. Nevertheless, there were instances of intense Jewish labour militancy which affronted the regime—because it was directed against Arabs, because it damaged the interests of property-owners, or because it violated public order. Under most such circumstances the administration was able and willing to effectively employ coercion against the workers. The annals of labour relations in the Yishuv, especially (but not only) where conflicts between Jewish and Arab labour were concerned, are full of instances of repressive police intervention.[15] The dual interest of the authorities—in defending governability and protecting employers—could thus be effectively served, where necessary, by the use of force rather than by co-operation with the organized Jewish working class.

Ambiguities in the Histadrut's role

Three motives—none of them unique to the conditions of the Yishuv—may be posited for inferring a Histadrut interest in seeking a peak agreement with organized employers. First, the protection of labour's economic interests, which may be assumed to have been most salient in periods (like the 1927 crisis) when workers confronted stringent labour-market conditions. Second, the top leadership of the Histadrut had a self-evident incentive to enhance the role of the labour organization's upper echelons in mediating labour relations. Had Ben-Gurion succeeded at the time of the 1924–5 strike wave in becoming party to a labour convention, local labour council influence would have been nipped in the bud. Such a development would have transformed the Histadrut centre into the indispensable guarantor of the local activity of labour exchanges, branch unions, and workers' committees, as well as enlarging the Histadrut's centrally-controlled resources (specifically, by employer participation in the Sick Fund). Third, as noted in our introductory survey, the labour-movement élite embraced a political agenda which, in the 1930s, gave pride of place to the pursuit of industrial peace and harmonious relations with employers' organizations as part of the struggle for Mapai hegemony.

Notwithstanding this powerful array of motives, in the sphere of industrial relations the Histadrut failed to impose its preferred corporate model of aggregating and centralizing labour activity. To understand why this was so requires, first of all, that we recall the peculiar status of trade unionism in the Histadrut's original institutional design when compared with the European experience of working-class mobilization.[16]

The problematic status of trade unionism

Historically, the impetus for trade unionism in the West arose out of labour's response to industrial capitalism and its corollaries of competition among workers for jobs, and employer control of the labour process. The propertyless Jewish settlers of late Ottoman Palestine confronted some of these problems in the rural sector, where they were concentrated, but the formative stages of labour organization largely preceded processes of urbanization and industrialization. Partly as a result, instead of skilled workers forming the vanguard of trade unionism in response to capitalism's assault on their craft skills, the Zionist labour movement's base was centred on the unskilled proletariat from the beginning. A second point to note is that whereas in the Western nations peak associations of labour emerged directly or indirectly from the fission of pre-existing local and occupational units, the Histadrut was organized from above. Third, rather than the trade union wing of the labour movement constituting an equal partner to the party wing on the one hand and frameworks of economic co-operation on the other, in Jewish Palestine it was overshadowed by them. Parties, not unions, created the Histadrut; and trade unionism was deliberately assigned a subordinate position within the panoply of functions which the Histadrut embraced.

As we have argued in Chapter 2, the founding of the Histadrut is best understood as a historic crystallization of the Jewish labour movement's strategy of defending workers' economic interests by means of a partnership with organized Zionism. The labourers, unlike the leadership and the majority of the Zionist rank and file in the Diaspora, had demonstrated their readiness to actually settle in Palestine. Their adaptation to conditions there contrasted strongly with that of the veteran independent farmers (*ikarim*). The worker-pioneers sought to supplant, or at least circumscribe, indigenous labour, rather than to promote an economic base dependent on the Arabs. They were committed to building a 'workers' economy' with the explicit aim of absorbing propertyless Jewish immigrants. And they were willing to establish and defend a Jewish presence on strategic but economically unenticing areas of the Land of Israel. While the labour movement's expectations of Zionist material assistance were never fully realized, the economic and service institutions of the Histadrut—in fact even its administrative apparatus—would certainly not have been viable without the financial aid of the World Zionist Organization and similar bodies. And crucially, the institutional fashioning of the Histadrut was decisively influenced by the requirements for attracting WZO subsidy. These included: (*a*) the creation of a single and authoritative framework through which the labour movement could negotiate and channel Zionist aid; (*b*) the formal distancing of party politics and purging of class-struggle ideology from this instrumentality; and (*c*) the placing of the Zionist tasks of immigration, absorption, and settlement at the head of the Histadrut's agenda.

These requirements go a long way to explaining the unity and centralization of the Histadrut, the dominance of Zionist and near-absence of socialist objectives in its founding charter, and its incorporation of virtually all worker political streams within a framework of formal autonomy from parties despite *de facto* party control. They also help to explain the anomalous marginality of trade unionism in the Histadrut's scheme of things. It is true that unionism's stunted early development was to some extent the result of objectively adverse conditions: the limited scope and unfavourability of the wage labour market, the scant development of factory production, the absence of stable occupational and geographical identities among the workers, and general pessimism about the immediate prospects for capitalist development. But this is not the whole story, as we may infer from the Histadrut's resistance to normalizing its trade union function even after many of these circumstantial limitations were removed. Rather, we must look to the genuine contradictions between the labour organization's role in the union sphere and its responsibilities to the Zionist enterprise.[17] Left to itself, labour's 'economism' would likely have drawn workers out of frameworks dedicated to the Jewish settlement effort and into more local and autonomous forms of collective action. The organized would have sought to protect their advantages at the expense of new immigrants. Also it was feared that successful trade union pressure for economic gains might price employed Jews out of their jobs. Perhaps most importantly, it could (and occasionally did) happen that Jewish workers would be tempted to cross the national boundary in defence of their immediate economic interests, a possibility which the Histadrut was determined to avert (see Chapter 2).

These in-built tensions between the model embraced by the Histadrut centre and the trade union instincts of its periphery posed evident difficulties for the leadership of the labour organization.[18] Veteran workers indeed wished to protect their jobs from the competition of newcomers; the skilled were more interested in wage differentials than in participating in co-operatives or fighting for a wage floor for the unskilled; all workers were tempted to gravitate towards opportunities for steady work and better pay rather than remain in 'conquest work' and endure the interminable wait for an opportunity to settle on the land. As a counterpoint to these centrifugal forces, the majority of Histadrut members were themselves recent immigrants whose position in the labour market was fragile and who accepted the need to keep jobs open for newcomers and to strive for equality of sacrifice and rewards. At a more concrete level, the labour organization's ability to provide access to subsidized employment and services had obvious appeal to those facing the trauma of absorption in a context of low wages and job scarcity. Yet the trade union impulse surfaced in spite of these strategic, material, and ideological attractions of the Histadrut model. The labour organization was unable to prevent the emergence of independent local mobilization in defiance of the tutelage of the Histadrut centre and the dominant Achdut Avodah labour party. In the early 1920s these tensions resulted in a bitter contest for authority in Jaffa, then the most advanced centre of urban Jewish settlement.[19]

During the early period of the struggle to establish the hegemony of the party and the Histadrut centre, symptoms of local unrest also surfaced in other urban areas in the form of defections from Histadrut membership, actual and threatened break-away unions, and the appearance of a loose coalition of dissident unions at the labour organization's second convention in 1923. These were indications that opposition to party control of labour councils and council control of unions, and rejection of the organizational linkage of unionism to the Histadrut's economic collectives and its settlement programme, extended beyond the radical left. Later in the decade, a variety of innovations to strengthen organizational and political control of the unions helped hold such oppositional tendencies in check. But even at this stage, the labour councils in Jaffa and Haifa (the main concentrations of urban Histadrut members) recognized that abdication from the advocacy of workers' interests in conflicts with employers would carry a serious risk of losing their rank and file. In turn, the Histadrut/party élite had to make some accommodation to the dialectical push and pull between trade unionism and their preferred model of worker organization.

The economic transformations wrought during the 1920s by the combined effects of British policy and a new wave of immigration (the Fourth Aliyah) deepened this dilemma. The initial commitment of the British administration to infrastructural activity such as road-building had precipitated a spectacular growth of producer co-operation under the auspices of the Histadrut. But the new regime also established for the first time legal and political conditions which enabled population expansion and the development of a modern capitalist economy in the Jewish sector. With the Fourth Aliyah, the Yishuv experienced the novelty of a substantial immigration of Jews with independent means and no interest in rural settlement. The result was a considerable extension of the boundaries of the urban labour market.[20]

The growth of wage work and private investment fundamentally altered the context for working-class collective action. Workers' dependence on the Histadrut's labour exchanges or its co-operatives for the ability to make a living lessened considerably. The labour movement could no longer claim a monopoly on the ability to attract and absorb immigrants, yet this was the central assumption on which the alliance between Zionism and labour had been constructed. One of the inevitable consequences of these trends was a belated recognition, on the part of the labour leaders, of the centrality of workers' trade union interests. At the same time, the political strategy hitherto adopted by the leadership was thrown into question by the emergence of new classes which could hardly be attracted by a labouristic programme—merchants, small businessmen, and other self-employed. This constituency was opposed to unrestricted labour militancy, and to woo it the labour movement sought new ways to exercise 'responsibility' in industrial relations.[21]

The barriers to corporate trade unionism

The plan for industrial-relations reform which was presented to the Histadrut's fourth convention in 1933 furnishes a concrete illustration of the conflicting forces buffeting the labour organization. The proposals of the Executive Committee would have radically altered the prevailing highly decentralized system of industrial relations. They envisaged the Histadrut entering into an overarching accommodation with organized employer groups on the basis of joint management of the labour exchanges and union consent to compulsory arbitration of labour disputes during the term of collective agreements. These concessions would have been complemented by a more active role for the Histadrut centre in providing uniform guidelines for wage negotiations and pressing for the aggregation of these negotiations along the lines of entire branches and/or regions.

We know that on earlier occasions when the possibility of imposing a 'peace obligation' on unions was raised, the Executive was sceptical of its ability to deliver the rank and file. It is true that there were many indications during the pre-sovereignty period that where the vital interests of the Histadrut centre and the political leadership were at stake, they could successfully mobilize the requisite material and political resources to impose their will—if necessary, coercively. But limits on the right to strike and plans to remove exclusive control of the labour exchanges from the Histadrut were consistently and vigorously opposed by exchange and labour council officials. Even more vocal opposition to proposals like those fielded in 1933 was expressed by the radical left and some of Mapai's own kibbutzim. Consequently, any broadly based attack on trade union and labour council independence would have imposed an unacceptably high political cost on the labour movement élite. In this respect, developments from the mid-1920s had strengthened the militants' hands. The growth of an urban working class employed in private enterprises, complemented by the formation of a new cadre of labour-movement activists with a class-struggle orientation, forced the leadership to accept the furthering of workers' immediate economic interests as a legitimate Histadrut activity—and a vital one for building up their loyalty to Achdut Avodah and later, Mapai. Moreover, since the Histadrut's local institutions became the most important bastion of the apparatus on which the party élite relied for mobilizing the party and the wage-earning public in their support, the wishes of the apparatus could not be flouted with impunity.[22]

The leadership of the labour movement did not abandon its efforts to ensure that trade unionism was placed under strong institutional and party control. But to make this control tolerable to those subjected to it, rank-and-file members in a position to make 'opportunistic' gains were permitted to do so. This was particularly important to the Histadrut so far as skilled workers were concerned. The labour organization's experience with contracting groups in the early 1920s had shown that once these groups found it necessary to attract additional skilled members, they began to tolerate very high wage differentials; and even so, many craftsmen (including those trained by the collectives) deserted to the private sector. More generally, skilled workers could do without Histadrut mediation to obtain employment and many could also dispense with Histadrut social services. Since ultimately the strength of the Histadrut (and the parties behind it) depended on its capacity to mobilize the Jewish working class *en bloc*, it was ready to make almost any concession necessary to keep privileged groups of workers (not only craftsmen but also white-collar and professional employees) within the fold. This was reflected, for instance, in the tolerance of labour councils towards the wide wage differentials achieved by these groups and the regressive structure of Histadrut dues throughout the 1920s and 1930s.

Decentralized wage negotiations were a further symptom of the Histadrut's accommodative stance towards the minority of workers who enjoyed a favourable bargaining position in the labour market. These workers were not impelled—as they would have been under binding multi-employer collective agreements—to accept fixed wage rates over long periods, and neither was their potential to make gains circumscribed by the economic capacities of marginal employers. An aggregated and unified system of wage-fixing would also have forced the Histadrut to confront the extremely wide pay differentials prevailing between more- and less-privileged groups of members. Finally, economic considerations also favoured preserving the status quo in wage determination. Given the role of immigration in determining the future of Zionism and the labour movement's own capacities for expansion, and the condition of chronic unemployment which prevailed among unskilled workers, the Histadrut was inclined to refrain from exercising solidaristic pressure to raise the wage floor. On the contrary, it exhibited a readiness to exempt weak enterprises from its wage standards. Moreover, the Histadrut's own business interests—made conspicuous by the collapse of its building company in 1927—provided the labour organization with an in-built sensitivity to the potential consequences of wage pressure for employment and investment.

In sum, the Histadrut's hesitation in embracing any far-reaching 'corporatization' of industrial relations is traceable to the very characteristics from which it derived its strength. The remarkable breadth of membership on which the labour organization based its capacity for political mobilization and its ability to commit the Jewish working class to the Zionist project, increased the potential for conflicts of interest among differentially advantaged groups and thus deterred the Histadrut from accepting responsibility for reaching an internal consensus on workers' wage demands. Its unique functions as an agency of settlement and an organizer of economic activities—critical pillars of the labour organization's internal and external power—weakened its credibility as a trade union and fed opposition movements. The Histadrut's structural permeation by political parties, whose consent had made it possible in the first place to aggregate such a broad range of functions and members, opened the door (for both the Mapai apparatus and the left-wing opposition) to party sponsorship of rank-and-file militancy.[23]

The sources of employer resistance to corporatism

There can be no doubt that the prospects for corporatist compromise in the Yishuv were limited by the characteristics of capital as well as organized labour.[24] It is evident from the prevailing economic structure that there was a marked diversity of interests between, and even within, the main 'fractions' of capital in the Jewish business sector. These differences hampered corporate collective action on the part of employers and discouraged uniformity in labour-relations arrangements. The three leading branches of production—construction, manufacturing, and citrus—each represented a distinctive economic basis for conflict or co-operation with organized Jewish labour, and each fielded its own employers' organization. In so far as there was a common denominator, it was the presumptive interest of all Jewish employers in some form of wage restraint. The most labour-intensive branches, agriculture and construction—not surprisingly, the principal concentrations of Arab and other unorganized workers—exhibited particular sensitivity to labour costs. Even manufacturing had to contend with the absence of high tariff walls, potential competition from local Arab producers, and pressures from the multitude of small-scale enterprises within the Jewish economy.

It is true that the large sector of production and services catering to the domestic Jewish market stood to gain from high wages, which would feed back into demand for their products and services. But there were no grounds for capital to anticipate supportive monetary and fiscal interventions by the state apparatus to stabilize this demand in periods of economic recession. Consequently, there was little scope for a Keynesian type of class compromise to meet the employers' interest in controlling labour costs. While the Zionist movement was more committed than the government of Palestine to counteracting economic downturns, it proved unable to mobilize sufficient resources to do so effectively. The Jewish political centre was also fiscally incapable of subsidizing labour costs sufficiently to bridge the gap between the 'Jewish minimum' and prevailing Arab wage levels. Not only were employers faced with limited positive economic incentives to enter into a historic compromise with organized labour, but the latter could exert only limited sanctions to prevent capital from exploiting labour-market conditions to its advantage. Despite the Histadrut's success in achieving a rate of organization encompassing about three-quarters of Jewish workers, it could not eliminate undercutting by rival labour organizations and the unorganized. Employers at large thus had a clear incentive at least to keep open the option of employing non-Histadrut labour. This explains their repeated refusal to accept the Histadrut's core demand to control hiring and firing.

In order to lend greater precision to the analysis and to highlight the sources of internal diversity within the capitalist class, we move now to an analysis of the three branches of the Yishuv economy which were most salient to labour relations.[25] The first of these, manufacturing, accounted for between a fifth and a quarter of total Jewish employment and product throughout the inter-war period.

A second key branch, construction, is the least charted of the three in terms of labour-market issues. But it was of great importance to the Yishuv because of the intimate connection between the building industry and cycles of immigration and economic growth. The scope of the construction industry was highly volatile, accounting for under 5 per cent of product towards the close of each of the inter-war decades, but more than 15 per cent during the boom periods coinciding with immigration peaks.[26] Finally, citrus growing possessed special importance for Jewish labour. The majority of new arrivals among the workers made their way initially to the Moshavot, the rural Jewish settlements which grew up around privately-owned agricultural plantations, where the Histadrut enjoyed a relatively high rate of organization. At the beginning of the 1930s, when citrus was at its zenith as an employer, it provided work to as many as one-sixth of all Jewish wage-earners in Palestine.

Manufacturing. Those manufacturers engaged in factory production had a tangible interest in accommodative industrial relations as a result of the superior productivity of a stable and experienced labour force under factory conditions. The relative harmony between labour and capital in this sector was reinforced by the fact that it generally eschewed Arab labour. Finding the local Arab market inhospitable, industry appreciated the purchasing power of a prosperous work-force and the co-operation of the Histadrut in its efforts to persuade the Jews to 'buy Jewish', the British to raise protective duties, and the Jewish Agency to allocate credit and subsidies.[27] Nevertheless, given the position of manufacturing within the Yishuv economy, there was little likelihood that it would set the tone for capital as a whole. The industrial sector was overshadowed by the service sector and until the Second World War its share of the economy stagnated.[28] More importantly, industry also suffered conspicuously from qualitative weakness. Production was almost entirely devoted to converting imported raw materials into products sold on the home market, the majority of which were consumer- or construction-related rather than capital goods. Private industry was also heavily dependent on credit, even to finance operating costs, and exhibited little capacity for internal capital accumulation.

In addition to the limited significance of manufacturing as a factor in the wider economy, it was internally divided into three tiers with quite different orientations towards labour matters. Consequently, not only the possibility of a leadership role for the industrial sector, but also the prospect of corporately organized industrial relations within the sector itself, was in doubt. In terms of capital concentration, manufacturing was markedly top-heavy. Modern industrialization did not begin until the 1930s, but even prior to that a very small number of large Jewish-owned firms in Palestine accounted for an impressive share of the capital stock. These big firms eschewed solidarity with the organized manufacturers, preferring to manage their relations with the authorities (Zionist and British) and the workers directly. By dint of their large size, monopoly privileges, and relatively heavy shield of protective tariffs and given their advantages of scale, they were able to opt for independent industrial-relations strategies. Large firms tended to pursue enterprise-level accommodation with the Histadrut and its work-place representatives in return for high productivity and labour peace. In a number of cases these co-operative relations were buttressed by an internally segmented labour market with unorganized Arabs occupying unskilled jobs.[29]

At the other extreme was industry's broad underbelly, that of workshop production, which as late as 1937 accounted for a quarter of all industrial employment.[30] This extensive economic periphery was entirely outside the spheres of influence of both the Histadrut and the Manufacturers' Association. This is not surprising, since, in addition to its small scale, much of the workshop sector was based on working proprietors and the labour of family members, rather than on wage work. It was thus only in the domain of medium-sized industrial employers that there was an impetus towards collective action. Even so, the mobilization of the industrialists was impeded because there was relatively little material benefit which they could hope to gain by lobbying the state.[31] And because it covered only part of a sector, which was relatively weak and internally variegated to begin with, the industrialists' associational activity was inevitably enfeebled. Crucial general meetings of the Jaffa and Tel Aviv Association at the height of the industrial-relations crisis of 1925 drew no more than two dozen participants.

As late as 1932 the Manufacturers' Association's own membership claims amounted to under half of the Jewish industrial establishments in Tel Aviv, and the rate of organization in the other main centres was far lower. Co-ordination among the Association's local branches was limited and neither the peak body nor regional organizations enjoyed any significant measure of authority. The associational problems which the Jewish industrialists of Palestine faced are to some extent germane to collective action by business interests in capitalist societies. Nevertheless, other forces in these societies may be capable of *imposing* coherent interests and collective organization on capital. But in the Yishuv, the limited incentives and supports for corporate action in labour relations, which were furnished by the Histadrut and the British authorities, had the effect of reinforcing rather than counteracting industry's internal weaknesses.[32]

Construction. The scope for harmonious relations between labour and capital in the building industry was far more limited than in manufacturing. Employers in construction had little incentive to feed demand via workers' wages, since building was largely paid for out of imported private and public funds. Moreover, whereas industrial employers operating at above workshop scale were interested in acquiring a reliable and relatively skilled work-force and paid their workers on a steady basis, conditions were quite different in construction. The demand for building was subject to sharp fluctuations, work was partly seasonal due to weather conditions, and production was labour-intensive and based largely on unskilled workers. Accordingly, the building contractors of Tel Aviv drew heavily on non-Histadrut Jewish labour—in the 1920s, religious workers and in the 1930s, Revisionists.[33]

As the turbulence of 1925 clearly illustrated, competition among workers, coupled with the boom-and-bust character of the industry, was capable of generating major eruptions of labour militancy at cyclical downturns—while simultaneously providing employers with the means to fight back successfully. But even in ordinary times, as long as employers were in a position to bypass Histadrut labour they felt no necessity to seek out an organized accommodation. For two reasons, it was also improbable that they would do so. First, construction was an intensely competitive branch in which there were few large and enduring private firms capable of sustaining a permanent employers' association and leading the industry into collective bargaining. Second, relations with the

Histadrut were perennially strained by the scope for conflict between private contractors and the labour organization's own activity in the construction field. The contractors naturally feared that if they conceded to Histadrut demands concerning labour exchanges and wages, these concessions would be exploited to put them out of business.

Citrus. The citrus growers of the Moshavot were by far the most important group of private employers in agriculture. They were also the source of the most intense opposition to the Histadrut's elementary wage and employment demands. This was the joint effect of the industry's particular labour requirements and its geographical proximity to the Arab labour reserve. In any case, the Histadrut proved to be an unreliable source for meeting the need of the larger plantations for masses of unskilled workers in the harvest season. Moreover, Jewish labour could not compete with Arab in either price or productivity—a condition which, as contemporary observers perceived, ruled out any move towards orderly collective bargaining. In addition, the fact that during the 1930s citrus became the only significant export industry in the Jewish economy meant that it was not dependent on either the Zionist institutions or its own employees as customers.[34] From a political perspective, only those of the Ikarim (farmers) who had been settled on 'national' land after the First World War, on the basis of a commitment to employ Jewish labour, were part of the mainstream of the Yishuv. Given their consequent isolation and sense of outrage at being accused by the Histadrut and the Yishuv at large of disloyalty to the Jewish community, the majority of the older-established (pre-war) Ikarim were willing to employ Arab labour on a large (although widely fluctuating) scale. They also made effective use of the coercive powers of the Mandatory authorities in order to combat Jewish labour militancy.[35]

Ironically enough, as Anita Shapira (1977: 262–8 and 307–30) has documented, by the mid-1930s the prospects for a corporatist resolution of class conflict were actually far greater in agriculture than in industry. Three trends after 1935 were behind this development: erosion of the export market for citrus, which for the first time rendered the possibility of Zionist economic subsidies attractive to the farmers of the pre-war Moshavot; the practical and ideological pressures to cut back dependence on Arab labour following the Arab general strike beginning in the spring of 1936; and the new availability and weak bargaining position of Jewish agricultural workers as a result of unemployment in urban areas. In addition, the Farmers' Association became a pivotal element in Ben-Gurion's political strategy of forging a consensus on the national issues of defence and partition. As a result Mapai was now more open to offering the Ikarim incorporation into the political institutions of the Yishuv.

While the Mapai-controlled Jewish Agency pressed for a peak labour agreement in agriculture and offered various forms of subsidy to the farmers, this last corporatist gasp of the inter-war period enjoyed no more success than its predecessors. The Histadrut was fearful of the internal repercussions of an open compromise on the sensitive issues of wage cuts and Hebrew labour. As the crisis in citrus deepened, the Ikarim came to doubt that Zionist funds would suffice to keep them afloat. In any case, conditions in the labour market were on the farmers' side: rising unemployment, availability of non-Histadrut Jewish labour, and the rapid return of striking Arab labour to the citrus groves. The Ikarim were thus able to fall back on the alternative of regulating wages and employment unilaterally or through negotiations with local labour councils. Market forces had triumphed over political will to frustrate once again the prospects for corporatism.

Class, markets, and conflict

We conclude that the weakness of capital in the Yishuv as a class *for itself* was to an important extent rooted in its objective weakness as a class *in itself*. To some degree the problem was one of internal diversity. As we have seen, profound differences in market and production conditions discouraged co-operation among employers, both across and within the different sectors. No single faction of capital or natural coalition, was capable of playing a leadership role for the capitalist class as a whole and directing its relations with labour. At the same time, as we have argued in the previous chapter, capital was not sufficiently hegemonic within society at large to confine the labour movement to a subsidiary role. Quite the contrary, even most non-labour groups—including the large *petit-bourgeois* stratum—accepted labour hegemony.

The juxtaposition of a highly mobilized labour movement

alongside a fragmented and non-hegemonic capitalist class might, under other circumstances, have led to extreme class polarization and conflict.[36] The sense of unity among Jews as result of the all-embracing national conflict and the labour movement's internalization of Jewish national interests, help explain why this did not occur. Still, had these forces been sufficiently potent, they would presumably have overcome the structural barriers to corporatist class accommodation. In reality the issue cannot be resolved for the simple reason that corporatism was objectively dispensable; even in its absence severe class conflict could be avoided. An alternative equilibrium was reached in the relations between labour and capital on the basis of economic rather than of political forces. Class relations were mediated, above all, by conditions in the labour market; and until World War II, these conditions generally favoured employer interests.

Part of the labour market's restraining impact on industrial relations stemmed from its unstable rhythm. The Yishuv economy was buffeted by severe cyclical swings broadly linked to trends in immigration and capital inflow. As the history of corporatist experimentation reveals, the moment that the conjuncture altered in capital's favour (i.e. rising unemployment), the employer side lost interest in any accommodation which would constrain its freedom to exploit this conjuncture. At such times it often appeared that agreement was stalled because of the inability of the employers' peak association to impose an internal consensus. But it was also true that the Manufacturers' Association's limited authority provided a convenient guise for evading undertakings opposed to its members' interests. Two severe economic crises (1926–7 and 1936–40) and additional periods of milder recession taught employers that institutionalized wage-fixing arrangements were either avoidable or could be revoked under changed conditions and that labour militants would be unable to sustain an aggressive posture over long periods.[37]

Not only the volatility of the labour market, but also divisions within the labour force, made the regulation of employment the most crucial—and intractable—issue in negotiations for a peak union–employer accommodation. Actual [illegible] potential recruitment of cheap and flexible labour, in a market which even in periods of prosperity was over-supplied with unskilled workers, more than compensated for capital's disorganization. A wide variety of 'marginal' types of labour acted to weaken the position of unskilled Histadrut members: Arabs, employed mainly in agriculture; minority labour organizations (religious, Revisionist, Yemenite); unorganized Jewish men (mostly Easterners), widely utilized in construction; and, in some specific industries and occupations, Jewish women who, even when organized by the Histadrut, were sharply discriminated against.[38]

Taken together, recurrent economic crisis, the reserve of unskilled labour incompletely organized by the Histadrut, and the willingness of the authorities to invoke police repression made it possible for employers to combat successfully the Histadrut if they had good reasons for doing so. The availability of these coercive levers did not necessarily rule out collaborative labour relations. But rather than developing in *a politically mediated framework of class-wide negotiation*—that is, along corporatist lines—collaboration, where it appeared, was based on collective relations at the level of individual enterprises. Within the business sector such collaboration was confined mainly to medium- and large-scale firms in manufacturing. This reflected not only the demonstrated potential of employers to combat labour militancy, but also the consequences of the *labour-market dualism* which coincided with the polarized structure of industry. The existence of a large workshop sector of production acted as a disciplinary influence on labour in enterprises exposed to its competition, while also enabling larger employers to derive benefits which they shared with their employees.[39]

Even though micro-level co-operation was not universal in industry and the industrialists failed to conclude any formal pact with the Histadrut, cordial relations generally prevailed at the élite level, particularly during the 1930s.[40] This cordiality was the product of convergent interests: on the one hand, the dependence of industry's market on workers' purchasing power, as well as on credit and orders stemming from the labour-controlled Zionist institutions; and on the other, the Histadrut's economic sympathy for the principle of 'employer ability to pay' and its political enthusiasm for harmonious relations with private capital. In short, the political economy of the Yishuv succeeded in stabilizing class relations by furnishing coercive alternatives to corporatism and by providing openings for class harmony in spite of the absence of a corporatist structure of labour relations.

Corporatism and the political economy of Wartime

Developments during World War II provide an apposite postscript to corporatism's inter-war failure. The war hastened several of the trends which had emerged during the two preceding decades: the rise of an urban working class, the growth of centre-periphery conflicts and left–right struggles on the terrain of the Histadrut, and the impulse to class collaboration generated by Mapai's political aspirations. Even more important, British interests shifted dramatically in favour of a more interventionist role for the state in the Jewish economy, including labour relations. In conjunction with an economic transition from prolonged depression to an inflationary boom, the result was a limited but unmistakable movement towards economy-wide collective bargaining and political exchange between the Histadrut and the authorities.[41]

The war was extraordinary, mainly because it provided an enormous boost to the Jewish economy—particularly industry, and to construction and food production. The near-closure of sea transportation to Palestine and its neighbours provided local manufacturers with a greatly expanded market. At the same time, especially following the establishment of a regional Supply Centre in Cairo in 1941, the economy of Palestine became a major factor in meeting war-related military and civilian requirements, not only locally but throughout the Middle East. Given its much larger size and scale, higher productivity, and more favourable branch composition, Jewish industry was far better placed than the Arab sector to benefit from these opportunities. Rapid industrialization together with the decline of citriculture, profoundly altered the composition of the Jewish labour force: the share of industrial workers rose from 22 to 24 per cent of all wage-earners in the 1920s and 1930s, to 32 per cent at war's end.[42]

The newly enlarged working class was ripe for trade union activity. Its members were increasingly thrown together by the expanding size of plants and the concentration of the bulk of the industrial work-force in the Tel Aviv area. By 1942 Jewish unemployment had vanished as a result of the absorption of manpower by the military and the recovery of the business sector. With industry booming, labour shortages ensured that even the unskilled had sufficient bargaining power to engage in collective bargaining and strikes, and to act autonomously in the work-place. The new urban workers were largely uncommitted to Mapai or any other political party and organized themselves from below. Plant-level workers' committees mushroomed, acquiring a new independence and importance as participants in collective bargaining. Many came into the orbit of the left wing within and beyond Mapai. Driven by an accumulation of material grievances from the depression period and the new conflicts engendered by rapid expansion and inflation, strike activity soared. In 1942–6 worker involvement in disputes rose to an annual average of 10,000—almost all concentrated in the industrial sector, in which the average organized worker spent five days on strike each year.[43]

These developments furnished the Histadrut/Mapai leadership with potent internal motives to further centralize and politicize the labour organization's trade union function. Moreover, the Histadrut recognized that the changed interests of the state in wartime created novel opportunities for corporatist political exchange. In return for labour restraint, the state could strengthen the Histadrut's internal and external authority, afford it a political role in the formation of economic and social policy, impose on hitherto recalcitrant and disorganized private employers the duty to bargain with the labour organization and abide by its standards, and assist trade union penetration of the growing public sector of the economy. Broader considerations also contributed to the Histadrut's corporatist aspirations. From a Zionist perspective, the common Nazi enemy and the sense that events were moving in favour of Britain relinquishing sovereignty to the Jews increased the political attractiveness of co-operation with the Mandatory authorities and strengthened the labour movement's determination to help lay the economic foundations for statehood. Finally, with Mapai courting the American Zionists in order to mobilize support for its political programme within the world movement, there was an additional reason for the Histadrut to display a spirit of class partnership.

The interests of the other potential partners to corporatist regulation of labour relations were less clear-cut. The leaders of the Manufacturers' Association faced similar incentives to their counterparts in the Histadrut: the opportunities for legitimacy and authority afforded by greater centralization of collective bargaining and dispute settlement, and the Zionist argument for class cooperation. Nevertheless, industrial capital continued to exhibit the same lack of internal cohesion as before the war. No more than about half of the Jewish labour force in industry was encompassed by the Manufacturers' Association membership. Palestine's few really large enterprises not only remained outside the Association, but temporarily formed their own roof organization. Individual manufacturers were divided between those favouring co-operation with the Histadrut, and others who—as a result of orders from the British—were now freed from dependence on labour's purchasing power and the benevolence of the national institutions controlled by the labour movement. Industrialists working under 'cost-plus' contracts had no need for industry-wide wage restraint and preferred independent enterprise-level wage agreements.[44]

According to Chana Levine (1985), there were also conflicting perspectives on the side of the British authorities. The military supply agencies were basically willing to pay whatever it took to 'deliver the goods', and thus had no pressing interest in wage restraint. In addition, since 1938 the authorities had become committed to developing a modern state apparatus in the fields of social and labour policy. Because it implied a more active and independent role for the state (to encompass Arabs and unorganized Jewish workers as well as the Histadrut), this new stance was also inhospitable to corporatist developments. However, stronger economic and political interests pushed in the opposite direction. Now that Britain was the Yishuv's major customer and employer, the government of Palestine was naturally concerned to restrain wages and prevent strikes. Moreover, with the local currency permanently fixed in parity with sterling, the British could hardly remain complacent while a higher rate of inflation than that at home drove up their indebtedness to Palestine. Pressure was also exerted from London to co-operate with the Jewish community for domestic and strategic reasons. A corporatist relationship with the Histadrut held out the prospect of promoting such co-operation while also combating wage push and industrial disorder.[45]

Corporatist experiments

Against the background of the sharp erosion of real wages by wartime inflation, the Histadrut and the Manufacturers' Association were, for the first time, drawn into multi-employer wage bargaining. In September 1940 they instituted a cost of living allowance which was, in principle, Yishuv-wide, although initially it covered only about half of the industrial labour force and fixed graduated increases for individual branches. Almost simultaneously the Executive Committee of the Histadrut established a central Trade Union Department, with the clear intention of centralizing wage determination. The government decided to encourage the trend towards nationally negotiated adjustments of wages to prices, while putting pressure on the parties to endorse only moderate wage increases. As the result of an initiative by the War Supply Board, in the spring of 1942 a consensus was reached between government officials and representatives of the Histadrut, the Manufacturers' Association and the Jewish Agency on an automatic system of compensation for price rises.[46]

Official recognition of the Histadrut's status as spokesman for Jewish labour (and to a lesser extent recognition of the parallel role of the Manufacturers' Association) was also affirmed by other state initiatives in this period. In mid-1941 the Histadrut was asked to comment on government proposals for stiff anti-strike emergency regulations. Just as they had done two decades earlier, the Jewish national institutions reacted to the threat of state intervention by pressing for voluntary arrangements—but their proposal for a master collective agreement for industry foundered once again on the labour-exchange issue.[47] In any case, the Histadrut's initial hostility to the government's proposal was softened by pressure from Mapai leaders, who were anxious to avoid any confrontation with the British. Moreover, Histadrut leaders found reasons of their own for co-operating with the proposed legislation. The Trade Disputes Order for the first time granted the labour organization the exclusive legal right to bargain with employers (albeit limited to work-places where its adherents constituted a majority of the work-force). It was also hoped that a recognized role in statutory arbitration would reinforce the Histadrut's sagging authority over its membership.

During 1942 the Histadrut participated in several government-sponsored forums charged with recommending wage policies for specific branches, and was the only outside body invited to sit on an official Wages Committee. By this time the labour leadership had become painfully aware of its limited control over rank-and-file militancy, and had taken steps to prepare itself for a more corporatist role in industrial relations. The Trade Union Department suspended the right of labour councils to authorize strikes and announced that any workers' committee, which rejected Histadrut authority, would be denied its negotiating services. The new Wages Committee held out the prospect that the state would take additional and complementary steps to strengthen the Histadrut's corporatist capacities, but these hopes were only partially realized. The Committee's report advocated establishing a legal framework for trade unionism and collective bargaining. But it stopped short of conceding the Histadrut's authority to negotiate on behalf of the unorganized, failed to support its demand for a uniform (Arab/Jewish) minimum wage, and refrained from calling for a more active role for the labour organization in public policy-making.

In spite of their modesty the government failed to implement the Wages Committee's recommendations, as by 1943 British interests were shifting again. After El Alamein, Palestine's strategic importance dwindled, and so did its role as a source of supplies and essential services. As a result, the authorities lost their most pressing motive for containing labour militancy.[48] There was as well a revival of earlier fears that granting the Histadrut political status for industrial relations purposes would indirectly succour the Zionist cause. This was seen as a liability in the later years of the war and immediately thereafter, when Britain's oil interests and Jewish pressure for independent statehood heightened the salience of Arab claims. In short, political exchange with organized Jewish labour was now neither necessary nor desirable.

As soon as British interest in consensual labour restraint faltered, the Yishuv authorities attempted to fill the vacuum and revived the idea of an intra-communal accommodation between labour and capital. In the spring of 1943 the Jewish Agency once again attempted to sponsor a master collective agreement and to engineer an agreement on bringing organized employers into the management of new 'general' labour exchanges. A series of marathon negotiating sessions was interrupted at mid-year when the Manufacturers' Association refused to contemplate any arrangement requiring industrialists to recruit labour exclusively via the exchanges. The Histadrut élite nevertheless continued to aspire to greater centralization of collective bargaining. To this end, in November 1943 the manufacturers were offered a six-month wage freeze during which pay increases for individual branches would be negotiated to supplement a national framework agreement on matters of principle. But, bowing to pressures from the rank and file and the labour left, the Histadrut was unable to consent to a Manufacturers' Association demand that strikes be outlawed during the negotiations for branch agreements, and the talks fell apart. With this, the long quest for a voluntary labour convention finally came to an end. In the course of the next two years the practice of collective bargaining in industry widened and deepened considerably[49]—but on the basis of relations at the enterprise level which left the peak associations of labour and capital largely confined to the sidelines.

This did not prevent Histadrut leaders from continuing to harbour hopes of being granted corporatist privileges by the Mandatory authorities. Their aspirations included a legal infrastructure which would provide a needed lever against employers, government subsidy for the labour organization's social services, and the possibility of pre-empting future Arab wage competition by making Jewish rates universally binding. However, the diluted Trade Union Law which finally came into force in 1947, with the end of British rule already in sight, emerged stillborn. Having made an indispensable contribution to the aggregation of collective bargaining up to the national level and to moving wage determination onto the terrain of political exchange, the authorities ceased their flirtation with corporatism.

The fact that such a flirtation had occurred at all can in large part be attributed to the forces that generated similar trends in other democratic nations during the war. The workers' first taste of sustained full employment (reinforced in the Yishuv by the maturation of labour-market segregation of Jews from Arabs) produced a shift in the power balance between labour and capital. This shift combusted with wartime inflation and job-related grievances to elicit a high level of grass roots labour militancy. The state, meanwhile, now had a direct interest—of massive proportion—in production costs and deadlines. In addition, the authorities were obliged to deal with a popular consensus strained by wartime privations in general and inflation in particular. Meanwhile, as a result of the war they had temporarily acquired much enhanced powers of intervention which could be used to reward compliant trade union and business élites. Under the variant of these circumstances which prevailed in Palestine, a limited (in time and scope) engagement in corporatist political exchange was an understandable development from the state's point of view.

Employers had a clear interest in pacifying labour, although not necessarily by moving industrial relations into the state arena. The Histadrut, however, was positively anxious to participate. Enlargement of its trade union function on a centralized and politicized basis would permit the labour organization to regain its authority and help Mapai earn the allegiance of the new working class. Overall, the matrix of motives and opportunities confronting labour, capital, and the state had altered dramatically in comparison to the pre-war period; but these changes were conjunctural rather than structural in character—at least so long as Palestine remained under British rule.

Conclusions

In Jewish Palestine during the inter-war period, a corporatist class accommodation failed to emerge because of institutional disabilities (especially on the part of the Histadrut and the national institutions) and a dearth of incentives (primarily in relation to employers and the Mandatory authorities). We have argued that the most important disincentive was the accessibility of viable alternatives to corporatist restraint of labour—in the form of barriers to worker militancy built into the labour market (above all the problem of unemployment) and the repressive interventions of the state. The common denominator shared by each of these sources of labour quiescence is their basis in *coercion* rather than accommodation. To the extent that class co-operation developed, it did so either within individual enterprises or between the élites of labour and capital—that is, without the active participation of the state.

It is true that the Histadrut was locked into intimate relations of political exchange with Mapai on the one hand and the Zionist movement on the other, and in this context was at least implicitly committed to keeping Jewish labour militancy in check. Yet both the potency of this restraint and its corporatist character, were profoundly qualified by two peculiarities of the Yishuv setting. One of these was the extreme decentralization of collective bargaining—and relatedly, the limited and contradictory nature of the Histadrut's trade union function, which imposed grave limits on its corporate authority in wage determination and strike activity. The other was, of course, the hostility which Jewish workers displayed towards *Arab* labour. In the framework of its unwritten compact with the Jewish political centre, the Histadrut was called upon to exercise aggression as well as restraint. Indeed, it was the Jewish–Arab conflict in the labour market that most routinely invoked non-corporatist sources of labour restraint, in the form of Arab competition (labour-market discipline) and police action against 'Jewish-only' strikes and picketing (state suppression).

Our case study of the Yishuv suggests several lessons for the theoretical and comparative study of the origins of corporatist class accommodation.[50] We pointed out at the opening of this chapter that historical studies of the small nations of Western Europe have found that trade union movements opted for centralization and self-restraint in industrial relations either from a position of social-democratic strength, or as a result of politically catastrophic internal or external threats. A different strand of the literature, which rests empirically on cross-sectional comparisons across countries, has tended to argue more narrowly that corporatism's emergence depends on the power of peak organizations of labour. Those with broad scope, unchallenged authority, and links with governing parties are believed most likely to engage in corporatist political exchange.[51]

Both the historical and the cross-sectional arguments, at least as interpreted here, would have erroneously led us to anticipate a transition to corporatism in the Yishuv, and neither would have shed much light on the nature of the watershed constituted by the Second World War. Major shifts in the balance of parliamentary forces, the organizational characteristics of union peak associations, and so forth may well contribute to corporatism's ascendancy, but comprise only part of the broader political–economic context requiring analysis. In this respect, our research on the Mandatory period underscores the limitations of adopting a primarily labour movement-centred approach to the prerequisites for corporatism. It is unwarranted to assume that the presence of an organizationally and politically strong labour movement (certainly a fair characterization of the Yishuv) is a sufficient condition for corporatism. *Both capital and the state must also be predisposed towards accommodating and tempering union power through bargained political compromise.* In the Jewish business sector in Palestine capital suffered from divided interests and weak solidarity. But employers also had reason to be satisfied with the status quo in the labour market, and correspondingly less interest in organizing on a class basis and entering into a formal class compromise. Under these circumstances the decisive significance of the role of the state became strikingly evident during World War II. This dramatically altered the interests and the resources of the British authorities.[52]

In the case of the Yishuv, analysis of the role of the state is complicated by the coexistence of two political centres. The quasi-state institutions, which represented the Palestinian Jewish community and the interests of world Jewry in Palestine, made great efforts to persuade the organizations of labour and capital to minimize class conflict through formal class accommodation, but the incentives at their disposal were insufficient for the task. The existence of such a gap, we have suggested, attests to the theoretically important possibility of a disjuncture between state *interests* and *capacities* with regard to corporatism. As we have argued for the inter-war period and as the dramatic shift in state-economy relations during the war shows conclusively, the Mandatory state was not disengaged from problems of class conflict in the Yishuv—but rather, tailored its involvement to (shifting) British interests. In the period between the wars, Palestine's rulers had little incentive to turn to corporatist regulation of class conflict because other mechanisms were operating or could be invoked to prevent serious outbursts of Jewish labour militancy. The authorities also lacked either the fiscal room to disburse subsidies or the ability to steer private investment and production. And, they feared the political consequences of recognizing and supporting the corporate power of the Histadrut. The result was a *laissez-faire* stance faithful to the contradictions of Britain's imperial aims in Palestine. These contradictions had obliged its local representatives to adopt a double-stranded policy: in the *political* realm their primary concern was Arab legitimation, while their main *material* interest was in the Jewish contribution to economic development and public revenues.

In this light it is clear that the effect of the Second World War was to reduce temporarily the political importance of Arab relative to Jewish consent, while at the same time furnishing the British themselves with strong economic motives for promoting labour restraint in the Jewish sector. Moreover, from the viewpoint of the state's menu of choices for achieving such restraint, it was critical that the new conditions prevailing in wartime labour markets had the effect of inciting industrial workers while virtually ruling out coercive mechanisms of restraint. The pressure for political regulation of industrial conflict even came close to overshadowing the secondary costs for the British of political exchange with the Histadrut. But it did not do so, and as soon as the material urgency of labour quiescence faded political exchange was prevented from becoming institutionalized or generalized. The Histadrut was once again frozen out of policy-making. For the heads of the labour organization this was a bitter blow. As Golda Meyerson (Meir) confided to her colleagues in July 1944, whatever their distaste for 'this imperialist, anti-Zionist, White Paper Government', they had to understand that 'without the Government, thousands upon thousands of collective agreements or gentlemens' agreements with the property-owners will not help us' (Rosen, 1974: 208).

Golda Meir's insider knowledge of the significance of the Mandatory state in the political economy of the Yishuv finds surprisingly little echo in mainstream Israeli scholarship. Most of this scholarship credits the Jewish political centre in Mandatory Palestine with having built up a well-functioning 'state in the making' in spite of the fact that the prerogatives of the state were vested in the British authorities. We have concurred that the problem of establishing authority without the benefit of sovereignty was genuine enough; so much so that for this very reason, the Jewish national institutions unambiguously *failed* in their repeated attempts to actuate a corporatist class compromise. We are thus rather more sceptical than most Israeli observers regarding the accomplishments of the Jewish quasi-state institutions in Palestine. This difference in judgement, moreover, goes together with an important divergence in analytical focus.[53]

Horowitz and Lissak's (1971; 1978) influential discussion of the prehistory of the Israeli polity can help clarify the nature of the debate. These authors contend that not only a deficit of sovereign powers, but also an exceptionally intense level of internal ideological conflict worked against the establishment of an authoritative political centre in the Yishuv. They then identify three major reasons why these difficulties were successfully overcome. First, the Mapai leadership's embrace of the consociational technique of regulating inter-group conflicts by means of inter-élite compromise and bargaining. Second, unity was fostered by the overarching consensus within the Yishuv regarding Zionism's essential objectives. The third factor in Horowitz and Lissak's model was the centre's extensive command of resources (especially 'national capital'), which it allocated in return for political support.

In our view, this analysis and others like it overestimate the roles of ideology and voluntaristic political action as sources of cleavage and integration in Yishuv society. The present case study has documented the emergence in the Jewish community of Palestine of vigorous *material/structural cleavages*, in the form of conflicts of interest both between and within the working class and the *bourgeoisie*. Although their forms and intensity of expression certainly differ, such conflicts are endemic to all capitalist societies. In the circumstances of the Yishuv, the combined forces of the politics of accommodation, Zionist solidarity, and even the political disposition of economic incentives were no match for inter- and intra-class divisions. As a result, the political centre was conspicuously incapable of either persuading or obliging organized Jewish labour and capital to commit themselves to class compromise. Rather than providing a demonstration of political culture, ideology, and political resource-allocation supplanting market forces, the chequered history of corporatism in the Yishuv therefore suggests the very opposite. For, despite its politicization and permeation by highly charged rhetorical conflicts, the labour-market arena was overwhelmingly governed by supply and demand—which on the whole favoured the rule of capital, in spite of labour's unquestionable organizational and political superiority.

Only sovereignty and its consequences were capable of fundamentally restructuring this balance of forces in the political economy and extending corporatism beyond the parameters attained during British rule, including the wartime interlude described above. In the chapter that follows we shall examine the strengths—and yet fragility—of the corporatist labour restraint which took root once the Zionist community succeeded in attaining statehood.

Notes

1. For a fuller introduction to the corporatist model see the discussion in the Introduction and the references therein.

2. The inter-war origins of corporatist class accommodation have been traced by Maier (1984). See Katzenstein (1985: ch. 4) for the common predisposing features of the small West European nations, as well as a historical survey (pp. 139–47) of the inter-war corporatist accommodations reached in these countries. The transition from overt class conflict to 'historic compromise' in Sweden is a major theme of Walter Korpi's work (e.g. 1983). Esping-Andersen (1985*a*: 193–204) places such developments in the context of the adoption of Keynesian policies of crisis management throughout Scandinavia.
3. For instance, see Rosen's (1974: 32–4) reiteration of Ben-Gurion's views. Katznelson (1948: 362) was among those who decried the alleged immaturity of the rank and file.
4. The history of corporatist experiments in this period was reconstructed largely on the basis of documentary evidence held by the Central Zionist Archives (CZA) in Jerusalem, located with the expert help of archivist Yoram Mayorek. Except in cases of direct quotation or very specific claims, detailed sources will not be cited in the text. The following is a list of the principal files consulted. Va'ad Leumi files: J1/7228, 7754. Files of the Labour Department of the Palestine Zionist Executive (and later, of the Jewish Agency): S9/17761–b, 1225, 1231, 1235, 1237, 1345, 2196. Files of the London Office of the Zionist Organization: S25/633–5, S30/2664/441–2. Other Zionist Organization files: Z4/1596I–II, 3487. In addition, at the Lavon Institute (Histadrut archive) we consulted selected reports and publications of the Histadrut and minutes of meetings of its Executive Committee. Relevant correspondence between the Palestine government and the Colonial Office was found in Britain's Public Records Office file PRO/C.O.733/152, a copy of which resides in the Israel State Archives. We obtained the minutes of meetings of the Manufacturers' Association of Jaffa and Tel Aviv between 1922 and 1925, held by the CZA as document number K11/94. Selective use was made of newspapers and magazines, especially *Ha'aretz, Kuntress*, and *Mischar veta'assiyah*. Finally, we also consulted standard sources on the Yishuv regarding economic conditions (especially Gross, 1979 and 1982; and Halevi, 1979) and industrial relations (Bar-Haim, 1972; Etkin, 1982; Kantor, 1966; Rosen, 1974; and Sussman, 1969*a*).
5. For further information on the Jewish 'national institutions' see Chapter 3, n. 2.
6. Data on labour disputes published by the Histadrut's Department of Information and Statistics confirm the impression of limited conflict in the industrial sector. In the period from the termination of the strike wave of 1924–5 until the end of 1932, the total volume of Jewish strike activity (number of striker-days) was generally

under 10,000 per year (excluding some important uncounted non-industrial strikes in 1931 and 1932). The exceptions were 1927 and 1931, although in each case a single major dispute was responsible for the higher figure (Nemirovsky, 1933). In the same vein, at a general meeting of the Manufacturers' Association it was reported that during 1931 and the first nine months of 1932, only a dozen affiliates had experienced work stoppages which the Association was called upon to mediate. Even the keynote speaker at this meeting, who claimed that Jewish industrialists suffered cruelly from labour militancy, pointed out that most strikes in industry occurred in small firms and were called in protest against the employment of non-Histadrut labour. (See the report in *Mischar veta'assiyah*, Oct. and Nov. 1932.) Finally, for data on the growth of enterprise-level collective bargaining during the early 1930s see Preuss (1935).

7. For a more extensive discussion of the rise of the Revisionist threat see Chapter 3. Shapira (1977: 252–7) specifically noted the potential for a right-wing alliance incorporating organized employers. Shapiro (1976: 241–6) has explained the political rationale for Mapai's espousal of labour peace in this period. Mapai's activity along these lines within the Zionist Organization is also documented by Shapira (1977: 264–6, and archival sources cited therein).
8. Stein to Kisch, 14 June 1923, CZA file S25/633.
9. The limits to the political centre's capacities which we have described should not be understood as contradicting the Zionist movement's ability to effect an alliance with organized labour, as discussed in Chapter 3. There we saw that what organized Zionism brought to the bargain was its capacity to subsidize and legitimize labour, which were not dependent on (although would doubtless have been augmented by) state power.
10. Sources consulted on the Mandatory state in Palestine, and specifically its economic interests and policies, include Biger (1983); Finegold (1978); Gross (1982); Horowitz (1948); Horowitz and Hinden (1938); Smith (1978); and Wasserstein (1974). A more recent study by Beilin (1987: ch. B2), which became available after the research for this chapter was conducted, largely confirms our interpretation of British economic policy towards the Yishuv.
11. For a survey of relevant theories see Crouch (1979).
12. Wasserstein (1974) has analysed the dualism of British policy and Finegold (1978: 81–2) points to the specific problem of mobilizing Jewish economic resources.
13. Support for the foregoing interpretation of British strategy is explicitly provided by Smith (1978: 23, 380) and Finegold (1978: 50–1, 81–2, 101). The popular and scholarly Israeli perceptions of British economic policy towards the Yishuv have been clouded by the

impression of an extreme bias in fiscal redistribution from the Yishuv to the Arab population. That impression rests on the undeniable fact that the Jews furnished the majority of tax revenues while Arabs were the beneficiaries of most of the government's social expenditures. However, this bias was actually much smaller than contemporary Zionist claims suggested (Gross and Metzer, 1978; Metzer, 1982), and, if expenditures on 'infrastructural conditions' are taken into account, it may well disappear (Smith, 1978: 105–6; also Finegold, 1978: 210–13).

14. The image conveyed by Zionist propaganda of a domestic economy mercilessly exposed to international competition was therefore unfounded. However, particularly with the rise of economic nationalism in the 1930s, protection of Palestine's (Jewish) industry was indeed weak by international standards. For a review of the issue see Gross (1982: 10–16).
15. Preuss (1953: 84–5), a contemporary observer, noted the authorities' extensive use of force against strikers, adding that the legal framework was deliberately permissive of police intervention. According to Smith (1978: 286–9), it was only in order to sweeten the impact of tough prohibitions on picketing that the major pre-Second World War labour laws (cosmetic protective measures which were barely enforced) were introduced in 1927.
16. Chapters 1 and 2 discuss the Histadrut's singularity in comparative perspective at greater length, but touch only briefly on the specific issue of trade unionism. See these chapters for additional bibliographical sources.
17. As Kolatt (1973: 212) put it, 'Both of the two main parties in the Histadrut, Achdut Ha'avodah, and Hapoel Hatsair, were apprehensive of an urban wage-earning proletariat which was not bound to constructive efforts [i.e. Zionist colonization]. Not only would this damage the Zionist objective of building up their own economy, employing Jewish labour—it would create a working class with narrow trade [union] interests in which both parties foresaw the danger of a drift towards communism.'
18. Because of its characteristic sympathy for the Histadrut and the labour leadership, much of the historiography of the Israeli labour movement has passed over the resultant conflicts between the labour élite and local/rank-and-file interests. However, Anita Shapira's (1977) thorough study of the struggle for Jewish-only labour provides a number of illustrations of grass-roots rebellion. In the discussion which follows we rely on the invaluable documentation of events following the Histadrut's establishment in studies by Yitzchaki (1974) and Tsachor (1979).
19. Achdut Avodah behaved with considerable ruthlessness in this

struggle. The party unilaterally disbanded the elected local labour council and reconstituted it only after its political opponents had been weakened by: (*a*) denial of employment; (*b*) stepped-up Histadrut subsidy of party-approved local activities; and (*c*) replacement of personal candidacy by the party list system in labour council elections.

20. On the character of the Fourth Aliyah and its implications see Giladi (1973); Carmi and Rosenfeld (1971); and Shapiro (1976). Biger (1983) demonstrates the importance of British policy for the Yishuv's development.
21. According to data from Sussman (1969*a*: 119, 137), in 1922 producer co-operatives had supported half of all the Jewish unskilled labour and construction workers in Palestine. The response of the labour movement to the challenges posed by the Fourth Aliyah is also discussed in Chapter 3.
22. Tokatli (1979: 240) illustrates the Histadrut executive's doubts about its authority in the trade union arena. On the labour movement's use of coercion against local labour autonomy and militancy, note in addition to the case of the forced dissolution of the Jaffa labour council in 1922 (n. 19 above) a similar episode in Magdiel in 1931 (Tokatli, 1979: 86–7). See Goldberg (1975) and Shapiro (1976: esp. ch. 8) on the role of the local Histadrut bureaucracy in the party machine and its defence of trade union autonomy.
23. On Histadrut policy *vis-à-vis* skilled workers see Sussman (1969*a*: esp. 99–100, 111–14, 127–9, 145–7). The same author also documents the problem of opposition to binding collective agreements (pp. 87–8), the extent of unemployment among unskilled Jewish labour (pp. 90–2 and 174–5), and the constraining effect of the Histadrut's business interests on its wage policies (pp. 177–8). For more accessible summaries of this important study see Sussman (1973*a* and 1973*b*). Shapira (1977: 323), on the specific case of the citrus plantations, points to the importance, for the Histadrut, of avoiding any wage policy which would have focused attention on the wage differentials enjoyed by skilled manual labour and the Histadrut's own functionaries.
24. Our understanding of the structure and interests of capital relies heavily on the work of Biger (1983); Finegold (1978); Giladi (1965); Gross (1982); Horowitz (1948); Horowitz and Hinden (1938), and Smith (1978).
25. Data underlying the observations in this paragraph were drawn from Halevi (1979: 65); Jewish Agency (1947: esp. 291); Preuss and Nemirovsky (1931); Smith (1978: 148–9), and, on citrus, Shapira (1977: 49–51 and 153–6).

26. In January 1926 the Zionist Organization estimated that fully half of the working population of Tel Aviv was occupied in the building industry!
27. See Beilin (1987: ch. B3).
28. Broadly defined as the residual outside of agriculture, industry, and construction, the services accounted for 50–60% of product throughout the mandatory period (Halevi, 1979: 65).
29. In 1927 the government reckoned that only a dozen enterprises in all of Palestine had more than 100 workers on their payroll (Finegold, 1978: 37). A Jewish Agency inquiry conducted two years later indicated that the seven largest firms (including several which were not strictly manufacturing in character) had two-thirds as much capital invested as all the rest of Jewish industry put together (Smith, 1978: 360). The relatively advanced institutionalization of labour relations in big private firms was attested in the mid-1930s by Katznelson (1948: 364) and Ben-Gurion (Jewish Agency Labour Committee, 11 March 1936, CZA file S9/1231). Smith (1978: 318, 366) and Ussishkin (Jewish Agency Labour Committee, 30 December 1935, CZA file S9/1231) noted the employment of Arabs in some prominent large enterprises. See also the testimony of a Nesher worker in the proceedings of the 26th Histadrut Council (4–8 Oct. 1931) at page 64. UN sources reported in 1947 that by then only one big company in the Jewish sector (the potash works) employed 'mixed' labour (cited by Flapan, 1979: 198). The positive attitude of big employers towards mixed labour in earlier years, even in the wake of the 1936 Arab revolt, was noted in Chapter 3, n. 13.
30. On the size distribution of industrial establishments see Jewish Agency (1947: 221). The Histadrut's failure to penetrate the workshop sector was noted, among others, by Nemirovsky (1935). The coexistence of small- and large-scale enterprise in the industrial sector is of course relatively common in other economies, including a number of those in which corporatist industrial relations took root. However in these cases (as well as in contemporary Israel), large-scale employers participate in employers' associations (often very actively) alongside medium-sized firms. The split in employers' ranks between medium- and large-scale industry is thus the distinguishing feature of the Yishuv case.
31. There is no doubt that the relatively non-interventionist economic role of the state before the war weakened the incentive for business to develop pressure-group capacities. The exception which proves the rule is tariff policy. As Smith (1978: ch. 7) shows, the really big industrialists could deal directly with state agencies, while for others

the Zionist Executive acted as a willing intermediary, again vitiating the case for collective action.

32. The Manufacturers' Association's membership claims are contained in *Mischar veta'assiyah*, Oct. and Nov. 1932. For theories of business interest 'associability' see Jessop (1983); Streeck, Schmitter, and Martinelli (1979).
33. This analysis of the contrasts between manufacturing and construction echoes that of a speaker at a general meeting of the Jaffa/Tel Aviv Manufacturers' Association on 1 March 1925; see CZA file K11/94. The use of non-Histadrut labour has been noted by Etkin (1982: 286) and Bar-Haim (1972: 40).
34. In the period 1932–8, the citrus industry consistently accounted for at least three-quarters of Palestine's export sales (Horowitz, 1948: 64). In this respect there is an interesting contrast to be drawn with the role played by economic openness in the small West European countries (e.g. Katzenstein, 1985; Crouch, 1988). In these settings, export industries typically led the way in both the early development and the contemporary functioning of industrial relations corporatism, since both employers and workers alike were under pressure to keep labour costs in line with international competitiveness. The citrus growers of the Yishuv, however, were well aware that their best hope of keeping wages down when world market pressures rose was by replacing Jewish with Arab labour.
35. For contemporary accounts of labour relations in citrus see the observations by Greenbaum (30 Dec. 1935) and Remez (25 Feb. 1936) in CZA file S9/1231. Bar-Haim (1972: 26) notes the planters' recourse to intervention by the authorities in labour disputes.
36. Compare Abraham's (1981) analysis of Weimar Germany.
37. The instability of the economy of (Jewish) Palestine has been chronicled by Halevi (1983*a*).
38. On labour-market discrimination against women see Horowitz (1936: 22) and Bernstein (1983*a*).
39. There are interesting parallels here to the post-war Japanese setting; see the concluding chapter.
40. Contemporary sources indicate that it was common for top Histadrut and Manufacturers' Association figures to arbitrate labour disputes informally. At a general meeting in 1932, the head of the Association himself testified to the high degree of understanding between the leaders of the two sides (*Mischar veta'assiyah*, Nov. 1932, p. 19).
41. Except where otherwise stated, source material for our analysis of the wartime period was drawn from the comprehensive study by Rosen (1974). Economic conditions of the period are also discussed by Horowitz (1948); Halevi (1979); and Finegold (1978: 142–97).

42. See Chapter 3, n. 23.
43. Between 1930 and 1942, the proportion of industrial workers employed in large enterprises (more than 100 employees) rose from one-tenth to at least one-third (*Bulletin of the Economic Research Institute of the Jewish Agency*, 6(3), 1942, 44). In 1943, 47% of Jewish industrial workers were concentrated in Tel Aviv, with an additional 24% in the neighbouring Dan Region (Rosen, 1974: 60). Etkin (1982) furnishes strike statistics, while the number of organized wage-earners in manufacturing was estimated from data for 1943 in Jewish Agency (1947: 293).
44. On employer organization during wartime see Palestine Government (1943: 8–11). See Rabinowitz (1962: 54) and Levine (1985: 46–7) for commentary on changes in the interests of individual manufacturers.
45. An additional means by which the authorities attempted to buy industrial peace and prevent wage increases was by heavy subsidization of consumer essentials. Here again the state had contradictory interests. The real cause of price increases was shortages, which were due in part to London's strategic desire to pre-empt Jewish demands for stepped-up immigration (Finegold, 1978: 177–8).
46. On the cost of living agreements see Jewish Agency (1942). For a discussion of the Histadrut's Trade Union Department (later, Division) see Shirom (1983: esp. 124–6). The Department was officially founded in 1941, but began to function *de facto* the previous year (Kantor, 1966: 313).
47. See Avniel (1943: 108).
48. See Levine (1985). The British may also have been in a position to actually benefit from inflation. Levine suggests that the Palestinian market became more attractive to British commercial interests following the loss of Burma, and that their penetration of this market was facilitated by the elevated level of local prices. Economist David Horowitz told Histadrut leaders in June 1944 that the British were trying to reduce their debt to Palestine by obliging it to accept their exports at artificially high prices. See the minutes of the Histadrut Executive Committee meeting of 21 June 1944.
49. The Histadrut's surveys in 1943 and 1945 of labour conditions in Jewish industrial firms point to dramatic changes in the space of only two and a half years (Histadrut, 1945). The proportion of workers covered by written collective agreements rose from 30% to more than 80%, and there were also very large increases in the prevalence of certain negotiated protective measures (severance pay and sick pay).
50. For related discussions see Chapters 5 and 7 and the Conclusions.

51. More recently, several commentaries on the historical record have indirectly lent support to an 'institutional' (as opposed to 'political') explanation of the origins of corporatist industrial relations. Thus, Lash and Urry (1987: 233) claim that in Western Europe corporatism developed only where union movements were dominated by industry-based organizations and entwined in a partnership relation with a labour party. Therborn (1988) has similarly characterized corporatism as a corollary of the 'Germanic' type of labour movement. However, in contrast to the mechanistic associations between types of labour mobilization and forms of class accommodation, which have been the hallmark of static comparisons, both of these studies point to additional contingencies which were historically necessary to corporatism's emergence (see also Therborn, 1985).
52. The intellectual tradition which focuses more or less exclusively on organizational and political features of the labour movement began with a pioneering article by Headey (1970), and was continued by scholars such as Crouch (1985); Marks (1986); and Korpi and Shalev (1980). Marin (1985) has also called for a 'comprehensive political–economic perspective' on the basis of an analysis which, like ours, began with a paradox. In Marin's case the puzzle was Austria's transition from bloody class confrontation to elaborate class accommodation between the First and Second Republics, in spite of major institutional and political continuities. It appears that it was not so much an increase of labour's power as a sharp clipping of capital's wings that brought to life a long-dormant potential for class accommodation following the war. Some other students of corporatism have also emphasized the role of capital. See, for instance, Fulcher's (1988) account of the origins of corporatist industrial relations in Sweden, and the role of employer dis/organization in the explanations offered by Flanagan, Soskice, and Ulman (1983) for the differential potential for corporatist wage restraint in Britain and West Germany. Finally, inattention to the circumstances and motives of state intervention has been identified as a major lacuna of neo-corporatist theory by many of its critics, and even one of its founders (Schmitter, 1985: 32).
53. Obviously, these competing perceptions of the extent to which the limitations of 'authority without sovereignty' (Horowitz and Lissak, 1971) were effectively transcended are influenced by the substantive arena under study. The issue of labour restraint is perhaps understandably peripheral for scholars whose primary puzzle is how the Yishuv acquired the political and military capacity to wrest statehood from the British and the Arabs. Nevertheless, the former problem is by no means irrelevant to the latter. Jewish unity and

consensus, seen as the achievement of a 'modern' and effectively managed polity, is explicitly regarded by Horowitz and Lissak and others to have been a cornerstone of Zionism's ultimate success at state-making.

5

From Corporatism to Crisis

This chapter is concerned with the strengths, weaknesses, and enigmas of the corporatist system of industrial relations which took root in Israel after its constitution as a sovereign state in 1948. Our introduction begins with an extended footnote to the historical era surveyed in the preceding chapter, the purpose of which is to show how—within significant limits—the transition to sovereignty made possible the corporatist evolution which was sought but not realized during the Mandatory period. Because it released the inhibitions posed by the labour market and the goals, structure, and endowments of the state, sovereignty set in motion innovations which finally gave a recognizably corporatist cast to labour organization and labour relations. But, we argue, the Israeli case cannot be understood without recognizing the remarkable idiosyncrasies—from a European perspective—of the corporatism which came to inhabit Israel's landscape, and why those quirks matter.

Following this introduction to the structural features of corporatism in Israel, we turn our attention to the dynamics of political-economic mediation of labour relations, focusing on the antecedents and consequences of a single historical moment. That moment was an acute bout of unemployment, in the mid-1960s, which Michal Kalecki (1943) would have identified as a 'political business cycle'. We shall use this case-study to demonstrate that during the decade of relative labour peace which followed the transition to sovereignty, corporatism functioned as part of a broader array of state-managed restraints on labour militancy; that each one of these restraining mechanisms decomposed in the course of the economic boom which began in the late 1950s; and that the result was a multidimensional crisis to which the state chose to respond with unemployment and recession. Paradoxically, though, while in some respects the mid-1960s recession achieved the restoration of labour-market discipline, in the longer run it could not prevent, and may even have contributed to, enduring instabilities of the Israeli political economy.

After sovereignty: Corporatism's maturation and its limits

The acquisition of sovereign powers by the Jewish political centre swept aside the diminutive state capacities which had earlier crippled the potential of the Jewish national institutions to mediate a class compromise. Not only sovereignty itself, but also the state's success in using it to gain access to extensive independent resources, freed the newly constituted political centre from the severe fiscal constraints which had shackled the Mandatory government. Politically, given the Zionist character of the state and Mapai's continuing dominance, the new regime was distinctly unlike its predecessor in being indebted to and sympathetic towards the Histadrut. In equally striking contrast, the agenda of the Israeli state was set with an unabashed Jewish bias, seemingly undisturbed by contradictions between Jewish and Arab aspirations. Finally, since the Palestinian Arabs had been transformed into a small minority with virtually no influence over the state, their potential to endanger the economic interests of Jewish workers was dramatically curtailed.

The effect of these transformations was to close the historic gap between Jewish labour's dominance in the political arena and its vulnerability in the labour market. The concrete result was that the Histadrut won the monopoly over worker representation to which it had long aspired and collective bargaining finally matured into an important and more centrally constituted function. Yet the Histadrut did not perform this function in a manner directly comparable to labour organizations in the Western nations. Institutionally, union wage policy was hammered out inside Mapai, where the party mediated between its emissaries in the Histadrut and at the pinnacle of state power. Ideologically, the frame of reference embraced by Histadrut leaders was neither 'pure-and-simple' unionism nor class-wide solidarity, but the trinity of nation, state, and labour. Substantively, a variety of specific constraints prevented the Histadrut from rushing headlong into the embrace of corporatist wage restraint.

To begin with, sovereignty unleashed painful conflicts between Histadrut and state élites over the division of public functions between their two spheres. As a result, the labour organization was anxious to assert its independence from government and party dictate. At the same time, the conditions which had hampered the assertion of central authority over rank-and-file workers during the

Second World War were not wholly eliminated. Despite the high *aggregate* unemployment which prevailed during the period of mass immigration, the labour-market position of *veteran* industrial workers remained substantially sheltered from the competitive threat of cheap immigrant labour. As a result, the Histadrut was obliged to actively court their loyalty. In addition, until the breakup of Mapam in 1954 and the entry of its two successor parties into the Cabinet the following year, the left-wing opposition to Mapai formed a powerful bloc backed by over a third of the Histadrut electorate, actively contesting the principle of wage restraint. Consequently during the first few years of statehood, wage equality, class solidarity, and the defence of the workers' standard of living against inflation were the hallmarks of official Histadrut wage policy. Following the winding down of hostilities at the beginning of 1949 and urged on by Mapam, the Histadrut launched militant bread-and-butter demands backed by strikes in several large, privately owned factories.

Israel's early years were, however, rent with acute macro-economic difficulties. Under pressure from the government the Histadrut agreed to co-operate with its austerity programme by limiting national wage increases to compensation for increases in the cost of living. (Payments to individuals under productivity-boosting incentive schemes were exempt from the policy.) Notwithstanding widespread although uneven wage 'drift', the result was a *de facto* lowering of average real wages. The Histadrut contributed to the cut by choosing to ignore the authorities' blatant manipulation of the official price index and by permitting the employment of new immigrants at below union rates.[1]

Beginning in 1952, the labour organization's (actually Mapai's) declarations concerning national wage policy for the Histadrut came increasingly to emphasize 'the good of the state' and 'the needs of the economy', and mostly continued to rule out across-the-board increases in real wages. There was no easing up on this score until the second half of the 1950s, after the national emergency associated with the invasion of the Sinai Peninsula had passed. By this time the quickening pace of economic growth had enlarged the scope for wage concessions, while in the secondary labour market —where employers remained tight-fisted—the places formerly filled by veteran manual workers had been taken by weaker groups. Accordingly, there was now greater willingness to countenance blanket demands for increased real wages. However, the new demands were carefully packaged within new constraints (longer wage contracts and less frequent compensation for inflation). And to take pressure off employers, from 1958 the government decided to exempt cost-of-living increases from income taxation. Corporatism had begun the transition from austerity to prosperity.

Internally, in keeping with its aspiration for unchallenged authority in the trade union sphere, the Histadrut leadership exploited the labour organization's strengthened position after sovereignty to try and insulate it from the militancy of industrial workers. Neither recommendations that party control of trade unionism be phased out nor a long-standing commitment to establish a single national union for industrial workers were implemented. Instead, the Histadrut created an all-powerful Industrial Workers' Section staffed by party appointees inside its Trade Union Department, which fixed wages in co-operation with leaders of the Manufacturers' Association and the government's economic ministries.[2]

These organizational changes were complemented by the exercise of coercion. A measure of control over unauthorized strikes was achieved by the open or implicit threat of cutting off medical services to wildcat strikers. In several dramatic test cases where rebels were not deterred by such sanctions, the authority of the Histadrut centre in trade union matters was asserted more aggressively. Mapai also launched a vigorous counter-attack on the opposition parties' substantial foothold in union affairs at the workplace and enterprise level. Left-wing militants were ousted from their leadership of a substantial minority of the workers' committees of the veteran working class. In new-immigrant work-forces Mapai bosses were implanted as tutelary committee heads. Once in office, the party's delegates were able to use the spoils controlled by the committees—such as dispensation of loans and the power to give or withhold recommendations for promotion—in order to perpetuate their influence.[3]

As a result of these manoeuvres, the Histadrut élite and its political patrons were notably successful in the 1950s in curbing the potential for manual-worker militancy which had come to the forefront during the 1940s. But they were unable to duplicate this success among the growing number of newly militant upper-level white-collar workers in the ranks of the Histadrut. The strong labour-market position of salaried professional and managerial workers, most of them employed in the public sector, and the difficulties experienced by Mapai in co-opting them into the party's sphere of influence, formed the background to recurrent collisions between the professionals' drive for organizational autonomy and advantageous wage differentials, and the labour organization's quest for exclusive authority to represent and bargain for the entire 'working public'. The Histadrut found itself torn between fear of the professionals' secession and the danger of undermining its own legitimacy in the eyes of the less-privileged mass of its membership by capitulating to the demands of university-trained employees. After failing to suppress the professionals' revolt despite informal concessions, the labour organization attempted to salvage its authority in the wage-policy field by institutionalizing the *status quo*, and adopted a system of formalized inter-occupational wage 'linkages'. Professional workers were also granted effective autonomy from the Histadrut system of party governance and the Trade Union Department's control of national unions.[4]

Peculiarities of Israeli corporatism

The foregoing sketch of developments during Israel's first decade is indicative of an important puzzle. While changes contingent on the transition from Yishuv to statehood favoured the emergence, at last, of an authoritative national wage policy, and while the Histadrut's central leadership was genuinely committed to a national wage policy and made great strides in 'corporatizing' (centralizing and monopolizing) trade unionism, the achievement in practice of corporatist labour restraint remained incomplete and to some extent contested. Moreover, it is clear that the labour-relations regime established in Israel in the 1950s was only a partial approximation of the corporatist ideal type. Three deviations of Israeli corporatism in this period from the European variant are especially striking.[5] First, party forums played an all-pervasive (although not necessarily all-powerful) role in the determination of Histadrut policy, at times down to the tiniest details and the lowliest levels of trade union activity. Mapai was also the pre-eminent channel for resolving conflicts between the labour organization and the government. Second, employer organizations had only marginal practical significance in the corporatist wage determination process. Third, alongside the Histadrut's extraordinary measure of formal authority, in the framework of relations between the top leadership and powerful sections of the membership its standing was decidedly precarious. In the sections which follow we discuss these peculiarities and also raise two subsidiary questions. Why did the Histadrut leadership see fit to embrace a posture of restraint? And in practice, how far was labour militancy actually curtailed?

The role of Mapai.[6] Labour parties everywhere enjoy some measure of influence over the trade union wing of the labour movement. It is not so much the weight of party influence, but rather its all-embracing character that constitutes the singularity of the Israeli case in the era of Mapai hegemony. The linchpin role of the party rested in the final analysis on Mapai's absolute majority in the Histadrut polity and its organizational penetration of the entire trade union hierarchy. The party's responsibility for filling elective and appointive positions in the Histadrut and also the weight carried inside party councils by its leaders in government naturally limited the Histadrut's options, without, however, ensuring the labour organization's subordination in trade union affairs. This was after all a two-way street in that the Histadrut provided a critical service in mobilizing popular support and other resources for both the party and the government. Consequently, its officials were able to exert bargaining leverage of their own, which they were tempted to enhance by cultivating an independent following among activists and in the wider Histadrut constituency.

That it would be mistaken to regard the labour organization as having been automatically subservient to party dictate is clear from the fact that Histadrut leaders often treated party circles as the domain of choice for their policy arguments with the government. Like other interest-groups operating within the party (including Mapai's own unofficial machine), the Histadrut was anxious to preserve its autonomy from the party's emissaries in the state and consequently was by no means opposed to party mediation. Quite apart from this, it was at least tacitly understood in Mapai that in order to preserve the Histadrut's value as a political resource, its rank and file had to be persuaded that party control and the blurring of union and employer functions in the Histadrut were not seriously at odds with their own interest in improving wages and other work rewards. Had the party been overly enthusiastic in supporting the government line, the ability of Histadrut leaders to garner the requisite popular legitimacy would have been seriously impaired. In practice the party indeed tended to impose limits on what the government could demand of the Histadrut, although it was unable to prevent it from periodically introducing unilateral policy decisions as *faits accomplis*. Overall, two things made the party an effective mediator. One was its ability to put brakes on both sides against the background of their shared interest in preserving Mapai's capacity to jointly rule the Histadrut and the state. The other was the fact that this mutuality was tangibly reinforced by exchanges of specific economic and political benefits between the labour organization and the state (discussed below).[7]

The employers' role. There was evident dissonance during the 1950s between the formal status of the Manufacturers' Association as a signatory to collective wage agreements, most notably the all-important cost-of-living allowance, and its absence from the political frameworks where wage policy was actually determined. With the labour-movement and public-sector economies employing about two-fifths of the labour force, employer interests were automatically represented at the bargaining table even without the participation of organized private employers. Furthermore, given the acute dependence of large private-sector employers on state subsidy, the Manufacturers' Association learned to concentrate its efforts on extracting compensation *ex post facto* for whatever wage concessions were agreed to between Histadrut and government élites.[8]

The industrialists therefore did not challenge the Histadrut's paramountcy in the field of wage determination, and neither did they insist on bringing it on to a more tripartite footing.[9] Nevertheless, the weakness of employer interests may have been more apparent than real. Influential private employers were determined that the Histadrut's trade union arm not be tempted to exploit its organizational might to attack their vital interests, particularly in preserving the secondary labour market within low-paying segments of manufacturing. This was the chief issue at stake in several of the few major confrontations between the Histadrut and private employers since the advent of sovereignty. These contests revealed that on matters affecting its most compelling collective concerns, capital could mount effective opposition to the Histadrut.[10]

The rank and file. All corporatist labour organizations face the problem of how to ensure the compliance of the mass membership with centralization of trade union authority, and how to reconcile them to the existence of legal or practical barriers against switching allegiance to a competing organization or opting out of trade unionism altogether. Institutional checks, state support, and ideological appeals are among the forces which have been discussed in this connection in the European context.[11] In Israel in the 1950s, the overarching role of parties in Histadrut governance, the interlocking of Mapai's influence across different spheres of citizens' lives, and the intensity of members' dependence on the Histadrut's non-union functions resulted at one and the same time in a distinctive capacity for steering the rank and file *and* a dangerous potential (rendered painfully evident by the revolt of the professionals) for rejection of Histadrut authority.

It must be remembered that most Histadrut members affiliated for reasons largely extraneous to their interests as trade unionists. Moreover, only as a consequence of their membership in the peak organization were they 'assigned' to unions, and these were typically led by party appointees rather than directly elected representatives.[12] Rank-and-file dissidence was denied any outlet in conventional forms of union democracy. Where dissidence did emerge, it either built up pressures for a radical severing of ties with the Histadrut or, for those who had no realistic exit option, was channelled into the opposition parties and devolved on to workplace and enterprise workers' committees.

In the first decade of statehood, the Histadrut's problems of internal authority were still relatively manageable. Conflicts with the professionals were fierce, but only one group (secondary school teachers) actually seceded. In the domain of manual and service workers, Mapai succeeded in bringing under its wing most of the large workers' committees which had come under the sway of the left during the war. Mapam's failure in this respect must be seen in terms of the trend towards its dissipation as a militant opposition. Among the symptoms of this trend were internal fissures (climaxing with the breakaway of Achdut Avodah), the party's coalition with Mapai within the Histadrut[13] and later also the government, and the left's overall inability to seriously challenge Mapai's hegemonic blend of nationalism, militarism, and statism.

The mainsprings of self-restraint

The content of the political exchange between government and unions which took shape in Israel during the period under discussion was very different to the 'social contracts' and incomes policy 'deals' which became so central to the discussion of corporatism in Britain and Europe in the 1970s. One of the most pointed expressions of this distinctiveness is a comment by an economist, Israel's leading expert on wage determination. He once chastised the Histadrut for having endorsed the principle of wage restraint with exaggerated enthusiasm—'without trying to obtain in return . . . gains in the area of social legislation, tax policy and so forth . . . which would have repaired its image in the eyes of its members' (Sussman, 1969*b*:334). Our analysis suggests, however, that such criticism rests on the mistaken assumptions that trade unionism is the Histadrut's primary function and that the rank and file is its primary constituency. On the contrary, it is the Histadrut's uniqueness that its trade union activity coexists with economic and political purposes of great (if not greater) significance; and that Histadrut leaders must answer not only to the mass membership, but also to the parties that gave them their positions, and the managers of the labour organization's enterprises and services. Consequently, the Histadrut trades off wage concessions not only, or even mainly, in return for compensatory material benefits for the working class. What it seeks in addition are state subsidies and concessions in favour of the labour-movement economy and the Histadrut's health clinics and pension funds.[14]

Generalized exchange. In contrast to the Histadrut's labour exchanges and its responsibilities for defence and education, all of which were absorbed by the state during the first decade, the labour organization's other non-union spheres were strengthened with the state's tacit or active assistance. In this manner, the formerly decentralized credit unions were incorporated into the 'Workers' Bank'. The worker-run provident funds, established on an enterprise basis during the war, were consolidated at the national level. And the Histadrut Sick Fund was buttressed by lavish operating subsidies and by continuation into the era of mass immigration of the pre-state system of automatic enrollment of newcomers. In the background to recurrent disputation on the public stage between the Histadrut and the Treasury over how wage increases were to be connected to inflation, productivity, and the government's macro-economic policies, there developed a crucial but highly private sphere of negotiation. It was in this sphere that wage restraint was traded off for cheap loans and free land for the Sick Fund's building programme or for special regulations permitting pension contributions to be converted into low-interest financing of investments by Histadrut enterprises. No less oblique to the outward ritual of wage determination were the services rendered by the Histadrut to Mapai and the Mapai-controlled state. These included the use of the Histadrut for nurturing or placing party activists, for mobilizing party funds, and for activity in the fields of foreign policy and the control of Israel's Arab minority.[15]

It is in the context of such labyrinthine trade-offs that an important aspect of the transition to statehood becomes interpretable from the vantage point of corporatist theory. One of the sources of diversity of real-world corporatisms is the scope of political exchange between trade union and state élites. In this respect a pointed contrast may be drawn between the pinnacle of corporatist experience in the Mandatory period during World War II and developments after sovereignty was attained. Paradoxically, the most institutionally visible corporatist compacts—of which the trade-offs between the Histadrut and the government of Palestine in the early 1940s are a good example—may well be the least substantial and enduring. In contrast, more covert and diffuse transactions—exemplified by what took place within the Histadrut/party/state nexus in post-statehood Israel—come closer to the ideal of concertation between state and society which has always been the special vision of corporatist thought. It is no accident that in this respect, as in several others, the closest referent to the Israeli experience among advanced capitalist societies is Austria. Theoreticians inspired by the Austrian case have employed the concept of *generalized political exchange* to signify the participation of organized interests in a far-flung network of policy trade-offs which does not depend on formal structures of incorporation into the state or explicit delegation of its authority.[16] The distinction between corporatism as a discrete form of barter, and as 'generalized political exchange', nicely underscores the limitations of Israel's pre-sovereignty experience in comparison with what followed.

Is restraint effective? Economists and economic observers of different theoretical and political stripes have presented dramatically opposing views of the Histadrut's influence on aggregate wage developments. Critics have claimed that the Histadrut's allegedly rigid defence of protective mechanisms has *pushed* inflation forward on the cost side and has stymied attempts to make Israel more internationally competitive. In this view, practices like the automatic adjustment of wages to price increases and the principle of job tenure for 'permanent' employees have prevented productivity increases and nullified the dampening effect of devaluations on comparative wage costs. More sympathetic experts maintain, however, that wage–price linkage through the COLA (cost-of-living allowance) is no more than a transmission belt *pulled* by pre-existing inflationary pressures on the demand side. They point out that if actual wage increases had been confined solely to the COLA and the Histadrut's official pay targets, then for much of Israel's history real wages would have been on a trend of stagnation or decline.[17]

The issue of whether wage restraint works in Israel has been subjected to sophisticated empirical scrutiny, but with mixed results.[18] The most robust findings are the least controversial ones: that wage increases have been modulated by supply and demand, on the one hand, and by the presence or absence of war-induced national unity on the other. It appears that at times of low unemployment, when there is no influx of cheap labour into the market, and/or when national security pressures are not compelling, the Histadrut's attempts to hold down aggregate wage demands have been vitiated by powerful wage drift. The real question, however, is what market forces would have done to wages *in the absence* of the Histadrut's commitment to wage restraint. It can be confidently argued in this connection, that the pattern of industrial relations which developed during the 1950s effectively pre-empted a number of counter-factual scenarios which could have transformed the labour organization into a more militant force.

In principle, the Histadrut might have used its organizational power solidaristically in the interests of the relatively powerless workers in the secondary labour market or, alternatively, left the field completely open to unco-ordinated activity by unions and workers' committees. Instead, despite a programmatic commitment to solidarism, the Histadrut's policies and practices made important contributions to labour-market segmentation. Moreover, at least in the 1950s, it was also successful in forestalling unbridled recourse to work stoppages. Strike statistics for the period indicate a low rate of worker involvement in disputes (only 60 per cent of the level which prevailed during the decade prior to sovereignty) and a very low proportion (only 10 per cent) of disputes lacking Histadrut authorization. This relatively high level of centralized labour discipline was, however, very unevenly spread. We have already seen how different constituencies within the labour organization have always enjoyed substantially different degrees of organizational autonomy and bargaining power. The Histadrut's readiness, and its capacity, to exert restraint have also fluctuated quite considerably in the course of time, reflecting external shifts from prosperity to depression, from war to peace, or from strong to weak governments.

It is precisely this element of historical contingency, at a particular phase in Israel's development, which it is the task of this chapter to illuminate. But before proceeding with that task, let us summarize the core features of post-sovereignty Israeli corporatism indicated by the preceding discussion.

1. The ruling labour-movement party (Mapai) played an exceptionally vital role. Although by no means the Histadrut's absolute ruler, in spite of its remarkable formal powers, the party's penetration of the labour organization was all-pervasive, and it was often able to mediate effectively between Histadrut and government élites.
2. Organized business interests were excluded from key processes of wage determination. Nevertheless, this was a reflection not so much of the impotence of business as its ability to rely on the paternalism of the state and its own determination to repel rare instances of Histadrut aggression.
3. Wage restraint developed as only one strand of a complex web of generalized exchange binding the Histadrut and the state. The labour organization therefore had powerful motives to exercise trade union discipline which were unrelated to the welfare of

workers. Nevertheless, as a result of internal contradictions, the Histadrut's practical capacity to deliver labour restraint was inherently limited.

4. The paradox which limited the Histadrut's authority was that the very forces which served to buttress its influence over the membership—organizational centralization, party control, and compelling material incentives—also had the effect of endangering its legitimacy and forcing rank-and-file protest into potentially destabilizing channels.

Corporatism and full employment

The emergence or revival of corporatist labour restraint in Western Europe during the post-war period took the characteristic form of commitments by trade union peak associations to voluntary wage restraint. These commitments were made in the framework of active participation by labour élites in making and legitimating the economic policies of the state. Full employment was the universal accompaniment to such developments, both as pre-condition and as consequence.

At first unemployment remained low only in the few nations in which America's conservative influence was limited and where democracy and working-class mobilization were already well developed by the 1930s and remained intact during the war. But from the mid-1950s labour-market conditions tightened throughout the Western nations as a result of conditions in the world economy favourable to sustained domestic expansion. In some settings, strong unions responded with wage pressures which squeezed profits and amplified the balance-of-payments problems of open economies. An alternative development, union engagement in corporatist self-restraint, was characteristic of those contexts where collective bargaining was highly centralized, the legal framework and the organizational structure of unions favoured the authority of union élites, and the labour movement had no ideological objection to co-operation with employers and the state. In effect, labour leaders agreed to boost profits by trading off wages for jobs. The most likely alternative was that declining investment and the state's refusal to sponsor growth-inducing macro-economic policies would reintroduce unemployment and, in consequence, force workers to accept involuntary wage restraint.[19]

In the wake of the severe economic difficulties which beset the Western nations in the 1970s there was a surge of interest in 'social-contract' solutions to distributional problems, and much admiration was expressed for the left-wing regimes which were apparently the most favourably disposed to produce such solutions. Nevertheless, many social-democratic parties suffered political setbacks and ran into severe fiscal constraints in paying for corporatist bargains in the post-1973 era. The acute trade-offs imposed by economic stagnation and a relatively hostile international economy raised similar doubts about corporatism's stability, to which was added the possibility that corporatism might in fact plant the seeds of its own disintegration. It could be argued that the maintenance of full employment, its most coveted achievement, also increased the risk of union leaders being challenged from below by rank-and-file workers unwilling to accept the burden of restraint in the face of labour market conditions favourable to their bargaining power. In this event, politically and organizationally mediated limits on labour militancy might well be obliged to defer to, or cohabit with, the discipline of the market—that is, renewed unemployment.[20]

The Israeli case

Israel provides an especially interesting context for examining relationships between social democracy, corporatism, and full employment. The protracted political dominance of the Labour Party and the Histadrut's exaggeratedly corporate structure resonate strongly with the expectation, grounded in two decades of cross-national research, that long-term social democratic rule together with trade union unity and centralization, favour a full-employment policy regime founded on corporatist political exchange.[21] Moreover, as we have already seen, the specific historical circumstances surrounding the conversion of what had been a binational community ruled by imperial Britain into a primarily Jewish national state, point in the same direction. In this light it is conspicuously anomalous to encounter in the mid-1960s a period of recession and mass unemployment in the midst of nearly two decades of rapid economic growth and an even longer era of full employment.

It is true that unemployment in Israel was already high (around 10 per cent) in the early years of statehood. But this was a trying period of massive expansion of the labour force through immigration. Beginning in the mid-1950s joblessness began to decline, and from the introduction of regular Labour Force Surveys in 1958 until the middle of the 1980s, the annual unemployment rate almost never exceeded 6 per cent. Typically, it fluctuated between 3 and 4 per cent—a low level considering the relatively depressed conditions on the country's economic periphery. The sharp deviation which afflicted the economy in the mid-1960s was officially designated as a period of *Mitun* or 'moderation'. But beginning in the autumn of 1966 unemployment reached double-digit levels which persisted for a whole year. Recovery began only in the wake of belated expansionary policies initiated in response to growing citizen unrest, and was unexpectedly consolidated by the economic consequences of the Arab–Israeli war of June 1967.

Contrary to theoretical expectations the leadership of the ruling Mapai Party and the Histadrut expressly and enthusiastically embraced unemployment as a policy instrument. We propose to unravel this apparent paradox with the help of an extended political economy perspective which goes beyond simplistic assumptions about the affinity between social-democratic corporatism and full employment. Two features of our approach, already previewed in Chapter 4, are especially relevant in this connection. First, we insist on identifying the national and historical characteristics and the contradictions of the *specific context* under study, rather than remain at the level of an abstract ideal type. Second, we emphasize the *strategic logic underlying the behaviour* of the cabinet ministers and upper-echelon bureaucrats responsible for the rise of mass unemployment. Their intention, we suggest, was not only to alter the terms of distributional conflict between labour and capital, but also to address acute political and organizational problems of the labour movement. And, in the process, to effect a fundamental restructuring of the political economy in order to establish a more viable pattern of politically steered economic growth.

The discussion which follows is divided into several parts. We shall turn first to the full employment norm which prevailed in Israel from the late 1950s until the Mitun, asking what it was that made full employment possible, desirable, and for the most part, also manageable. This is followed by an analysis of the crisis which stimulated the mid-1960s recession, in which the argument is developed that the Mitun can be interpreted as rational, problem-solving behaviour by the state. Finally, we shall assess the extent to which the labour-market goals set by the architects of the Mitun were achieved in practice, and speculate on the longer-term repercussions of the recession and its theoretical implications.

Full employment as a structural predisposition

There is a structural bias towards full employment in Israel's political economy. Crucial *national* and *geopolitical* features of the Israeli context have generated motives and resources capable of offsetting inherent economic weaknesses. Among these long-term infirmities we may cite: (*a*) relative poverty of natural resources; (*b*) the limited size of the domestic market and the existence of political barriers to penetration of regional markets; (*c*) a comparatively modest industrial base characterized by predominantly small-scale operations and a lack of international comparative advantage in most sectors; (*d*) substantial dependence on imports for (in changing proportions) basic consumption goods, production inputs, and military *materiel*; and (*e*) Israel's relative unattractiveness to foreign investors due to geopolitical instability, direct pressure by Arab states, high labour costs compared with other peripheral economies, and the small local market.

In view of these handicaps, Israel would at first sight appear an unlikely candidate for full employment, especially since the state could not and would not adopt an authoritarian strategy of labour repression in order to attract foreign corporate investment. Nevertheless, since Israel's establishment in 1948, as well as during the preceding era of colonization, unemployment has been viewed by élite figures as inimical to fulfillment of the Zionist programme. Particular fears have been voiced concerning its implications for the flow of Jews into and out of the country. Thus, joblessness has always been seen as a dangerous disincentive for Jewish citizens to desert Israel. Similarly, in periods of substantial actual or potential immigration, rapid employment growth has been regarded as essential to the economic absorption of newcomers. These perceptions are also built on the importance of sheer numbers for staffing the citizens' army and regulating the demographic and territorial balance between Jewish and Arab Israelis. They relate as well to the fact that the legitimacy of the Israeli state is closely bound to its demonstrated ability to provide a viable Jewish 'national home'. Not surprisingly, then, there is no political debate in Israel regarding the desirability of full employment as a policy aspiration.

Moreover, since the 1970s potentially explosive socio-economic cleavages, and a strongly competitive political climate to which ethnic inequality among Jews is highly salient, have made governments acutely aware of the social and political costs of unemployment. Despite all this, it was by no means inevitable that the political aspiration for full employment would be converted into an economic reality. For the missing links we must look to several other distinctive features of the Israeli setting.[22]

Ramifications of the geopolitical context. It might have been assumed that Israel's enormous military commitments would necessarily have drained the resources necessary for creating and maintaining jobs. However, prior to 1967 direct defence costs—at no more than a tenth of GNP except in the year of the Sinai campaign—were a relatively manageable constraint on a growing economy. Since then, this burden has grown to reach a modal level of about one quarter of the national product. Yet the cost of the sizeable import component of increased defence expenditures has been met by foreign aid. Spiralling domestic military spending following the wars of 1967 and 1973 was largely financed by raising taxes and running deficits, rather than by macro-economic policies which would have precipitated unemployment.[23]

The Arab–Israeli conflict has other profound consequences for the political economy besides its fiscal dimensions. Two of these are especially relevant to the issue of full employment. First, Arab–Israeli hostility has provided an ideological foundation for establishing severe limitations on the social, political, and economic activities of the Palestinian Arabs under Israel's jurisdiction. As we saw in Chapter 2, the subordination and dependence (in different ways) of Arab citizens and the inhabitants of the occupied territories have been of particular importance for the formation of a flexible Palestinian work-force occupying the least favourable positions in the labour market. One other very significant implication of Israel's character as a 'nation in arms' is the role of the army and the wider military economy as sources of employment. In fact the influence of the armed forces alone is so substantial that for Jewish prime-aged men in the mid-1980s, soldiering accounted for the equivalent of one-sixth of the effective labour force. In addition, military procurement from the business sector coupled with the extremely rapid growth in military-related exports, which procurement helped to stimulate, were responsible for the lion's share of job creation in the industrial economy between the 1967 and 1983 wars.[24]

International economic relations. The condition of permanent geo-political tension between Israel and its neighbours has contributed greatly to both the need for foreign aid and its 'production'. The latter has also benefited from the sympathy which Israel evokes among world Jewry and the claims Israel is able to make on other nation-states (especially Germany) as the political objectification of the Jewish people. In addition, for the last several decades the strategic implications for American interests of Israel's position in the Middle East and the opportunity to exploit Israel and the conflict as a proving-ground and a dumping-ground for US armaments, have triggered heavy American involvement in weapons sales and their funding. The joint effect of these factors has been large-scale inflows of financial capital—'unilateral transfers' (gifts) and long-term loans—which have made it possible to sustain Israel's persistent trade deficit. While both the forms and the sources of capital inflows have varied over time, direct foreign investment—particularly that part which is not disguised charity—has typically constituted only a minor component. And despite the fact that the value of exports relative to imports has risen in the long-term, absolute expansion of imports and a rising burden of debt service have prevented any secular decline in Israel's dependence on outside economic assistance.[25] But in the context of this dependence the Israeli economy was historically able to sustain levels of investment, and therefore employment, far in excess of domestically generated resources.

The engines of economic growth. The roots of the long cycle of economic growth which began in 1954 and ended with the Yom Kippur War in 1973 were, in varying combinations at different times, capital inflow, mass immigration, military-industrial activity, and territorial expansion—all corollaries of the particular features of the Israeli setting reviewed above. The first growth-inducing factor, capital inflow, had a variety of impacts. Transfers to and by individuals helped feed consumer demand, but even more notable was the stimulation effected by the state's redistribution of its own foreign income. This took innumerable forms, including subsidies to producers and consumers, direct and indirect public employment, and large-scale expenditures on economic development and immigrant absorption. Acting as a channel for domestic savings and imported capital alike, the state also dominated the private-sector investment process.

The second key ingredient of rapid growth was the mass Jewish immigration of the first decade of statehood, during which the population increased two and a half times. In the product market, newcomers injected demand for basic consumer goods and services, notably construction. Those immigrants who entered the labour market, in particular men of non-European origin, provided a ready-made and relatively (to veterans) cheap labour force when rapid construction and industrialization efforts commenced around the mid-1950s. Moreover, the burdens of mass immigration provided an essential basis for appeals to foreign philanthropy.

Third is Israel's territorial expansion which has taken place both internally and externally. Particularly in the first decade, there were large-scale state take-overs of land formerly or currently occupied by Arabs. This appropriation provided a substantial basis for extending economic activity in agriculture and construction. Later, the economic benefits of Israel's occupation of added territory were coupled with rapid expansion of its military economy. This was the major new ingredient in the growth process after the Six Day War (1967).

Buffers against the consequences of declining unemployment

At the end of roughly the first five years of Israeli sovereignty, as these engines of growth began to operate, there indeed followed a pronounced trend towards full employment. The economy entered a phase of remarkable expansion, in which for more than a decade there were very large annual gains in per capita GNP. Correspondingly unemployment fell progressively, from an estimated 11.5 per cent in 1953 to only 3.5 per cent by 1961. This low level was maintained or even bettered during the five years which led up to the recession of 1966–7.

As Kalecki (1943) and other observers pointed out at the dawn of the post-war period, a transition to sustained full employment like that which occurred in Israel around the late 1950s and early 1960s could be expected to alter fundamentally power relations in the labour market between workers and employers, causing erosion of both profit shares and managerial authority. Nevertheless, there were political–economic mechanisms operating in the Israeli setting which counteracted the augmentation of labour's power and militancy normally associated with full employment and protected the interests of employers and private investors. One of these mechanisms, corporatist labour restraint, was discussed at length early in this chapter. We now introduce two additional buffers against the destabilizing consequences of declining unemployment: state subsidy and labour market segmentation.

Patterns of state subsidy

The state, it may fairly be said, exerted enormous influence over the very construction of Israel's systems of stratification and distribution—by creating investment and jobs, by allocating individuals (especially newcomers) to positions in the economic and political structure, and by fixing living standards. This influence in turn stemmed from its access to extensive foreign grants and loans on the one hand, and the weakness of both private capital and a large segment of the citizenry (the newcomers) on the other.

From the outset, there were strong biases in the way the state managed these activities. Those who were ethnically, temporally (in terms of arrival), and politically closest to the labour-movement élite enjoyed definite advantages. That this was true for the veteran working class which led the state-building effort is not surprising. But there was also an enduring split within the post-sovereignty mass migration along 'Eastern' (Middle Eastern/North African) versus 'Western' (European and American) lines. This had to do with the fact that a larger proportion of the Westerners enjoyed independent means and/or ties (cultural, familial, organizational) with the pre-statehood Jewish population and were not handicapped by being perceived as 'primitive' and culturally alien. Like members of the veteran working class, the more advantaged elements (primarily Western) among the new immigrants were offered privileged routes of entry into the Israeli economy. These included mobility into skilled and supervisory jobs in the business sector, the opening up of managerial and professional positions in expanding public bureaucracies, and a strengthening of the *petite bourgeoisie* and bourgeoisie in response to consumer and state demand.[26]

Employers, who in theory stood to lose most from full employment, were handsomely compensated by protected markets, access to cheap credit and machinery, and a variety of other forms of state subsidy. The occupants of entrepreneurial, managerial, and other well-remunerated positions were thereby freed of the obligation to convert their profits/incomes into the savings normally necessary to capital formation.[27] The state also made available subsidies to private consumption, to the benefit of the Jewish working class. New immigrants were provided (often with political strings attached) with the basic means of existence, which helped persuade many of them to accept marginal locations in the spatial, economic, and political systems—thus protecting vital interests of the state and the ruling party, and their veteran supporters. The state thus succeeded in simultaneously creating stratificational disparities and easing distributional conflicts.

But by the same token, the problems of full employment were primarily *problems for the state*. The more that labour was protected from market forces and employer discipline, the greater the cost of subsidizing business and the greater the dependence on outside support to finance this generosity. And the more that workers were allowed to become independent of labour-market dictates, the harder it was to sustain both their material dependence on the ruling party and the territorial and economic roles assigned to them in state-building strategies. Nevertheless, these effects were mitigated for a time by institutional mechanisms—specifically, the confinement of marginal groups to the secondary labour market and the corporatist response of politically-engineered labour restraint.

Labour-market segmentation

The literature on dual or segmented labour markets posits the existence of qualitatively distinct clusters of job locations between which there is little worker mobility.[28] A distinction is typically posited between mirror-image 'primary' and 'secondary' labour markets, with the latter consisting of jobs characterized by instability of occupancy, low pay, limited intra-organizational career prospects, and lack of institutionalized job rights. The empirical relevance of such a perspective to the Israeli job structure in the period under discussion is suggested by evidence of wide gaps in wages and employment stability—between large and small enterprises, and also within enterprises—between 'temporary' and 'permanent' employees. There has also been a clear and persistent demarcation between economically sheltered places of employment in the Histadrut and state-owned sectors, and the more exposed and smaller-scale private sector. Finally, interaction between this dual structure and the social division of labour is strongly suggested by systematic ethnic and gender inequalities in access to the job hierarchy and job rewards.[29]

Particularly striking in this connection was the fact that industrialization and economic growth were accompanied in the labour market by a strong bias towards assigning Eastern Jewish newcomers to less skilled, less rewarding, and less secure jobs. Without the protection of severance pay, in the absence of reliable and adequate citizen entitlements to income replacement, and given their characteristic poverty and disorganization on arrival in Israel, the Easterners were especially vulnerable *vis-à-vis* both employers and the state. Furthermore, their labour-market marginality was often tied up with and reinforced by spatial marginality, especially for the many Easterners who ended up in 'development towns' planted in outlying areas.[30] But while the Jewish ethnic division in the labour market was certainly conspicuous, the economic position of Israel's Arab population was still more precarious. Most Palestinian citizens were effectively barred from working in Jewish areas until the labour market had accommodated the bulk of the new immigrants, in the late 1950s. Subsequently, a limited range of unskilled and poorly paying job slots (initially in construction and agriculture) opened up to Arabs willing to commute from their towns and villages to the Jewish economy.[31]

The existence of secondary sector jobs held by socially disadvantaged groups made important contributions to protecting employer profitability, and to sustaining the privileges enjoyed by workers in the primary sector. Labour-market segmentation performed more than a distributive function, however. It also helped meet important state objectives. In the case of Arabs, employment in the proletarian jobs on offer from Jewish employers served to ease the economic pressure generated by confiscation of much of their agricultural lands and to cement their fate to that of the state by making them dependent on the Jewish economy. Labour-market marginalization of Eastern Jews neutralized the competitive threat which they potentially posed to the veteran working class, but the Easterners were not left to the mercy of the market alone. The ruling party was able to help forestall challenges to its legitimacy in the eyes of the Easterners by providing for their minimal consumption needs in return for electoral loyalty. In the development towns, where jobs were insecure as well as scarce, unemployed men were offered relief work—to keep them in place (to further the objective of dispersing Jews territorially) and to keep them in the habits of manual labour (for the developing industrial economy).

The origins of the mid-1960s crisis

Our case so far has rested on three arguments about why full employment was workable in its early stages. First, the manner in which the state managed and participated in economic development provided powerful and privileged groups—including business—with substantial material and social gains. This helped foreclose the emergence of serious distributive conflicts, which might otherwise have been provoked by the advantages of declining unemployment for even the less-privileged sections of the working class. Second, the potential bargaining power of the weaker groups of workers, and hence the profitability of weak sectors of the economy, were regulated by labour-market segmentation. Third, the Histadrut lent its corporatist endorsement to freezes and other forms of wage restraint, nominally on the grounds of its responsibility to the national economy and respect for party authority, and substantively in return for institutional and economic power. The irony is, though, that as the 1950s came to a close, with abundant evidence that the state's strategies for creating and managing full employment had proven their efficacy, these same strategies began to fail as their external pre-conditions weakened or internal contradictions came to the fore. The problems thus confronted were not limited to the sphere of industrial relations. They also concerned the political–economic mechanisms which had hitherto provided the material basis for full employment, and particularly the paternalistic role of the state.

Limits of the paternalistic growth model

The state's role as a motor of economic expansion had been threefold: as the source of tremendous direct and indirect demand;

as provider of diffuse subsidies which promoted a favourable environment for business generally; and as the author of selective incentives designed to stimulate the production of exports and import substitutes, and the flow of private (especially foreign) investment. For the state to sustain the massive scale of these activities as consumer, investor, and subsidizer it needed both the special policy problems of the 1950s (population expansion) and a hard currency income sufficient to cover the bill. In the early 1960s these exogenous prerequisites began to evaporate. Aliyah (Jewish immigration) fell sharply in 1964 and 1965, and there was little prospect of any large-scale exodus from the Diaspora in the foreseeable future. Meanwhile, unilateral transfers and long-term loans—on which the state relied for cheap capital inflow—had reached a plateau. And two of the most attractive sources (US aid and German reparations) were scheduled to dry up altogether.

The alarm bell rang when the trade deficit twice experienced a 30 per cent jump, in 1962 and again in 1964.[32] Even though revenue from exports had risen by the 1960s, it was still equivalent to only half the cost of imports. It became necessary to resort to short-term loans or to dip into foreign exchange reserves in order to fill the gap. The trade crisis served notice on policy-makers of the inadequacy of their past efforts to foster an industrial economy with import-saving and export-augmenting biases. In general, industry was inefficient and overcapitalized (to no small extent as a result of the state's generosity), under-competitive internationally (in part because of the dual policy of domestic protection and export subsidy), and unwilling to fight to retrench labour costs (since the state gave its backing to the power of workers in the primary labour market while also making good to employers the costs of conceding to their demands).

An economic system which, regardless of formal ownership, was nurtured and protected by the state could evidently not operate cost-efficiently. Moreover, it imposed distinct liabilities on the state. Among those noted by contemporary observers were: demands for bail-outs when managerial incompetence threatened jobs, pressure on state planners to grant incentives not justified by declared national priorities, the failure of most firms to honour commitments given in exchange for export subsidies, and a tendency for only the weakest industries to locate in the outlying areas where public subsidy was greatest. With both private and

Histadrut investment dependent mainly on government-directed credits and grants, rather than on the (very limited) capital market or on reinvestment of undistributed profits, economic growth was painfully unable to sustain itself. The labour élite had long recognized this weakness, but pinned its hopes on attracting overseas (especially Jewish) investors. Little came of this until the first half of the 1960s, when direct foreign investment surged to a quarter and more of the level of unilateral transfers. In 1965, however, net foreign investment fell by half, just at the point when it was needed most. The desire to restore and enhance its role undoubtedly helped to shape the new economic strategy behind the slowdown.[33]

The rise of labour in the market

Israeli economic observers in the early 1960s were universally distressed by the growth of strikes, absenteeism, 'unco-operative attitudes', and the workers' steadfast holding to established protective devices (seniority provisions, job tenure, the COLA).[34] These practices were seen as undermining the prospects for export-led growth by pushing labour costs above those of Israel's competitors and preventing more productive allocation of labour. This critique is sustained by data on labour costs in industry which show that their rate of growth intensified between 1955–60 and 1960–5. Prior to the 1960s wages had been restrained while government subsidies simultaneously kept profit rates high. In contrast, in the first half of the new decade 'wage increases accelerated while the growth of the profit rate slackened off' (Gaathon, 1971*a*: 115). By 1964 the capacity of employers to counteract wage push by raising productivity was exhausted.

These developments accord well with Kalecki's prediction that sustained full employment would result in profit squeeze and eroding employer control of the labour process. However, not only the direct effects of declining unemployment were at work here, but also the failure of the other mechanisms which in the past had operated alongside job scarcity to restrain labour militancy, namely, labour-market segmentation and corporatist industrial relations. The main source of the weakening of the first of these two buffers was that various groups of Eastern Jews, predominantly males, had been drifting out of the secondary labour market. This exodus took several forms. Some secondary locations—notably in the construction industry—became characterized by labour shortages, high pay, and opportunities to move into self-employment. In addition, there were sections of the new-immigrant working class, mainly in industry, which began to utilize independent collective action at the work-place level, successfully demanding the benefits of the primary market. Still others left the proletarian labour pool by entering clerical and service jobs at the lower levels of the expanding public bureaucracies. Finally, particularly in the development towns and on the urban periphery, there emerged a kind of lumpenproletariat on the margins of conventional labour markets or totally outside them.

The last of these trends was in part the consequence of expanded welfare state provision targeted to disadvantaged Eastern Jews, particularly following a serious outbreak of urban slum riots before the 1959 elections. The problem of rejection of secondary jobs also became more acute with the emergence of an Israeli-born generation led to expect upward mobility by the ideology of integration propagated by the schools, the army, and other organs of the state. It is true that stepped-up participation of other socially marginal groups (non-Jews, women, the aged, the handicapped) to some extent offset the diminution of the labour pool which had hitherto manned the secondary labour market. But many of the newcomers were 'misallocated'. Most of the Arabs (virtually all men) entering the labour force were drawn into construction, and the sharpest growth in female employment was in service jobs. Apparently the industrial economy's preference for secondary labour intensified over the period, but was increasingly unsatisfied. The manufacturers responded with a recommendation to transfer unemployed workers from the development towns to the prosperous centre of the country. A plan to import foreign 'guest workers' was also floated. But for a combination of political and technical reasons, neither of these solutions was feasible in the 1960s.[35]

The challenge to corporatism

The Histadrut's centralized structure and multi-level politicization, built up so assiduously during Israel's first decade, were severely undermined during the second. In a context in which labour organization and representation were organized from above by a leadership which repeatedly preached restraint to its captive audience, full employment gave a tremendous boost to processes of grass-roots self-organization. Quantitatively, this was translated into a 150 per cent increase in the number of workers' committees between 1960 and 1965. Concurrently, direct party control of the committees disintegrated. By 1964, more than 80 per cent of Histadrut members reported non-partisan elections in their places of work. There remained settings—such as Histadrut-owned enterprises or localities with strong, co-ordinated municipal and Histadrut machines—where the party retained a virile and explicit presence. But even in these cases, pressure from below obliged Mapai's delegates either to defy Histadrut wage policy themselves or to see it challenged by an alternative form of work-place representation, the 'Action Committee'. Wage drift in the form of supplements negotiated by workers' committees was rife, especially in large factories. And there was a veritable upsurge of rank-and-file militance. The proportion of strikes lacking Histadrut authorization rose from 25 per cent in 1960 to an average of 60 per cent during the remaining full-employment years. And while the overall volume of industrial conflict remained unchanged, there was a major decline in the duration of disputes which augured a lasting change in Israel's strike profile.[36]

Another revealing feature of the new conflicts is that they were increasingly directed towards Mapai's own dominion—that is, the Histadrut and state sectors of employment. The unrest among public employees was sparked both by the issue of equity between sectors (because of the greater effectiveness of wage freezes in the public service), and inter-occupational differentials (professional and managerial workers continued to complain that the pay structure was far too flat). Unions of university-trained employees had long since become proficient at using their relative advantage in the labour market and the threat of secession from the Histadrut, in order to openly challenge official wage policy. The government was especially susceptible to their pressure, since it was anxious not to alienate the professionals politically and was not insensitive to the wishes of its senior bureaucrats.[37]

These inter- and intra-sectoral grievances accumulated, and by the early 1960s the government faced the wrath of both contending groups in its employ—the large mass of clerical and manual workers, and the managerial and professional élite. An attempt to devolve the responsibility on to a commission of inquiry bequeathed a reform mechanism ('Reclassification Committees') which sanctioned very high pay increases for workers in the non-professional grades. Not to be outdone, the 'academicians' won promises to restore their former advantages. The result was a massive increase in the public-sector wage bill, due to stretch over 1965–6, which placed a weighty new burden on the fiscal system. The affair clearly exposed the inherent weakness of a centralized system of wage determination in the absence of effective Histadrut control over members with their own power base.

The politics of full employment

Students of Israeli politics generally agree that the most important reason for Mapai's initial success in attracting the loyalty of the Eastern Jews who arrived during the post-1948 influx, was their material dependence on the bounties of the Mapai/Histadrut machine. However, by the 1960s most of the newcomers had acquired the necessities of life, economic growth had opened up opportunities for their autonomous advancement, an indigenous leadership was developing (especially in local politics), and public agencies were more accessible to their claims. These circumstances gelled with the enhanced work-place power that went along with full employment to generate a rank-and-file revolt which for the first time encompassed ordinary workers. It was hardly surprising that Mapai's economic ministers felt powerless to prevent the wage explosion of 1965–6, considering that the demands were raised in the shadow of forthcoming elections which were absolutely critical to the party's future. In the balloting for the 1965 Histadrut elections, held six weeks prior to elections for the Knesset (parliament), the right-wing Gachal (forerunner of the Likud) gained an opening wedge into the Histadrut polity, and Mapai barely managed to sustain its traditional majority. The party saved itself from still greater losses only by concluding a pre-election alliance with Achdut Avodah, a former rival on the left.[38]

Among the political factors which had facilitated Mapai's prolonged hegemony were the party's strong leadership and tight internal organization, the weakness and fragmentation of the opposition parties on the right, and Mapai's success (particularly in the Histadrut) in co-opting the parties immediately to its left. All but the last of these props had weakened considerably by the time of the 1965 round of elections. Mapai was still suffering the after-effects of a fierce and protracted leadership struggle, which as much as anything else hinged on opposing positions on two issues: whether the party should continue to rely on the Histadrut as its principal power base and how to check the erosion of Histadrut authority and its politically and economically destabilizing consequences.[39] When Ben-Gurion and a coterie of ambitious younger men lost their bid to strip the labour organization of most of its functional and political importance, and also proved unable to prevent Mapai's leftward confederation with Achdut Avodah, they broke away to form *Rafi*. Meanwhile the opposition to the right of Mapai had been greatly strengthened when Menahem Begin's Cherut Party joined with the pro-bourgeois Liberals to create Gachal. Rafi and Gachal both denounced the existing structure of labour representation. Independently, they called for depoliticization and internal democratization of the Histadrut, transfer of its non-union functions to the state, and statutory controls over labour disputes. Israel's corporatist arrangements were thus condemned not only to suffer the penalties of their own shortcomings, but also to come under attack in the parliamentary arena.

In spite of the blows which Mapai suffered during the run-up to the Knesset elections, the results ironically strengthened its capacity to govern in the face of the gathering political–economic storm. While the Labour Alignment's constituent parties forfeited five of their former fifty seats, the sponsoring parties of the new bloc on the right lost even more ground (not only to Rafi but also to the 'Independent' Liberal Party formed in protest against the Gachal alliance). Nevertheless, the new-found unity of the two biggest right-wing parties helped to encourage the opposition parties to Mapai's left to drop much of their traditional anti-Mapai demeanour. Achdut Avodah formalized this transition in its Alignment with Mapai, while Mapam—perhaps anticipating following suit at a later date—had already dropped its usual contestational stance prior to the elections, and stood ready to join the Cabinet. Under these circumstances Mapai's Levi Eshkol was able to put together a government enjoying such broad support that it faced only a 41-seat opposition (out of 120 Knesset seats in all). The state's economic managers were now in a position to contemplate the pursuit of unpopular policies with relative equanimity.

Recession as problem-solving behaviour

We have seen that full employment gave expression to, and aggravated, decay of the mechanisms by which the state and the ruling party had become accustomed to preserve political and economic stability. Under circumstances in which organized labour was able to push costs upwards and resist attempts to raise productivity, and in which the supply of cheap marginal labour was insufficient or at risk, the weakness of state-subsidized capitalism became strikingly evident. The problem was particularly acute because 'hard' means of meeting external obligations (exports and direct investment) were insufficient to compensate for declining 'soft' sources of capital inflow. Moreover, immigration could no longer be expected to act as a catalyst to growth.

But the developing crisis was not only related to the state indirectly, because of its responsibilities for steering the economy. It also encompassed the state's administration of its own economic affairs—particularly, the high cost of simultaneously subsidizing capitalists and trying to buy political popularity through wage increases, in a context of diminishing inter-governmental transfers. Beyond this, the labour movement's political élite was forced to confront the damage done by full employment and the party and voter realignments of the mid-1960s to the power of the Histadrut and Mapai's control over the Histadrut—the pillars of the party's capacity to mobilize mass support and govern the political economy.

The essence of the slow-down policy was a two-pronged response to these problems: ending 'over-employment' in order to break workers' grass-roots power and strengthen the hands of both the Histadrut and employers; and shaking up business to squeeze out redundant and uncompetitive industries and enterprises. The plausibility of this interpretation rests on the following claims: that a recession was the only feasible palliative to industrial disorder; that the state was openly in favour of high(er) unemployment; and that injecting new vigour into Israeli capitalism was an integral part of the policies pursued.

The indispensability of recession. Only an economic slow-down could bring about severe unemployment, the sole force believed capable of reliably defusing the crisis in labour relations. As Greenwald

(1972: ch. 8) has shown, the alternatives suggested by past experience were unworkable, intolerably costly, or else would have addressed the balance of payments problem without providing a solution to the labour-relations problem. Capital subsidy at past levels was now beyond the state's means and so was the option of state support for maintaining the advantages of the primary labour market while enlarging its secondary segment. Experience earlier in the decade had already shown that any attempt to revive corporatism by tinkering with its particulars would either fail outright or provide no more than a temporary stopgap.[40] A good example of the dilemma facing policy-makers was the Treasury's attempt in 1966 to offset the government's pre-election concessions to public employees by denying similar rises to the business sector and by raising indirect taxation. The result was a rash of strikes, the re-emergence of multi-plant action committees, and successful resistance to having the inflationary effect of the new taxes kept out of the COLA system. A consensual agreement capable of countering these forces was impossible given the Histadrut's diminishing authority, erosion of Mapai's influence, and the competitive tensions between different groups of workers. Devaluation was advocated by many experts, but unless labour militancy had already been stilled by unemployment a rise in import prices would have been quickly translated into wage increases by indexation and/or unauthorized bargaining and strikes.

Unemployment as an explicit goal. The state itself did not conceal that the solution sought was what Kalecki had called a 'political business cycle'—a deliberate withdrawal of the policy supports on which sustained full employment depends in a Keynesian economy. Leading official spokesmen stated publicly that labour militancy was a (if not *the*) fundamental cause of Israel's economic malaise and that a dose of unemployment would be the most effective cure. It is true that a recession was well-nigh inevitable at about this time due to forces beyond the state's immediate control (i.e. the running down of immigration and capital inflow). The critical question is how policy responded to these trends, and the evidence is unambiguous. In July 1966, when 40,000 work-seekers were already registered at the labour exchanges, the Minister of Finance was reported as stating that his economic programme would require 95,000 unemployed. Moreover the authorities continued to delay, for roughly a year, the adoption of counter-cyclical policies oriented towards easing unemployment, which had by then passed a quarterly peak of 12.5 per cent of the civilian labour force.[41]

The desirability of capitalist efficiency. In Kalecki's scenario, the state was viewed as playing the role of understudy for capital. Its choices were seen as limited to either repairing the damage full employment had caused to 'business confidence' or facing a collapse of output and employment in the wake of declining private investment. Since in Israel most of the investment of the business sector had hitherto been directly or indirectly financed by the public sector, the state found it necessary to raise profits by disciplining labour and also to encourage the captains of industry to accept capitalist responsibilities for driving economic performance. In itself, unemployment could be expected to help employers halt the growth of wages, gain access to a larger pool of labour, and re-establish managerial authority over lay-offs and work practices. But capital would also have to make sacrifices. For instance, the Mitun intentionally shrank the formerly highly profitable construction and kindred industries. Most importantly, vigorous domestic demand—which under Israel's high tariff walls had hitherto shielded most producers from the export imperative—was deliberately run down or simply not revived. There was much talk of exposing industry to the whip of international competition, and insistence that the state's benevolent assistance would no longer be made available to lame ducks.[42]

Recasting the political economy through crisis

The state's strategy, in essence, was to shift the crisis out of its own jurisdiction and into the domains of labour and capital. The implementation of this attempt at reformulating key elements of Israel's political economy suggests that there were in fact significant limits to how far the state could go in asserting itself *vis-à-vis* society. One noteworthy indication was the lack of success enjoyed by the attempt to use the slow-down to pressure industrialists into voluntarily embarking on an export drive. Only positive rather than negative incentives turned out to have the desired effects.

Apparently for this reason, no serious practical steps towards trade liberalization were taken during the recession. In general, policy towards business was softened relatively early, towards the end of 1966. Even so, discernible increases in investment and exports did not occur until after the June 1967 war. It is doubtful that this can be attributed to a lag in the working through of recessionary incentives. In the end it took a devaluation to make production for overseas markets attractive enough to yield the desired response. The state also adopted a range of new and expanded incentives aimed at encouraging private investment generally. Above all, without the stepped-up militarization following the war, which gave an enormous 'cost-plus' boost to industry and construction, neither productive capacity nor exports would have grown as fast as they did.[43]

Factors enhancing labour discipline

The discipline of the market proved to be much more effective on the labour side. As the Bank of Israel concluded in its annual report for 1966 (p. 262), the recession 'undoubtedly induced workers to adapt themselves to employers' demands and to tone down their own demands'. In part this reflected labour's declining ability to resist wage cuts, lay-offs, and deterioration of working conditions in direct confrontations with employers. Labour effort was intensified by the raising of production quotas, lowered absenteeism and turnover, and enforced co-operation with efficiency measures. Starting in the building industry, wage drift ceased and even became negative. Data on labour disputes also reveal a sharp Mitun-induced turnaround from early in 1967, when the number of both strikes and strikers fell substantially, remaining below earlier levels for several years. Simultaneously, the causes of conflict altered radically in favour of more defensive issues, and there was a dramatic fall-off in worker recourse to strikes without Histadrut backing.[44]

The decline of wildcat strikes is indicative of how the Mitun enhanced the Histadrut's capacity to implement a policy of restraint.[45] In several celebrated cases it was forcefully made clear that henceforth no deviations from official policy by hitherto powerful rank-and-file groups would be tolerated. The leadership of the labour organization even agreed to co-operate with employers and the Treasury in sanctioning effective real wage cuts, confident in the knowledge that most workers now had little choice but to accept its authority. And renewal of the peak organization's corporatist capacities did not stop here. The Histadrut also performed what might be termed a 'shock-absorbing function' for the state, shielding it from the workers' wrath by: (*a*) publicly supporting official economic policy; (*b*) trying to reassure rank-and-file members that the Histadrut was safeguarding their interests; and (*c*) actively discouraging protest actions.[46] In the short term, then, the Mitun was instrumental not only in producing the outcomes desired of corporatism, but also in recreating the pre-conditions for the Histadrut's very participation in corporatist intermediation between labour and the state.

The much improved viability of corporatism under recessionary conditions was the mirror-image of the directly corrosive effects of high unemployment on worker power which have already been noted. The Mitun also showed promise of refurbishing labour market segmentation, another factor supportive of industrial peace. During the recession the social hierarchy in the labour market—which under full employment had become less closely associated with the job structure—reasserted itself. Arab workers suffered the most, partly as a result of discrimination and partly because of their concentration in 'temporary' jobs and in the hard hit construction-related industries. The Arab unemployment rate, after falling sharply during the boom years, rose faster and further than that of other groups. Much the same forces which worked to the detriment of Israel's Palestinian citizens also operated (but less virulently) on Eastern Jews, especially those trapped in the 'development towns' with their chronic job deficits. In addition, the revival of the secondary labour market was abetted by the fact that the state, which since 1948 had successfully ruled out the introduction of national unemployment insurance, offered quite different remedies to 'weak' and 'strong' groups among the unemployed.[47]

The limits of labour discipline

By their actions the Histadrut, and even more so the employers, clearly succeeded in regaining the initiative in labour relations. Labour discipline was sufficiently tightened to bear tangible fruit in the form of a decline in wildcat strikes and a growing profit share. However, by the late 1960s, workers' readiness to struggle against the ongoing redistribution of income from labour to capital had been dulled. This was due not only to fresh memories of mass unemployment, but also resulted from developments in the sphere of national security—first the euphoria of military victory and then the hardships caused by the 'War of Attrition' on the Suez Canal.[48] Nevertheless, neither the restraining effect of the troubles on Israel's borders nor the chastening impact of unemployment on rank-and-file assertiveness were capable of outlasting the conditions which brought them into being. Indeed, it may be that workers became increasingly desensitized to both types of discipline.

There is certainly evidence along these lines so far as unemployment is concerned. Even in the midst of the Mitun some of the workers weakened by the labour-market crisis, discovering that the Histadrut was unwilling and unable to defend them, turned their anger against the labour organization and subsequently the government as well. Finding other channels blocked, the stronger workers' committees co-operated on a regional and even national basis to launch extraparliamentary protest actions. While the potential of these challenges to radically transform the status quo in labour relations turned out to be short-lived, many workers drew the conclusion that self-reliance was their most effective weapon. In an action which was to become emblematic of the post-1967 revival of rank-and-file labour militancy and its anti-Histadrut and anti-government flavour, construction workers hired to build the new port at Ashdod launched a bitter struggle at the end of 1966 to demand that they receive permanent employment as dock workers. They were transformed by their success into a labour pressure-group of considerable significance. In this and numerous other cases the Mitun's delegitimizing consequences, together with the favourable labour-market conditions invoked by the resumption of economic growth, overpowered the 'lesson-teaching' legacy of unemployment.[49]

It is also instructive in this context to compare the initial triumph of the wage policy ambitions of employers and the state with subsequent setbacks. The Mitun successfully broke the automatic linkage of wages to prices (in fact the COLA was suspended for four years). It also dealt a heavy blow to the prevalent practice of unofficial sub-national wage bargaining (in 1967 wage drift came to a complete halt). The practical result of these trends was that, in striking contrast to the abortive 1962 devaluation, the next depreciation of the currency five years later directly enhanced the profitability of exports without the usual inflationary side-effects. Nevertheless, in order to increase workers' effective incomes without forcing employers to foot the bill (and pass on the costs in prices), the state found it prudent to compensate for the 1968–9 wage freezes with tax cuts and increased family allowances. By the early 1970s there was no choice but to put the COLA back into operation. Even before this, in fact by 1968, wage drift reappeared as workers succeeded in offsetting the punishing effects on their purchasing power of both official wage-restraint policy and periodic devaluations, by winning supplements negotiated at the branch, occupational, and work-place levels.[50]

Conclusions

The thrust of our discussion of the aftermath of the Mitun is quite clear: of the economic objectives which we have attributed to the state, only those pertaining to the labour-market arena met with success. The state's attempt to wean capital of dependence on public funds foundered on its inability to steer the business sector *except* by means of subsidies. But even the trend to labour quiescence, significant though it was, proved to be incomplete and short-lived. Neither the Histadrut's internal authority nor the credibility of peak wage agreements was strengthened more than temporarily by the trauma of the Mitun. Instead, as we show in Chapter 6, a new pattern of labour relations emerged. This pattern was characterized by costly attempts at severe corporatist wage restraint in the strike-ridden public sector, coupled with conditions of relative tranquillity in the self-governing business sector.

Despite our focus on the labour-market sphere, it is important not to lose sight of the fact that the Mitun was motivated by political as well as economic objectives. Did the recession succeed in restoring Mapai's ability to rely on bonds of material and organizational dependency as a means of capturing the loyalty of less advantaged citizens? The answer is that it did not. In fact there are grounds for arguing that the punishment which the recession meted out to the weaker strata of Israeli society was an important contributory factor in the decline of mass political support suffered by the ruling Labour Party, and its ultimate eviction from office.[51] This was not merely a case of backlash on the part of the specific individuals who suffered hardship. The protracted economic stagnation experienced during the Mitun generated a widely felt 'crisis of morale and spirit' (Medding, 1972: 284) which gravely undermined the government's prestige. This malaise received forceful extra-parliamentary expressions—collective hunger strikes and demonstrations protesting unemployment and austerity, and a wave of individual 'exit' in the form of emigration—which undoubtedly contributed to the process of Labour's delegitimation. The new mood also symbolized the beginning of a new crisis for the monopoly of parties over articulation of the political energies of the mass public.

In keeping with the overall objectives of this book, our analysis of the Mitun implies lessons for both students of the Israeli case and more general scholarly controversies. So far as the literature on Israel is concerned, we have offered a corrective to previous research, which is notable for the absence of contributions by social scientists or historians from outside the economics discipline. By embracing orthodox perspectives on business-cycle swings, Israeli economists have presented a narrow and sometimes even jejune view of the Mitun. While the majority echo our assumption that the state acted intentionally to deepen the economic downturn, they are divided on the issue of whether this policy was worthwhile. It is commonly held that the state over-reacted, that the major objectives of the recession could have been achieved by means of a devaluation once the economy cooled down, and that the 'industrial-relations benefits' of prolonged unemployment were far outweighed by its social and economic costs.[52]

This chapter has presented a different view. On the substantive controversy, we have argued that macro-economic policy was profoundly constrained by the breakdown or inefficacy of alternatives to unemployment as a regulator of labour unrest. Our analysis has also shown that it would be mistaken to interpret the economic problems which policy-makers addressed in the mid-1960s as conjunctural setbacks amenable to 'fine tuning'. They were instead *structural* difficulties which invited a *qualitative break* in policy. The Mitun was a critical test—of the state's ability to oblige labour and capital to bear the costs of economic failure, of capital's ability to become a partner in policy-making and reinstate authority and profitability in the factories, of the Histadrut's ability to revive its influence at the grass-roots level of the working class, and, finally, of the possibility that in the future the whip of unemployment might once again be employed on a large scale in order to impose labour restraint.

The investigation of the Mitun in this chapter provides reinforcement for the premise that in the current state of the discipline, progress in the macro-level study of labour movements and labour relations will necessitate greater reliance methodologically on historically grounded case studies, and theoretically on a broadly conceived political economy approach. The methodological point can be phrased quite simply as *the indispensability of context.* A recurrent concern throughout this work is to demonstrate that while general conceptual categories are vital to analytical progress, caution is necessary in assigning real-world contexts to these categories. Even the conditions for, and the functions of, full employment have their own contextual specificity. Thus in the Israeli setting during the late 1950s, the commitment of the state to containing unemployment was not a 'compensation' or 'guarantee' won by the trade union movement in return for good behaviour in the industrial relations arena, as corporatist theory would anticipate. Instead, a transition to full employment was made *desirable* by considerations of state-building and domestic politics, and *possible* by a unique combination of factors favouring economic expansion.[53]

Our principal theoretical conclusions can best be conveyed in relationship to Kalecki's brilliant and prophetic conceptualization of the political business cycle. Our case study lends strong support to Kalecki's view of the labour market as an arena of old-fashioned class struggle—a view which is also consistent with research in other settings.[54] As Figure 5.1 makes clear, in Israel in the 1960s worker militancy, and capital's ability to control and profit from labour, were both powerfully conditioned by swings in the unemployment rate. In the first half of the 1960s, when joblessness stabilized at a low level (shown as a high point in the graph, in which unemployment has been refracted), the rate of wildcat strikes rose and increases in labour productivity were cancelled out

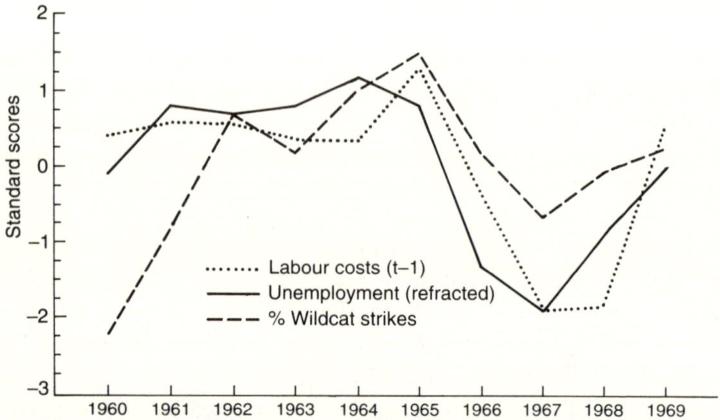

FIG. 5.1. Labour militancy and the business cycle in the 1960s

Sources: The *Statistical Abstract of Israel* for unemployment figures. Publications of the Histadrut's Institute for Social and Economic Research for strike data. The Bank of Israel's *Annual Report* for 1982 (p. 57) for real labour costs per unit of business sector product for 1963–9. Estimates for 1960–2 were made on the basis of the ratio of wages to output per man-day as published in the Bank's 1967 report (p. 301).

Note: The three series were plotted on a common scale using standard scores (number of standard deviations from the mean). To facilitate interpretation of relationships between the series, unemployment was 'refracted' (standard scores were computed by deducting each observation from the series mean, instead of the opposite).

or even overtaken by rising wage costs ('unit labour costs' reflect the joint impact of wages and productivity). The sharp rise in unemployment during the Mitun was followed by a correspondingly dramatic fall in both wildcat strikes and labour costs. Whereas on the upswing of the cycle, when the demand for labour began to recover in the late 1960s, these effects were predictably reversed.

Our disagreement with Kalecki, however, concerns the role of the state in 're-equilibrating' the labour market. Kalecki's view, which was similar to later neo-Marxist accounts of the contradiction between the state's dual responsibilities for accumulation and legitimation, left no room for the pursuit of 'state-centred' ends relatively autonomous from class conflict. His emphasis—important as it is—on the state's obligation to protect capital's interests by safeguarding labour restraint, cannot in itself explain public policy's retreat from full employment in the Israeli case. For, in this instance not only capital accumulation, but also the Histadrut's institutional integrity and political potency, the electoral strength of the ruling party, the fiscal health of the state, and its overall ability to direct the economy were all at stake.

A second aspect of the role of the state in Kalecki's analysis which deserves to be questioned is its unsatisfactory treatment of alternative responses to crises of full employment.[55] In the case analysed here, the state's choice between sustaining or retreating from its commitment to full employment was softened for a whole decade by a variety of *buffers* which, it will be recalled, rested on the inflow of gift capital, a ready supply of 'marginal' labour, and the advent of generalized political exchange between the Histadrut and the state. Such defences against the political business cycle are certainly not inviolate, and the Israeli example suggests that when they do weaken the result may indeed be a deliberate defection from full employment, providing that the government is strong enough politically to pursue unpopular policies. But it is clear that substitutes for the political business cycle are important enough to warrant fuller theorization than Kalecki offered. Later authors posited *corporatism* as an alternative for contemporary economic crisis managers. This is an important step forward, but raises a further difficulty. For, our analysis has shown that the Mitun was not merely a new phase in the regulation of labour in which market discipline replaced bargained consensus. Instead, unemployment was intended to (and initially did) *strengthen corporatism*—along with other props which had earlier helped to contain full employment's destabilizing potential. To view corporatism and market discipline —and for that matter also, labour-market dualism—as simple alternatives is thus to close our eyes to the scope for interplay between them.

Running through our studies of corporatism in Palestine and Israel, with deliberate intent, is an insistence on breaking down the boundaries between economic and political perspectives on labour markets and industrial relations and addressing mediating forces which are grounded in both the state and market arenas. In discussing the inter-war period in Chapter 4, we showed how economic and political features of the Yishuv and its wider environment rendered a shifting combination of unemployment, labour market segmentation, and state repression a viable alternative to corporatist class accommodation—in spite of the fact that in many respects the Jewish community in Palestine was congenitally 'preconfigured' for corporatism. Conditions after sovereignty had the effect of finally bringing this potential to fruition. Nevertheless, it was the *juxtaposition* of Israeli corporatism with labour-market segmentation and state subsidy which made it possible—until the crisis which gave birth to the Mitun—to limit substantially open confrontation between labour and capital.

Along with the potential complexity of the political–economic bases of labour restraint, both this chapter and the preceding one have underlined the essential *fragility* of such mechanisms of regulation. Changes in the underlying political and economic pre-conditions of any given system, as well as processes of internal decay, sooner or later lead to a crisis accompanied by struggles to establish new patterns of labour/capital/state relations. In the chapter which follows we shall have occasion to return to this historical dynamic, showing how in the shadow of a more recent crisis the state's increasingly limited options for managing the problem of labour restraint contributed to its inability to revive economic performance. But we shall also begin to consider evidence that, by the 1970s, the problem of disciplining capital had become even more of a barrier to economic stability than the renewal of worker militancy.

Notes

1. Information on early wage policy was drawn from Kantor (1977: esp. 132); Sussman (1973*a*); and Rubner (1960: esp. 20–1). In addition, Wasserman *et al.* (1961) provide a detailed survey of Mapai/Histadrut wage policy pronouncements.
2. On the Industrial Workers' Section see Kantor (1977: 271); and on party control, Tokatli (1979: 105).
3. The disciplinary uses of medical care were noted by Robinson (1966: 195), although compare Shirom (1983: 153). The most celebrated 'test cases' were the merchant seamen's strike at the end of 1951 and the strike at the *Ata* textile firm in 1957. Trade union autonomy and relations between the Histadrut's upper and lower echelons were, however, not the only issues at stake in these complex and intense conflicts. On Mapai's successful bid to win control of the workers' committees see Almogi (1980: 86); Kantor (1977:

273); and Medding (1972: 50). See also Tokatli (1979: esp. 237) on the heavy-handed manner in which Mapai took charge of the committees.

4. The Histadrut's relations with professional employees have been analysed by Derber (1963); Ben-David (1965); and Medding (1972: 59–65).
5. The discussion which follows is, strictly speaking, relevant only to approximately the first decade of Israeli sovereignty. However, many of the generalizations made refer to structural features and where important changes did occur over time, these will be noted in due course. For a more comprehensive analysis of the peculiarities of Israeli corporatism and the developments during the formative period under discussion see respectively Grinberg (1991*a*; 1991*b*).
6. The formal relations between union and party are described in Chapter 1 and Appendix 3. For fuller discussions of the dynamics of party involvement in the period in question see Tokatli (1979); Medding (1972); and Shapiro and Grinberg (1988). There were substantial ups and downs in the extent to which the Histadrut leadership was willing to co-operate with party and governmental élites, which Yanai (1981: ch. 11) and other observers have linked to the coming and going of different Histadrut Secretary-Generals. While not belittling these regime variations, we regard them as reflecting underlying political and economic trends more than the characteristics of individual leaders, and in any case as being secondary to the overall evolutionary thrust depicted here.
7. In this respect we depart from assumptions, quite prevalent in Israel, that the 'responsibility' of Histadrut leaders, the 'socialist' inclinations of government leaders, and Mapai's primacy at the institutional level were the keys to the success of corporatist wage restraint in the period concerned (e.g. Medding, 1972: 205–6).
8. On the significance of the Histadrut's role as employer see Sussman (1973*a*: 76). The private employers' reactive stance in wage determination was observed by Greenwald (1972: 16); Glatt (1973: 226); and Shapiro and Grinberg (1988: 32–3).
9. Tripartism, sometimes mistakenly considered a *sine qua non* of corporatism (e.g. Kut, 1987), was somewhat more developed outside the field of wage determination. The Histadrut and the Manufacturers' Association participated in a large number of tripartite (or similarly structured) 'advisory committees' attached to specific government ministries. The formulation of five-year development plans in which most of these committees participated, was, however, largely a symbolic exercise. Tabb's (1964, 1966) description also indicates that in the Treasury (the most important factor in economic policy) they were relatively marginal, whereas the most

influential committees—those attached to the Ministry of Agriculture—were dominated by the producers and apparently had no Manufacturers' Association representatives.

10. Early in 1951 the labour organization for the first time sponsored a national strike against private employers (in the metal industry). But as a result of the government's opposition to compensatory price increases and a 'defensive' lock-out launched by the Manufacturers' Association, the Histadrut was forced to compromise its demands (Kantor, 1977: 154–6). It never again resorted to militancy on an industry-wide scale. Two decades later, in the summer of 1972, the Histadrut's left-wing Secretary-General threw all his prestige behind a strike against the large and profitable Elite confectionery company in which the central issue was low pay (specifically for women). As a result of united employer opposition (informally involving even Histadrut employers) and the apathy, or even antipathy, of key Labour Party ministers, the 53-day stoppage was a failure (Shirom, 1974). One other dispute, at Ata textiles (at its peak the largest private employer in Israel), has already been mentioned. This was the site of the most severe confrontation between organized labour and private capital in Israel's history (nearly 1,700 workers participated in a 107-day walkout). While also regarded by all parties as a test case, the Ata strike differed from the other two incidents in both the issue at stake (which was a struggle over the prerogatives of workers in the *primary* labour market) and the position taken by the Histadrut's national leadership (which was determined to prevail against the labour organization's local boss). Ata management won the Histadrut's agreement, in principle, to its main demands (Tabb, Ami, and Shaal, 1961: 226–30).
11. See Lange (1984) and Armingeon (1986).
12. See Chapter 1. In principle, officials holding elective positions were (are) voted into office by the membership. But in practice, as a maverick Histadrut Secretary-General commented derisively in the early 1970s, party functionaries 'nominated themselves and appointed themselves' (Ben-Aharon, 1972: 35).
13. As Mapai leaders were wont to complain, Mapam played a double game within the Histadrut, carrying the mantle of grass-roots opposition to imposed wage restraint, while simultaneously participating in the system of governance which so hobbled rank-and-file initiative. Particularly noteworthy in the latter respect is the fact that when the Histadrut belatedly established limited branch-wide unions in the early post-sovereignty years, Mapam in many cases co-operated in the 'postponement' of elections in these unions (as well as in others, already established) in favour of appointment

of top union officers by informal agreement between Mapai and Mapam leaders (Ben-Shoham, 1985).

14. Theories of corporatism and political exchange in industrial relations (e.g. Crouch, 1977; Pizzorno, 1978) recognize that measures to increase the institutional power of the union peak association inevitably figure, at least implicitly, in horse-trading between governments and labour organizations. Their emphasis, however, has correctly been on the issue of organizational capacities, with the role of the state in this regard being to safeguard the national labour organization's monopoly and internal authority by granting it statutory or *de facto* recognition and taking legal steps to minimize its 'free-rider' problems. The Israeli state has been no exception in these respects—as indicated, for instance, by its initial refusal to bargain with the few professional unions operating independently of the Histadrut, its introduction of the concept of 'most representative union' into Israel's labour legislation, its use of ministerial 'extension orders' to widen the coverage of collective agreements, and its statutory imposition of an 'organization tax' on non-members assumed to benefit from contracts negotiated by the Histadrut (for documentation see Shirom, 1983). The singularity of the Israeli case derives from the importance of state 'licensing' and subsidy for the labour organization's *non-union* activities.
15. Greenberg (1986) and Yitzchaki (1970), respectively, have recorded the remarkable post-sovereignty consolidation of credit unions and provident funds. The direct linkage between wage restraint and the government's protection and subsidy of such activities is documented by Grinberg (1991*b*) and Shapiro and Grinberg (1988). Zalmanovitch (1981: 48, 59–77, 85) furnishes relevant data and analysis of the case of the Sick Fund. In his controversial memoirs, Asher Yadlin (1980)—a front-rank Mapai politician/technocrat convicted of embezzlement while heading the Histadrut Sick Fund—provides some fascinating illustrations of the more diffuse forms of political exchange which passed through the party nexus.
16. For theoretical discussions of 'generalized political exchange' see Lehmbruch (1984) and Marin (1986). The parallels between Israel around the 1950s and Austria in the 1960s and beyond should not be overdrawn. The political regime, the scope of the state, the structure of labour representation, and the breadth of the peak labour association's role in political exchange all bear certain similarities; but the institutions and key players in generalized political exchange were significantly different.
17. Good examples of the critical view are Lerner (e.g. 1957) and Riemer (1960). Subsequently, building on econometric work and a

closer familiarity with the institutional framework, local experts like Gaathon (1971*b*) and Sussman (e.g. 1973*a*) took odds with this perspective.

18. A watershed study by Artstein and Sussman concluded that wage freezes in the 1955–74 period had 'considerably dampen[ed] the wage–price spiral set off by [devaluations]' (1977: 24). However, that study's choice of four 'controls-on' periods was to a large extent arbitrary. The year 1974 was defined as 'on', even though restraint only began following the devaluation in November of that year. Furthermore, in 1974 and 1967 wage movements were clearly affected by war as well as economic crisis. Artstein's (1980) more fully specified model and Brauer's (1987) more up-to-date investigation yield results which verify the effect of the security situation (see also Reshef and Bemmels, 1989). They suggest in addition that restraint was more circumscribed than implied by the Artstein–Sussman study. Finally, as Sussman and Zakai (1985) have demonstrated, the exercise of Draconian formal restraint in the absence of supportive economic conditions actually has the effect of eroding the ability of central wage negotiators to control and co-ordinate wage movements. The tendency of 'market forces' to defeat wage-restraint policies, except in the very short run, is also the theme of a survey of the Israeli experience in the 1970s and 1980s by Artstein and Sussman (1989).
19. The foregoing sketch follows the, by now, classic studies of Apple (1980); Panitch (1981); and Salvati and Brosio (1979). Other comparative work, for instance by Lange (1981); Armingeon (1986); and Esping-Andersen (1987), points to the need for a more nuanced formulation in a number of respects. However, there remains a broad consensus of opinion behind the notion of full employment as both cause and consequence of post-war transitions to corporatist industrial relations.
20. Panitch (1976) and Sabel (1981) are representative of the substantial literature on rank-and-file revolt. In concluding their magisterial study of incomes policies in Europe, Flanagan, Soskice, and Ulman (1983) pointed to coexistence of corporatism and unemployment as a distinct future possibility.
21. The pioneering study linking corporatist union restraint to variations in social-democratic and trade union strength across countries was that of Headey (1970). For later examples see Crouch (1985) and also Marks (1986).
22. For additional discussion of the issues raised below see Chapters 6 and 7.
23. Standard sources on military expenditure and its economic consequences are Barkai (1980) and Berglas (1983).

24. For data on the position of Palestinians (citizens and non-citizens) in Israel's labour market see Farjoun (1980) and Makhoul (1982). The ratio of armed forces to total employment among prime-aged men was calculated from estimates of conscripts and career soldiers published by the International Institute for Strategic Studies (London), minus the presumed number of women soldiers, plus the number of reservists on active duty as determined by Labour Force Surveys. The reference year is 1985, a relatively quiet period between the Lebanon War and the *Intifada* (Palestinian uprising). See Barkai (1987*a*) on Israel's military industries.
25. For data on Israel's balance of payments and its component flows see Halevi (1983*b*).
26. On 'East-West' inequality among Israeli Jews see Hasson (1981) and Smooha (1986). Additional sources within the extensive literature on this topic are cited elsewhere in this and other chapters.
27. This point was recognized explicitly—and rather incredulously— by a foreign economist, Howard Pack (1971: ch. 8).
28. See the beginning of Chapter 2 for a fuller discussion of theories of labour-market segmentation, including distinctions between different approaches which need not concern us in the present chapter.
29. Leventhal-Shartal (1985) provides a comprehensive survey of labour-market segmentation in Israel (especially as it bears on ethnicity) which includes the period in question. On gender inequality in the labour market see Bernstein (1983*b*) and Izraeli (1983). The sectoral line of differentiation was noted by Barkai (1964) and Kleiman (1964*b*), and its contemporary manifestations have been evaluated by Farjoun (1983) and Stier and Lewin-Epstein (1988). The prevalence of secondary labour-market conditions in small privately-owned enterprises was noted by Greenwald (1972: 100). Ginzberg (1968: 4) reported the phenomenon of discrimination against the 'temporary' tier of the work-force.

    The practice of collective bargaining respected these demarcations. In its Annual Report for 1967 (266) the Bank of Israel stated that one-fifth of the labour force was not covered by collective agreements. A work-place survey in 1969 indicated that even in the Tel Aviv area, small plants in the metal industry did not pay supplements to the basic wage mandated by the applicable contract and honoured by larger plants (Shirom, 1969).
30. On the ethnic division of labour see especially Bernstein and Swirski (1982). Protection of the interests of the predominantly Western veteran workers was not limited to the allocation of jobs. After three years of unrestricted immigration immediately following sovereignty, some economically motivated limitations were imposed (Friedlander and Goldscheider, 1979: 90 ff.). Once inside Israel,

many immigrants—again, Easterners in particular—were kept outside the labour market altogether in transit camps or on relief works (Bernstein, 1981; Bahral, 1965). As noted in the text, others were shunted to economically backward areas or neighbourhoods (e.g. Spilerman and Habib, 1976).

31. See Ben-Porath (1966); Rosenfeld (1978); and Chapter 2 of this volume.
32. On the economic developments and problems which preceded the Mitun see Halevi and Klinov-Malul (1968).
33. Halevi and Klinov-Malul (1968: 246–7, 280); Patinkin (1960: 85); Kanovsky (1970: 22–3) are among the numerous observers who commented on the problems of employer inefficiency and over-subsidization of capital. Tamari (1980: 91) documented the absence of ploughed-back profits as a mechanism of capital formation. Soon after sovereignty the Mapai élite was chastised by none other than Michal Kalecki (1950) for harbouring unrealistic expectations regarding foreign investment.
34. For a survey of contemporary views see Kanovsky (1970: 21–3).
35. Weinshall (1976: 965–6) provides evidence of the recruitment of new 'marginals workers' to the secondary labour force. The manufacturers' proposals to increase the supply of cheap labour were reported by Lev Grinberg in a personal communication.
36. The developments concerning workers' committees summarized in this paragraph are documented and discussed by Tokatli (1979: 134); Friedman (1963 and 1976); and the Histadrut Yearbook (*Shnaton Hahistadrut*) for 1965/6: 356. For further data and discussion regarding strike trends see Chapter 6.
37. See n. 4 above for studies of professional employees. For histories of the related topic of public-sector wage policy and labour relations see Glatt (1973); Reuveni (1974: chs. 3 and 4); and Harel (1976).
38. The magnitude of the near-upheaval in the Histadrut in 1965 was such that the Mapai–Achdut Avodah 'Alignment' lost *20 percentage points* of the votes won by its component parties for the preceding (1959) convention. More than half of the loss was to Rafi, a Mapai breakaway which was in part a response to the very alliance which saved Mapai from electoral calamity. It also appears that Achdut Avodah's alliance with Mapai drove a number of that party's former supporters into the Cherut camp. More detailed election results and descriptions of the various labour parties may be found in Appendix 4.
39. For general background on the split in Mapai see Medding (1972: ch. 12). A brilliant reconstruction by Shapiro and Grinberg (1988) has recently brought to light the remarkable extent to which

Histadrut-related struggles were at the bottom of the turmoil inside the party.

40. Among the initiatives that failed were the following: (*a*) Histadrut efforts early in the decade to bring the centre of gravity in wage determination back to the national level, for instance by formalizing the linkage between aggregate wages and productivity, and by freezing the inter-occupational wage structure; (*b*) attempts by the Histadrut leadership to break rank-and-file autonomy by a combination of uncompromising resistance and the co-optation of more union people to the labour organization's governing bodies; (*c*) The government's endeavours in 1962 to try to soften the relative militancy which the Histadrut felt obliged to embrace, by offering it 'package deal'-type inducements such as indirectly financing part of a wage increase and extracting an employer promise to hold down prices.
41. For some relevant public statements see *Divrei Haknesset* (41: 584); *Kol Ha'am*, 18 July 1966; and Kanovsky's (1970) well-documented account.
42. For illustrative declarations of the new policy towards capital see *Hata'assiyah*, Oct. 1966; and Beham and Kleiman (1968: 32).
43. The fate of the state's policy towards capital was documented by Remba (1969: 60), Kanovsky (1970: 31), and Greenwald (1972: 61).
44. For convincing micro-level evidence of the new climate in labour relations see Weinshall (1976: 965–8). At the macro-level, wage and productivity trends were documented in the Bank of Israel's annual reports for 1966–8, and strike statistics were compiled and analysed by Michael and Bar-El (1967). Whereas in the first half of the 1960s only 20% (at most) of strikers were involved in authorized actions, by 1968–70 this proportion had risen to 70% or more.
45. See the discussion in Greenwald (1972: 130–9).
46. See Shalev (1984: 41–3) for additional details regarding the Histadrut's role *vis-à-vis* worker protest.
47. The differential impact of the Mitun on different social groups is documented in Shalev (1984: 36–8). State responses to unemployment among Arabs and women were tokenistic at best. Unemployed Jewish men (mainly Easterners) who had previously held menial secondary jobs, or were seen as fit for them, were offered relief work. In contrast, a temporary system of cash grants was reserved mainly for educated white-collar employees or skilled manual workers judged 'unaccustomed to unemployment' (Chermesh, Bar-Tsuri, and Barzilai, 1972).
48. The association over a period of time between military tensions and individual and collective 'anomic behaviour' has been demonstrated in studies by Kimmerling (1974); Cahane and Canaan (1973); and Landau and Pfeffermann (1988).

49. For additional details regarding workers' committee actions see Shalev (1984: 43–4) and Shirom (1971). For a case study of the Ashdod Port workers, see Mars (1980).
50. For data on wage drift in this and later periods see Sussman (1974) and Sussman and Zakai (1985). See also Tsaban (1978), who argues that the squeeze on labour in the late 1960s was the major factor precipitating an explosion of labour militancy in the early 1970s.
51. For elaboration see Shalev (1990*b*); and, in less detail, Chapter 7 of this volume.
52. For examples of diverse views of economists regarding the Mitun compare Halperin (1968) and Lerner and Ben-Shahar (1975) on the role of government policy in instigating the downturn, and contrast the views of Beham and Kleiman (1968) and Greenwald (1972) on the costs and benefits of the recession and its accompanying unemployment.
53. On the concepts of compensation and guarantee in the analysis of corporatist exchange see Lange (1981). Therborn (1986) is a valuable study of the divergent foundations and methods of 'institutionalized commitments to full employment'.
54. See Boddy and Crotty (1975) and Cameron (1984) for American illustrations.
55. At the close of his famous article, 'Political Aspects of Full Employment', Kalecki raised but rejected the possibility that the Western states would resolve the political–economic dilemmas of full employment by imitating the Nazi synthesis of Fascist discipline and full-employment militarism. His tantalizing but vague conclusion was instead that the increased power of the working class would—or at any rate *should*—receive new institutional expression after the war (1943: 331).

Part III

Policy and Political Economy

6

Policy Outcomes

Dualism and Disorder

This chapter seeks to establish the impact of long-term Labour Party incumbency on the 'revealed preferences' of the Israeli state in key areas of domestic policy.[1] Theoretically, our endeavour is inspired by one of the central themes of recent research in comparative political economy—namely, the debate over the scope for, and consequences of, 'political control of the economy' in advanced capitalist societies.[2] In the 1970s, at least, it appeared to a number of political scientists and sociologists that politically mediated economic steering might be both possible and beneficial for overcoming the strains of global economic crisis. This optimistic outlook came under attack from both right and left. Conservatives berated the economic myopia of popularity-hungry politicians and claimed that the fiscal capacities of governments had been 'overloaded' by uncontrolled popular demands. Radicals, on the other hand, were sceptical whether governments could do any more in the macroeconomic realm than reproduce favourable conditions for the long-term welfare of capitalism and the capitalist class.

Two overlapping theses of new political economy emerged to counter these claims. The answer to the radicals was that despite their pessimism about the autonomy of the democratic state from the capitalist economy, well-entrenched social democracy does make a palpable difference to public policy, concretely benefiting the working class and gradually shifting consumption (and perhaps in future also production) along a socialist path. The retort to the conservatives was that, if anything, only *more* politicization of the economy could save the market from its own irrationality and fragility in a conflict-ridden world. A 'neo-corporatist' interleaving of state and economy, mediated by powerful associations of the major classes, makes possible co-ordination, consensus, and a sufficiently long-term horizon for successful economic adaptation, even in the face of powerful external shocks.

With these claims in mind, we might reasonably expect that Israel should be an exemplar of politico-economic stability and socially protective public policy. By all normal criteria of comparative measurement, the Israeli labour movement was for most of its history both very strong and exceptionally closely integrated into state and society alike. Nevertheless, Israel's welfare state embodies features which are alien and even antithetical to the social-democratic model of social policy.[3] Moreover, neo-corporatist order and stability have been noteworthy for their absence from the politics of distribution and economic adaptation in Israel, most particularly in the period of crisis after 1973. Accordingly, the paradox which we seek to resolve in this chapter is that in neither respect are public policy expectations derived from comparative research consistent with the Israeli experience. In Israel, a distinctive form of social-democratic corporatism has coexisted with a relatively undeveloped and dualistic welfare state, disorderly industrial relations, and spiralling hyperinflation and budget deficits.

The pattern of outcomes

In order to come to grips with the apparent incommensurability between Israel's institutional superstructure and its pattern of domestic policy, it is necessary to begin by elaborating on the policy profile itself. What have been the main characteristics of public priorities and outcomes in respect of the economy, welfare, and distribution?

The economy

In characterizing Israel's economic performance we adopt the self-imposed limitation of excluding the first decade of sovereignty, a transitional period of modernization and take-off, and the years since the taming of hyperinflation in the mid-1980s, which may or may not project an altered future.[4] Israel's economic performance between 1960 and 1985 (see Figure 6.1) presents a dramatic contradiction between developments before and after 1973. From the mid-1950s until 1973, barring the very sharp recession of the mid-1960s, Israel enjoyed a more rapid growth rate than any of the

18 core OECD countries except Japan. The puzzle is that after 1973 the growth of per capita product, at little more than a percentage point a year, dropped to the lower reaches of the OECD group. As a result, Israel's historical trajectory in terms of the standard of living (per capita income) started to turn. That trajectory had been upward, moving Israel from a Third World to a First World level. Since 1973 it has been sinking down again, to the point of being overtaken by several of the newly industrializing countries.[5]

Quite the opposite contradiction characterizes Israel's labour-market performance. Israeli unemployment rates were relatively high by OECD standards throughout the pre-1973 period. That may not be such an unremarkable achievement, given the fact that at the outset the labour force doubled over a short period due to mass immigration; but comparatively speaking, it was not a particularly impressive record. However in the 1970s, precisely when the economy was bogged down in crisis, Israel's unemployment performance got better rather than worse—so much so that until the late 1980s it ranked just below the select group of nations which embrace what Therborn (1986) terms an 'institutionalized commitment to full employment'.[6] This is puzzling, since for two reasons the economy's capacity to create jobs should have been severely impaired after 1973. First, in the course of the 1970s the cost of Israel's oil imports rose from 1 per cent to 12 per cent of GNP—a massive outflow of resources. Second, in 1973–4 defence spending shot up in the wake of the surprise 'Yom Kippur War'. Despite stepped-up American aid, the resultant balance of payments problem was very grave, and in the face of a domestic downturn the growth of productivity and output abruptly ceased. As indicated in Figure 6.1, this stagnation of domestic product persisted over most of the next decade.

Figure 6.1 also reveals that 1973 was a turning-point in terms of inflation. In the preceding decade or so, price increases had barely reached double digits and their fluctuations were 'well behaved' with respect to trends in unemployment. But beginning in 1973 inflation soared, to the peak of nearly 450 per cent reached in 1984 (simultaneously, unemployment was actually rising, albeit modestly).

Figure 6.2 offers a comparison with seven representative OECD countries to highlight the peculiarity of Israel's major economic trends since the October 1973 war and the coincident oil price

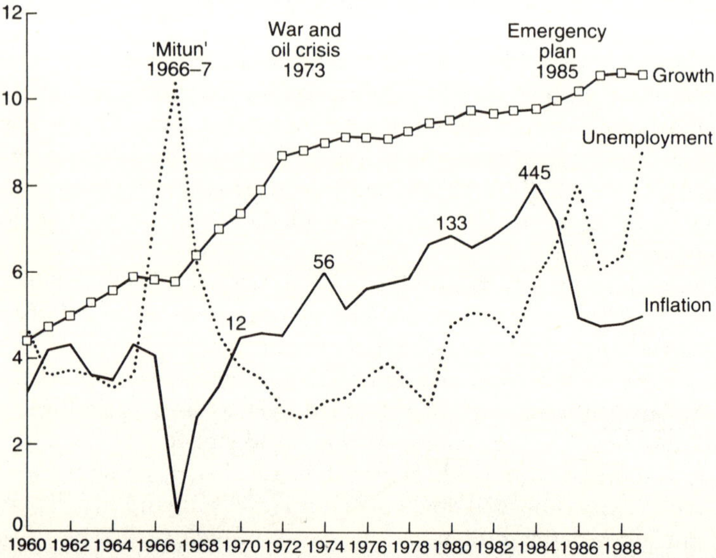

Fig. 6.1. Economic performance indicators: 1960–89

Source: *Statistical Abstract of Israel.*

Note: To graph all three series on a common scale, two of the indicators were transformed: inflation (natural log plus 2); and per capita GDP (thousands of constant 1980 shekels). Inflation is measured as the percentage change in the Consumer Price Index in the course of each year.

shock.[7] On the basis of changes between the five-year periods before and after 1973, it emerges that both the slow-down in growth and the increase in inflation in Israel were three times the seven-country mean; whereas Israel's success in forestalling rising unemployment was paralleled only in Sweden.

Welfare

According to the social-democratic view, where a labour-movement party has been in power for a long period of time (and there is nowhere in the West other than Sweden where that has happened more remarkably than in Israel) one can also expect a large welfare state which offers a high degree of social protection along solidaris-

FIG. 6.2. Deterioration in economic performance after 1973: Israel and seven OECD countries

Sources: *Statistical Abstract of Israel* for Israel. OECD Economic Outlook, *Historical Statistics 1960–1985* (Paris, 1987) for OECD countries.

Note: The underlying data are ratios of the mean for 1973–9 to the mean for 1968–73. (For the growth rate the ratio was reversed.) These ratios were then standardized as a percentage of the country average for the seven OECD nations. The growth indicator used is the year-to-year change in real per capita GDP. The unemployment figures were 'standardized' by OECD in a manner comparable to Israel's Labour Force Surveys, with the important exception that OECD uses total rather than civilian employment as the denominator in calculating rates of unemployment.

tic lines. For example, Esping-Andersen (1985*b*) has found empirical support for a model which associates strong social democracy with social security (income maintenance) systems characterized by high expenditure, state rather than private provision, programme uniformity, and an emphasis on insurance rather than relief. But in fact Israel's social security spending is such that, in Wilensky's (1975) rather narrow terms, it is a pronounced 'welfare state laggard'.[8] Moreover, Israel is distinctive not only in its

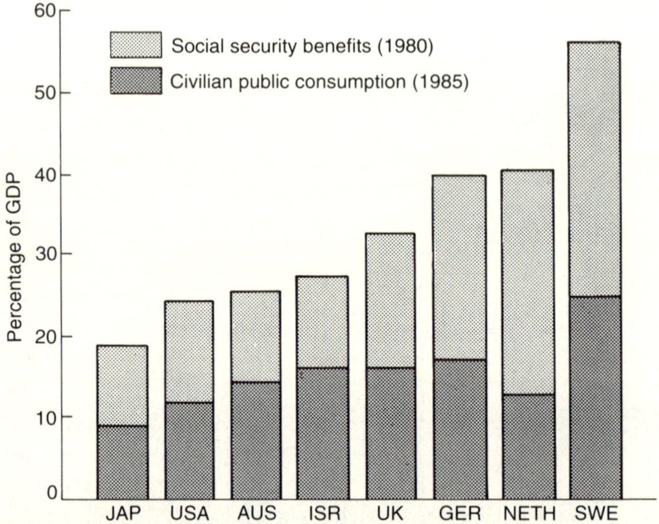

FIG. 6.3. The size of the welfare state: public expenditure in Israel and seven OECD countries

Sources: The Bank of Israel's *Annual Report* for Israel. *The Military Balance*, published by the International Institute for Strategic Studies (London) and the OECD's *Historical Statistics* for the other countries.

Note: Data for both series are percentages of GDP. The social security measure indicates expenditure on benefits as defined by the ILO in its 1980 survey, published in 1985 by the International Labour Office (Geneva) as *The Cost of Social Security*. Public 'consumption' (in 1985) is government expenditure other than transfer payments or investment. Civilian expenditure was calculated as a residual after deducting military spending from total expenditure.

modest overall commitment to income maintenance, but also the relative emphasis it places on different target groups. As in European nations with a pronounced Catholic influence, social policy has favoured benefits to children over pensions for the retired.[9]

Figure 6.3 demonstrates not only Israel's laggard status with respect to social security spending, but also the fact that in contrast, expenditure on direct social services like education and health is within the OECD mainstream. A broad indicator of the scope of this kind of state activity is the national accounts category known as 'public consumption'. At 16 per cent of GDP (1985), Israel's *civilian* public consumption is squarely in the middle of the range captured by the other seven countries. (Its 22 per cent of

GDP allocated to *military* consumption, not shown in Figure 6.3, is, however, more than triple the high US figure.)

As for the underlying rationale or principles governing Israel's welfare state (i.e. the qualitative features of social policy which are no less important than its quantitative dimensions), they seem to fly in the face of the most hallowed principles of the social-democratic model. There is a noticeable degree of non-uniformity of policy provisions for different population groups, particularly so far as Arabs and Jews are concerned.[10] Jews get all the benefits and Arab citizens get some of them. Arab non-citizens, which means Palestinians in the occupied territories (nearly one-quarter of the overall population under Israeli control) are entitled to virtually no income maintenance support and are offered a limited range of public social services which bear no comparison with those in Israel proper.

While the Palestinians of the West Bank and Gaza have been exposed to Israeli law and social service arrangements with deliberate selectivity, Israel's Arab citizens, in principle, enjoy the same standing in the welfare state as the Jewish majority. In practice they are strongly discriminated against, although typically indirectly, and to a varying extent—least of all (although far from trivially) in income maintenance and education; and most of all (to the point of near exclusion) in employment creation, housing, and the personal social services. This tendency towards segmentation of the welfare state is undoubtedly related to the long-standing hostility between Israel and the Arab states and the national conflict with the Palestinians. This has encouraged state agencies to adopt a restrictive policy of rationing benefits of all kinds to the Arab sector in return for 'good behaviour', and has legitimized the opinion held in some Jewish quarters that the Arab minority are not deserving of full citizen rights. As we shall argue below, however, the nationality-based segmentation of social policy has also served concrete material and political interests of the Jewish majority.

However one cares to explain the second-class standing of Arab citizens in Israel's welfare state, given Israel's Zionist ideology it is much less surprising than the phenomenon of more attenuated but still significant discrimination within the Jewish population. In comparison with other countries' welfare states (and not just the social-democratic ones), Israel's has been strongly permeated by particularism and selectivity. This was especially so in the period of mass immigration, the 1950s and the early 1960s, when a two-tier system of welfare developed for Jews.[11] Essentially, the upper tier was reserved for the veterans of the period before sovereignty, most of whom were Ashkenazim (of European or 'Western' origin). Here social protection depended primarily on the employment relationship. The veterans had access to the best jobs and enjoyed a high degree of job security as a result of strong organization and punitive severance pay agreements. In turn, with employment stability went entitlements to a variety of insurance-based income maintenance schemes, some public and others negotiated with employers. In contrast, recent arrivals naturally lacked job seniority and a great many were unemployed, in temporary jobs, or administratively barred from entering the labour market. Instead of the employment-linked system of social protection, they were dealt with harshly by means of a 'residual' system of niggardly means-tested benefits and manipulative forms of so-called treatment and rehabilitation.[12] The ones who suffered the most were those who had the least, mostly the 'Eastern' Jews who immigrated to Israel from North Africa and the Middle East.

In the 1970s there was some movement towards a more 'institutional' welfare state, like past reforms largely a response to political violence in the slums. Compensatory education for the children of Eastern immigrants was greatly expanded. There was also a major jump in income maintenance provision, mainly in the form of progressive family allowances geared to the concentration of poverty in large Eastern-Jewish families. The Likud government which entered office after Labour's election defeat in 1977 introduced a universal minimum income guarantee and embarked on an ambitious programme of urban renewal. These elements of change were, however, accompanied by significant continuities. For instance, the exclusion of Arab neighbourhoods from the renewal scheme and the concentration of new educational opportunities for Easterners in 'dead-end' vocational schools.[13]

Social protection in Israel is noticeably *dualist* (in the sense of Goldthorpe, 1984) not only in discriminating between citizens on primordial grounds, but also in relation to the balance between private and public provision. The 'private' (although state subsidized) social services offered by the Histadrut are especially significant. The clinics and hospitals of the labour organization's health plan serve as much as 80 per cent of the population and have traditionally overshadowed the activities of the Ministry of Health. Similarly, while public pension expenditure is noticeably low in Israel compared with OECD countries, this universal form of social insurance coexists with a Histadrut-operated supplementary pension scheme which largely bypasses the secondary labour market. Israel's atypically low concentration of elderly citizens undoubtedly diminishes its pension and health requirements (just as large cohorts of children have invited relatively high spending on family allowances). But laggard public 'pension effort' also reflects the fact that the state again made space for an employment-based system. Increasingly, this has been true of a broad spectrum of 'occupational welfare', the growth of which has accentuated the split between conditions in the sheltered (primary) and secondary segments of the labour market.

Distribution

A comprehensive perspective on social welfare cannot ignore the fact that public and private forms of social protection are both supplementary to the outcomes of prior distributional processes in the market arena. Social democracy may be thought of as a particular model of linkage between the labour market and the 'political market', characterized by full employment and generous social spending on the one hand, and on the other a high degree of trade union solidarity and self-restraint.

Here again, Israel constitutes an exception. The labour movement's historic self-image of its wage policy as ultra-egalitarian was in reality only a half-truth. More recent evidence regarding wage differentials and the overall distribution of income shows that inequality has been on a rising secular trend, and is high in Israel in comparison with OECD countries. This is not terribly surprising in view of the depth of labour-market segmentation and its well-documented complement, the existence of a persistent national and ethnic hierarchy in the division of labour and the distribution of economic rewards in Israeli society—the same hierarchy encountered in our earlier discussion of welfare state segmentation. Transfer payments and progressive taxes attenuate these inequalities to some extent, although less so than in nations with more far-reaching and less uneven welfare states. Consequently, both the 'market' and the 'final' distribution of income in Israel resemble those of bourgeois-dominated polities far more than the relatively egalitarian social-democratic nations.[14]

In democratic capitalist societies, disputation in the labour relations sphere is the most important quantifiable indicator of how distributional conflicts are pursued and managed. From a cross-national perspective, strike activity in Israel is high. By the measure of relative wage-earner involvement in conflicts, Israel has been close to the top of the OECD league table since the late 1960s. The 'political' shape of strikes—typically brief but broadly based—also stands out, and is symptomatic of the high concentration of labour disputes in the public sector (including state-owned transport, communication, and utilities). In fact over the last two decades Israel has ranked poorly on *all* the components of what Schmitter (1981) once referred to as 'ruliness'—reflecting not only labour strife, but also extra-parliamentary protest and governmental turnover.[15]

To conclude, what we have in the Israeli case is a dominant Labour Party only partially accompanied by a Keynesian welfare state. We see labour organized in a highly corporate way, but without industrial peace. Israel's labour market operates with unmistakable dualist tendencies, again posing a paradox because, at least according to Goldthorpe (1984), political economies and particularly their labour markets tend to be structured along either corporatist or dualist lines. Yet in Israel a corporate labour organization enters into social contracts with the state, while at the same time members of marginalized social groups form an exposed underclass in the labour market, with clearly inegalitarian consequences.

Historical and institutional distinctiveness

Enough has been said already to make it plain that the Histadrut and the long-dominant Labour Party hold the keys to unlocking many of the mysteries of Israel's domestic policy exceptionalism. As we have sought to show throughout this work, in common with the nationally unique institutions which have shaped public policy profiles elsewhere, the Histadrut (and the broader labour movement of which it is a part) defies understanding unless placed in historical context. There is no need to specify that context again here. Instead, we shall move directly to the task of identifying some of the most significant linkages between historical experience and the central features of Israel's subsequent social policy regime.[16] Those features of particular relevance are: (*a*) the preference for provision of welfare by the labour movement rather than the state; (*b*) the pattern of national and ethnic segmentation of social protection; and (*c*) the labour leadership's aversion to income maintenance entitlements.

Delegation. The assignment of social policy tasks to the labour movement during the pre-state period was consistent with, although not the direct result of, the prevailing structure of the state. While the British regime in Palestine following the First World War possessed the necessary authority to tax, spend, and regulate, to a great extent its hands were tied by the immense material and organizational differences between the condition of the Arab and Jewish working classes, by stringent fiscal restraint imposed from London, and by the virtual stalemate on British initiative caused by the Arab-Jewish conflict. But at the same time, within the Yishuv a sectoral social policy operated by and for Jewish labour possessed compelling attractions. From a Zionist point of view it was desirable that only Jews, more specifically Jews willing and able to serve the Zionist cause, would benefit. For the labour movement, control over access to its manifold programmes of so-called 'mutual aid' was a potent incentive to rank-and-file political loyalty. Given Mandatory conditions, there was no possibility for labour parties to foster clientelistic political mobilization except by using the Histadrut as their vehicle. The practical fusion of Zionist and partisan political motives is exemplified by two new measures introduced to strengthen the workers' Sick Fund soon after Mapai's David Ben-Gurion gained command of the Jewish Agency in 1935. It now became obligatory to join the Histadrut in order to participate in the Sick Fund; and in addition, the practice was instituted of granting new immigrants free initial membership in the Fund, at Jewish Agency expense.

Dualism. Although the Histadrut was, in principle, open to all Jewish workers, the Arabs were not alone in being left outside the labour movement's subsidized system of 'voluntary' social protection. To an important extent this was also true of those Jewish immigrants (mostly from Arab countries) deemed unfit to participate in land settlement or the organized labour market. The policy of exclusion was based on fears of the presumed susceptibility of the excluded to the influence of anti-labour political trends, and also on a certain reluctance to share Zionist subsidies with 'outsiders'. The result was a tripartite division of welfare. Jobs or help in finding them, health care, some housing, workers' education, and even soup kitchens were provided through the Histadrut on a members-only basis. Far less comprehensive services were dispensed to non-members, with the framework dependent on who they were—Arabs were cared for (if at all) by the British authorities, while the unorganized Jewish poor were assisted by local volunteers and social workers supported by foreign philanthropy.

'Constructivism'. The labour movement's ideologists coined this term to emphasize its commitment to the 'constructive' tasks of Jewish colonization and employment-creation, in contradistinction to the orthodox socialist view that workers' collective action should be directed towards confronting the bourgeoisie. As previous chapters have elaborated, this was essentially a strategic and self-interested choice, arising from the economic vulnerability of the Jewish working class in Palestine. As a corollary to the labour movement's compact with organized Zionism, its social policy programme was distinguished by an overriding concern for the absorption of immigrants and a deep distaste for 'handouts'. The debilitating effects of economic deprivation on the feasibility of Jewish settlement were well known to the long-time leaders of the Histadrut and Mapai, most of whose contemporaries had long ago abandoned Palestine. Moreover, while cash in hand might enable the unemployed to stay on and affirm their attachment to Zionism and the labour movement, only 'constructive' activity could simultaneously meet the further objective of building up the Jewish enclave. Consequently, the labour movement was opposed to income guarantees, preferring to devote collective resources to job creation and service provision.

The impact of nation-statehood[17]

As a result of Britain's withdrawal from Palestine, Israel's unilateral declaration of independence (ratified by the UN), and its success in repelling the armies of the surrounding Arab states and conquering additional territory, Israel emerged during 1948–9 as a fully-fledged nation-state. Because of the obvious threads linking the pre- and post-sovereignty eras—in particular, an almost unaltered balance of electoral forces—it is tempting to exaggerate the elements of continuity and to treat sovereignty merely as an incident which facilitated the enlargement and consolidation of the prior social formation. That would be mistaken. Statehood vastly enhanced the overall range of the political élite's activity—its scope for forging inter-state alliances, opening or closing the gates to immigration, and modifying the distribution of power and economic resources in civil society. Also, the circumstances attending sovereignty created a new social map in the Israeli part of Mandatory Palestine by setting in motion the flight of four-fifths of the Arab population and, immediately afterwards, inviting a doubling of the Jewish population after just three years of immigration. Taken together, these new parameters had the potential for radically altering the contours of the economic structure, state-society relations, and mass politics in the 'post-revolutionary' era.

Three specific issues require attention. First, what happened to the Yishuv pattern of social protection? Specifically, why is it that such hallmarks as clientelism, segmentation, opposition to income guarantees, and the centrality of the Histadrut persisted without any major overhaul? State, party, and class interests in the new circumstances implied by sovereignty all played a part in reproducing the broad features of pre-1948 social protection. Second, the focus thus far on social policy issues has necessarily deferred consideration of economic questions, and in particular the way that public policy led the Israeli economy first along a path of rapid expansion and later into a quagmire of hyperinflation and stagnation. Here we shall note how crystallization of the role of the state in the political economy after 1948 laid the basis for swift economic growth. The third and last puzzle sketched in our introductory review of policy outcomes was why it is that in Israel, the combination of long-term social-democratic political pre-eminence and a highly corporate labour centre has failed to bring about industrial peace. In this connection we shall review, and place in longer-term perspective, the argument of Chapter 5: while sovereignty transformed the Histadrut into a fully 'corporatized' intermediary, from the very outset the disciplinary capacities of the new corporatism were damagingly incomplete.

The social policy transition

Israel's establishment as a sovereign political entity dissolved the contradiction between the aspirations of the Histadrut and other Yishuv institutions to perform state *functions*, and their profoundly limited state *capacities*. As a result, the dependence of the Zionist political centre on the intermediary role of the Histadrut was, in principle, at an end. Those who remained at the helm of the labour organization took a different view, however. They now expected to reap the benefits of the successful struggle for national liberation, in the form of delegation of state authority and a flow of other privileges to strengthen the Histadrut and its allied institutions.

In the event, despite a strong inclination to concentrate authority and resources in the new state apparatus, its leadership recognized that the old partnership with the Histadrut still had its uses. For macro-economic reasons the Histadrut was needed for restraining workers' demands. The labour organization's affiliated enterprises, which had become a major economic power during World War II, constituted a flexible means of steering the economy in the service of state objectives. Above all, straddling both Histadrut and state was the party. The Yishuv experience had demonstrated the Histadrut's value to Mapai as a potent instrument for mobilizing both resources and voters. These advantages were now as crucial as they had ever been. The decade or so prior to sovereignty had already posed new challenges to the labour movement, notably the growing size and self-confidence of the urban Jewish working class and the partly related rise of left-wing opposition to Mapai. To these the attainment of sovereignty added the loss of labour's indispensability to the national cause, now that this cause was won; and a greatly enlarged population, over much of which Mapai had no a priori claim.

Given this vector of political and economic incentives for keeping the Histadrut intact, a compromise was reached over the role of the labour organization in performing quasi-state functions. While the Histadrut did not emerge unscathed, 'nationalization' bypassed the Sick Fund and the Provident Funds. The former proved to be remarkably effective in bringing newcomers into the Histadrut and Mapai's sphere of influence. The significance of the Provident Funds was limited at first, but grew rapidly. They provided for a variety of contingencies (sickness, lay-off) which otherwise would have been candidates for state social insurance. And they spawned the supplementary pension scheme which soon came to embrace more than half of all wage-earners, locked in by their employers under the terms of national collective agreements. The authorities permitted the Histadrut to exploit much of its vast accumulation of pension fund contributions as a convenient means for financing new investment in the labour organization's own economic enterprises. In this way, the survival of 'voluntarism' in social policy became part of the political-economic dynamic around which Mapai reconstructed its political dominance in the post-sovereignty era.

Sovereignty not only posed the issue of whether social policy functions would now be taken over by the state, but in principle also raised the spectre of an end to the politicized and particularistic ethos of pre-1948 social protection. A small cadre of policy advisers inside the Histadrut indeed urged the labour movement to embrace a progressive, Beveridge-style programme; but the implications of transition to a universal, social insurance-based set of income entitlements would have been intolerable to Mapai. For one thing, the division between Arab and Jewish citizens would have been rendered irrelevant and invisible. The state was, on the contrary, anxious to apply the nationality criterion to social policy as an aid in the subordination of Arab citizens to Jewish territorial and political domination. Discrimination against Arabs was, moreover, temptingly easy to carry out as a result of the willingness of the Zionist institutions of the Yishuv era to continue raising funds and supplying welfare services on a Jewish-only basis.[18]

The state's reluctance to embrace a comprehensive 'citizen's wage' did not originate solely in the national conflict. Material motives were also at work. As a result of both prejudice (Eastern Jews were widely assumed to be work-shy) and the formulation of plans for labour-intensive industrialization, the political élite was anxious to maintain economic discipline among the Jewish poor. Consequently, for more than two decades the state successfully resisted the introduction of unemployment insurance. Benefits under social assistance and the preferred solution, relief works, were deliberately held below the minimum market wage. Since both the Mapai leadership and its most powerful mass constituencies were composed of pre-1948 veterans, public policy was at the same time naturally sensitive to veterans' economic interests.

Given the desperate straits and lower customary living standards of Arabs and, to a lesser extent, Eastern Jews, established workers had good reason to fear labour-market competition. Bifurcating social protection between a residual welfare state and a sheltered labour-market segment with privileged access for veterans was a way of assuaging these fears. It was also a means of ensuring that employers (including those within the labour-movement family) would retain their access to cheap labour.

Its approach to the distributional conflicts inherent in the meeting between veteran, immigrant, and Palestinian workers is illustrative of the wider political problem faced by Mapai, of how to simultaneously retain the loyalty of its former supporters while drawing masses of new citizens into the party's orbit. Had social policy moved in a more social-democratic direction, it would have taken most of the sting out of the clientelism on which Mapai was so heavily reliant. Instead, the party's far-flung network of officials in the public and Histadrut bureaucracies, working closely with street-level 'bosses', was able to bargain life-chances for votes with considerable political effect. The most susceptible clients were the groups which were most disorganized and impoverished, and the least familiar with their surroundings—Eastern immigrants and the remnant of the former Arab majority. Mapai also found ways of cementing the effects of this dependency on political loyalty—by appealing to the national sentiments of the Easterners and by exploiting the system of military rule which governed the Arab population until the mid-1960s.

The economic transition

With the acquisition of sovereignty by the Jewish political centre and the transformation of the Palestinian Arabs into a subordinate minority, the balance of power between capital and organized Jewish labour in the market arena moved sharply in labour's favour. Moreover, the classic economic barrier to eliminating private ownership—the state's dependence on the bourgeoisie for the performance of crucial economic functions—was far from imperative. Private investment capital was at a premium and there was little objective hope of attracting foreign investors because of Israel's obvious economic handicaps and uncertain future. Nevertheless, for a variety of political reasons Mapai chose not to infringe on the private sector, and most of the entrepreneurial activity which the state regarded as properly belonging within the public sphere was delegated to the labour-movement economy (see Chapter 3). The chief political–economic issue in Israel's early years was not whether to appropriate the appropriators. What was at stake was instead how to divide the means of capital formation suddenly concentrated in the hands of the state—the result of its take-over of Palestinian refugees' former land and property, economic aid from world Jewry and foreign states, and the extensive regulatory powers acquired by the authorities.

The ruling party responded with a share-out that respected the existing tripartite (public, Histadrut, and private) ownership structure and encouraged a loose division of labour between the sectors. Newly created *state* enterprises were utilized mainly to build and administer infrastructure. 'Movement' enterprises (Histadrut factories, agricultural collectives, and related institutions) were encouraged in so far as they were expected to give the politicians control over the economy's true commanding heights; and equally important, because of their capacity to furnish the party with funds, spoils, and a sizeable captive audience of workers and farmers. Finally, Mapai opted to maintain the status quo *vis-à-vis* the large existing sector of small and medium-sized *private* business, also making it possible for some large, new private concerns to flourish provided they embraced the sponsorship of the party/state.

The early post-sovereignty years saw the formation of the main lines of economic policy as well as structure. It soon became evident that the economy was in danger of being permanently crippled by severe balance-of-payments deficits. Largely ignoring economists' advice, the government by the early 1950s had forged its own solution to the problem, in the form of foreign 'unilateral transfers'. The mechanisms were varied: new forms of fund-raising in Jewish communities overseas; American gratitude for Israel's effusive support in the Korean conflict; and, above all, the government's sponsorship—in the face of intense political controversy—of an agreement under which large quantities of West German goods, machinery, and raw materials were to reach Israel over a 12-year period as collective compensation for the Holocaust.

With the major sources of both liquid capital and physical plant entering the country from abroad via Mapai-controlled public bodies, the state became the dynamo powering the country's economic engine. The government and its economic ministries were consequently in a strong position to manage distributional flows in the interests of the governing party. Among the symptoms were a pronounced 'electoral business cycle'; generous overt and covert funding of Mapai and its allies; and the ability to grant economic favours to individual citizens or whole communities. So far as business interests were concerned, by virtue of its near-monopoly over new sources of investment finance and its ability to give or withhold access to a vast array of government contracts, concessions, exemptions, and incentives, the state also acquired 'the potential power to destroy any firm or to make it extremely profitable' (Aharoni, 1976: 357).

The macro-economic consequences of the political–economic arrangements put into place after 1948 are starkly clear from a single datum: between 1954 and 1965 per capita GNP rose by an average of 7 per cent a year in real terms. Without question, this exceptional performance resulted from the encounter between the extensive inflow of gift capital to the state and the rapid growth of consumer demand and labour supply attendant upon mass immigration.[19]

The transformation of labour relations

As Chapter 4 has documented, in the Jewish Yishuv between the two world wars trade unionism and collective bargaining were highly decentralized. The Histadrut's policy of obliging employers to recruit labour solely through its employment offices was only partially successful. And, the existence of small rival labour organizations and an unorganized minority belied its pretensions to a monopoly of representation. Together with the threat of Arab competition, this placed the Histadrut's unskilled members (by far the majority) in a highly exposed labour-market position. Employers relied on this weakness together with the readiness of the authorities to come to their defence, to act as brakes on labour militancy. They, therefore, had little interest in organizing or bargaining along corporatist lines, even though the Histadrut leadership would have liked to extend organizational centralization to the sphere of labour relations. During World War II the British authorities for the first time acquired a major interest in limiting trade union struggles. But this corporatist evolution was nipped in the bud as a result of hesitation on the part of employers and the regime itself.

Sovereignty changed this (see Chapter 5). The Histadrut and the state took a variety of steps aimed at strengthening the labour organization's political capacities and its authority in labour relations matters. Monopolization and centralization of trade unionism was complemented by a national wage policy, negotiated between top Histadrut officials and government ministers within closed party forums. Within this framework, Mapai's Histadrut leaders periodically acceded to Treasury demands for wage restraint in the form of freezes, foregone indexation rights, and so forth. But unlike post-war neo-corporatist developments in Western Europe, union-government political exchange in Israel was not based on the sacrifice of bargaining power for a full employment commitment—since this commitment was dependably strong for reasons of state-building. It is true that Histadrut leaders, accustomed to advocating worker self-sacrifice in the name of the national interest, articulated the same rationale which Olson (1982) has discerned in the 'encompassing' interest organizations of Europe's corporatist societies. Nevertheless, the underlying reasons for wage moderation were to an important extent peculiar to the Israeli context: the fact that until 1977 the Histadrut's officials owed their positions to the ruling party; the Histadrut's built-in appreciation of employer interests in view of its own substantial role as an employer; and the leverage enjoyed by the Treasury as a result of the dependence of Histadrut economic institutions and social services on state subsidy.

From the beginning, this system produced only limited labour peace. In the early years well-organized veteran workers supported by the left-wing opposition forced the top leadership to embrace their demands or else pressed these demands independently. At that time the labour market position of the Eastern and Israeli Arabs who rapidly became the mainstay of the unskilled manual labour force was very precarious. They were either excluded from Histadrut union protection or brought under the tutelage of party appointees. The major disciplinary problem for the Histadrut and the state (which for the most part was their employer) originated among the rapidly growing white-collar labour force, especially salaried professionals. The enormous expansion of state activity after sovereignty, not least in the 'absorption' of the mass immigrations, had transformed educated labour into an economic and political pressure group of major importance. Confronting the

Histadrut's insistence on representing the entire spectrum of wage-earners within a single comprehensive framework, upper-level public employees repeatedly went to bat over the issues of wage differentials and union autonomy. Their pressure paid off, but not before the eruption of many bitter labour disputes.

By drawing on more than sixty years of statistics on labour disputes, it is possible to place the developments which followed sovereignty in the perspective of the *longue durée*, including more recent trends yet to be discussed. Industrial conflict in Israel (and earlier, within the Jewish community of Palestine) has experienced some major conjunctural surges. The first great peaking of labour militancy, in the mid-1920s, was coincident with the beginning of systematic record-keeping by the Histadrut and, economically, with a short-lived boom. Two subsequent peaks were also ushered in by exceptional bursts of economic activity: the first in the course of World War II; the second during the 'crisis of full employment' in the first half of the 1960s.

Of most interest from our perspective are the secular transitions which the data in Table 6.1 reveal. During Israel's first decade of sovereignty strike activity was significantly lower than it had been in the Yishuv. In part this was a reflection of the fact that many of the post-1948 entrants to the work-force were effectively beyond the pale of collective action, although it also resulted from the development of corporatist labour restraint. But a proliferation of short strikes in the context of the labour shortages of the early 1960s signalled the entry of many formerly powerless workers (other than Arabs) into the orbit of industrial militancy.[20] In the process, the form of conflicts was permanently altered, away from relatively sparse involvement in somewhat protracted disputes towards more frequent and dispersed—but much briefer—participation.

The Israeli experience is thus quite different from the diminishing historical path of strike activity in the corporatist nations of Western Europe. Instead it came more closely to resemble the traditional French and Italian pattern of broadly based but demonstrative conflicts.[21] In Israel two different phenomena were behind the growing reach of strikes and accompanying attenuation of their intensity: the mobilization from below of narrowly constituted groups acting outside of the Histadrut's corporatist framework; and a proliferation of mass actions by workers in the state sector. Later,

TABLE 6.1. *Long-term indicators of strike activity, 1924–88*

	1924–5	1926–47	1948–59	1960–73	1975–88
Worker involvements[a]	218	39	23	80	218
Average duration[b]	13.8	11.4	7.7	2.5	2.1

Source: Etkin (1982), with updating for the 1980s on the basis of figures supplied by the Chief Labour Relations Officer in the Ministry of Labour.

Notes: Period averages are geometric means, to reduce the impact of occasional and unrepresentative years of hyperactivity within sub-periods.

[a] 'Worker involvements' are the number of persons involved in strikes and lock-outs for every thousand workers, the latter calculated on the basis of total employment (and before 1948, the total *Jewish* labour force in Palestine, since the strike data used pertained only to the Yishuv).

[b] 'Average duration' is the number of working days on strike per worker involved.

in the 1970s and beyond, there was a major escalation of distributional conflicts generally. These reflected both the declining political coherence and legitimacy of the ruling Labour Party and the difficult macro-economic choices facing the state. These new conditions did not alter the *shape* of industrial conflict, but resulted in marked increases in its *magnitude*. In fact, as Table 6.1 shows, in the contemporary period the reach of labour militancy across the workforce has come full circle to precisely the level recorded when urban trade unionism first mushroomed in the Yishuv in the 1920s.

Let us now pause to sum up the implications of the transition from settlement to statehood. The political economy of post-1948 in some respects reinforced and in others modified the basic thrust of earlier policy legacies. In social protection the transition to sovereignty had particularly conservative effects. Mapai's leadership in the state was impressed more by the benefits than by the costs of perpetuating the Histadrut's triple role as bearer of the functions of state and capital as well as working-class representation. The temptation to exploit segmented and selective social policy for exerting political and economic control over subordinate groups further closed the potential opening to a universalistic welfare state and reinvigorated the old ideology of constructivism. In contrast, access to the powers of state fundamentally changed the role of the political centre in relation to the economy and the labour market, by making it possible for the political élite to realize aspirations hitherto outside the realm of the possible. The economic role of the state was enlarged far beyond the limited dimensions adhered to by the government of Palestine (at least in peacetime). The import of people and capital continued to drive economic growth but acquired new forms. With state stimulation, immigrants poured into Israel while concurrently, institutional transfers took over the earlier role of personal assets in capital import. Buoyed up by the state's redistribution of these transfers, private business became in a sense just one more client of the party/state.

From sovereignty to crisis

How significant are developments subsequent to the formative period of state-building for explaining contemporary policy patterns and consequences? So far as social policy is concerned, it would be mistaken to exaggerate the changes introduced during the 1960s and early 1970s. The welfare state altered over time, but the alterations were more form than substance. Certainly, income maintenance became more generous, less politicized, and less selective; yet without modifying the broad lines of Israel's comparative singularity. Except for child allowances (an instrument of population policy as well as social security) the state continued to provide relatively low levels of income support by OECD standards. Social protection remained partially segmented between Ashkenazim, Easterners, and Arabs. Finally, the role of Histadrut and employer-linked provision grew rather than contracted.[22]

In the sphere of labour relations, there were far more significant innovations during the period between the onset of rapid economic growth in the late 1950s and its cessation in the mid-1970s. It has already been pointed out that with the advent of full employment worker militancy permeated beyond privileged public-sector groups. It embraced sections of the blue-collar labour force in the business sector who succeeded in sloughing off their dependence on the Histadrut and demanded the conditions of the primary labour market. The chastening experience of the mid-1960s recession had no more than a temporary effect on these workers' susceptibility to traditional corporatist controls; but there were other reasons why, by the early 1970s, their propensity to strike was once again substantially curtailed.

One important source of relative labour quiescence in the business sector was that Israel's occupation of the West Bank and Gaza introduced a new pool of marginal labour to the secondary labour market, which substantially weakened those citizen-workers who were unable to escape to more attractive jobs. Second, the emergence of more co-ordinated and combative action by the private-sector Manufacturers' Association during the recession was subsequently consolidated, with the encouragement of the state. And it did much to block the earlier trend towards co-ordinated worker-committee militancy and to discourage the Histadrut from filling the resultant vacuum. Indeed, co-operation from above came increasingly to characterize industrial relations in the private sector, facilitated by growing linkages between the managers of private and Histadrut firms. A third source of restraint stemmed from institutional change. The Histadrut introduced a number of organizational reforms which made it possible to bring trade unionism and collective bargaining more firmly under its control, at least in those occupations and enterprises where workers lacked independent bargaining strength. Those workers who did enjoy such strength were in many cases silenced at the work-place level by the payment of special wage supplements and fringe benefits, along with management's partial co-optation of workers' committees.[23]

Very notably, most of these new sources of labour quiescence bypassed the public sector, where worker militancy had increased substantially by the early 1970s.[24] Nearly all public enterprises and services refrained from employing Palestinian labour. At the same time, the state's behaviour as an employer tended to stimulate rather than discourage strike activity. Weakened by the labour parties' loss of their collective Knesset majority in 1969, the government invited conflict when it attempted to control inflation in an overheated economy by holding the lid on public-sector wages. On the workers' side, the state faced not only long-standing pressures from salaried employees for wider pay differentials, but also had to contend with the growing power of big workers' committees in the publicly owned monopolies responsible for crucial infrastructural services.

The Histadrut leadership, the state's traditional partner in political exchange, experienced waning credibility with the rank and file generally and particular difficulties in imposing restraint on the strong public-sector workers. As a result, Histadrut-government relations became so strained that the Labour Party's mediational role turned increasingly peripheral. The irony was, of course, that the growing inadequacy of corporatist restraint in the public sector was paralleled by precisely the opposite trend in the remainder of the labour market. The pattern of intimate co-operation and complex trade-offs, characteristic in the past of corporatist Histadrut–state relations, now became the hallmark of the deepened bilateral relationship between the leaders of the Histadrut and the private employers. Tellingly, with a tripling of public-sector strike involvements in the early 1970s, the government veered towards imposed statutory remedies for labour unrest, the very negation of its traditional policy of backing the Histadrut's exclusive role as intermediary between workers, employers, and the state.[25]

To return to our initial question, it thus appears that the continuity of policy and policy outcomes was relatively substantial for the welfare state, and rather less so for labour relations. The peculiarities of Israeli social policy, viewed in comparative perspective, altered little in the course of time, particularly since in most respects the pace of reform in other countries more than matched what was happening in Israel. In contrast, Israel's distinctiveness in terms of industrial conflict has shorter roots. It dates essentially from the period of rapid economic growth following the first decade of sovereignty. The further strike explosion of the mid-1970s and beyond reflects the concentration of industrial conflict in the public sector which was set in motion during the new cycle of growth that followed the 1966–7 slow-down.

From the more contemporary perspective of the decade which ended in the mid-1980s, the sharpest discontinuity is to be found in the area of economic policy and performance. Israel's response to the global problems of economic stagnation after 1973 exhibits a notable contrast to the earlier period, at least in terms of outcomes. The economy's severe structural problems and the dismal accomplishments of adjustment policies, except in terms of unemployment, reflect a sea change of major dimensions. This change can be interpreted as the transformation of the state's role in the political economy from a pre-condition for growth to a hindrance to economic adaptation. That there has been (at least up to the mid-1980s) such a transformation is treated as axiomatic among virtually the entire economics profession, and increasingly also by 'public opinion' at large. But the reasons for the shift in state–economy relations are by no means self-evident. Israeli economists have tended to view the problem as one of cabinet ministers' alleged myopia and the readiness of politicians generally to succumb to popular pressure. Most political scientists have simply ignored the issue. We shall outline three explanations, each plausible, each consistent with our account of historical developments, but each suggesting an inadequacy which we intend to tackle in the final chapter of this book. In order to prepare the ground for these discussions, we first need to consider the principal economic trends prior to and during the crisis.

Economic disorder and decline

Israel's first wave of rapid growth, which lasted until the recession of 1966–7, rested essentially on the same foundations as the booms of the Yishuv period—namely, the onset of a major influx of people and money from outside the country. However, although by the early 1970s migration to Israel had recovered to the relatively high levels experienced a decade before, even providing the economy with a substantial stock of ready-made human capital, the magnitudes were greatly diminished compared to the immediate post-1948 period. Far more salient to the economic recovery of the late 1960s and the boom of the early 1970s were a range of factors contingent (as was the upturn in immigration, to some extent) on the Israeli victory in the war of 1967.

To begin with, Israel's conquest of the West Bank, Gaza Strip, and Sinai Peninsula enabled it to develop highly advantageous terms of trade with the occupied territories: the import of cheap labour and oil, and the export of merchandise to a literally captive market.[26] Of still greater importance was the economic stimulus resulting from the militarization of Israel's economy. After the 1967 war, weapons-related production (along with construction projects and a variety of other 'civilian' services paid for by the military) became the hub of Israel's rapid economic growth. Boom conditions in the international market for armaments encouraged the belief that expansion of the domestic military industries would serve the needs of the economy as well as the armed forces. Requirements for the latter multiplied in the context of the arms race which overtook the Middle East and Israel's geopolitical elevation to the status of a regional power.[27]

From an economic policy viewpoint, the strategy adopted during the pre-war 'Mitun'—curtailing domestic demand, tolerating high unemployment, and cutting back capital subsidies—was effectively turned on its head after 1967. At first the evident inflationary potential of the new expansion was avoided, even though wages lagged decisively behind the recovery of output and profits. By 1970, however, a number of factors including wage pressures caused a sharp rise in the rate of inflation, to an alarming 10 per cent (more than twice the level then typical of the OECD countries). The economy was thus already on an inflationary course when in 1973 Israel was surprised by an expensive war (and further massive rearmament in its wake) and by the drain on its resources due to the rising cost of oil and other imported commodities.

The response of the last Labour government, in the years 1975–7, was a series of deliberate price increases, wage freezes, and other austerity measures, alongside the preservation and even expansion of military commitments and civilian services alike. This combination was what initially produced the pattern that came to characterize Israel's economic performance for more than a decade—spiralling inflation and stalled growth, but virtually no increase in unemployment.[28] The Likud governments which ruled Israel between 1977 and 1984 embraced a bewildering series of economic policy zigzags, which, however, were tied together by several recurrent threads.

1. Despite continuing stagnation of the national product, there were large increases in private consumption and wealth (although they were unevenly distributed among different classes and followed a pronounced electoral cycle).
2. No cutbacks were effected in either military or civilian public expenditure and employment, necessitating big budget deficits and heavy borrowing.
3. Incomes policy achieved only intermittent and temporary

restraint of real wages, typically enforced by highly inflationary means (devaluations and cuts in price subsidies).

4. Vast windfall profits accrued to banking and other business interests as a result of the state's failure to adjust its tax, credit and subsidy policies to rapid inflation.

The common failure of the Labour and Likud governments to adopt effective stabilization policies, and the underlying continuity of policy between the two regimes, contrast rather strikingly with the clashing normative visions of Israel's left and right in relation to the national conflict—the domain which increasingly came to monopolize the very meaning of the left–right continuum. It is true that party rhetoric in the field of domestic policy is also characterized by ideological discord, partly along the lines of the usual left–right polarities on the classic issues of the role of the market and the desirable scope and form of the welfare state. But the Labour Alignment and the Likud are also equal partners in the full-employment consensus. They are divided primarily by their conflicting interests in the continued vesting of key economic and social functions in the Histadrut. That is why Israel's political history is replete with such ironies as the right's vigilant advocacy of 'nationalization' of the health system, and its attacks on the Histadrut's role as an employer on the grounds that this compromises the interests of rank-and-file workers.[29]

In practice the 'political upheaval', as the 1977 change of government came to be known, had surprisingly little short-term impact on the entire range of distinctive features of domestic policy with which this chapter has been concerned. The Likud took office seemingly determined to savage the Histadrut, but often found it prudent to avoid head-on confrontation. In economic affairs the new regime at first embraced the cause of deregulation, but its fervour was decidedly tempered by the exigencies of the electoral cycle and also by the tension between the party's bourgeois and lower-class wings. Two Likud terms of office and four of the party's finance ministers failed to delimit the breadth of state involvement in the economy or to turn back the tide of stagflation.[30]

While irrespective of its political stewardship the state was seemingly incapable of preventing serious economic deterioration, this should not be interpreted as evidence of the irrelevance of the state. It was not the sheer weight of the blows inflicted by the shocks of 1973 that determined the economy's fate. Rather, these new constraints served to exacerbate an ongoing process of transformation of formerly successful motors of growth and distribution, into fetters on economic success. In this respect, the role of the state in economic steering was critical to the failure of stabilization policy. Assuming that the main lines of economic orthodoxy are correct, the state needed to do two things after 1973 for successful economic adaptation to occur. It had to be able to discipline civil society—to restrain the demands of capital, organized labour, the poor, etc. And it had to discipline itself—to reduce public-sector spending and jobs and to roll back the authorities' domination of Israel's money and capital 'markets'. In the event, public policy failed on both counts.

Accounting for the destabilizing role of the state

To explain these policy failures fully would require a historical and institutional analysis of some complexity. For present purposes, our goal is the more limited one of suggesting some fruitful avenues of explanation to account for the destabilizing consequences of economic policy after 1973. A promising starting-point for this endeavour is to return to those motivating forces—*political*, *distributional*, and *national*—which repeatedly reared their heads earlier in discussing the origins of Israel's policy distinctiveness. From these, there follow three arguments. The first is an Israeli version of theories of overloaded government. It points to Israel's transition to a new era of competitive politics, in which governments gave in to a rising tide of popular demands upon the state. For relevant evidence, we turn to changes in the composition of public spending, the rising magnitude of which is widely regarded as having 'crowded out' business-sector growth and driven inflation upward since the 1973 turning-point. A second hypothesis also stresses the declining independence of the state from societal forces. However, it focuses not on the mass public, but on the failure of political mechanisms of interest intermediation, which formerly had shielded the state from the demands of powerful collectivities. The obvious empirical referent here is the inadequacy of labour restraint in the public sector after 1973, and the resulting resistance of both wages and employment to downward adjustments. Third, in both the present and previous chapter we have emphasized how Israel's national identity and the Arab–Israeli conflict provided critical mechanisms for past economic growth. But arguably, by the 1970s these same defining characteristics of the Israeli context had come to have a depressing rather than a facilitating effect on the state's ability to steer the economy.

Populist excesses

Earlier, we explained the importance of political clientelism and the unique institutional triumvirate of Histadrut, party, and state in the formation of Israel's domestic policy regime. But it was also pointed out that the labour movement's very successes gradually eroded its chief instruments of power. Not only did the material dependency of the electorate diminish in the face of rising prosperity, but also Mapai's internal functioning was impaired by its achievements in co-opting opposition parties and containing challenges from a new generation of would-be leaders. Meanwhile, the right reorganized, embraced new issues (especially the future of the occupied territories), and turned into both a mouthpiece for anti-establishment sentiment and a respectable contender for power. The results of these changes in the political constellation were growing factionalism, party competitiveness, and extra-parliamentary mobilization. It has been widely contended that these trends in turn stimulated the rise of a populist imperative in the economic and social interventions of the state. From the late 1960s, public policy responded defensively to political flux by re-sanctifying the full-employment norm, enlarging the welfare state, and providing conditions for rising private consumption. The fact that this occurred in an inhospitable external environment—which imposed debilitating price rises and greatly increased defence costs on Israel—is said to have magnified the economic consequences of giving in to popular pressure.[31]

The growing political weakness of Israeli governments in their relations with the mass public cannot be denied. Perhaps its most impressive manifestation has been the vigour of the stop–go policy cycle associated with the electoral calendar, in spite of the damaging consequences of pre-election expansion in periods when macroeconomic rationality necessitated restraint.[32] However, the primary structural burden alleged to have been inflicted by the politics of

TABLE 6.2. *Selected fiscal indicators for three periods* (proportions of GNP)

	1962–6	1968–72	1976–84
Total expenditure	36.3	53.1	73.0
Financed domestically	32.1	44.0	55.5
Financed abroad	4.2	9.1	17.4
of which, gifts	(2.9)	(3.4)	(10.8)
Major expenditure components			
Transfer payments	9.1	14.8	31.4
Other civilian expenditure	16.0	15.0	15.5
Military expenditure	10.5	22.4	24.7
of which, imports	(5.3)	(10.5)	(10.3)

Source: Adapted from Meridor (1988: tables 1–3).

Note: Meridor's figures are original estimates which attempted to reconcile government budgetary data with broader national accounts statistics. Debits due to the repayment of debts which are refinanced and the matching revenues from new loans, are both ignored. 'Transfer payments' comprises transfers to households and non-profit organizations, the subsidy implicit in budgeted loans to investors, price subsidies paid to local producers, and real interest on the government's domestic debt. 'Total expenditure' is actually total receipts plus the three components of the deficit in Meridor's table 3. 'Other civilian expenditure' is civilian consumption plus investment.

populism is the growth of the welfare state. It is, therefore, of some importance to clarify changes in the fiscal commitments of the state since the onset of stagflation. That these commitments have grown to almost unbearable proportions cannot in itself be doubted. By 1985, when the deficit peaked, Israel's domestic public debt was one and one-third the size of its GNP. In the same year, more than 40 per cent of the government budget had to be set aside for the settling of past obligations. Table 6.2, which disregards transactions contingent on the rolling over of debt, demonstrates the tremendous net growth over time in the share of national resources allocated by the state.[33] More precisely, that share rose to new plateaus following two major wars—increasing by 17 percentage points of GNP after 1967, and by a further 20 points after 1973.[34]

Even more informative than the overall rise in the state's commitments is their uneven distribution across specific categories. If we set aside what happened in the unrepresentative years immediately following the October 1973 war, it emerges that almost

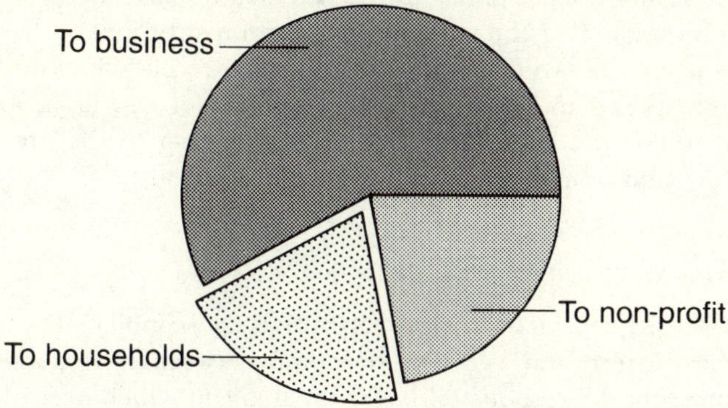

FIG. 6.4. The increase in transfers 1970–80: how 18% of GNP was redistributed

Sources: Meridor (1988) and additional unpublished estimates (dated 24 July 1989) kindly made available by the author.

Note: The three divisions in the figure were created by aggregating Meridor's detailed expenditure categories. In instances where the benefits from transfers flow to both businesses and households, we arbitrarily established a 50–50 split. (This was the case for interest on the domestic public debt and price supports on 'essential' goods and services.) Different ratios would have little effect on the overall result.

all the relative growth in public spending since the crisis (other than debt service) is accounted for by transfer payments. But as Figure 6.4 shows, contrary to the populist hypothesis this evolution was to a great extent due to a spectacular expansion of the welfare state for business.[35] Moreover, in contrast to wage-earners and consumers, who were forced to bear a heavy burden of additional taxes and compulsory loans after 1973, the growing cost of state support for business was not balanced by any offsetting rise in tax receipts. On the contrary, the opportunities for tax avoidance under inflation actually diminished the contribution of the corporate sector to financing its own benefits. So far as social transfers are concerned, the circumstances surrounding the growth of income maintenance do not support the view that the government behaved with rampant economic irresponsibility.[36] It is also noteworthy that only part of the expansion derived from cash transfers to households. An even larger amount was diverted to non-profit organizations—Sick Funds, universities, and parochial schools—whose leverage over the state derived from institutional power and coalition considerations, not popular pressure on the state. Even so, in response to the resource constraints of the crisis period, by the 1980s the state had virtually put a stop to the growth of spending and employment in education and health.[37]

Distributional struggles

We have argued that, historically, material conflicts of interest between Eastern and Western Jews and between Jews and Arabs bear much of the responsibility for the dualism which pervades the welfare state, the labour market, and industrial relations in Israel. Dualism was in turn a mechanism of great importance for the containment of such distributional conflicts, including those that found expression in the labour market. Workers in the secondary market, made even more vulnerable by relatively limited access to public social protection, were constrained from pressing their interests. Concurrently, labour in the primary market was disciplined, at least to some extent, by the corporatist self-restraint exercised by the Histadrut in the context of its relations with the Labour Party and the state. It has also been pointed out, though, that by the late 1960s, growing crystallization of dualist tendencies around the split between public- and private-sector workers led to labour militancy reaching new heights in the state's own domain. Among public employees the always restive professional workers were now joined by newer loci of economic privilege and union autonomy—manual and technical workers employed in state-owned and exclusively Jewish work-places lying on the most sensitive nodes of the political economy (including transport and communication, energy, and the giant state arms and aircraft factories). These trends—which pre-dated the shocks of 1973 and beyond—inevitably had an even greater impact in an environment of powerful economic constraints.

Indeed, there is little doubt that barriers to imposing corporatist restraint on the more powerful sections of the working class made it extremely difficult after 1973 for the state to reduce public-sector employment or to more than temporarily restrain the real wages of public-sector employees (and hence real wages generally). The fact that from mid-1977 onwards the reins of the Histadrut and the state were held by rival parties potentially heightened the difficulties even further. The problem was not so much the absence of Labour Party co-ordination, since by the 1970s party forums in any case played a declining role in Histadrut-state relations. It was also not the case that the traditional enmity between the labour movement and the Revisionists made political exchange impossible; on the contrary, at times trade-offs of wage restraint for favourable concessions to Histadrut enterprises and services were as robust as ever. Nevertheless, since Histadrut and government élites now had no shared interest in enhancing each others' power bases in the long term, by the end of the 1970s a damaging potential for non-co-operation had become evident.[38]

At the same time, the problem faced by the state went well beyond its difficulties in enlisting the Histadrut to help impose moderation on public-sector workers and to publicly endorse the government's economic policies. The difficulty, increasingly, was the evolving collusion between private employers and the Histadrut's managers and officials. In discussing the period leading up to the crisis, we pointed to a tendency for the Histadrut and private industry to conduct quasi-corporatist deals of their own, without the necessity of state mediation. While the state was thus partially deprived of its steering role, it was still called upon to provide the wherewithal to underwrite the internal deals of the business sector.[39]

Undoubtedly, workers employed in the primary labour market of private and Histadrut enterprises also formed an important component of the 'robbers' coalition' facing the state, just as the power of their counterparts in the public sector frustrated attempts to control that sector's wages and employment. However, had the state's economic managers been able to rely on employers outside the public sector to oppose wage demands in their own jurisdiction and to fight the mutual 'contagion' of public and private militancy more resolutely, then the workers could have been restrained. As it was, the state behaved as if it had little choice but to compensate employers for the cost of wage concessions. This was particularly evident so far as exporters were concerned, since policy-makers apparently felt compelled to prevent any deterioration of profitability in order not to impair precious foreign currency earnings. The result was a highly inflationary cycle of devaluation followed by pressure on wages as workers sought to recover purchasing power and catch up with exporters' windfall profits, resulting in a further 'corrective' devaluation. In short, it was the autonomy and cohesion of capital, as much as the leverage enjoyed by well-placed groups of workers, that impaired the state's ability to dampen distributional conflicts in the crisis period.

The national conflict

Zionism and the conflict between Israel and the (Palestinian) Arabs, have long had implications of major importance for the economy of Israel (and before that, the Yishuv). In different ways, Israel's military success in 1967 and near-failure in 1973 delegitimized Labour and catalysed the right, thereby reinforcing the political trends—fear of electoral punishment, intensified coalition bargaining, and responsiveness to organized pressure groups—which fed 'populist' economic policies. But the national conflict has also been directly incorporated into the economy, with definite consequences for Israel's economic decline.

We argued earlier that Israel's occupation of the West Bank and Gaza, coupled with rapid military industrialization fed by a regional arms race, constituted a new formula for economic growth to replace the earlier (and by the mid-1960s no longer workable) model based on the import of inexpensive human and financial capital. But this new formula was not without its disadvantages, which emerged with full force in a later period of highly constrained economic development. Precisely because of the relatively exposed and unsophisticated nature of the markets and sources of labour opened up by the occupation, they had the effect of reinforcing the more 'backward' elements of the Israeli economy. In addition, the almost exclusive concentration of high-tech resources in the military-related domain exacted a heavy price, as did the highly subsidized character of arms production and the volatility of the international arms market.[40]

Because of the potentially damaging consequences of these two mechanisms under the difficult economic conditions which prevailed after 1973 and given the fact that both were so obviously dependent on the state for their very existence, it is important to understand why public policy failed to respond with appropriate structural adjustments. Israel's failure to distance itself economically from the occupied territories clearly followed from its political commitment to continuing the occupation, and the concomitant need to prevent civil unrest. But it also reflected the vested interests of the occupation's economic beneficiaries (producers and employers as well as workers) in Israel. To understand the failure to sponsor conversion from military to civilian production again depends on perceiving the role played by capital—in both senses of the term. As we shall demonstrate in the chapter which follows, the state's vital contribution to the profitability of arms production in Israel needs to be interpreted in the broader context of the growing power of *business interests* in relation to the state. Additionally, the changing composition of the *liquid capital* passing through the state—i.e. the growth of American aid earmarked explicitly or implicitly for Israel's military aggrandizement—had the effect of adding to the pressures to engage in arms production and of diminishing the overall economic reach of the state.

Conclusions

The paradoxical aspects of the Israeli policy regime which have been the central concern of this chapter are a reminder that typological abstractions are precisely that—abstractions from nationally distinctive contexts formed by specific historical trajectories. The comparative study of political economy has increasingly recognized the confounding but inescapable truth that there exist diverse roads to similar policy outcomes.[41] A second verity, the logical obverse of the first, is that like polities are capable of generating unlike outcomes. The proposition axiomatic to this chapter, namely, the disjuncture in the Israeli case between the apparent strength of working-class mobilization and the major thrust of domestic policy is, of course, a case in point. We have tried to show the indispensability of a historically and institutionally grounded perspective for illuminating such a paradox. Israel's departures from the norms of social-democratic corporatism can be understood only in terms of the peculiar origins and formative experiences of the labour movement, the particular purposes and modalities which it attached to the state in the context of overarching national and distributive conflicts, and a highly ramified set of interactions between Israel and the international system (including immigration, capital import, and geopolitical alignment and disputation).

It would be fair to say that in Israel both social democracy and the welfare state have developed more along *dualist* than socialist lines. The fundamental mainspring of dualism is the deeply embedded cleavage between Arabs and Jews, the legacy of the entwined economic and national conflict which became internalized and institutionalized in the organizational and political mobilization of the Jewish working class in Palestine/Israel. But the pronounced competition and inequality among ethnically different Jews has also played a role, exemplified during the period of mass immigration by the interest of the dominant (European-born) veterans in blocking new immigrants from North Africa and the Middle East from affluence and mobility in the market arena. Coinciding with the Labour Party's inclination to exploit social policy as an instrument of voter dependency, this distributional struggle resulted in a double system of social protection: market-based economic advance and security backed up by an array of social entitlements for the stronger groups of wage-earners; and a particularistic, tight-fisted public welfare system for the needy. For more than two decades following the attainment of sovereignty in 1948, Labour succeeded in reaping sufficient political credit from both groups to sustain a broad popular base.

Complementing the peculiarities of Israel's variant of social democracy is the flawed character of Israeli neo-corporatism as a paradigm of politico-economic stability. In spite of theoretically favourable pre-conditions for corporatist intermediation by the peak labour association, labour relations are comparatively—though not uniformly—unruly. In those sectors where labour peace is the norm, this is in large measure due to labour-market dualism, i.e. a combination of 'micro-collaboration' between private business and the Histadrut (which itself is a major employer) together with the political weakness of the groups typically employed in the lower tier of the market.

The incomplete scope and effectiveness of political exchange between the Histadrut and the state is one of the reasons why it took more than a decade to engineer a political consensus around a comprehensive economic stabilization policy for the post-1973 era. In the interim, Israel's long spurt of rapid economic growth abruptly ceased, and its *monthly* rate of inflation rose to double-digit levels. It has sometimes been argued that the striking cross-national differences in these and other indicators of economic adjustment to post-1973 conditions can be explained, at least in part, by differences in countries' vulnerability to oil price hikes and other shocks of the period. In the Israeli case, not only was the economy already heavily dependent on imported oil, but as a result of the Yom Kippur War military commitments were greatly expanded.

In studying these new burdens, Israeli economists have contended that despite their traumatic character, the underlying growth path of the Israeli economy could have been maintained if economic policy had responded appropriately.[42] That the problem may indeed be traced to the state's role in economic steering is also suggested by the specific ways in which it responded to the new challenges. Subsidizing the business sector in a futile attempt to revive growth, attempting to contain inflation by generating still more inflation, and other demonstrably inefficient policy responses were far from constituting technical necessities. Moreover, the evidence assembled in this chapter indicates that it would be naïve to regard the economic burden of Israel's military commitments solely in the context of the requirements of national defence. Roughly half of Israel's post-1973 military spending has been devoted to purchasing American arms paid for by the American government. As the next chapter will show, the other (domestic) half of expenditure was a critical element in the rising profitability of big business.

The discussion in this chapter contributes in a number of specific respects to unravelling the puzzle of Israel's distinctive pattern of economic performance between 1974 and 1985. This pattern, it will be recalled, combined low/no growth and high/hyper inflation with comparatively full employment.

Israel's relatively *low unemployment* is closely bound up with the operation of its 'defence economy'. In the period under discussion, the overall military labour market (including manpower absorbed by arms-related industries) was Israel's most important antidote to unemployment—although not the only one. Particularly in the initial few years of the crisis several other mechanisms also operated, either to cut supply (the rapid growth of the commuter labour force from the occupied territories was temporarily halted), or to create demand (most notably in the form of new public-sector jobs in education and health).[43]

Our analysis also offers several pointers for explaining the *growth slow-down.* Beyond the external shocks of the 1970s, we argue that this can best be understood in terms of the exhaustion of a specific political–economic formula for economic growth. That formula rested on the fruits of conquest, massive demand for military-related products and services, and (at the start) labour quiescence. Expansion of the protective activities of the state, both military and social, undoubtedly contributed to the measured stagnation of the economy (in part simply because activities of this type always translate conservatively into estimates of economic output). But no less important, the state's extensive subsidies to capital (and the captive markets and manpower provided by the occupied territories) had the effect of impeding efficiency in the business sector. Meanwhile as inflation rose, financial and industrial enterprises alike found it more profitable to devote their resources to speculation in financial markets (including the 'gray' and black markets not reflected in the national accounts) than to production.[44]

Lastly, *inflation* was stoked by the state's responses to the power of both labour and capital. In responding to past inflation, governments led by Labour and Likud alike periodically induced further price rises by administrative means in the hope of cutting real wages. However, in the face of strong worker resistance and heavily cushioned employers, this tactic yielded only transient benefits at the cost of pushing up inflation to a still higher notch. At the same time, Israel's self-defeating cycle of costly public borrowing and rising public expenditure had enormously profitable side-effects for business. These profits were dependent on institutional arrangements which pegged interest rates on private loans to fluctuations in the cost of living, while leaving the interest due on loans issued by the government unencumbered by linkage. The question which must be asked in this context is *why* the state was unable to impose the procedural adjustments needed to lower the burden of inflation on its fiscal balances and economic stability generally. By the same token, it is necessary to question why the state proved to be so ready to expand the welfare state for big business; and equally, why military industrialization—arguably a grossly inefficient path to increased employment and economic growth—was so generously encouraged. These are the puzzles which will be taken up in the next chapter.

Notes

1. Unless otherwise stated, data cited in the text of this chapter were derived from two standard sources: The Bank of Israel's *Annual Report*, or the Central Bureau of Statistics' *Statistical Abstract of Israel.*
2. As noted in the Introduction, the phrase 'political control of the economy' was coined by Tufte (1978). While the specifics of the debate have altered, the issues are clearly defined in two volumes published more than a decade ago; namely, Lindberg, Crouch, and Offe (1975), especially the essay by Andrew Martin (1975); and Crouch (1979), especially the introductory chapter.
3. For discussions of the 'social-democratic model' see Shalev (1983*a*) and Esping-Andersen (1989).
4. Special measures introduced by Israel's 'Government of National Unity' in 1985 succeeded in reducing inflation from triple- to double-digit levels and in initiating some significant economic reforms. These trends have already had important reverberations for both the structure and the mode of operation of the Israeli economy, but by the end of the 1980s their depth and durability was still uncertain. The successes of the emergency Stabilization Plan introduced in July 1985 were undoubtedly dependent in part on potentially fragile conjunctures in both the international economy and domestic politics. During the first two years of stabilization, the economy not only experienced dramatic disinflation, but this was accompanied by very little increase in unemployment and even some resumption of growth. However, after two more years the Israeli economy entered the throes of a severe recession, and despite this, the rate of inflation, the balance of payments deficit, and the budget deficit remained at problematically high levels. Many economists have questioned whether the long-term structural objectives of stabilization are in fact in the process of realization. See on this point the virtually continuous discussions in the pages of the leading forum for policy debate among economists, the *Rivon Lekalkala.*
5. For economists' discussions of the causes and dimensions of the post-1973 crisis see Ben-Porath (1986).
6. More recently, in the period which lies beyond the purview of this chapter, Israel's position has altered quite dramatically. As a result of the pronounced slow-down which began in the middle of 1987, by

the end of the decade unemployment had reached a level (*c*.10%) unprecedented for two decades. By way of contrast, the OECD's comparative data for 1988 identified only four countries with double-digit levels of unemployment.

7. For in-depth analyses of domestic public policy in the seven countries included in Figures 6.2 and 6.3 see Castles ed. (1989).
8. Wilensky's study referred only to government spending on social security, as defined by the ILO, as a proportion of GNP. A number of qualifications surround the ranking of Israel *vis-à-vis* the OECD nations in this manner. Israel's relatively youthful demographic profile (which could have been captured by standardization in terms of 'need' rather than resources) explains part of its laggardness in pension spending. On the other hand, Israel's 'effort' is significantly inflated by the ILO's inclusion of expenditures in the framework of the Histadrut Sick Fund (Kupat Cholim), in direct contradiction to its declared criteria for 'public' programmes. Another bias in the same direction is introduced by the use of GDP, rather than 'total resources', including foreign gifts and loans, to standardize the level of welfare spending (although it might be argued that these additional resources merely compensate for Israel's exceptional military burden). For further discussion see Shalev (1983*c*).
9. See Moab (1982) for a detailed comparison of Israeli and OECD social security spending. Israel's relative generosity in child allowances has been in part contingent on increases granted in lieu of the cancellation of income tax benefits. When both forms of assistance are taken into account, Israel is closer to the European norm than to the leaders (see Messere and Owens, 1979). For reliable comparative evidence of the strikingly low level of Israel's social insurance pensions see Achdut and Tamir (1985).
10. Appendix 1 shows the contours of Israel's 'political demography'. The background to, and significance of, the Arab–Jewish cleavage was analysed in Chapter 2. For surveys of the treatment of Arab citizens in Israel's welfare state see Haidar (1987); Reiss (1988); and Cnaan (1985). A further although more dated source is a series of mimeographed reports prepared in 1976–7 for the Arab Affairs Working Party (Dr Sami Jerasi, Chairman) of the Prime Minister's Advisory Committee on Social Welfare Matters.
11. See Klein (1959) and Shlonsky (1971).
12. The contrast between 'institutional' and 'residual' welfare states enjoys wide currency in discussions of comparative social policy. It originated in work by Titmuss (1974: 30–2, 121–31) and Wilensky and Lebaux (1965: 138–41).
13. The innovations of the early 1970s have been analysed by Avizohar (1978 and 1982) and Hoffnung (1982). However, Avizohar's useful

survey glosses over the continuing elements of dualism in the reformed social security system, especially instances of differential entitlement for Jewish and Arab citizens and selective privileges concealed in occupational welfare (on which see the following paragraph). On the conservative implications of educational reform for the 'ethnic gap' see Shavit (1984) and Nahon (1987).

14. For a statistical portrait of Israel's national/ethnic division of labour see Semyonov and Lewin-Epstein (1987: ch. 2). The comparable differentials with respect to income distribution are particularly striking. One reasonable indicator of relative inequality between population subgroups is the ratio of per cent in the top quintile to per cent in the bottom quintile of the aggregate distribution. The Central Bureau of Statistics' *Survey of Incomes* for 1980 (limited to urban wage-earners and calculated on a 'per standard equivalent adult' basis) yields the following ratios: veteran (immigrated pre-1948) Ashkenazim 8.1; other Ashkenazim 2.8; Eastern Jews 0.3; Arab citizens 0.1 (comparable data are unavailable for Arabs in the occupied territories). Contrary to once-prevalent 'melting pot' expectations, the income gap between Ashkenazi and Eastern parents (immigrants since 1948), and the gap between their Israeli-born children, is almost identical. This is consistent with research documenting intergenerational stability or even widening of ethnic inequality in the occupational distribution (Nahon, 1987). The most reliable indications of Israel's comparative standing regarding income inequality, on which the observations in the text are based, come from the Luxembourg Income Study (e.g. Uusitalo, 1989: ch. 8). For comparative data on wage differentials see Jerusalem Institute of Management (1987: 234). The pronounced limits to the Histadrut's historic commitment to wage equality were exposed by Sussman (1973*b*). Trends in income inequality have been analysed by Hanoch (1961); Roter and Shamai (1971); and Fishelson (1983).
15. Relative involvement in strikes in Israel, compared with 15 OECD countries for which data are published in the ILO's *Yearbook of Labour Statistics*, ranked fourth highest in 1967–73 and second in 1977–82 (Giladi, 1980; Bar-Tsuri and Batsri, 1985). The ILO's branch-disaggregated data for representative years in the 1980s show that relative involvement in 'public and community services' was well over *ten times* the OECD median, whereas the figure for all other industries was only one-third higher than the median. On the rise of extra-parliamentary protest in Israel outside the labour-relations sphere see Lehman-Wilzig (1981); Sprinzak (1977); and Wolfsfeld (1988).
16. For other discussions of the labour movement's historic orientation

towards social policy see Kellner (1976); Doron (1967: ch. 1); and Schindler (1976).

17. For additional, complementary discussions, of the implications of sovereignty for Israel's political economy see Chapter 2 (concerning Arab–Jewish relations in the labour market), Chapter 3 (for the political regime and the political economy), and Chapter 5 (on industrial relations). References cited in earlier chapters are not repeated here.
18. On the post-1948 formation of social policy, including the debate within the labour movement see Doron (1967). Lustick (1980) has analysed the context in which policy was formed after 1948 in relation to the Arab minority.
19. The standard source on Israel's economic policy and performance in the early decades of its history is Halevi and Klinov-Malul (1968). Most evaluations of the state's initial policy choices (e.g. Barkai, 1983 and Gross, 1988) have been concerned with their economic soundness, rather than with their implications for the structure of ownership (Bichler, 1985) or capital import (Yago, 1977).
20. We are aware that the decision of the recording authorities to extend their net to work stoppages of two hours or more (prior to 1960, the threshold was a full day) contributed to the apparent multiplication of brief strikes in the early 1960s. Despite this, the trend cannot be dismissed as artefactual. A calculation of average strike duration before and after 1960, limited to disputes approximately within the old threshold, also indicates a modest decline in the length of stoppages. More importantly, the procedural change may itself be assumed to have reflected a genuine transition in forms of workers' collective action.
21. Compare Shorter and Tilly (1974: ch. 12) or Korpi and Shalev (1980).
22. See Doron and Kramer (1991); Achdut and Carmi (1981); and the annual reports of the Center for Social Policy Studies in Israel (beginning with Kop, 1983) on major trends in social policy. The persistence of the Histadrut's social-policy role and the growth of employer-linked ('occupational') welfare have been discussed by Doron (1984).
23. For evidence of the disciplinary impact of the influx of commuter labour from the occupied territories see Artstein and Sussman (1977) and Semyonov and Lewin-Epstein (1987). See Shirom (1974 and 1984) on employers' associative action; and on co-ordination between private and Histadrut employers, Galin and Harel (1978: 22); Shirom and Jacobson (1976: 471); and especially, Grinberg (1985). The Histadrut's organizational initiatives included the revival of party-controlled national unions for blue-collar workers,

closer links to and controls over workers' committees, and the creation of a central role in sub-national (branch-level) wage bargaining. Regarding the changing standing of workers' committees, compare surveys carried out by Friedman (1963) and Kaminka (1974). On the growth of unofficial wage drift and social benefits see Dubin and Aharoni (1981) and Shirom (1971: 72).

24. As a result of these trends, the proportion of work stoppages originating in the private for-profit sector, which had been in excess of 60% in the first half of the 1960s, fell to only half that proportion in the later 1960s, and dropped again (to little more than one-fifth) in the 1970s. This emerges from data presented by Michael and Bar-El (1967) together with later Histadrut and Ministry of Labour statistics. See also Reshef and Fried (1986).
25. Grinberg (1991*a*) provides a fuller analysis of the trends under discussion. See Galin and Tabb (1971) and Artstein and Sussman (1989) on the disintegration of centralized wage discipline in the 1970s. Shirom (1977) furnishes a case study (albeit from a slightly later period) with revealing indications of collusion between the Histadrut and the Manufacturers' Association. The deterioration of Histadrut–government relations and the erosion of the party's co-ordinating role are documented by Reshef (1981 and 1986) and Yanai (1981: ch. 11). The estimate of a threefold increase in public-sector strike involvements compares the period from mid-1966 to the third quarter of 1970, with the subsequent interval up to the 1973 war. The conservative geometric mean was used; the raw data were kindly supplied by Yonatan Reshef.
26. For a survey of the economic effects of the 1967 war see Kanovsky (1970). The economic relationship between Israel (proper) and the occupied territories has been analysed by Cohen (1986) and Tamari (1980).
27. See Chapter 7 for further discussion of the militarization of Israel's economy. The magnitude of increases in military-related demand can be gauged from Central Bureau of Statistics data (published in periodic issues of the Supplement to the *Monthly Bulletin of Statistics*), which indicate that in the interval between the wars of 1967 and 1973, both foreign and domestic military procurement were nearly fourfold higher in real terms than during the preceding period (1964–6). Barkai (1987*a*) discusses a number of the factors that contributed to the growth of local military production. He also presents data showing that in 1972 the number of workers employed in the manufacture of military equipment was two and a half times the level of 1966, and exports in this field had risen four and a half times. (By way of comparison, in the same period the country's real GDP increased by one-half.)

28. Within the substantial 'mainstream' literature on economic crisis and stabilization policies in post-1973 Israel we have found Ben-Porath (1986*a*); Bruno (1984); Tov (1988) and Yoran (1987) particularly helpful.
29. On the political meaning of the left–right cleavage in Israel see Arian (1968) and Arian and Shamir (1983). Ishai (1977) has performed a content analysis of party platforms regarding specific domestic issues. The politics of health care have been analysed by Arian (1981) and Halevi (1980).
30. For analyses of economic policy continuity and change following the 'political upheaval' see Ben-Porath (1983); Reuveni (1985); and Sharkansky and Radian (1982).
31. For the views of a leading exponent of this interpretation among academic economists in Israel see Barkai (1984 and 1988) and an interview of this author in the *Ha'aretz* special supplement of 1 June 1988.
32. For evidence regarding Israel's 'electoral business cycle' in the period under discussion see Ben-Hanan and Temkin (1986).
33. According to the original source of these data (Meridor, 1988), 'the state' in principle includes the central bank and such 'intermediary institutions' as the Jewish Agency. In practice, however, this was not entirely feasible—most notably in the case of 'directed credit' distributed by the Bank of Israel. Note that our use of more recently published data means that Table 6.2 differs somewhat from the comparable one (based on Meridor, 1987) which appears in Shalev (1989*b*: 137).
34. It could be argued that relative increases in state expenditure are more appropriately viewed in the context of 'total resources' (i.e. GDP plus imports, which in Israel, during the period under discussion, were only some one-half to two-thirds financed by export earnings). Using national accounts data published in the *Statistical Abstract of Israel* to make appropriate adjustments to Meridor's GNP-based ratios, the post-1967 increase was equal to 9.6% of total resources (cf. 16.8% of GNP) and the post-1973 rise was 11.3% (19.9% of GNP).
35. Consult the note to Figure 6.4 for sources and an explanation of how we constructed the crude estimates on which it is based. It is important to recognize that, even allowing for a reasonable margin of error in the magnitude of transfers to business, they are undoubtedly underestimated in Meridor's data. For instance, the latter include only one form ('development loans') of the subsidized credit increasingly made available to the business sector during the hyperinflationary years. Berglas (1986: table B2) has estimated that

export subsidies (including the subsidized credit which became a partial substitute after 1977) averaged 3.3% of GNP during the 1976–84 period.

36. Increases in the burden of family and old age allowances, to a significant extent, reflected a trend towards broadened eligibility which preceded the economic crisis. The rise in generosity of core social security programmes also began before the crisis, reflecting decisions made under conditions of rapid economic expansion. The onset of stagnation caused these increases to appear especially large in relation to the national product, but in fact rises in their value in real terms quickly began to taper off. Finally, in the case of family allowances part of the growth in expenditure resulted from an administrative reform in 1975, which converted a tax benefit into a transfer payment. See Kop (1983 and 1987) and Berglas (1986) for details. Somewhat ironically, the qualifications noted here are echoed in a valuable survey by a major critic of 'populist' profligacy (see Barkai, 1987*b*: 124–5).
37. For evidence of the freeze (actually a decline in per capita terms) in real expenditure see Kop (1988). Ben-Porath (1986*a*) shows that by the 1980s, 'public-sector' employment (in practice, the data referred mainly to education and health) no longer played the sharply anti-cyclical role of the mid-1970s.
38. Thus, Likud Finance Minister Yigael Hurwitz encountered stiff Histadrut resistance when the leadership of the labour organization found that it could make political capital out of mobilizing public sentiment against his unpopular austerity policies. (He reacted by abolishing the most important form of state subsidy to the labour-movement economy, a step which was one of the major causes of the catastrophic difficulties that befell Histadrut enterprises in the late 1980s.) When Hurwitz's successor tried to vitiate the Histadrut's corporatist status by launching an authoritarian incomes policy backed up by direct relations with popular workers' representatives, both he and those representatives paid a heavy price. On the other hand, there is no doubt that the Labour Party's return to the Cabinet in the first National Unity coalition was a major factor in obtaining the Histadrut's consent to the successful disinflation programme of 1985. This was due, in part, to the complementarity between the interest of Labour ministers in supporting the re-election of the Histadrut's political leadership, and the latter's need for a strong voice inside a government on which the Histadrut relied to salvage the labour movement's key economic bastions. For a full account see Grinberg (1985) and Shalev and Grinberg (1989). See also Reshef (1986) and Shirom (1983) on the impact of the 'political

upheaval' on labour relations in Israel; and Sussman and Zakai (1985) and Artstein and Sussman (1989) on the unresolved dilemmas of wage policy in the post-1973 period.

39. For a pointed illustration see the discussion in Grinberg (1985) of the private 'package deal' concluded by the Histadrut and the Manufacturers' Association in 1979. The labour organization's leaders traded wage restraint and credit to private industrialists for enlargement and guaranteed exclusivity of the Histadrut-administered supplementary pension scheme for the entire manufacturing sector. In doing so, the Histadrut imposed heavy costs on the Likud's Finance Minister: it sabotaged his policy of a credit squeeze on production for the domestic market; scuttled his hopes of forcing the Histadrut to share the pension field with commercial banks; and, having effected wage discipline within the business sector, left him to his own devices in the battle with public sector labour. Crucially, the economic resources which enabled the Histadrut to court private industry with offers of bank credit were in part the consequence of a special exemption which Histadrut pension funds had long enjoyed from the requirement of converting almost the entirety of their accumulations to Treasury bonds. In this case, however, as mentioned in the previous note, the Histadrut was subsequently punished by the unilateral cancellation of the exemption.
40. For an attempt to demonstrate the braking of technological advance associated with employment of Palestinians from the occupied territories see the study of Israel's construction industry by Bar-Natan (1984). For a systematic empirical study of the economic costs of Israel's over-commitment to military industries see Halperin (1986).
41. Not surprisingly, this maxim is more readily acknowledged in the context of comparative historical research than in abstracted quantitative comparisons of many nations. For some insightful recent illustrations see Therborn (1989) and Schmidt (1988).
42. For discussions of Israel's changing energy and defence costs and their consequences see respectively Barkai (1984*a*) and Berglas (1983).
43. For fuller discussion of these undeclared military and civilian instruments of the state's full employment policy see Ben-Porath (1986*a*) and Rein and Shalev (1985). Quantitative indications of the scope of military employment in Israel were cited in Chapter 5 (pp. 202–3).
44. For a discussion of the problematic nature of estimates of economic growth in contemporary societies see Block (1985). Kondor (1986) has attempted to estimate the scale of Israel's 'black economy'.

7

The Crisis of the State

In this concluding chapter we argue that a crisis of the state lay behind both acute economic disorder, which has afflicted Israel over much of its recent history, and political instability, which began earlier with the decomposition of Labour Party rule.[1] Analytically, we interpret this crisis as the result of impairments to the state's *autonomy*, especially in respect to capital. In positioning relations between the state and business interests at the centre of the discussion, we seek to highlight an issue which has been largely invisible in accounts of the spectacular political and economic failures in Israel over the last several decades.

The substantive issues discussed here reopen questions which were raised, but not fully addressed, in earlier chapters. In Chapter 3 we saw how closely Mapai's political hegemony after 1948 was tied to the interface between politics and the economy. The extensive economic prerogatives and resources at the disposal of the state, complemented by the Histadrut's intermediary role *vis-à-vis* both capital and labour, made it possible for Mapai to mobilize voters, restrain distributional conflicts, and steer economic growth and its long-term political consequences. We speculated that just as Mapai had won its pre-eminence with the help of 'political control of the economy', the loss of this capacity was at the heart of the party's diminishing power to rule. Along similar lines, it was argued in Chapter 6 that the changing relationship between the state and the major economic actors was the principal cause of the state's inability to avert the economic disorder of the 1970s and beyond. The loss of its directive capacities over the economy was signalled by escalation of labour militancy within the public sector, profligate expansion of 'the welfare state for business', and growing co-operation between the Histadrut and private business.

There is a rich theoretical literature relevant to the theme of declining state autonomy and the ascent of capital within Israel's political economy. For our purposes, a brief review of the central themes of this discussion will suffice to set the scene.[2] State autonomy, in Skocpol's (1985: 9, 11) formulation, is present in a given context to the extent that the state is free 'to formulate and pursue goals that are not simply reflective of the demands or interests of social groups, classes, or society'. The autonomy of the state is subject to wide variation—across polities (depending in part on the wealth of states), over time (autonomy is greatest in periods of societal crisis), and between issue areas (the state's independence from domestic social actors tends to be highest in the domain of foreign affairs). In conditions of exceptional autonomy, the élites in command of the state[3] may realistically aspire 'to direct and restructure society and politics'.

There are, however, good reasons not to anticipate such a high degree of discretion and initiative in relation to economic affairs. Skocpol and others are correct to argue that state autonomy is a more *general* and potentially much more *variable* phenomenon than the Marxian concept of 'the capitalist state' tends to imply. Nevertheless, the fusion of liberal democracy with an economic system which, in principle, places the power to determine the economic fate of the mass of citizens in the hands of a very small minority of resource-rich investors and large corporations, inevitably constrains the degrees of freedom with which public policy-makers may independently set domestic policy priorities. As Kalecki put it, to the extent that output and employment depend on 'the so-called state of confidence' of private investors, 'this gives to the capitalists a powerful indirect control over Government policy: everything which may shake the state of confidence must be carefully avoided because it would cause an economic crisis' (1943: 325). Moreover (and the more so in our time than Kalecki's because of the growing scope of multinational enterprises and international markets), no national state is in the position to ignore what capitalists and governments *elsewhere* do—to exchange rates, labour and other costs, and investment subsidies. Nevertheless, the mechanisms by which business interests are reconciled with democratic process cannot be fruitfully analysed without recognizing the historical and national specificity of 'capital' and 'the state', the scope for a variety of relationships between them, and the degree to which the power of each is mediated by working-class mobilization, position in the world system, and other contextual variables.

In many respects the Israeli political economy under what might be termed 'the system of 1948' may be considered a case of extreme state autonomy. The new Israeli state forged a number of quite remarkable relationships with collectivities and nation-states elsewhere in the world. These relationships yielded major inflows of resources which passed directly through the state but imposed relatively few reciprocal obligations upon it. Partly as a result, the state was in the position to fix the pace and direction of economic growth broadly in accordance with two sets of criteria—the interests of the governing party, and the territorial and geopolitical priorities of the state *per se*. In addition, working largely through the Histadrut, mechanisms were fostered to place limits on labour militancy and other forms of distributional conflict. We shall argue, however, that during the 1960s and 1970s the state's relatively autonomous standing in relation to domestic classes and the international system alike was badly undermined. In turn declining state autonomy, especially in relation to capital, helped precipitate both Labour's decomposition as a governing party and the state's mismanagement of economic policy in the post-1973 period. Let us begin with what was chronologically the first of these two problems, that of Mapai's fall from power.

The unravelling of one-party dominance

The death blow wielded by Israel's 1977 elections to Labour's standing as a natural party of government serves as a dramatic reminder that a dominant party—to borrow Maurice Duverger's widely quoted dictum—'bears within itself the seeds of its own destruction' (1964: 12). Building directly on the historical analysis earlier in this book of Mapai's rise to dominance, it is possible to identify a number of 'seeds of destruction' in the Israeli setting. Indeed, the very bulwarks of Mapai's strength in an earlier epoch—its capacity to form dependency ties with economically less-advantaged voters, its reliance on the Histadrut, its control of an independently wealthy state, and specifically its nurturing of state-made capitalists and relatively privileged middle strata—ceased to be effective or even became counter-productive to the perpetuation of Labour rule. First, sections of the electorate originally recruited to Mapai as indifferent or reluctant supporters ceased to vote Labour once they acquired personal and political choices. Second, the viability of the Histadrut as a mobilizer, legitimator, and political–economic instrument was damaged by rank-and-file alienation, friction between party leaders in the Histadrut and governmental arenas, and the growing independence of the managers of the labour-movement economy. Third, there was a significant change in the character of the funds made available to the state by foreign benefactors, which had constituted the mainstay of the economic leverage underpinning Mapai's hegemony. Finally, due in no small measure to the cumulative effects of the state's own benevolence, big business grew and solidified and the state's capacity to control the economy according to political criteria was correspondingly impaired.

Sources of electoral realignment[4]

In the course of three elections—in 1969, 1973, and 1977—the number of seats in the 120-member Knesset held by the Labour Alignment (including its Arab satellites) plummeted from 60 to 54 to 33.[5] Concurrently, the number gained by the Likud or its forerunner Gachal rose from 26 to 39 to 45. Evidently, while 1977 was the year Labour was actually forced to leave office, the right had already made its major gains in the previous elections. Labour's fate was sealed by the appearance of the Democratic Movement for Change (DMC), a new party which succeeded in winning 15 Knesset seats in 1977. Although the DMC soon disintegrated, in all three electoral contests of the 1980s Labour and the Likud remained evenly matched, each with about one-third of the popular vote.[6]

In retrospect, it is not difficult to see why the Labour Party's mass support had so eroded by 1977. Already in the 1960s survey research had revealed that *substantial numbers of voters chose Mapai reluctantly*, under pressure or because no existing party embodied their aspirations. Others preferred not to vote at all. The decline of personal dependency on Mapai's bounties and the emergence of credible vehicles for frustrated constituencies, were pre-conditions for the mobilization of disaffected groups behind opposition parties. Three such realignments came to a head in 1977. One of these, the culmination of a trend which first surfaced in the 1965 elections, was that many former Labour voters of Eastern origin crossed over to the Likud. At the same time, a large bloc of the Ashkenazi

(Western-origin) middle class deserted to the DMC (most of them subsequently returned to Labour). In addition, close to one-fifth of Labour's electoral losses were suffered among Israel's Palestinian citizens, many of whom switched loyalties from Labour and its associated Arab slates to the Communist Party.[7]

In our discussion of Mapai's climb to hegemony in Chapter 3, we pointed out that the nexus between politics and the economy, state and market, has been largely foreign to scholarly analysis of single-party dominance in Israel. This is equally true of the electoral triumph of right over left in the 1970s. It has been understood almost exclusively in terms of three explanatory arenas: the dynamics of parties and party élites, the political culture of voters, and the interface between domestic politics and the Arab–Israeli conflict.[8]

The leading hypothesis of the *political dynamics* approach[9] is that in time Mapai's leadership in the government lost its sensitivity to public opinion and grass-roots political trends. As a result it was taken by surprise by protest movements which created a new extra-parliamentary political arena free of party control. The arrogance of power kept alive Labour's intolerably oligarchic mode of internal governance, and also was expressed by revelations of impropriety among prominent figures in the party. Concurrent with Mapai's degeneration from within, the right-wing opposition engineered a successful course of regeneration. This was epitomized in 1965 by Cherut's alliance with the pro-business Liberal Party and a few years later by Mapai's public recognition of the right as worthy of a legitimate role in government.

Other theorists, particularly opinion-poll analysts, see the motor of political change in the mass public rather than in the behaviour of élites.[10] They have argued that Mapai's decline originated in its failure to adjust to changes in the composition and orientation of the electorate which shifted Israel's *political culture* to the right without any corresponding adjustment by the dominant party. From this perspective Labour's descent was, at root, the result of demographic shifts which proliferated the kinds of voters who tend to be sympathetic towards the right and antagonistic to the left—namely, young and/or Eastern-origin Jews.

Another, more novel, approach to explaining partisan realignment in Israel starts from the assumption that the 'external' *national conflict* decisively structures the parameters of 'internal' politics.[11]

The conquest of new and symbolically highly charged territory in the June 1967 Arab–Israeli war reopened divisive issues concerning the fundamental character of Zionism and the concrete problems of national security. In this context the right easily fell heir to the very elements, which in the pre-state context had succoured Mapai's own ideological dominance—nationalism, militarism, messianism, and settlement. Mapai, historically so adept at shaping and exploiting the Jewish national struggle for its own political benefit, reacted ambiguously to the dilemmas introduced by the occupation. As a result, it lost support from both the war-weary middle class and the nationalists pressing for annexation.

Managing the political economy

Our purpose is not to adjudicate between these differing explanations for the decomposition of Mapai hegemony, but to complement them with a political-economy analysis. It is not enough for dominant parties to be on top of key political issues and to function with internal consistency and effectiveness. In order to enjoy legitimacy, a political regime must also be capable of satisfying voters' material interests and responding to the economic demands of organized collectivities. Furthermore, political legitimacy is only one of the pre-conditions for successful governance. Both pluralists and Marxists, although they emphasize different requirements, agree that no party can dominate the state unless it is capable of managing the economy to the mutual satisfaction of capital, the mass public, and the party's own interests. By the early 1970s, three specific requirements of effective political–economic management were notable by their absence in Israel. We refer to the state's needs to: (*a*) develop a workable and politically profitable formula for economic growth; (*b*) find solutions to problems of distributional conflict, especially as they bear upon its relations with organized labour; and (*c*) establish an economically supportive relationship with the international environment. Behind these difficulties lay a momentous decline in state autonomy as its former foundations suffered damaging erosion. Of particular importance in this connection were the declining usefulness of the Histadrut as an arm of the party/state; the political élite's receding discretion concerning the disposal of gift capital flowing into Israel from the outside world; and the increasing difficulties encountered in harnessing the actions of business interests to the priorities of party and state.

The Histadrut. The waning of the Histadrut's ability to meet the needs of the governing party was discussed in earlier chapters. Despite the emergence in the 1960s of a major right-wing challenge to Mapai's control of the labour organization, the party maintained a firm grip on the Histadrut by incorporating its major rivals on the left into electoral alliances.[12] Nevertheless, it will be recalled that the labour organization's influence over its mass membership was seriously weakened by the rapid economic growth and relatively full employment that prevailed for most of the period between the late 1950s and the Yom Kippur War. Its leaders were obliged to become more attentive to rank-and-file sentiment, and all the more so because the right was now a potentially serious contender for power inside the Histadrut. The labour organization became correspondingly less susceptible to party direction. And the ability of Labour governments to rely on receiving popular assent to their domestic policies via the Histadrut suffered accordingly. Histadrut leaders also became less effective at restraining public employees in order to protect the state from inflationary deficit spending and politically embarrassing strikes. By the 1970s industrial relations inside most private and Histadrut enterprises had been brought under managerial and union control, while the state was left to contend with a rising tide of labour strife within the public sector.

In the meantime, the contributions of the labour-movement economy to Labour Party dominance were also curtailed. Many blue-collar Histadrut employees, whose material dependence exemplified the basis of Mapai's traditional captive vote, began to turn against Labour with a vengeance.[13] A new generation of profit-oriented executives at the head of Histadrut-owned corporations drew strength from joint ventures and informal co-operation with the heads of other large concerns. Partly because of this, the party was hurt by heightened resistance to its treatment of the posts and profits of Histadrut enterprises as political spoils. Exemplifying their conflicts with the Mapai old guard, Histadrut magnates were among the prime movers behind the DMC's challenge to Labour in the 1977 elections. In effect, the new party's emergence represented a further round of the debate, which had been simmering in the labour movement since 1948, over the issues of leadership succession and the status of the Histadrut. Like the challenge posed by Ben-Gurion, Dayan, and their allies in the 1960s, the DMC stood for rejection of the Mapai tradition of mobilizing voters through the Histadrut and relying on its enterprises for political leverage over the economy. Instead, the new party's leaders favoured a self-serving programme of economic liberalization aimed at enhancing the independence of managers and salaried professionals alike.[14]

Capital inflow. A second, very striking trend in the political economy originated in the arena of inter-state relations—specifically, the growing ties between Israel and the United States in the context of the military escalation which followed the 1967 Arab–Israeli war. Beginning in 1971 American aid to Israel rose to major proportions in order to finance sales of US-made aircraft and other high-priced military hardware. During the decade following the October 1973 war, Israel typically received about one billion dollars' worth of free American-made war *matériel* each year together with substantial dollar loans to offset the burden of additional arms imports on the country's chronic current account deficit. In part this reflected the extension to an overseas market of the Pentagon's traditional nurturing of the interests of large American arms manufacturers. But America's generosity also embodied a fundamental change in its expectations of Israel's strategic role in the Middle East.[15]

Unlike the German reparations and Jewish philanthropy which fed Israel's economic growth machine in the late 1950s and early 1960s, the inflow of foreign capital in the form of American arms contributed relatively little to the economic reach of the state. The far-reaching significance of this change in the Israeli political economy can be illustrated by a simple comparison.[16] In the late 1950s, the time of Israel's first wave of industrialization, the state was the beneficiary of foreign aid equivalent to about one-sixth of GNP. Half of this sum comprised donations and loans from world Jewry, a third was reparations from Germany, and the remainder consisted of cheap loans and grants from the US government. These funds would have sufficed at the time to finance not only the defence budget, but also most of the investment bill of the business sector.

By the mid-1970s a very different pattern had taken root, one of enlarged foreign assistance (approaching a quarter of GNP) which, except for Jewish philanthropy, was dominated by the United States government. The most salient feature of the US aid package has been its close relationship to the cost of Israeli purchases of American arms.[17] Consequently, instead of having a major portion of foreign assistance at its disposal with which to direct economic development, the state routinely turns over almost the entire inflow of aid for military purposes. This inability to freely channel US aid in the most economically and politically rewarding directions eliminated one of the most important sources of the dominant party's power. It also emerged as a major constraint on policy responses to the rapid rises in Israel's energy costs and military expenditures which followed the 1973 war.

The fact that most US aid to Israel is returned to the American economy as payment for armaments does not mean that the 'special relationship' between the two countries has had no effect on Israel's domestic structures. In fact, it was one of the forces which stimulated the economy's far-reaching militarization in the years following the 1967 Arab–Israeli war. There are several reasons for this. Most obviously, the fact that the bill for Israel's burgeoning arms imports came to be paid for by the United States made it easier for the Israeli government to devote a high proportion of the state's domestic revenues to local procurement. But other implications, both strategic and economic, must also be considered. From a *strategic* viewpoint, the stream of big-ticket arms from the USA encouraged the view (which was presumably shared by Israel's American mentors) that other components of Israel's military effort should be upgraded to the advanced level of its imports. It was logical, and at the beginning also rational from an *economic* viewpoint (given boom conditions in the international arms market), to meet this need from domestic production. In addition, the magnitude of Israel's purchases from American arms manufacturers has encouraged it to demand compensatory benefits, in the form of local production and co-production arrangements which directly stimulate the Israeli arms industry.

Capital steering. Partly because of the large-scale, monopolistic nature of sophisticated weapons production, and other features characteristic of 'military-industrial complexes', neither Israel's political élite nor its defence establishment were able to prevent massive and wasteful drains on state funds by enterprises producing for the military. The arms-makers were also unable, or unwilling, to deliver votes to Labour with the same facility as state-supported firms and communities had done in an earlier era. Military industrialization thus proved to be a far less potent lever of Mapai hegemony than the political–economic axis built up by the party's long-time economic policy czar, Pinchas Sapir who, in countless informal deals with local and foreign investors, had traded diverse forms of state largess in return for entrepreneurial activity and political support. Nevertheless, in the longer term this form of *dirigisme* also proved to be of limited effectiveness. Under the Sapirist regime state aid was targeted to a very limited range of individual and corporate beneficiaries. The major banks and other large concerns were especially strengthened by the coddling of their interests, with the result that the concentration and cohesion of capital grew at the expense of the state's autonomy. As we shall see, this had profound implications for the political (un)manageability of the economic crisis which erupted in the 1970s.[18]

To conclude, by the mid-1970s Labour had not only exhausted its success with the politics of nationalism and other sources of popular legitimacy. It also no longer possessed the capacity to reproduce the political–economic underpinnings of its hegemony, including high rates of economic growth, a workable political consensus on economic issues, and the state's maintenance of the party's socio-economic base. These failures were not the private property of the dominant party, however; *they had become internalized into the state itself.* Indeed, the severity of the problems faced by Mapai as a party was in large part due to the fact that its hegemony had been founded so directly upon the state. But it also followed that the difficulties surrounding macro-economic management in the face of declining state autonomy did not cease when Labour was forced to surrender its political supremacy. Coupled with the constraints inherent in American aid, the state's inability to break free of class interests severely limited policy responses to the economic shocks of 1973 and beyond. In spite of the damaging fiscal implications, capital subsidy increased dramatically and remained high, notwithstanding the failure of this policy to trigger renewed economic growth or its offsetting benefits for state revenues. Finally, the state was also prevented by the militancy of public-sector labour from making lasting wage cuts or cutting back public-sector employment. There was thus a costly symmetry in the state's relationship to the strong sectors of labour and capital—*neither* could be subjected to sufficient political discipline to assist in resolving the economic crisis. The origins of the difficulties that confronted the state in its management of labour relations have already been discussed in Chapter 6. We are now ready to take a closer look at the changing balance of power between business interests and the state.

The ascent of capital

Now that we have outlined fully the relationship between business and the state as a central motor of change in Israel's political economy, it is important to gain some insight into the historical evolution of the structure of capital and its interdependence with the state. Unfortunately, due to the paucity of existing research this is a task for which only limited evidence can be gathered, most of it drawn from a few pioneering works. Let us recall, to begin with, the forces that protected the state from becoming hostage to 'investor confidence' under the conditions which prevailed after the transition to sovereignty.[19] Foremost among these were powers to bestow riches vested in the state by virtue of its receipt of gifts and loans from foreign well-wishers, its inheritance or confiscation of Arab land and property, and its extensive regulatory powers and highly centralized apparatus. Large private investors were few in number and heavily dependent on the state to bankroll their entrepreneurial activities, while the most concentrated and strategic sectors of capital (public and Histadrut-linked enterprise) were directly accountable to political masters.

The privileged position characteristically enjoyed by the bourgeoisie in Western societies is not only a product of its technical indispensability to the economic fortunes of society as a whole, but also reflects capital's hegemony at the level of ideas and consciousness. However, in the new-born state of Israel by far the strongest political force in society was the labour movement, which espoused a blend of labourist and statist ideologies. Moreover, it was the state rather than capital which was most readily identifiable with the collectivity's most urgent and universal interests.The government, the bureaucracy, and the military had accepted responsibility for an extremely broad and fateful agenda—populating and defending territory in the face of external hostility, attracting and absorbing masses of immigrants, and so forth. Also, the state had powerful allies outside the domestic political economy who were willing to help provide the financial means for carrying out this agenda. To this must be added a cohesive political party apparatus in control of all of the society's key institutions, with little or no obligation to private capital for either material or ideological resources, and with its own internal networks of élite recruitment and interchange.

Yet the 'system of 1948' did not end here. For economic and political reasons, the leadership of the labour movement recoiled from exploiting its position of strength in order—let alone to eliminate private capital altogether—to discriminate against the private sector. The state's patronage of business interests broadly perpetuated the sectoral divisions of the pre-1948 political economy. It also had the effects (partially intended, partially the result of the system itself) of benefiting big over small business and encouraging co-operation between the large enterprises of the different sectors. As this system matured, the political élite frequently found itself hard pressed to maintain control over the 'institutional entrepreneurs' at the head of state- and Histadrut-owned enterprises. They found it equally difficult to prevent private investors from appropriating capital subsidies without fulfilling their economic obligations to the state, and were also obliged to contend with offensive coalitions between the different wings of big business. Despite that, Mapai's influence over the private, public, and Histadrut-owned sectors alike remained very strong, because of capital's dependence and also as a result of the continuing elements of competition between the private and collective sectors and within the private sector.

The second half of the 1960s turned out to be a watershed for both the structure of capital and its relationship to the state. During the first half of the decade the state's external sources of revenue contracted. As a result its dependence on foreign loans and overseas investors to finance the import surplus grew sharply. As Chapter 5 recounts, responding to its lack of necessary resources to maintain past levels of business subsidies, the state attempted to wean capital of this dependence in the framework of the 1966–7 Mitun (recession). The slow-down failed to achieve this aim, which was subsequently abandoned in the era of renewed economic expansion that followed the June 1967 war. Nevertheless, the recession left a lasting imprint on the structure of business by intensifying an already high degree of capital concentration and monopoly.[20] The economic strain of the Mitun had naturally been disproportionately borne by weaker enterprises; then, in the recovery, there was a rash of mergers and take-overs. When the dust settled, three formidable financial–industrial conglomerates, each linked to one of the country's leading banks, gained clear pre-eminence at the apex of the economy. Despite competitive frictions, the 'big three' were increasingly bound together by structural interlocks (a dense network of ownership and other business connections) and by their virtual monopolization of state subsidies.

Its failed attempt to employ market discipline as a means of steering capital, which after 1967 was joined by the revival of old hopes of attracting Jewish investment from abroad, led Mapai's senior economic policy-makers to conclude that the state should strive to encourage foreign investment and strengthen domestic big business. In accordance with this strategy the state retreated from the course it had followed in the period preceding the recession, of expanding the business activity of the public sector and diversifying its reach. Instead, government companies—other than those devoted to infrastructure or armaments—were sold off. At the same time, as we have already noted, a new and aggressive managerial cadre was installed at the head of the Histadrut's industrial and financial corporations. Soon after the war Histadrut political leaders joined their counterparts in the government in praising the virtues of profitability and private enterprise. The labour organization also officially proclaimed its economic affiliates free to participate in joint ventures with private investors. Consequently, at the same time as state ownership was shrinking, the ties between private and Histadrut-owned capital became markedly stronger.[21]

The Mitun also turned out to be a turning-point for the solidarity of capital. In strengthening the employers' hand in the labour market, the recession emboldened the Manufacturers' Association to show new mettle in its relations with both the Histadrut and unofficial trade unionism. The trend towards more co-ordinated and combative employer action intensified after the war. In the late 1960s, with the blessing of the state, the first umbrella organization for the private sector was born. Simultaneously, a potential was becoming evident for the kind of informal solidarity between private and Histadrut executives that later produced quasi-corporatist 'package deals', consummated without the state's mediation but at its expense.[22]

By the time Israel had to confront the problems of commodity price rises, stagnating world trade, and escalating military commitments in the 1970s, the structure of capital and its standing *vis-à-vis* the state had altered inexorably. As the sole empirical study of the period concluded (Aharoni, 1976: 118), not only had the economy become increasingly split into a competitive periphery and a dominant core of big conglomerates, 'the big companies and ownership groups have a great deal of influence on economic policy and on the manner in which the resources of the state are allocated, and the state apparatus is often turned into being dependent on them when it wants to implement some action or other'. It was this political economy, revolving around increasingly powerful concentrations of capital, that can now be seen to bear much of the responsibility for Israel's slide into extreme stagflation and fiscal crisis, and specifically for the counter-productive role of state policies. We now present this case in broad outline for the two most important divisions of Israeli business–industry and banking.

The nurturing of big industry

During the decade of economic stagnation following 1973, official Israel noisily promoted the manufacturing sector as the indispensable centre-piece of healthy economic growth. Industry, it has long been argued, holds the key to creating 'productive' employment and weaning the economy of reliance on foreign gifts and loans for balancing its external deficit. Yet in this same period, industry's share of national output and employment actually declined. Table 7.1, which brings together diverse indicators of the fate of the manufacturing sector before and after the turning-point in the macro-economy, helps explain this gap between theory and praxis. The table shows that, as the result of a growing but badly underutilized stock of capital equipment, the growth of industrial output fell drastically after 1973 in spite of continued increases in labour productivity. Moreover, this unimpressive performance occurred even though industry modernized (larger and more mechanized factories) and became far more export-oriented (accompanied by a major shift from 'traditional' to high-tech exports). To explain these paradoxes, it is necessary to reckon with three closely related institutional characteristics of industry as it had developed in Israel by the 1970s: first, its dual structure; second, the scope of the government subsidies which it came to enjoy; and third, its increasing reliance on defence-related production.[23]

A dual economy.[24] Israeli industry has long been characterized by coexistence between a growing 'big economy' and a multitude of small firms and self-employed proprietors. By 1985 the reported turnover of the hundred largest industrial firms was said to be equivalent to as much as 40 per cent of Israel's GNP.[25] Within industrial branches the leading firms command an extremely high share of both domestic sales and export production. But the full extent of capital concentration is in fact far more pronounced than this, since in most cases the key firms in each branch are owned by the economic giants—the Histadrut, the state, and the banks. As of the mid-1980s, a handful of government-owned producers of arms, aircraft, electricity, and minerals accounted for more than one quarter of the combined activity of the top 100. The share of the enterprises owned by *Koor*, the Histadrut conglomerate, was also close to one-quarter. Two of the three largest banks, one owned by the Histadrut and the other privately controlled, held most of the shares in Koor's rival, the *Clal* conglomerate (with nearly one-tenth of top 100 turnover). Each of the big banks also had a direct stake in individual manufacturing firms.

In fact, already by the 1970s the division between 'core' and 'peripheral' capital had largely transcended the traditional sectoral cleavage within industry based solely on ownership (private, public, or Histadrut). It is true that each of these sectors continues to embrace somewhat different priorities and strategies (limited, however, by real difficulties of exerting centralized control over salaried executives), and that they sometimes compete fiercely among themselves. Nevertheless, irrespective of their firms' parentage, the senior managers of core enterprises share a common business philosophy, the same social milieu, and very similar levels of remuneration. Above all, as Rowley, Bichler, and Nitzan have pointed out:

> Structurally speaking, the big concerns are closely bound together by complex ownership/control ties among the holding groups, reciprocal

Table 7.1. *Industry before and after the crisis of 1973*

	1965–72	1973–80
Profits		
(1) Overall rate of return	18.1	19.8
(2) Profits of big three conglomerates (% GNP)	0.4	1.0
Performance (% change)		
(3) Real output	10.0	3.0
(4) Total factor productivity	1.6	0.5
(5) Labour productivity	5.3	4.7
(6) Capital utilization	2.2	−1.9
Structure		
(7) Capital-intensity (% change)	2.3	6.7
(8) Three-firm concentration ratio	50.3	49.1
(9) Size (employment per plant)	43	57
(10) Export to output ratio	23.0	31.8
(11) Military branches as % of exports	16.1	36.8
Role of the state		
(12) Public consumption as % of output	15	21[a]
(13) Public subsidy as % of investment	7.3	27.8
(14) Public funding as % of investment	27.9	42.6
(15) Export subsidies (% GNP)	2.0	3.1
(16) Credit subsidy (% GNP)[b]	0.7	5.9
(17) Price subsidies (% GNP)[b]	1.9	2.9
(18) Index of protection	1.41	1.23

[a] 1973–5 only. (Average for 1976–83 = 15%)
[b] (16) and (17) are subsidies applying to goods sold on the local market.

Source: Most of the data were derived from tables constructed by Bregman (1986), located at the following pages: (1), (3), (9), (10) at p. 54; (4)–(7) and (13) at p. 20; (8) at p. 32; (14) and (18) at p. 13. In addition, (2) is taken from Bichler (1986: appendix 1 and an update supplied by the author), (11) uses data published by the Ministry of Industry and Commerce (1987: 27), (12) is from the Bank of Israel's 1986 Report (p. 134 of the Hebrew edition). Sokoler (1984: 21) is the primary source for (16). (15), (17) and part of (16) are from Berglas (1986: 3, 32).

Note: Full details on construction of the indicators are available in the source works. The rate of return (1) is total value added less labour costs, as a proportion of capital stock. (2) is based on the collective net profits of Koor, Discount Investments, and Clal, essentially as published in their balance sheets. Capital utilization (6) is measured by electricity consumption per unit of equipment. The three-firm concentration ratio (8) is the three largest establishments' share of sales of locally-produced output (the figures cited here are weighted averages for 95 detailed industrial branches). As Bregman points out, an index calculated solely in relation to domestic output ignores the growth over time of competing imports (which is indicated (18)). (11) aggregates the metals and metal products, machinery, electronics, and transport equipment (aircraft) branches. The proportion of investment publicly funded (14) takes account of only two forms of funding, explicit investment grants and 'development loans'. Public subsidy (13) is the *cost* of these two instruments, which for loans is the deviation from market rates of interest. (15) is the sum of direct export supports and the implicit subsidy in special loans to exporters granted after 1977. (16) was constructed by deducting Berglas' figures for the credit subsidy to exporters, from Sokoler's figures for total long-term credit subsidy to business (not including housing finance). (18) comprises estimates of the ratio of local to international prices of protected goods.

Nearly all indices refer to the manufacturing sector exclusive of diamonds (a high export, labour-intensive, small plant, low value-added branch with often deviant conjunctural behaviour). Following Bregman, the 'before' period is 1965–72 and 'after' is 1973–80. (In most cases it would have been impossible to avoid this confounding of somewhat disparate sub-periods.) There are certain exceptions to the periodization, in addition to the major one noted in the table itself. (4)–(7) and (13) compare 1965–72 with 1972–9. (8) is available for two benchmarks only, 1965 and 1979. Similarly, (11) refers to 1970 contrasted with the average for 1975 and 1980. (16) compares 1966–72 with 1973–80. (15) and 17 relate to the standard dates, but the 'before' averages had to be calculated by combining average figures for 1966–9 with annual data for the other years.

---

buying and selling arrangements, financing relations among the banks, the government and the industrial groups, property rights enjoyed exclusively by the largest groups and, finally, explicit collusion. (1988: 15)

In addition, the representatives of state- and Histadrut-owned firms have been openly active alongside major private industrialists in the Manufacturers' Association. In the 1970s and early 1980s, this dense network of ties between the seemingly disparate components of industrial big business was vividly expressed in the convergent level and trend of the profits of the three dominant private- and Histadrut-owned conglomerates.[26]

State subsidies. As Table 7.1 shows, despite industry's record of stagnating productivity and output after 1973, its overall profitability emerged unscathed; while the profits of the big industrial conglomerates linked to the Histadrut and the banks actually *increased* dramatically. The largely implicit industrial policy of the state can explain this puzzling combination. The core of that policy, which was oriented almost exclusively to big industry, had two planks:

capital subsidies, both direct and indirect; and orders from the defence establishment.[27]

Lavish increases in government subsidies on credit, investment, and, in many cases, production costs made it profitable for firms to maintain or increase their output and to buy equipment they did not need. Even production for the local market (officially a low priority) was treated generously, in part as compensation for the increased exposure to imports necessitated by new trade agreements. Exporters, meanwhile, enjoyed their own earmarked subsidies and privileged access to incentives to new investment. This wealth of state aid undoubtedly bolstered corporate profits, but was of dubious effectiveness in advancing the declared goals of economic policy. By the end of the 1970s subsidies had reached the point that the cost in local currency of an additional dollar of export earnings was estimated to be fully 30–40 per cent higher than the market price of a dollar bill.[28] The target of attracting manpower out of the services and into manufacturing was also badly missed. Whereas in the early 1970s the industrial labour force had been growing at the healthy rate of 5 per cent a year, in 1973–80 it expanded by an average of only 1 per cent. This achievement compares poorly with the rapid (5–6 per cent) annual growth of employment in banking and public services. In the event it was the welfare state, and even more so the *warfare state*, which had to bear most of the burden of job creation.

The militarization of industry. The warfare state was also decisive for the profitability of big industry. During the difficult first few years after the shocks of 1973, military procurement played an indispensable counter-cyclical role in buoying up the manufacturing sector in the face of depressed consumer demand. Following a temporary fall-off, procurement resumed its upward course after the Likud took office in 1977. Throughout, orders were directed almost exclusively to firms affiliated with core capital (although with an eye to awarding each of the big conglomerates a fair share of the action), and were based on generous cost-plus arrangements which the authorities proved unable (and for the most part unwilling) to control. The result, as we can see in Figure 7.1, was that until 1983 the collective profits of the big industrial groups followed the trend of local defence spending with quite extraordinary fidelity.[29]

The surge in domestic procurement attendant on the Yom Kip-

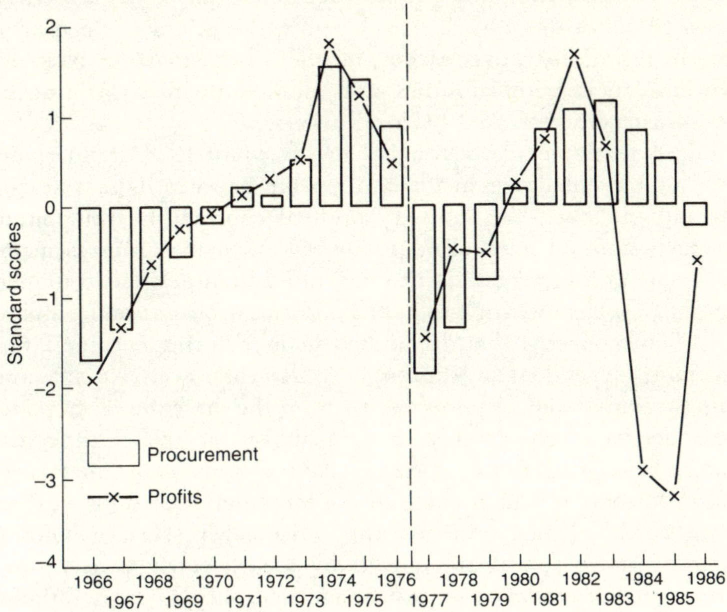

FIG. 7.1. Local defence procurement and profits of the big three conglomerates: 1966–86

Sources: Supplements to *Monthly Bulletin of Statistics* for local defence procurement (including expenditure on construction). Bichler (1986: appendix 1) and Rowley, Bichler, and Nitzan (1988) for profits.

Note: The 'big three' conglomerates are Koor, Discount Investment, and Clal. Profits are net of taxes. Both series were calculated in constant 1980 shekels and then converted to standard scores. As Bichler (1986) has demonstrated, 1977 marked a 'structural break' in the relationship between conglomerate profits and defence spending. For that reason we computed standardized scores separately for the pre- and post-1977 periods.

pur War and the re-equipment and redeployment which followed it lent renewed impetus to the post-1967 process of rapid military industrialization led by accelerated defence spending. The growth of local demand for weaponry also facilitated export sales, including diversification into some related science-intensive product lines for civilian uses. The volume of exports by the branches of manufacturing closest to military production quadrupled twice over—once in the first flush of growth (between 1967 and 1970) and again in the course of the 1970s. By all accounts, the profits were fabulous. Much of this was due to the state. It not only helped arms exporters find lucrative niches in the world market, but also showered them with subsidies and allowed them a free ride on the infrastructure created by local orders.

These developments of roughly the first post-1973 decade point to a notable imbalance in the relationship between industrial capital and the state. Big industry profited enormously from public contracts and subsidies. But it was able to make progress in exports only at a very high cost to the state and largely failed to meet the state's objectives of expanding industrial output and employment. The concerns that dominated manufacturing became larger and more dependent on the public purse than ever. At the same time the state's capacity to steer them in the direction of its policy goals declined considerably. Responsibility for this decline ultimately belongs to the changes we have already noted in Israel's political economy which came to the fore after 1973. One of these might be called the 'sorcerer's apprentice effect'. Having built up an industrial sector characterized by an extremely concentrated core, acute dependence on patronage and subsidy, and intimate formal and informal links with the political élite, the state had unwittingly created a centre of power capable of making compelling claims on its resources. The problem was naturally compounded by the shrinkage of these very resources. And what is particular to the Israeli case in this respect, is the fact that the material constraint was not primarily the result of the fiscal implications of the slow-down in economic growth (although those implications were certainly real enough). A more fundamental limit to state autonomy, and one which had already surfaced a decade before the 1973 war, was the waning of *discretionary* capital inflow and the rise of non-discretionary gifts tied to Israel's military commitments. These commitments, in turn, provided the state with a strong incentive to continue to promote the military industries in spite of the questionable macro-economic benefits which could be obtained thereby.

The big banks

The significance of Israel's largest banks as stakeholders in industry has already been commented upon; but they also play a remarkable role in the economy in their own right.[30] Like manufacturing, banking in Israel experienced a secular trend (accelerated by the mid-1960s recession) towards growing concentration, with the active support of the authorities. By the 1980s the three most important commercial banks—Leumi, Hapoalim, and Discount—had together cornered some 90 per cent of both assets and deposits, and monopolized almost the entire gamut of financial functions. One of the 'big three', the smallest, was privately controlled. The other two, officially the wards of the Histadrut and the Jewish Agency, were for the most part effectively run by their salaried top executives.[31] Even before the economic crisis, all three had long enjoyed a special relationship with the authorities. They were obliged to channel the vast majority of their deposits and other funds to the state, and in return were provided with opportunities to profit and grow. Under the conditions which came to prevail after 1973, this framework was highly conducive to a mutually reinforcing spiral of inflation on the one hand and aggrandizement of the banking industry on the other. In the course of this the growing weakness of the state in relation to the big three became painfully apparent.

The new inflation after 1973 received perhaps its most important boost from the first economic policy initiative of the Likud-led government which took over from Labour in 1977.[32] Until that time, stabilization policy had followed conventional remedies for a balance of payments crisis—principally, devaluation, wage freezes, and restraint of domestic demand by fiscal means. Only five months after taking office, the first Likud Finance Minister (the leader of the pro-business Liberal Party) introduced a dramatic shift in economic policy emphasis by announcing far-reaching measures to 'liberalize' Israel's foreign currency regime. Potentially the most significant aspect of this programme of deregulation was its simultaneous elimination of Israel's system of multiple exchange rates (a traditional indirect means of encouraging exports) and of administrative regulation of the terms of trade by import levies and export subsidies.

The immediate fate of this far-reaching programme affords eloquent testimony to the state's inability to impose market discipline on the business sector. In practice the fixing of new exchange rates was distorted so as to preserve the heavy protective shield enjoyed by domestic producers. At the same time, since exporters gained little or nothing from the convergence of exchange rates, the authorities immediately authorized a compensatory increase in off-budget export subsidies. Deregulation did, however, have dramatic effects on the monetary system. With the removal of hindrances to the import of foreign funds, 'hot money' streamed into Israeli banks in pursuit of high interest rates. In addition, because Israelis were now free to purchase dollars, the Treasury came under pressure to increase the attractiveness of its bond issues, the mainstay of public debt service. As a consequence of these developments, the authorities were effectively left with almost no means of restraining interest rates, the money supply, or erosion of the state's foreign currency reserves.

The liberal economics introduced by the Likud's self-styled policy revolution arrived at the close of a year in which inflation had been high (34 per cent), although no more so than over the preceding 12 months. But during the year which followed, prices rose considerably faster (54 per cent), marking the beginning of an acceleration which was to continue (with a temporary interruption at the beginning of the 1980s) until the emergency Stabilization Plan of 1985. The banks were the most spectacular winners from this unleashing of inflation. By 1980 their share of Israel's barely growing GNP was close to double the level of five years earlier. The same period also saw the collective net profits of the big three increase nearly fourfold in real terms. The trend of the big banks' profits in close proximity to Israel's accelerating inflation may be clearly observed in Figure 7.2.[33]

Yet instead of reining in the banks, the state increasingly gave them its business.[34] The big banks became the conduit for the rising tide of local and foreign funds necessary to service the public debt and maintain foreign currency balances. When added to their pivotal role as investors, these developments generated considerable sympathy for the banks' requirements on the part of the authorities. By leaving tax loopholes open and failing to enforce legal prohibitions on the banks' manipulation of their own share values, politicians and senior public officials knowingly became implicated in the soaring growth of bank profits. When the bank share bubble finally burst in the autumn of 1983, the rest of the stock market collapsed with it. Nevertheless, indicative of the leverage enjoyed by the banks and the big institutional investors which were the major holders of bank shares, the government intervened

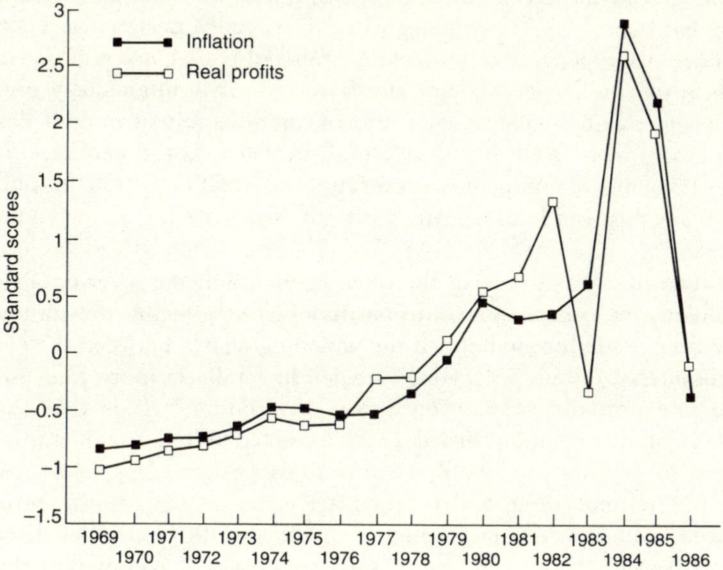

FIG. 7.2. Inflation and the profits of the three largest banks: 1969–86

Sources: *Statistical Abstract of Israel* for inflation. Bichler (1986: appendix 1) for profits.

Note: Inflation is the year-to-year change in the Consumer Price Index. The collective net profits of Bank Leumi, Bank Hapoalim, and the Israel Discount Bank were pooled and then recalculated in constant 1980 shekels. Both series were transformed into standard scores.

with special guarantees which made good a substantial part of the paper losses brought about by the 1983 crisis.

The banks' price-fixing practices have commonly been misinterpreted as the result of reprehensible standards of personal conduct on the part of bank executives and public officials, rather than as a symptom of the power wielded by the big three in the framework of their symbiotic relationship with the state. A parallel error has been to explain the banks' growing size and profitability as no more than the unintended by-product of accelerating inflation. Certainly, the awesome scope for holders of liquid assets to turn a profit, as well as the desperate need for ordinary citizens to manage their money, vastly expanded the scope for banking services as inflation reached double- and then triple-digit levels. Yet it was the state that furnished the most important pre-conditions for expanding bank profits. Many categories of specially designated beneficiaries were permitted to take out unlinked bank loans paid for by the authorities, even though the latter were simultaneously obligated to pay out index-linked interest on government bonds. This generosity was itself due in no small measure to the necessity for the Treasury to compete with alternative destinations for the public's savings—and above all, with the share issues of the major banks.[35]

Given the persistence of the phenomenon and the severity of the problems of external and internal indebtedness facing the state at the time, its failure to abolish the widening chasm between the cost structure of public borrowing and lending reflects more than just the unexpectedly rapid progression of inflation.[36] It is true that much of the resultant fiscal burden was deferred to the future. Even so, by the early 1980s the annual cost of repaying the domestic public debt alone had reached a level equivalent to the entire central government budget for education, health, and other direct social services.[37] In the face of such real costs, it is apparent that the state had no choice but to acquiesce to inflation's magic circle: higher deficits leading to more profitable opportunities in money markets and also to more inflation, leading to further profits from unlinked government loans and tax benefits, leading once again to higher deficits. Moreover, the banks were not the only winners from the joint availability of subsidized credit and attractive savings opportunities. Resource-rich industrial concerns, most of them directly linked to the big three, found it far more profitable to invest in the financial markets than in production.[38]

Conclusions

For more than a decade following the shock waves of 1973, the state's stewardship of the Israeli economy had the effect of aggravating rather than warding off destabilization. In attempting to account for this policy failure, this chapter has focused attention on the growing strength and integration of big business and its increasing power in the nexus between capital and the state. Prior to the crisis, both the underlying structure of the business sector and its associational activity became increasingly concentrated. After growing to maturity in a secure climate of massive public support, Israel's largest financial and industrial enterprises were compensated for the onset of economic slow-down by enormously increased state subsidies. When combined with the militarization of foreign aid and the state's increasing dependence on the big banks, this had the effect of greatly aggravating other motors of hyper-inflation and fiscal strain.

No doubt the impact of imported price rises in 1973 magnified the potential for economic crisis, just as the unanticipated challenge to Israel's military superiority mounted by Egypt and Syria in the same year brought an incipient political crisis that much closer to maturity. Nevertheless, these and other conjunctural developments should be understood as having intensified an *ongoing* process of eroding state autonomy in relation to business interests. The decomposition of Mapai's post-sovereignty regime of single party dominance was symptomatic of the same process, part of an overall decline in state control of the economy.

What are the broader implications of our case history for understanding the relations between capital and the state? Should Israel's early experience be interpreted as a transitory exception which proves the rule of the inevitability of state subservience to capital in democratic capitalist societies? It is indeed evident that in the longer term, just as in the metaphor of the sorcerer's apprentice, a weak and dependent capitalist class gained a substantial degree of mastery over its mentors. It would be tempting to interpret this as evidence for the proposition that, sooner or later, the state necessarily runs headlong into the interests of capital and gives way. In the lexicon of statistics, that is a statement which is asymptotically true; but it is not terribly useful as a guide to what happens in the interface between capital and the state under any given set of concrete historical conditions. This can be argued both on *theoretical* grounds, and in view of the actual *empirical variability* of political–economic contexts.

Theoretically, there simply is no unique and unambiguous policy imperative which flows from the structural constraints which have fascinated modern political economists from Kalecki to Lindblom. The reasons have been discussed extensively in the literature which succeeded the initial wave of radical theorizations of the state in the 1970s.[39] *Different sectors* ('fractions') of business have different and sometimes opposed interests. Moreover, the structure of incentives facing *individual* capitalists in the short term may dictate quite different policies from those which are in the longer term interests of capital *as a class*. Consequently, the implications of public policies for 'the interests of capital' are by no means unambiguous. In any case, 'what's good for General Motors' is not necessarily inconsistent with the interests of non-capitalists—that depends on the scope for and possible terms of *class compromise*. 'Positive sum' policies may be found which serve the interests of the working class and the state without harming those of business—although they can never eliminate the zero-sum elements inherent in this triangular relationship.

From an empirical perspective, different states (and the same ones at different points in time) clearly face significantly different opportunities and constraints. State autonomy from capital is *contingent*—it depends on the structure and solidarity of capital; the extent to which the independent agenda of the state is societally hegemonic; the state's capacity to extract and harness sufficient economic resources to implement its agenda; the power mobilized by labour and intermediate classes and their standing in the state arena; and the national economy's vulnerability to the whims of foreign investors and international markets.

Our analysis of Israeli trends pinpointed a number of changes in precisely these types of contingency, which had the effect of substantially altering the character of capital–state relations. Three of these developments were especially significant.

1. The ascent of capital in Israel was in part the consequence of a structural development predicted by the *Communist Manifesto*—namely, a growing concentration of capital in the wake of takeovers, mergers, and the purging effects of cyclical crises.
2. Capital also succeeded in augmenting its structural power by institutional means. Examples of this tendency include the increasing significance of the Histadrut as an instrument for transmitting the common interests of private and labour movement capital to the state; the growing strength of the work-forces of big business and their participation with employers in 'robbers' coalitions' to extract state subsidies; and the enhanced presence of business interest organizations, especially the Manufacturers' Association, as participants in policy networks.
3. Developments at the interface between the Israeli state and the

international system were of particular importance. They included the interlocking military and economic implications of Israel's increasingly close relationship with the United States; the decline of foreign gifts linked to the state's national identity (as opposed to its geopolitical role); and the economic aftermath of the 1973 Arab–Israeli war.

The ebbing tide of unrestricted gift capital from abroad and the growing linkage of foreign receipts to military aggrandizement, placed severe limits on the state's discretion in steering capital formation. But in addition, its own policies had the effect, both implicitly and explicitly, of promoting the growing solidification and power of Israel's economic core. The state's paternalistic relationship to a dependent class of 'quasi-entrepreneurs' (Ben-Porath, 1986*b*: 15), earlier a reflection of its relatively broad autonomy, was succeeded by a pattern of increasing dependence on large financial and industrial concerns, especially once the shocks of the 1970s ended Israel's era of effortless economic expansion.

Thus was eroding state autonomy *vis-à-vis* capital generated by the unintended consequences of the actions and policies of state élites, and the emergent contradictions between the system of 1948 and the geopolitical and geo-economic realities of the 1970s and beyond. A similar dialectic explains the declining capacity of the state to mediate the Labour Party's political hegemony over citizens. In its heyday, Mapai's exploitation of the state's political control of the economy had served to create dependency and buy loyalty. But the expanding economic choices of individuals and whole communities or strata and their successful efforts at self-organization transformed political assets into liabilities. It is true that the emergence of a credible political alternative on the right also played a crucial role. In this respect a good part of the Likud's success undoubtedly stemmed from its ability to capitalize on the cultural and geopolitical issues raised by warfare and conquest. But the rise of competitive party politics was also due to the second-order effects of the domestic policies which had once served the ruling party so well. The institutionalization of national and ethnic inequality by Mapai's segmented social and economic policies was bound eventually to generate a potential for political backlash. It was thus the Labour Party itself which turned both Eastern Jews and Israel's Palestinian voters into sitting targets for oppositional political entrepreneurs.

Notes

1. As in Chapter 6, data cited in the text for which no source is indicated have been drawn from either the *Statistical Abstract of Israel* or the Bank of Israel's *Annual Report*.
2. The revival of concern for relations between the state and capital is properly credited to neo-Marxism (e.g. O'Connor, 1973; Offe, 1975) although, as indicated by Charles Lindblom's (1977) seminal contribution, radical interpretations are by no means confined to Marxists. Theda Skocpol and her collaborators (Evans, Rueschemeyer and Skocpol, 1985) have been particularly influential in the development of a more 'state-centred' (as opposed to 'society-centred') approach to state autonomy. For reviews of relevant literature and major issues see Crouch (1979); Alford and Friedland (1985); and the symposium on 'The Return to the State' in the *American Political Science Review*, 82(3), 1988, 853–901.
3. We speak of 'élites in command of the state' whereas state-centred analysis has tended to emphasize the state's bureaucratic apparatus, apparently on the grounds that elected officials tend to be more reflective or captive of class and other 'societal' interests. This seems to us theoretically unnecessary and unduly limited in application to the Israeli case.
4. For a fuller treatment of the voting swings which generated the turnabout in the relative fortunes of Labour and the Likud see the original version of the study on which this part of the present chapter is based (Shalev, 1990*b*).
5. Figure 3.1 (Chapter 3) graphs the relative voting strength of Labour and the Likud before and since 1977. Appendix 4 has detailed information on changes in the Knesset representation of left-wing parties.
6. A significant concentration of the literature on voting trends in Israel may be found in the series of *Elections in Israel* volumes edited by Asher Arian (e.g. Arian, 1980).
7. The earliest survey enquiry, which lends clear support to the reluctant-voter thesis, was that of Antonovsky (1963*a* and *b*; 1966). The swings in the Jewish electorate referred to in the text are evident in both survey and ecological data—see respectively, Shamir (1986) and Diskin (1980). Cohen (1985) has compiled a large quantity of data on Arab voting trends. For evidence of a Jewish 'ethnic vote' well before the 1977 elections see Matras (1965) and Lissak (1969) among others. Note, however, that despite the existence of an ethnically structured vote, as late as 1977 ethnicity itself was not perceived as a major election issue (Ishai, 1977: 17). Also,

there are grounds for believing that the ethnic vote was in part a class vote in disguise (e.g. Swirski, 1984; Farjoun, 1983). Unfortunately, most of the considerable empirical research on voting in Israel since the rise of the ethnic vote has either ignored class effects or mis-specified or misinterpreted them (e.g. Shamir and Arian, 1982; Peres and Shemer, 1984).

8. For a related, but somewhat different analysis, see Shamir (1986).
9. For diverse illustrations of this approach see Aronoff (1977); Shapiro (1980); and Goldberg (1986).
10. See especially Etzioni-Halevy and Shapira (1977) and Arian (1980).
11. For examples of this kind of reasoning see Kimmerling (1983*b*) and Shafir (1984).
12. Since 1948 Mapai and its successor parties have never obtained less than 50% of the popular vote in Histadrut elections. The governing coalition in the labour organization has consistently enjoyed the large majority necessary to control constitutional provisions. For a long-term view of voting trends in the Histadrut arena see Figure 3.2 (Chapter 3).
13. Political scientist and Labour Party Knesset member Shevach Weiss presented striking evidence on this point from an undocumented survey, in a newspaper article in *Davar*, 9 Sept. 1981.
14. On the DMC see Urieli and Barzilai (1982) and data in Arian (1980).
15. For a survey of US aid policy see Laufer (1987). The estimate in the text of one billion dollars of free arms imports a year reflects only genuine gifts to Israel from the USA (including foregone loan repayments), after deducting the cost of servicing past loans.

    The economic interests supportive of US aid are explicated by Rowley, Bichler, and Nitzan (1989). They argue that the Arab–Israeli arms race resulted from the end of Vietnam-generated demand for arms and the emergent common interest of powerful US arms and oil companies in a cycle of interconnected military and oil crises in the Middle East. Arnon (1986*a*) has made a strong case for the role of American geopolitical interests in stimulating aid to Israel. These encompassed not only Israel's potential role as a surrogate policeman, but also the American interest in fostering regional alliances that would extend the US sphere of influence. These two interpretations—political–economic and geopolitical—should be seen as potentially complementary, as in Schuldiner's (1982 and 1983) modified dependency model of the American–Israel connection.
16. The data cited hereafter are annual averages for two periods, 1955–60 and 1975–7. The principal sources were Halevi (1983*b*) and

Bank of Israel annual reports. Dollar values were converted to proportions of GNP using 'effective' exchange rates.

17. The assertion that US aid has been indexed to Israel's purchases of American arms can be substantiated as follows (see also Razin, 1983: table 3). If the aid 'package' for a given year is defined on a cash-flow basis, as the sum of US grants and loans (irrespective of their designated purpose) less the cost to Israel of servicing past debts, then over the 1973–84 period it emerges that aid has generally exceeded arms imports by only 10%. (The 'Camp David supplements' of 1979–80 were excluded from this calculation.) It should, however, be noted that as a result of the emergency economic aid of 1985–6 (which played an important role in the success of Israel's stabilization plan) and the trend which crystallized at about the same time to replace loans with outright grants, the non-military surplus in the aid package has increased substantially in recent years.
18. On both the magnitude and dynamics of state subsidization of military-related production see Hadar (1988). Mintz (1983) and Peri and Neubach (1985) are among the many informative sources on Israel's 'military-industrial complex', but, typically, they pay insufficient attention to the economic interests which sustain it, to be discussed later in this chapter. On 'the method' (as it is still typically called in Israel) practised by Pinchas Sapir see Schecter (1972) and Shimshoni (1982: ch. 5, esp. 241–7).
19. For a fuller discussion see Chapter 6.
20. These trends have been documented by Aharoni (1976: esp. 96–100), and their interpretation sharpened by Bichler (1986).
21. Aharoni (1976: 123–46) provides details on the post-1967 retreat from public enterprise and Kanovsky (1970: 71–2) discusses the Histadrut's post-war orientation to the private sector.
22. Shirom (1983: ch. 7; 1984) has documented the markedly favourable treatment awarded to business interest associations by the state during the period of Labour Party hegemony. Illustrative of this tendency, in the closing years of Labour's reign legislation was passed granting the Manufacturers' Association corporatist privileges (dues check-off and a compulsory representation fee for 'free riders') comparable to those which had long been enjoyed by the Histadrut. For further discussion of co-operation between the managers of large Histadrut and private enterprises see Chapter 6.
23. For overviews of trends in Israel's manufacturing sector in the period under discussion see Shaliv (1981) and Bregman (1986).
24. For a theoretical exposition and overview of the sociological literature on 'dual economies' see Hodson (1983).

25. Dun and Bradstreet, publishers of the 'Top 100' listings, define 'industry' to include not only manufacturing but also electricity generation and mineral extraction and processing (but not oil refining and distribution). Dun and Bradstreet make no mention of it, but their 40% estimate is almost certainly inflated by the inclusion of full turnover figures for partly-owned subsidiaries.
26. For indications of the shared social milieu which not only binds the executives of the three sectors but also links them to the political élite see Frenkel and Bichler (1984) and, in an earlier period, Schecter (1972). Aharoni (1984) has gathered extensive attitudinal evidence for the convergence in managerial strategies and outlooks between the different ownership sectors. Building on the work of Bichler (1986), Rowley, Bichler, and Nitzan (1988) document the convergence of profits both within and between the three top banks and the three largest non-governmental industrial conglomerates. They withhold judgement regarding government corporations due to a lack of reliable information on profits and the fact that public-sector business sometimes appears to function as a 'loss leader' in the service of the private sector.
27. Detailed surveys of state subsidies are available in Jerusalem Institute of Management (1987) and Hadar (1988).
28. This was the conclusion of a re-analysis of the financial reports of a sample of large industrial firms by Levy and Lerman (1984).
29. Hadar (1988) substantiates the equality of privilege among the largest firms in the three ownership sectors, and also details the institutional arrangements underpinning the close relationship between profits and procurement. For a muckraking exposé of the profits of war reaped by a wide array of enterprises in the specific case of Israel's invasion of Lebanon see Frenkel (1982).
30. For a description of Israel's banks see Landau (1989). Our principal sources on industrial capital, Aharoni (1976) and Bichler (1986), also furnished important background material regarding banking.
31. To some extent both the ownership and operation of the largest banks was altered by the aftermath of a major crisis in 1983. A certain measure of publicity and accountability has been imposed on senior executives, and the terms of a government bail-out may ultimately induce some dispersal of the traditional high concentration of effective ownership rights within the three biggest banks.
32. We rely here mainly on the comprehensive study of the Likud's 'liberalization' initiative by Tov (1988).
33. As Figure 7.2 indicates, the otherwise close relationship between the rate of inflation and real bank profits was suspended between 1981 and 1983—the result first of the culmination and then the collapse

of the banks' so-called 'regulation' of their share prices. For additional data on the growth of banking see Marom (1988).

34. The most valuable source on the pivotal role of Israel's banks in the era of economic crisis is the report of the 'Beijski Commission', which was charged with investigating the banks' illegal price-rigging practices (Commission of Inquiry, 1986). Arnon's (1986*b*) article on the report provides some insightful commentary.
35. On the evolution of competition between the banks and the Treasury to attract savings see Galai and Brenner (1984) and Brenner and Ruthenberg (1987).
36. On this issue compare Meridor (1987, 1988).
37. Calculated from Kop (1987: tables 2 and 4) using Bank of Israel data on the break-down between domestic and foreign debt service.
38. See Yoran (1987) for an orthodox but trenchant critique of the self-defeating policy that he terms 'injection-absorption'. The reversal of fortunes suffered by many large industrial firms in the wake of Israel's 1985 disinflation constitutes powerful indirect evidence of the role played by the opportunities for corporate profits furnished by the state in the context of hyper-inflation. The real cost of credit suddenly became distinctly positive, and the tax burden on corporations rose sharply. The banks' gains from the public indebtedness generated by unreformed inflation are indicated by the close correlation over the period 1971–82 between the big banks' profits and the level of state expenditure dedicated to servicing the domestic national debt ($r = .91$ when both series are adjusted for inflation).
39. Three noteworthy contributions to this debate are essays by Block (1986); Pontusson (1983); and Przeworski and Wallerstein (1988).

Conclusions

At the outset of this book, it was suggested that by arming ourselves with the breadth afforded by history and the depth provided by theory and comparison, this study could cater to the interests of two distinct audiences: political economists without any special affinity to the Israeli case and students of Israeli society in search of new findings and alternative perspectives. The purpose of these concluding remarks is to extend the discussion in earlier chapters of what we take to be the central issues for each one of these audiences. We first address the concerns of those whose primary interest is in the implications of our study for theories of social-democratic corporatism (SDC). In part this involves returning to the problem of inconsistency between theoretical expectations inspired by the West European experience and the Israeli record. But we also offer some suggestions for augmenting the analytical power of SDC by incorporating insights from additional strands of political-economic theory.

After this the discussion turns to the claim that for researchers of Israeli society, political economy provides an especially insightful perspective, one that is capable of addressing significant lacunae in previous scholarship. Then, in the third major section of the chapter, we raise a question relevant to both of our audiences—namely, how to situate the Israeli case within the universe of the rich liberal democracies. Our answer is that Israel is neither a unique case nor one which directly corresponds to a single recognizable type of political-economic regime. Finally, we close with some observations on what those interested in speculating about Israel's future might learn from the theoretical and methodological postulates of this study.

This book has been self-consciously motivated by two contemporary perspectives on labour movements and the political economy. The social-democratic model has sought to demonstrate that class politics decisively shapes key political-economic outcomes, including inequality, economic performance, and the pattern of class conflict. The corporatist model argues that under certain conditions —especially where unions are encompassing and solidaristic, and social democrats dominate the government—class accommodation can develop on the basis of bargaining among the corporate representatives of labour, capital, and the state. Here too, practical benefits are envisaged—industrial peace, and a markedly resilient tendency towards political and economic stability. The question which we found puzzling in this context, was why Israel, in many respects an exemplar of synthesis between social democracy and democratic corporatism, has in large part failed to generate the benign outcomes anticipated by theory.

In trying to use theory constructively to illuminate a deliberately limited empirical terrain, we have consciously veered from several well-trodden paths. The theoretical literature on social democracy and corporatism has been much preoccupied, respectively, with the thorny questions of whether social democracy advances or retards prospects for a transition from capitalism to socialism and whether corporatist labour restraint serves or sabotages the interests of the working class.[1] At the same time, empirical work in the field has placed inordinate emphasis on quantitative comparisons of large samples of countries. Both of these predilections result in issues being posed at a global level and encourage a search for context-independent generalizations. Yet in order to lend due weight to the diversity and the individuality of national settings, there is a clear need for contingent theorizing and case-study research.[2] For this purpose the literature on SDC is most inspiring and useful when formulated as a series of limited and empirically manageable hypotheses. Having put this approach to work in the present volume, it must now be asked what lessons arise for the social-democratic corporatist model from its confrontation with the Israeli case.

One obvious result of this encounter is the evidence it has brought to light of notable inconsistencies with at least some of the expectations of the model. Some of these divergences suggest a need for modifying theoretical expectations. In other cases, they imply that the distinctiveness of the Israeli case is simply too great to permit direct comparison with other seemingly parallel Western societies. More important theoretically, however, is the fact that the analytical tool-kit provided by SDC proved seriously deficient unless supplemented by insights drawn from other sources. We have found state theory and models of labour-market segmentation to be especially helpful for this purpose. The former is a badly needed corrective to the over-concentration of theories of SDC on the labour movement, and their adoption of an 'instrumental' view of the state as little more than a tool of governing parties. The latter complements the focus of SDC on the politics of class mobilization and conflict by insisting that labour movements and industrial relations both shape, and are shaped by, the character of the labour markets in which they are embedded.

It will be recalled that the first major question posed in this study concerned what is arguably the Israeli labour movement's most central peculiarity—its early internalization of the Arab–Israeli conflict in a comprehensive but nationally exclusive labour organization. This brought us face to face with a major oversimplification of the social-democratic theory of working-class mobilization, which effectively posits a dichotomy between social homogeneity and solidaristic labour organization at one pole, and 'cross-cutting cleavages' and labour disorganization at the other. The very notion of *cross-cutting* cleavages presents racial and other ascriptive lines of social division as disruptive forces which originate outside the arena of class formation and conflict. In Palestine and Israel, however, it is precisely the *entanglement* of 'economic' and 'primordial' cleavages which explains the pattern of collective action by Jewish workers. Their mobilization and the emergence of the national conflict were chronologically and causally interlaced as labour sought and acquired the vanguard role in a broad movement for Jewish separatism. But this dynamic was instigated more than anything else by the fact that the line between Arabs and Jews ran parallel to conflicting material interests—the division between cheap and expensive labour.

In Bonacich's 'supply-side' interpretation of labour-market dualism, we found a theory that embodies precisely this understanding of internal conflicts within the working class. It is important to recognize the distinctiveness of this perspective in comparison with the better-known demand-side perspective on labour-market segmentation. According to the latter view, the varied technological and market conditions facing different types of employers drive them to adopt differing strategies of recruiting, rewarding, and managing labour. The members of subordinate social groups are preyed upon by peripheral capitalists in search of fluid pools of cheap labour; and also by core capitalists intent on weakening their work-forces by a policy of 'divide and rule'. This perspective has demonstrated validity, but pays insufficient attention to objective 'pre-labour market' differences in the labour costs of disparate ethnic groups. The demand-side view also fails to face up to the role played by 'expensive' labour in confining the disadvantaged to undesirable jobs. This is not a moral judgement about the culpability of labour versus capital. Rather, Bonacich's analysis is premised on the view that segmentation is one of a *variety* of defensive strategies which may be pursued by more expensive workers in a cost-split labour market. What needs to be explained is the choice between those strategies.

When the focus of our analysis shifted from the market to the political arena, the social-democratic model proved to be a more useful guide. As the model predicts, successful working-class mobilization was the most important source of the historic rise of workers' parties within the Jewish community of Palestine. Theory has also recognized that in order to govern democratic polities, labour parties depend on the support of allies from outside the working-class, either as voters or coalition partners. Mapai's success during the 1930s in forging such alliances was not dissimilar in principle to the better-known story of Swedish social democracy. In both cases the party transcended the limits of the working-class vote by combining economic incentives to non-workers with a demonstrated capacity to resolve key existential issues on behalf of 'the nation' as a whole.

In the course of time, however, Mapai/Labour became first a multi-class party and then a party of the middle class, with a hegemonic formula more resemblant to right-wing than left-wing dominance. This is one of the reasons why domestic policy priorities and outcomes in Israel are so inconsistent with the expectations of SDC. Yet this very inconsistency also provides a clue to Mapai's ultimate political failure. It has been persuasively argued—at least for conditions of relatively effortless economic growth—that successful social-democratic corporatist regimes perpetuate their hegemony by a 'politics of virtuous circles' (Castles, 1978: 118 ff.). The contention is that by dint of their social and economic policies, stable left-wing governments reinforce the most important pivots of their rule: working-class solidarity, inter-class co-operation, and state steering of the economy. In a long-term view of the Israeli case, one observes something closer to a politics of *vicious circles*. This is particularly true of the labour movement's role in the creation of deep distributional inequalities and conflicts between ethnic and national communities—divisions which contributed appreciably to the electoral realignment which removed the popular basis for one-party dominance. Another fateful legacy was the labour movement's sponsorship of a prodigiously concentrated capitalism, which the state's political and bureaucratic managers found increasingly difficult to direct.

It was in the changing relationship between capital and the state that we discovered a source of Israel's political and economic upheavals largely overlooked by earlier analysts. We shall have more to say about the specific sources of this neglect later. The important point for the present discussion is that this is also a blind spot of the SDC literature to which we turned for theoretical inspiration. Working from the assumption that the collective mobilization of *labour* essentially determines the relative class power of labour *and capital*, theorists have tended to gloss over the real barriers in capitalist societies to 'political control of the economy'. This has instead been conceptualized as contingent on the political weight carried by socialist governments, and their readiness to perceive that distributive policies can be powerful instruments for shaping political opportunity structures and the contours of social solidarity.

But this is actually only part of the story. What is missing is an analysis of the relative power of the state *vis-à-vis* capital. In this respect a good place to start is the contention that only some states at some moments are sufficiently autonomous so that they have the power to steer society. Conceptualizing Israel's regime of dominance in terms of state autonomy proved especially valuable in this study for interpreting the crises of the 1970s. It helped us to see that in basing its penetration of society so heavily on the state, Mapai banked its pre-eminence on a degree of autonomy which could not stand the test of time. What is more, declining autonomy could be identified as the source not only of the Labour Party's loss of hegemony, but also the state's inability to induce economic stability and growth. The fact that Israel's economic crisis only came to a head after Labour's eviction from office is consistent with a fundamental tenet of state theory: that while governments come and go, the state and its contradictions are enduring.

The centrality of the state as both concept and actor became equally apparent in studying the historical dynamics of industrial relations in Palestine and later, Israel. The favoured explanatory variables of SDC—the growth of encompassing labour organization and the political ascendancy of a social-democratic party—proved to be blunt instruments indeed for predicting the appearance and elaboration of corporatist relationships between labour, capital, and the state. Without a grasp of changing state agendas and capacities, it would have been impossible to analyse the inscrutable twists and turns of Israeli corporatism: the inability of the pre-state institutions of Jewish self-government to bring about a 'historic compromise' between labour and capital; the transforming effect of World War II on the readiness of the Mandatory government to contemplate corporatist solutions; and the burgeoning co-operation after 1948 between the political élites of the Histadrut and the sovereign State of Israel.

The greatest paradox of all was the failure of SDC in Israel to overcome the 1960s crisis of full employment and the labour movements's consequent recourse to a 'political business cycle'. Michal Kalecki was correct in anticipating, nearly fifty years ago, that a prolonged absence of unemployment could ignite labour militancy to the point that the state would have no choice but to repair the damage to profits and employer authority by restoring market discipline. Nevertheless, Kalecki's interpretation erred in presenting the state in capitalist society as little more than a transmission-belt for conflicting class interests. Israel's crisis of full employment came to a head, because of the increasing turbulence of industrial relations and also as a result of parallel challenges to both the political authority of the ruling party and the state's ability to stage-manage economic growth. However, whereas the theory of political business cycles at least anticipated in broad outline the mid-1960s recession, this is a case which confronts the corporatist model with a far more serious challenge. It has, after all, been a central claim of this model that corporatism developed in the post-war period as a more advanced *alternative* to the discipline of 'the sack'. We argued that, on the contrary, in Israel this discipline was invoked precisely in order to *revive* a flagging corporatist regime.

A further theoretically unanticipated conclusion of our study of the Mitun was that corporatism was not alone in upholding labour quiescence prior to the coming of stable full employment. Until that time militancy was jointly inhibited by the Histadrut's posture of self-restraint and by the precarious position of the Arab and Eastern-Jewish workers employed in the secondary labour market —just as in Israel's more recent experience, industrial relations have been simultaneously mediated by corporatism and dualism. Yet in one of the few attempts to place corporatism and dualism under a single theoretical umbrella, John Goldthorpe (1984) has argued that the two make unlikely bedfellows.[3] He points out that whereas (social-democratic) corporatism 'decommodifies' the working class as a whole by upholding full employment, under dualism these benefits are denied to less-privileged workers, who permanently labour under the shadow of job insecurity and employer domination. The Israeli experience shows, however, that the seemingly contradictory logic of corporatism and dualism by no means prevents their cohabitation.[4]

These reflections suggest that if corporatism is to have theoretical utility in the analysis of labour restraint, it needs to be conceptualized *in relation to other regulatory mechanisms* (at a minimum, both political business cycles and labour-market dualism). Moreover, such a conceptualization should be geared to clarifying the differences between corporatism and other mechanisms, and also to facilitating analysis of real-world situations in which regimes of labour restraint potentially have multiple components that alter over the course of time. Progress in these directions has to no small extent been hampered by a basic ambiguity of the contemporary literature on neo-corporatism. Much of the motivation behind the revival of scholarly interest in the subject was prompted by the search for a new paradigm for analysing relations between organized interests and the state. In this context the politics of industrial relations were important primarily as illustrations with particular contemporary relevance. It is only for those who turn to corporatism as a model of class compromise that it must necessarily be contrasted with other mechanisms of labour restraint and not with other modes of interest organization or public policy-making.

Unfortunately, as we have seen, the most influential responses to this challenge—Kalecki's classic contribution and Goldthorpe's more recent formulation—offer evocative but unduly dichotomous solutions.

One essential requirement for a more integrated view is a solution to the perennial issue of how corporatism is to be defined. In an industrial-relations context, what distinguishes corporatism from other vehicles of restraint is that it draws *organized* labour and capital into a fundamentally *political* resolution of class conflict. Corporatism is political in a double sense—with respect to the labour movement's reliance on the state as an arena for the pursuit of workers' class interests, and the process (of political exchange) which underlies class compromise. Industrial peace in non-corporatist settings may, however, originate not in bargaining but in *coercion*, exercised by private employers (intimidation) or the state (legal prohibitions and police repression). Alternatively, *consensual* labour relations may be achieved through bargains struck not in the state arena (the *sine qua non* of corporatism), but within individual enterprises.

These four possibilities are summarized in Table C.1. Under this scheme, both the political business cycle and labour-market segmentation are cases which fall between two cells. In the former, market forces are unleashed by public policy (cells 2 and 4). Segmentation, on the other hand, signifies a combination of enterprise-level 'micro-collaboration' in the primary labour market (cell 3) and the repression of workers in the secondary market by means of unemployment and employer duress (cell 4). Should these distinctions appear overly abstract, a good case for their face validity can be made by referring back to our study of the failure of corporatist initiatives in the Jewish sector of Mandatory Palestine. A major conclusion of that investigation was that political exchange was rendered unnecessary by the robustness of alternative sources of labour restraint. As examples, we pointed to the state's use of force against strikers and the threat of cyclical unemployment. And we also distinguished a tendency towards work place-level co-operation in the larger manufacturing firms, while elsewhere the pressure of competition for scarce job opportunities curbed the power even of well-organized workers.

The typology proposed here is intended to serve not only as a classificatory scheme, but also as a reminder that it is essential to

TABLE C.1. *Mechanisms of labour restraint*

Basis for restraint	Arena mediating class relations	
	State	Market
Accommodation	(1) Corporatism	(3) Micro-collaboration
Coercion	(2) State repression	(4) Business cycle Employer repression

consider the politics and the economics of labour restraint within a unified conceptual framework. One reason why such a reminder is needed is that in its effort to bring politics to centre-stage in the analysis of industrial relations, the theory of SDC risks detaching class conflict from its roots in the market arena. Undoubtedly a corrective was needed to the distorted view offered by the orthodoxy of the 1950s and 1960s. According to this view labour relations and class politics had parted company, the former to be contained by institutional arrangements and the latter by political incorporation. The literature on SDC has rightfully drawn attention to the possibility that strongly organized and politicized labour movements might successfully exploit the state arena as a means of pursuing labour's interests without industrial strife. But this insight is of limited value for analysing settings in which SDC never took root. It is also inadequate to the task of comparing the fate of social democracy itself in the post-war years of rapid economic growth to developments under the far more constrained circumstances of the last several decades. Even in Sweden, the paradigm case of SDC, labour relations have diversified out of cell 1 of our table and into cells 2 and 3.

The fact that political analysts have tended to downplay market forces and relations in the market arena as sources of labour quiescence is, however, only one side of the problem. There is an equally critical linkage which operates in the other direction, in that the emergence and effectiveness of market-based mechanisms of restraint are inherently conditional upon the role of the state. The fact that this is typically a role of omission rather than commission makes it less transparent, but no less significant. The best known examples of state non-intervention as a bulwark of labour-market discipline come from the United States. Political and institutional conditions in America have left employers considerable freedom to recruit 'guest workers' and launch cycles of unemployment as tools of labour management.[5]

Palestine under the British Mandate is also a source of relevant illustrations. As the Histadrut was eager to point out at the time, the authorities' failure to police immigration from neighbouring Arab countries or to enact legislation protecting union rights had the effect of exacerbating the competitive struggle between Jewish and Arab labour. On the other hand, when wartime conditions finally brought full employment to Palestine, the undeveloped character of public social protection was an essential (albeit unplanned) pre-condition for the spread of 'micro-collaboration' based on the establishment of miniature welfare states within individual enterprises. After sovereignty, gaps in social policy continued to leave room for the very same development. At the same time dualism in the labour market fed upon the unwillingness of either the state or the Histadrut to enforce the *de jure* rights of Arab labour to wage equality. In short, as with action, so also with inaction. To understand why a given state plays the role that it does we must complement abstract insights into state/economy relations with empirical enquiries into how policy is conditioned by variable political conjunctures, economic growth formulas, state agendas, and state capacities.

It is time now to turn the spotlight and to consider more explicitly what the political economy approach brought to bear in this study has to offer students of Israeli society. In reflecting on Israel's past, traditional scholarship on the labour movement placed extraordinary weight on the realm of ideas and the 'great men' who were their carriers. Ours is not the first attempt to critically rewrite this history. Nevertheless, some of the most influential earlier reassessments were flawed by having succumbed to the temptation of economic or political reductionism.

This can be most clearly seen in the seminal works of Zvi Sussman (1969*a*) and Yonathan Shapiro (1976). Sussman's study of Jewish/Arab relations in the labour market was the first to systematically unveil the starkly competitive realities which made a mockery of the Histadrut's claim to have implanted a regime of wage equality in the Yishuv. But in echoing the labour movement's own conception of politics as ideology, and presenting his study as a demonstration of the vanquishing of politics by economic realities, Sussman closes from view the crucial interaction between market forces and *realpolitik*. Shapiro's analysis, which took *realpolitik* as its starting point, contends that the political supremacy of labour in Jewish Palestine resulted from its organizational power—the success of the labour movement élite in building an effective party apparatus in control of key economic institutions. But rather than bringing to the fore the economic conditions which spurred this political dynamic, Shapiro (1976: 4) attributes it primarily to the 'collectivist political culture' imported by the original labour leaders from their native Russia.

Our analysis is indicative of the missing links between those of Sussman and Shapiro. We have argued that the competitive threat posed by Arab labour propelled the Jewish working class towards collectivism and political organization and led it to seek a historic alliance with the Zionist movement. But this alliance, in turn, added political incentives to the economic rationale for struggles to isolate Jews from Arab competition. In return for assistance that would ameliorate the condition of Jewish workers and their organizations, the Histadrut accepted a binding obligation to infuse the many spheres of its activity with Zionist criteria. Moreover, the dialectic of economic and political forces did not end here. For, as it unfolded, the struggle for 'Hebrew labour' was exploited by the labour movement's leadership as a decisive means of strengthening its political base.

The case for political economy is as strong for interpreting the contemporary problems of Israeli society as it is for analysing its prehistory. We have argued that the decline of the remarkable capacities of the Israeli state for steering capital accumulation and the life chances of ordinary citizens alike, removed an essential underpinning of Mapai's political dominance and the state's management of economic performance. This thesis is at odds with the trend among political scientists to seek 'purely political' explanations for Israel's political upheaval. It also squarely contradicts the parallel tendency among economists to see Israel's hyper-inflation and stalled growth after 1973 as the legacy of 'short-sighted' politicians and the insatiable appetite of 'the public'. In our view the most puzzling aspects of the counter-productive role of the state in economic adjustment are those bearing upon its relationship to big business. When this relationship is subjected to scrutiny, it is evident that the same practices and policies that bore the responsibility for stagnation and 'uncontrollable' inflation also made definitive contributions to the increasing power and prosperity of Israel's industrial conglomerates and big banks.

The theoretical implication of this analysis—although we took care to link it to specific characteristics of the Israeli case in the period analysed—is to redirect attention to what Lindblom (1982) has called the 'imprisonment' of public policy by business interests. Both neo-Marxist political economy and what has been called 'the new political science of corporate power' are united in the view that even in democratic societies, capitalism impels the state to place the interests of capital at the forefront of its agenda. There has, of course, been a lively disagreement among different theorists concerning the mechanisms which bear responsibility for sustaining the privileged position of capital *vis-à-vis* the state. In recent years, moreover, crude notions of the inevitability of business dominance have been justifiably criticized.[6] Nevertheless, few participants in these debates have questioned the centrality of relations between capital and the state for the functioning of democratic-capitalist political economies. This is an issue which analysts of the Israeli case have evaded for far too long. It is worth while considering what accounts for this evasion. In this respect, comparison to the American context is enlightening. There, the emergence of business power in the state arena as a focus of scholarly concern followed 'the cumulative impact of Vietnam and racial conflict in the late sixties, the drama of Watergate, and . . . growing economic difficulties', all of which 'served to make the exercise of power in American society widely visible' (Block, 1987: 23).

Israel has certainly not been spared similar cataclysms, although they arrived on the scene at a somewhat later date. Such phenomena of delegitimation in Israeli society have, however, failed to cause an accusing finger to be pointed at capitalist interests. An important reason for this is that in contrast to the USA, Israeli scholarship draws no inspiration from a tradition of popular and intellectual mistrust of business influence. Quite to the contrary, it is one of the many ironies of labour politics in Israel that the dominant wings of the left have done much to bury the realities of

Israeli capitalism under myths of socialist rule and economic egalitarianism.

Academic discourse in Israel reflects—and contributes to—prevailing ideologies in other ways as well. While Israeli political scientists have traditionally treated the economy as an *excluded* category, most economists have analysed politics, if at all, as a *residual* category. The outlook characteristic of political science has much in common with the exaggerated popular perception in Israel of the freedom of political choice carved out by the founding fathers in the realm of economic affairs. It is still widely believed that even though it was eventually overcome by 'reality', labour-Zionist ideology succeeded in creating new social frameworks in spite of, rather than *because of*, material constraints. In contrast, as newer generations of Israelis have become cognizant of the dark underside of the achievements of the founders, neo-conservative tenets—closely akin to the ontological biases of professional economists—have found fertile soil. Increasingly, academic and popular discussion have been pervaded by the glorification of market forces and a view of state 'intervention' as inherently harmful. This book suggests that the result of these biases is a misreading of the sources of Israel's economic problems and a theoretical misrepresentation of the essential interdependence of state–economy relations.

In undertaking this study we aspired not only to probe a range of specific issues in the development of the labour movement and labour relations in Israel, but also to locate the political economy of Israel on the international map of democratic, capitalist societies. Our choice of SDC as a role-model for analysis of the Israeli case was made in full awareness of the dangers of simplistically equating model and case. It should by now be clear that institutions (the Histadrut and Mapai) which are outwardly similar to their counterparts elsewhere conceal what is at least in *some* respects a very different logic. Nation-building, statist, and middle-class Mapai may only at great risk be directly equated with the labour-movement parties of the West. The Histadrut's blend of colonizing, entrepreneurial, political, and labour-representation functions renders it at least partially incomparable to peak associations of trade unions in Western Europe.

Does this mean that the Israeli case is *sui generis*? We believe that it does not. The very possibility of comparative analysis in any setting is dependent on navigating between the Scylla of a retreat to 'exceptionalism' and the Charybdis of ignoring the contextual specificity of 'real existing' societies. From a comparative perspective we interpret Israel as straddling two seemingly opposed models of political economy—SDC and dualism. We have already discussed the contrast between these two models, and their coexistence in the Israeli setting, in the context of labour restraint. That argument can now be broadened to encompass a wider range of attributes. For this purpose, it is enlightening to contrast social-democratic corporatism in Sweden, Norway, and Austria to the dualist political-economic regime which is common to Switzerland and Japan.[7]

Both the overall pattern of class power and politics and the specific underpinnings of labour restraint in Japan and Switzerland could scarcely be more different from the characteristic features of SDC. The working class in both countries lacks either political dominance or comprehensive corporate labour organizations. The competing peak associations of Japanese labour play only a marginal role as co-authors of public policy. Their Swiss counterparts enjoy far more substantial participation rights, yet public policy itself exerts only limited leverage over economic affairs. In both contexts industrial peace is rooted not in macro-level political bargaining, but in the joint effects of the market discipline which prevails in the secondary labour market and the micro-level accommodation characteristic of the primary segment. The state may operate (as in Japan) to rationalize long-term investment planning, but its fundamental stance is one of maximizing the role of the market in distributional processes. Accordingly, the welfare state is sufficiently circumscribed to allow space for enterprise-level 'occupational welfare' to flourish in the primary labour market—quite different from social democracy's massive public-sector role in social protection. Finally, under dualism the maintenance of full employment at times of economic crisis rests more on disemployment of the vulnerable than on state interventions to stimulate job creation or enhance the skills and availability of the unemployed.

Table C.2 offers a deliberately simplified picture of similarities and differences between Israel and the other two settings with reference to underlying features of the political economy and their

TABLE C.2. *A comparison between three political–economic regimes*

	Dualism (Switzerland and Japan)	Social-democratic corporatism (Sweden, Norway, Austria)	Israel
Class politics			
Political strength of labour	Low	High	High (pre-1970s)
Organization of labour	Low	High	High
Policy involvement of labour	Varies	High	High
Organization of private business	High	High	Increasing
The labour market			
Job allocation and conditions	Segmented	'Solidaristic'	Segmented
Unemployment	Low	Low	Usually low
Regulation of labour militancy	Labour-market mechanisms	Political exchange	Political exchange *and* labour market
Overt conflict (strikes)	Low	Low	High
Distributional politics			
Wage and income inequality	High	Low	High
Welfare state type	'Residual'	'Institutional'	Segmented and partly 'residual'
State involvement in markets	Low	High	High
State steering of investment	Varies	High	High

correlates, the policy preferences and outcomes which were surveyed in Chapter 6.[8] The classification not only evokes the 'contradictory' elements of the Israeli case, but is also a reminder of the limits to generalizing about relationships between contexts and consequences across nations. The pervasiveness of relatively low unemployment across all six of the countries represented in the table is a good illustration of the fact that similar outcomes are possible under diverse political–economic regimes. Conversely, and particularly salient to the Israeli case, it is evident that similarities of context are no guarantee of like outcomes. The superficially close resemblance between the pattern of class politics in Israel and the corporatist nations of Western Europe is consistent with the similarly broad role of the state in the economy observed in the table, but not with the divergence which characterizes social policy and labour-market dynamics in the two settings.

What this book has tried to show is that, once placed in its particular historical context, Israel's 'perverse' distinctiveness becomes readily comprehensible. The Israeli labour movement is so outwardly resemblant to its counterparts in the social democracies of Western Europe because its founders employed institutional and cultural blueprints that originated in the context of capitalist and democratic development in Europe in order to meet the very different challenges posed by the exposure of propertyless settlers to the competition of 'native' labour. Compared to the social-democratic analogy, there has been far less recognition of the dualist motifs which pervade Israel's political economy. To a great extent these motifs too can be traced to their origins in the economic and political conflicts between Arab and Jew unleashed by Zionist colonization of Palestine. More precisely, it may be said that dualism in Israel has three overlapping foundations, each of which has not only clear historical antecedents, but also theoretical precedents in the study of social stratification and political economy.

1. The habits of the colonization period, the course of the Israeli/Palestinian conflict since 1948, and the state's Zionist prioritization of Jewish interests have combined to provide both a rationale and an institutional structure supportive of pervasive discrimination against Arab citizens. The result is akin to a political caste system, similar in principle to other contexts in which different ethnic or

occupational groups enjoy unequal standing in relationship to the state.[9]

2. Conflict-oriented theorists of status formation from Weber to Bonacich have argued that economic competition is a powerful motivating force for establishing socio-political boundaries between differentially powerful groups. This is the dynamic which has informed the struggle of the dominant ethnic group in Israel to insulate itself from 'cheap labour', ever since the pre-sovereignty era. The predictable result has been the caste-like hierarchy which structures the participation of Palestinians (and to a lesser extent also of Eastern-origin Jews) in Israel's labour market.

3. The uneven development of capital in Israel has had effects anticipated by demand-side theories of segmentation, especially the dependence of the economic periphery on the labour of socially marginal groups. But the particular technological and market conditions faced by core employers, and the pressure exerted by their unionized employees, explain only part of their tendency to exclude Arab labour. In addition, receipt of the state sponsorship which is the lifeblood of Israel's core economy has always been at least implicitly conditional on its incorporation of the political caste system favoured by the state.

In Israel, then, dualism is both theoretically and historically over-determined. Hence it is hardly surprising that in many respects Israel shares features characteristic of Switzerland and Japan—labour-market segmentation, wide wage differentials, and a relatively small and selective welfare state. The puzzle which remains is that in the experience of other Western nations, not only dualism but also SDC have been accompanied—although for different reasons—by two widely noted successes: comparatively quiescent labour relations and relatively minimal disruption in the wake of the global economic storms of the last two decades. The conspicuous absence of these accomplishments from the Israeli experience demands explanation.

Israel's problems of economic adjustment have already been discussed at some length against the backdrop of the declining economic autonomy of the state. So far as the turbulence of industrial relations is concerned, the very juxtaposition of elements of SDC and dualism appears to bear much of the responsibility. An example is that in contrast to 'pure' dualist regimes, large sections of the core of Israel's dual economy are located directly inside the public sector. Under any circumstances, a large and expanding sphere of state employment connotes a high risk of labour disputes. All the more so when it includes large-scale monopolies responsible for transport, energy, and other infrastructural services where worker militancy rests on a potent combination of economic and political clout.

There are, it is true, a number of large enterprises in Israel (including some state-owned ones) in which Japanese-style labour peace prevails on the basis of secure employment, generous social benefits, and co-opted worker representatives. But this potential has often been frustrated by the corporatist face of the Israeli Janus—the unity and encompassingness of labour organization, the crucial party-political role of the Histadrut, and the highly centralized character of collective bargaining. For the sake of preserving its organizational and political strength, the Histadrut can neither abandon nor discipline the militant work-forces of the core. And because centralization renders wage differentials painfully transparent, the particularistic gains of the strongest workers inevitably give rise to demands for parity on the part of weaker groups covered by the same framework of national wage agreements. In effect, Israeli conditions serve to heighten the risks of corporatism, in particular what might be described in reference to recent experience as the 'Swedish disease' of growing trade-union sectionalism and unmanageable public sector militancy.[10] In contrast, the comparatively small public sectors, non-encompassing unions, and decentralized wage bargaining of the dualist political economies have prevented such divisions from erupting (Switzerland) or enabled employers and the state to utilize them as weapons against labour assertiveness (Japan). Because Israeli conditions are only partially consistent with the dualist model, these 'benefits' have been prevented from materializing.

Thus far our discussion has focussed on those relatively enduring characteristics of Israel's political economy which appear most striking from a comparative vantage-point. For those whose interests lie in second-guessing Israel's future, it is equally important to consider what might be learned from our interpretation of historical dynamics. The common denominator underlying this book's analyses of changes in politics, economic performance, and industrial relations is a conception of the political economy as a dynamic and potentially contradictory *gestalt* that encompasses a broad range of institutional spheres. In this respect our approach overlaps with a number of contemporary attempts at developing a synthesis between Marxism and institutional economics, particularly the 'regulation school' in France and the mature work of leading radical economists in the United States. Members of the latter group have employed the concept of *social structures of accumulation* to convey the insight that in the real world a web of global and domestic institutional arrangements, with the state at its hub, provides the social and political underpinnings for stable functioning of the economy.[11] No less important, as Block has pointed out, is the approach to historical dynamics propounded by regulation theories, in particular their insight that

> social structures of accumulation are always time-limited in their effectiveness . . . Particular patterns of social and economic development will face a law of diminishing returns . . . [S]ome of the positive synergies that occurred during the phase of expansion can turn negative under changing historical circumstances. (1986: 182)

This description accords very closely with our studies of the Mitun and the post-1973 crisis era in Israel. We have emphasized how political–economic change in Israel has been generated by the strains of changing environmental conditions coupled with the contradictions of domestic political regimes, mechanisms of labour restraint, formulas of economic growth, and patterns of state/economy relations.

It would be mistaken to read into these dynamic processes an underlying determinism of the kind proposed by over-abstracted theories of 'the capitalist state' or attempts to mechanistically link political–economic evolution to 'long swings' of capital accumulation. Faced with diminishing effectiveness of prevailing forms of articulation between politics and the economy, class actors and the state need not be passive. In particular, when declining autonomy threatens the vital interests of the state as an institution and the élites who direct it, new policies and arrangements can be expected to emerge. To return to the case of Israel in the mid-1960s, state managers were faced with a breakdown of the pre-conditions for stable rule, including threats to Labour Party dominance, deteriorating fiscal capacities, and a serious decline in the macro-economy's ability to pay its debts to the outside world. They responded by abandoning the state's cherished imperatives of full employment and rapid growth.

By the mid-1980s, Israel was in the grips of an even graver crisis. While its most dramatic outward symptom was a hyper-inflationary spiral, the critical considerations from the standpoint of the state were: the growing difficulty of meeting the public sector's domestic and foreign obligations; the pressures exerted by the US administration and its willingness to proffer generous economic aid; and the threat to party government posed by declining public confidence in the legitimacy of the parliamentary regime. The severity of these challenges together with a number of fortuitous political circumstances which have been analysed elsewhere,[12] gave birth to an emergency Stabilization Plan in July 1985. Assisted by favourable trends in the world economy, the Plan succeeded almost instantly in bringing hyper-inflation to an end. The theoretical significance of this development was that the state had launched an auspicious opening to a campaign to regain its capacity to control the economy. This implied a dramatic reversal of the *modi operandi* of the previous decade. Thus, the programme adopted in July 1985 mandated depoliticization of economic policy, authoritarian restraint of real wages, and, most significant of all, the trimming of capital subsidies.

In the mid-1960s, the counter-attack of the state was successful only in the short-term. Longer-term gains were conditional on factors (the June 1967 war, the American connection, militarization of the economy) which we have argued were central to the downfall of Israel's economic growth model in the next round. It would be foolhardy to try to predict the ultimate outcome of the thrust to revive state autonomy in the second half of the 1980s. The safest prognosis from our theoretical perspective is that of a renewed dialectic. By the beginning of the 1990s, despite the achievement of five years of relative economic stability, it remained an open question whether the Israeli state would prove capable of breaking free of a debilitating contradiction: that it has steadfastly remained the centre of gravity of the political economy, while lacking the capacity to steer itself and the principal actors in civil society towards a fundamental reform of the social structure of accumulation.

Notes

1. For competing interpretations of social democracy compare the optimistic views of Stephens (1979) or Higgins and Apple (1983) with more pessimistic assessments by Wolfe (1978) or Fulcher (1987). Pontusson (1987) offers a sophisticated appraisal in relation to Swedish developments in the 1970s and 1980s. Crouch (e.g. 1982*a*) and Panitch (e.g. 1981)—pro and con respectively—have been leading voices in the debate on corporatism.
2. For a powerful exposition of the value of 'case-oriented' (as opposed to 'variable-oriented') comparative research see Ragin (1987). Francis Castles (1988 and 1989) has discussed more specific reasons for moving beyond quantitative large-sample studies in the field of comparative political economy.
3. For a similar analysis see Lash and Urry's (1987: ch. 8) comparative study of the rise of dualism ('disorganization' in their terms) in Western Europe.
4. See also Regini (1984) and Hyman (1989: ch. 8), who have discussed the potential for coexistence between corporatism and dualism in the context of developments in Italy and Britain, respectively. Another 'anomaly'—and a particularly suggestive one—is the Austrian case, in which it appears that 'social partnership' has played an important role in regulating a patently dualist flow of immigrant labour (Bauboeck and Wimmer, 1988).
5. See Boddy and Crotty (1975); Cameron (1984); and Kaufman (1978) on how labour's political weakness and capital's strength have given rise in the USA to a weak state commitment to Keynesian counter-cyclical policies and a comparatively flimsy statutory framework of employment rights. Together with the presence of an independent central bank, which is a strong advocate of the interests of finance capital, these have left business relatively free to respond to labour militancy and profit squeezes by invoking unemployment. Piore (1979) has documented the implicit guest-worker policy of the USA *vis-à-vis* Mexican labour migration and Bonacich (1980) has discussed how the law permits employers access to cheap labour.
6. For a review and a critical reassessment of neo-Marxist theories of business dominance see respectively Carnoy (1984) and Block (1987: ch. 1). Contrasting evaluations of Lindblom's non-Marxist approach are offered by Crouch (1979) and Vogel (1987).
7. The choice of Switzerland and Japan as counterpoints to SDC requires further comment. These were not the exemplars suggested by Goldthorpe's (1984) analysis, which was concerned with inter-

preting what might be called the *liberal* variant of dualism embodied by Thatcher's Britain, with its deliberate assault on putatively social-democratic elements of labour organization, social policy, and state involvement in the economy. We, however, find the *conservative* dualism of Switzerland and Japan, associated with working-class fragmentation and long-standing labour-movement weakness, to be a more interesting point of comparison to the Israeli case. It is true that some observers regard these two countries, and particularly Japan, as exemplars of merely another form of corporatism, and in that sense as less distinct from SDC than we wish to imply. This contention is rebutted in a study of the Japanese case by Shalev (1990*a*). For a penetrating analysis of the Swiss political economy see Katzenstein (1980), whose work was one of the inspirations for our interpretation. But for the purposes of analysing labour-market questions we take issue with his classification of Switzerland as corporatist.

8. Obviously, the parsimony which is achieved by grouping countries in a typology necessitates glossing over internal differences within its categories. The very different standing in public policy-making of the Swiss and Japanese labour movements and the contrasting role of the state in steering investment in these two countries, are so striking that in these instances no single designation could reasonably be applied. Another instance of divergence within the same category, although a less dramatic one, is wage and income inequality. The Japanese case does not entirely fit the 'high' designation in our table, because despite large individual wage differentials Japan ranks comparatively low in terms of inequality of income between *households*. In the social-democratic category, it is probable that both wage and income inequality are significantly higher in Austria than in Norway and Sweden.

   While our taxonomy is thus somewhat flexible, it is so within definite limits. In particular, we drew the line at including the USA as a third exemplar of dualism. Despite evident similarities, in the absence of the conservative bias which characterizes state and employer strategies in Japan and Switzerland, employer and state coercion and market discipline have historically played central roles in American industrial relations. Symptomatically, unemployment has typically been high and strongly counter-cyclical to labour militancy. And, when it occurs, industrial conflict has been exceptionally intense.

9. We have in mind here such phenomena as the state's definition of divergent military roles for the members of different ethnic groups (Enloe, 1980), or its sponsorship of 'corporativist' differentiation between the social welfare rights of different occupational groups

(Esping-Andersen and Korpi, 1984). In such cases, quasi-caste political boundaries are designed to subvert challenges to the control of the state by a particular class, ethnic group, or dynasty. For an analysis of state policy towards the Arab citizens of Israel from a similar general perspective see Lustick (1980).

10. Rising industrial conflict and declining trade union solidarity in Sweden have been documented and analysed by Lash and Urry (1987: ch. 8); Ahlen (1989); and *The Economist* (3 March 1990, special section on 'The Swedish Economy').
11. We prefer this more generic formulation to the narrower focus on the socio-political requirements of capitalism suggested in works by Boyer (1979) and Gordon, Edwards, and Reich (1982). Compare on this issue Schatz (1984). In a wide-ranging review of no less than six schools of regulation theory, Jessop (1990) has pointed out that despite considerable diversity among the schools, they have in common an analytical emphasis on 'intermediate concepts' and an empirical emphasis on detailed case studies—orientations clearly shared by the present volume.
12. See Shalev and Grinberg (1989); cf. Bruno and Piterman (1987).

Appendix 1: The political demography of Palestine/Israel[1]

In 1880 there were nearly 500,000 Arabs and only about 24,000 Jews in Palestine. The First Aliyah or wave of immigration recognized by modern Zionism took place at the turn of the century. Motivated primarily by anti-semitic legislation and pogroms, the newcomers from Russia and Romania had the effect of doubling the Jewish population. Traditionally Jewish in their outlook, the First Aliyah settlers purchased their own land and worked it using European and subsequently French-colonial methods. The 35,000 or so immigrants of the Second Aliyah, emanating mainly from Russia, followed during the decade prior to World War I. Largely because of their lack of capital and the competition of cheaper Arab wage labour, the overwhelming majority of these socialist and secular Zionists abandoned the country. But their remnant founded and later continued to head the institutions of the Israeli labour movement.

The Allied victory over the Turks in the First World War ended 400 years of Ottoman control of Palestine. With the sanction of a League of Nations 'mandate', control over Palestine passed to Britain. On the eve of British rule, an official declaration of support was issued for 'the establishment in Palestine of a national home for the Jewish people'. To the 60,000 Jews remaining in 1919 were added the 35,000 of the Third Aliyah, the first organized Zionist immigration. Still, in 1923 the ratio of Arabs to Jews was about eight to one.

The masses of Jews leaving Russia and Eastern Europe had until now gravitated mainly to the United States. With the closing of America's gates the first to be affected were the Polish *petit bourgeois* who formed the core of the Fourth Aliyah, which brought more than 60,000 immigrants to Palestine in the years 1924–6. A far greater mass immigration of no choice (190,000 between 1932 and 1936) was prompted by the rise of Nazism and economic depression in Europe, and included a large number of German and Austrian refugees. Subsequently, except for a pause during 1941–2, this stream continued but at a substantially reduced rate. Violent Arab opposition, economic crisis, and British restrictions curtailed the entry of additional refugees.

In accordance with its economic and geopolitical interests in the region and in response to Arab sentiment, by the time of the Second World War Britain had effectively rescinded its commitment to a Jewish national home. In 1942 the Zionist movement officially accepted the idea of partitioning Palestine between Arabs and Jews, which was endorsed by the United Nations in 1947. When Britain abandoned Palestine and Israel's independence was unilaterally declared in the following year, there were some 650,000 Jews in Palestine—a more than fourfold rise in only two decades. But natural increase and immigration had also swollen the Arab population. They still outnumbered the Jews by more than two to one in the whole of Palestine and by a factor of one-third within the subsequent borders of Israel.

As a result of the first Arab–Israeli war the land base of the State of Israel increased by 20 per cent, while the Arab population within its new borders fell by a massive 80 per cent. By the end of 1948 Israel's armed forces had successfully combated both local resistance and armies of invasion from the surrounding states, in the process helping to thwart the UN plan for an independent Palestinian state. In the context of the former borders of Mandatory Palestine, little more than one-tenth of the prior Arab population remained under Israeli jurisdiction. Some 600,000–750,000 Arabs were driven out or fled, while others had been located before 1948 in areas which now came under Jordanian or Egyptian control.

Mass immigration between 1949 and 1951 brought as many Jews to Israel as had been within its borders when sovereignty was proclaimed. Half of the newcomers were European Jews (the majority from Poland and Romania), many of them refugees whose homes and families had been destroyed during the war. The others originated in the Middle East, principally Iraq and the Yemen. This inflow was due in part to the political backlash and upsurge of anti-Semitism in most Arab states following Israel's creation and its military victory. But both components of the mass immigration were actively recruited and transferred at Israel's initiative in order 'to deepen the nation's military manpower reservoir, to preempt the vulnerable empty places in the land, to garrison the new

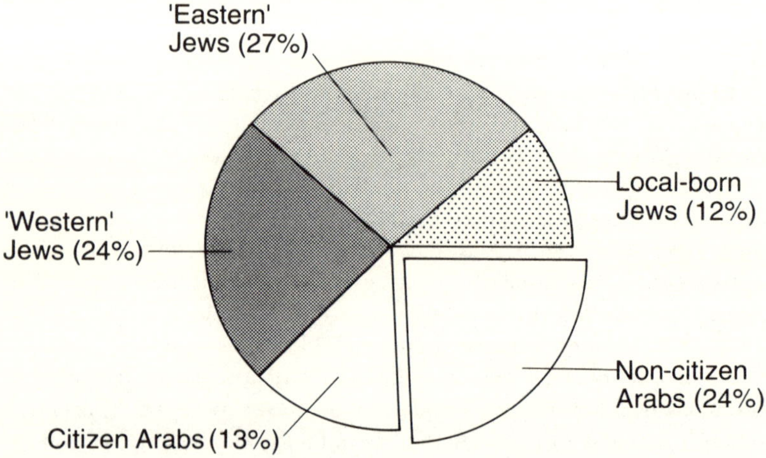

FIG. A1.1. Israel's major national and ethnic divisions, 1985

Source: Table A1.1.

agricultural colonies, and to create the modernized economy that was indispensable for achieving a Western standard of living' (Sachar, 1979: 395).

After a temporary weakening of the 'push' and the 'pull' factors which had prompted the initial immigration wave, close to half a million Jews immigrated to Israel in the ten year period 1955–64. About half originated in North Africa, principally Morocco, and more than a third came from Europe, again mainly Poland and Romania. By 1965 Israel's population had reached 2.5 million, nearly nine-tenths of it Jewish. In the succeeding years immigration fell to comparatively insignificant levels (although nearly 150,000 Soviet Jews entered Israel during the 1970s). Meanwhile, Israel's occupation of the West Bank and Gaza Strip during the Arab–Israeli war of June 1967 brought nearly a million more Palestinian Arabs under its control. Figure A1.1 depicts the demographic structure which had crystallized by the 1980s: over one-third non-Jewish and a Jewish population now more than half of Eastern origin.[2]

For purposes of comparison, the data underlying Figure A1.1 are presented in tabular form alongside earlier benchmarks in Table A1.1. These are no more than estimates intended to indicate

TABLE A1.1. *Historical shifts in Israel's major national and ethnic divisions*

	Jews			Arabs		Total	
	Local born	Eastern origin	Western origin	Citizens	Non-citizens	%	Millions
1947	17	4	22		57	100	1.45
1951	29	32	25	14		100	1.23
1985	12	27	24	13	24	100	5.61

Sources: Estimates derived from data published in the *Statistical Abstract of Israel*, and Kamen (1987: 457).

changing orders of magnitude. The distribution in 1947 refers only to the part of Mandatory Palestine that fell within Israel's future (1949–67) boundaries. The distribution in 1985 refers to all territories under Israeli jurisdiction. Another important difference is that whereas in the early years origin among Jews refers to country of birth, in 1985 Eastern (or Western) origin refers to Jews who immigrated from Eastern (or Western) countries *and* the children of those immigrants.

Appendix 2: The labour movement economy (Chevrat Ovdim)

Since the early years of statehood, the Histadrut-linked sector of the economy has employed roughly a quarter of the entire labour force, dispersed across a wide variety of economic branches.[3] This represents a substantial increase in both size and scope in comparison with the pre-sovereignty period. In that period, with some exceptions (notably in construction and transportation), Histadrut-owned or affiliated economic activity was concentrated in the agricultural collectives or activities ancillary to agriculture. Until the 1940s the major activity of the labour-movement economy was thus confined to branches which did not attract private capital. As a result, it failed to participate in the two sectors of the economy which experienced the most rapid secular growth during the inter-war period, namely, citrus growing and manufacturing.

Nearly all the economic activities of the Histadrut are carried out within the framework of a special roof organization, Chevrat Ovdim (literally, 'Workers' Society'). Beginning in the mid-1980s the labour-movement economy experienced an unprecedented crisis, the long-term consequences of which are still uncertain. However, in the more typical circumstances prevailing earlier in the same decade, Chevrat Ovdim claimed at least one-third of employment in four key branches of manufacturing—basic metals, non-metallic minerals, electrical and electronic goods, and plastics. In addition, Histadrut-linked enterprises accounted for 15 per cent of construction activity. Moreover, the labour organization's bank was the biggest lender in the country and its affiliated collective settlements produced 86 per cent of agricultural output. The settlements, which operate in industry as well as agriculture and are employers in their own right, contribute about a third of the total labour force encompassed by the Histadrut sector. Economically they are neither owned nor controlled by Chevrat Ovdim, although they are active in its administration and are its principal ideological defenders. The strictly corporate component of the Histadrut sector, comprising about 30 per cent of its work-force, is known

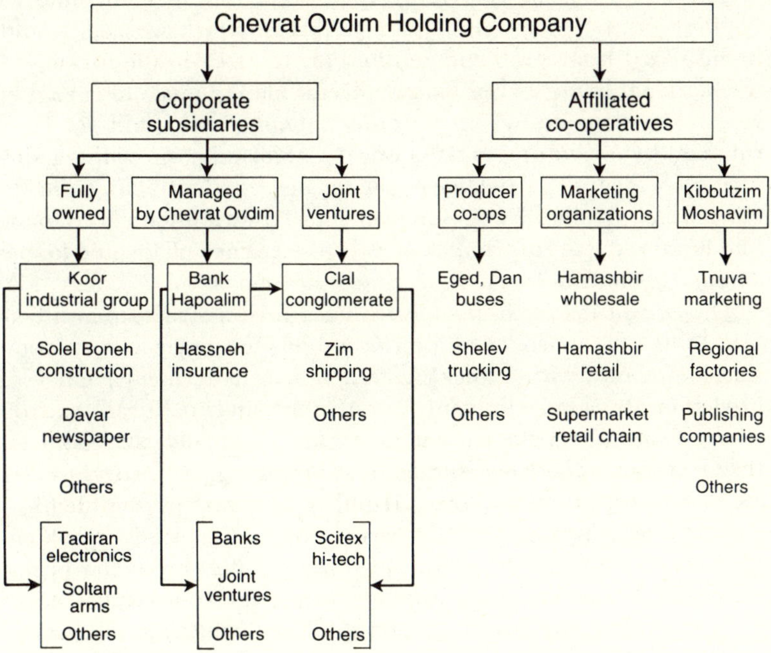

FIG. A2.1. The structure of the labour-movement economy

Source: Based on a chart that appeared in *Ma'ariv*, 19 April 1989.

internally as the 'administered economy'. It is made up of large enterprises or holding companies of which the Histadrut is typically the sole or majority owner.[4] The overall structure of Chevrat Ovdim, and some of the prominent concerns and activities associated with it, are indicated in Figure A2.1.

Historically, the labour-movement economy owes its origins to the economic difficulties faced by the early waves of would-be Jewish settlers in Palestine, rather than to any preconceived ideological project. Some voices within the labour movement genuinely believed in the virtues of decentralized self-management, and left-leaning elements hoped that the labour economy would eventually become the cornerstone of a future socialist society. But collectivism as an end in itself played only a secondary role. The principal original functions of Chevrat Ovdim were: (*a*) to contribute to building up a Jewish-only labour market in which workers would be insulated from Arab competition; (*b*) to assist in the making of the 'national home' by providing jobs for immigrants and engaging in land settlement; (*c*) to aid the Labour Party (and its forerunners) by facilitating mass political mobilization, providing gainful employment to party leaders and loyalists, and attracting outside recognition of the labour movement's contribution to nation-building; and (*d*) to promote a political culture of loyalty to the labour movement.

The realization of these objectives required a structure antithetical to the frameworks of producer and consumer co-operation that developed within the Western labour movements. Chevrat Ovdim was based on central direction and political control. Thus, while all Histadrut members are nominally shareholders, they receive no dividends and have no voting rights. Instead, under its 1923 constitution Chevrat Ovdim is governed by the identical structure which rules the Histadrut proper. Practically speaking, however, centralization was always problematic. From the beginning, the kibbutzim and other co-operatives resisted Histadrut authority. The executives responsible for managing the labour organization's corporations also came to enjoy considerable operational autonomy in return for expanding their enterprises and respecting political criteria in staff appointments.

It was only in the course of World War II that the Histadrut's direct activity as an employer and entrepreneur expanded into industry. Subsequently, during the first decade of statehood, with the aid of especially favourable treatment by the state, the labour-movement sector of the economy achieved its contemporary dimensions. In the same period there was also a process of internal concentration, with most of the remaining independent producer and credit co-operatives (outside of agriculture) being swallowed up by the 'administered economy'. The aggressive expansion of the Histadrut's construction and industrial holding company (Solel Boneh) led by the late 1950s to party-imposed organizational and personnel changes which reaffirmed Chevrat Ovdim's politicization but were followed by an effective halt to its expansion. From the mid-1960s a new efficiency-oriented cadre of managers took over in Histadrut companies. By exploiting the labour organization's relatively easy access to investment funds and taking greater recourse to joint ventures with private capital, they stimulated a new phase of growth and managerial autonomy.

Officially, the labour movement defends the 'administered economy' on the grounds that it is a more generous employer than the private sector, that its wages and conditions play a vanguard role in collective bargaining, and that it offers greater opportunities for worker participation in management. Each of these claims is only partially true at best. Wage levels in Histadrut firms are no higher than could be expected in view of their size, capital-intensiveness, monopolistic advantages, and mostly-Jewish labour forces. Their usual practice in wage-setting is to adopt standards already set by collective bargaining in the private sector, with the addition (as in other large companies) of negotiated enterprise-level supplements. Numerous experiments in worker participation in management have been intended mainly to appease left-wing circles within the Histadrut. In practice, participation is far closer to the precepts of 'human relations' than to syndicalist ideas of workers' control. Finally, informed opinion is unanimous that the Histadrut's interests as an employer have exercised a substantial restraining influence on its pay demands as a union, an effect with far greater macro-significance than any reverse influence of Chevrat Ovdim as a 'pattern setter' in collective bargaining.

Appendix 3: Linkages between union peak organizations and labour parties (after Bahat, 1979)

	Israel	Norway	Germany
(1) References to party in peak organization's constitution.	Specifies party's role in elections.	Commitments to co-operation, but party not named.	None.
(2) References to peak organization in party constitution.	Union membership requirement; party cells in unions; union officials subject to party discipline.	Union membership expected; unions affiliated collectively; union is primary party cell.	None.
(3) Legitimate party role in union elections.	Party-list elections.	Personal elections, but party factions allowed.	None.
(4) Legitimate union role in financing party.	National level only.	Both national and local levels.	None.
(5) Proportion of union members who vote Labour (*c*.1970).	*c*.70%	*c*.70%	*c*.60%
(6) Proportion of union members belonging to party (*c*.1975).	20% (15%)	16% (11%)	8%

(7) Proportion of party members belonging to union (*c.*1975).	90%	70%	55%
(8) Party role in nominating candidates for union office.	Official and determinate.	Only partly official, but determinate.	Unofficial, but determinate.
(9) Presence of party members in top union bodies.	Virtually universal.	Vast majority.	Vast majority.
(10) Framework of party delegates' activity in union.	Official party factions.	Nothing official; some covert factional activity.	Nothing official; some overt factional activity.
(11) Dual office in top union and party bodies.	Very common.	Common.	Common.
(12) Dual office in top union bodies and Parliament.	Rare simultaneously, can occur during career.	Uncommon simultaneously, common during career.	Very common simultaneously, common during career.
(13) Importance of union support for party finances.	More important than both dues and state support.	More important than both dues and state support.	More important than dues, less important than state support.
(14) Union–party policy co-ordination.	Party traditionally set union policy and mediated union–government conflict.	Ramified network of formal co-ordinating bodies.	Close informal ties between union and party leaders.

Sources Notes

This table is derived from findings reported by Shmuel Bahat (1979). Bahat's research utilized secondary analysis of official publications, opinion polls, and so forth, complemented by interviews and observation in the field. Below is a list of the items in the table, referenced by number, indicating the appropriate source in Bahat's thesis and (where necessary) adding explanatory remarks. In general, note that 'union peak organization' means the Histadrut in Israel, LO in Norway, and DGB in Germany. 'Labour parties' refers to Norway's Labour Party and the German SPD. The reference in Israel is to the Labour Party and not its Alignment with Mapam, except for items (5) and (9).

(1) From ch. 3.

(2) From ch. 3.

(3) From ch. 2 and 5.

(4) From ch. 7.

(5) pp. 71 and 72 for the results of voter surveys in Germany and Norway respectively. For Israel, we have indicated a compromise between the divergent findings reported by Arian (1973) and Burstein (1973). The figure in the table is indicative of the order of magnitude *c.*1970, which has undoubtedly declined since then.

(6) From pp. 85–6. The German figure refers to DGB members only. Figures in parentheses were adjusted by Bahat to take account of inflated claims and involuntary affiliation.

(7) From p. 87.

(8) From p. 116.

(9) From ch. 5. Refers to both elective and appointive positions, the characterization holding in each case for both types.

(10) From p. 115.

(11) From ch. 6.

(12) From ch. 6.

(13) From ch. 7. Reflects both monetary and in-kind support.

(14) From ch. 8.

Appendix 4: The left-wing parties of Jewish Palestine and Israel

In the period in which the Histadrut was established, the major parties of the Jewish working class were the two founded in 1906 during the period of 'pioneering' immigration (the Second Aliyah).[5] One of these (*Hapoel Hatsair*—the 'Young Labourer') embraced a non-Marxist orientation, while its stronger rival (Poalei Tsiyon or 'Workers of Zion') initially defined itself as orthodox Marxist. In 1919 Poalei Tsiyon incorporated associations of agricultural workers and other non-partisan elements to form the Achdut Avodah (Unity of Labour) Party. In the elections to the Histadrut's founding convention held at the end of 1920, Achdut Avodah received 43 per cent of the vote and Hapoel Hatsair 31 per cent. In the two subsequent elections, Achdut Avodah enjoyed an even greater (two to one) advantage.

In the 1920s three minority movements constituted the major left-wing opposition. They were the Communists, who enjoyed substantial but short-lived popularity in the large towns (Miller-Rubenstein, 1985); 'Left' Poalei Tsiyon, which doctrinally was located more or less midway between the Communists and Poalei Tsiyon; and the *Gdud* ('Jewish Labour Battalion'), an experiment with large communes led by idealistic Zionist radicals who later returned to Russia (Shapira, 1984).

In 1930 Achdut Avodah and Hapoel Hatsair merged to form Mapai (Palestine Workers' Party), which easily controlled the Histadrut and soon became the dominant political party in both the Palestinian Yishuv and the world Zionist movement (Chapter 3). During the early 1930s the expanding collective settlements associated with the *Artsi* ('nation-wide') kibbutz movement turned *Hashomer Hatsair* ('Young Watchman') into a significant political opposition. Hashomer was to an important extent anchored within the Zionist consensus articulated by Mapai, but it embraced a Marxist world-view and supported militant, binational trade unionism (Margalit, 1970). Mapai's own 'United' (*Meuchad*) kibbutz movement was also to the left of the party on trade union issues, although much of the quarrel between the two came to revolve around the Meuchad movement's hawkish position on defence and territorial issues. During the late 1930s both of these kibbutz-based oppositions joined forces with urban opponents of Mapai. Hashomer Hatsair co-operated with the Socialist League. The Meuchad kibbutzim allied with dissident urban trade unionists and party activists centred in Mapai's Tel Aviv branch. They formed a semi-official opposition ('Faction B') within Mapai, which in 1944 left the party to establish (confusingly) a new Achdut Avodah Party. Soon afterwards (1948) this party merged with Hashomer to form Mapam (an acronym for 'United Workers' Party').

At the more radical end of the spectrum, Left Poalei Tsiyon ultimately accepted the labour-movement consensus by officially joining Achdut Avodah in 1946. At its inception in 1921, the party's left wing had broken away to form the Palestine Communist Party. The PCP itself split into a Zionist and a non-Zionist wing, which reunited to facilitate the party's admission into the Comintern in 1924. From this point the PCP became a binational party whose Jewish and Arab adherents were both opposed to Zionism, but differed over how to appeal to Jewish workers and how far to embrace Arab nationalism (Beinin, 1990). During World War II the party split openly along national lines. But in 1948, after the USSR had shifted positions and supported the partition of Palestine, a united Communist Party of Israel (Maki) was established. In Knesset elections during the 1950s the Party's constituency was split two-to-one between Jews and Arabs. In the early 1960s, however, Maki became increasingly torn between the alternatives of an Arab and a Jewish national orientation and in 1965 split between an exclusively Jewish stream, which retained the Party name, and the larger, predominantly Arab *Rakach* Party (New Communist List, subsequently running as the Democratic Front). In 1981 a new primarily Arab party, the *Mitkademet* (Progressive List for Peace), emerged in direct competition with Rakach (Rouhana, 1986).

Within the Zionist camp, the more conservative Achdut Avodah left Mapam to resume a separate existence in 1954, and was a coalition partner in cabinets formed from the 1955 elections onwards. In 1965 the party entered into an electoral 'Alignment' with Mapai and then in 1968 it consented to the full-scale merger which created the Israel Labour Party (ILP). With the exception of an 18-month period during the early 1960s, the residual Mapam also participated in all the Mapai-led coalitions of the 1955–77 period. Mapam retained its separate existence as an organization, although beginning in 1969 it too contested Knesset elections under the banner of the Labour Alignment (Ma'arach).

The formation of the original Alignment with Achdut Avodah was accompanied by a split on Mapai's right. In 1965 David Ben-Gurion led a group of younger leaders out of Mapai to form Rafi (Israel Workers' List), but they subsequently returned to the mother-party upon the formation of the ILP. (A minority formed the 'State List', which later joined forces with the Likud).

Figures 3.1 and 3.2 in Chapter 3 illustrate the most significant electoral trends involving the parties of the left: in national elections since sovereignty, the stability of the Mapai (Alignment) vote until the 1977 upheaval, contrasted with the improving fortunes of the right from 1965 onwards; and in Histadrut elections, the long-term dominance of Mapai and, during the 1960s, the simultaneous rise of the right and decline of the independent left. Tables A4.1 and A4.2 below supply more detailed data for the post-1948 period on the fortunes of the parties of the left in each of these electoral arenas.

Notes to Appendices

1. Sources consulted include: Jewish Agency (1947); Sicron (1957); Eisenstadt (1967); and Shapiro (1976); on the period prior to sovereignty; Flapan (1987); Friedlander and Goldscheider (1979); and the *Statistical Abstract of Israel* for the period since 1948; and Kimmerling (1983*b*).
2. It is safe to assume that a majority of second generation Israeli-born Jews are, like the first generation, of Eastern origin.
3. Barkai (1964) is the only comprehensive study of the economic magnitude and composition of the labour-movement economy. Corresponding information on the pre-sovereignty period is available in Meunzner (1942); Horowitz (1948); and Sussman (1969*a*). The contemporary data cited in this appendix are drawn from an official

Table A4.1. *The parliamentary representation of Israel's left-wing parties* (out of 120 Knesset seats)

Knesset	Election Year	Rakach and P.L.P.	Maki and radicals	Mapam	Achdut Avodah	Ma'arach	Mapai	Rafi	Arab satellites	Total labour movement
1	1949		4	19			*46*		2	67
2	1951		5	15			*45*		5	65
3	1955		6	*9*	*10*		*40*		5	64
4	1959		3	*9*	*7*		*47*		5	68
5	1961		5	9	*8*		*42*		4	63
6	1965	3	2	*8*		*45*		10	4	67
7	1969	3	3			*56*			4	60
8	1973	4	1			*51*			3	54
9	1977	5	2			32			1	33
10	1981	4				47				47
11	1984	6				*44*				44
12	1988	5		3		*39*				42

Source: *Statistical Abstract of Israel*.

Notes: Numbers in italics indicate seats held by parties participating in the cabinet coalition formed following the election in question. Lines with arrowheads denote splits, other lines denote mergers.

Rakach is the New Communist List; P.L.P. is the Progressive List for Peace; 'Maki and radicals' means the Israel Communist Party plus predominantly Jewish radical-left parties (1 seat in 1965, 2 in 1969, 1 in 1977); Ma'arach is the Labour Alignment; Rafi is the Israel Workers' List; Arab 'satellites' are all-Arab lists affiliated with Mapai. 'Total labour movement' includes satellite Arab parties but not Communist parties.

Table A4.2. *The representation of Israel's left-wing parties at Histadrut conventions* (out of 100% of delegates)

Convention	Election Year	Rakach and P.L.P.	Maki and radicals	Mapam	Achdut Avodah	Ma'arach	Mapai	Rafi	Total labour movement
7	1949		3	34			57		91
8	1955		4	13	14		58		85
9	1959		3	14	17		55		86
10	1965	1	2	14		51		12	77
11	1969	2	4			62			62
12	1973	4	2			58			58
13	1977	3	1			56			56
14	1981	4				63		1	64
15	1985	5							
16	1989					67			67

Source: Ben-Meir (1980: 121–5) and the Organization Division of the Histadrut.

Notes: Parties and symbols are as explained in Table A4.1.

publication (in Hebrew) entitled *Chevrat Ovdim 1982*. The organization and rationale of Chevrat Ovdim are reviewed by Daniel (1976); Kleiman (1964*a* and 1987); and Barkai (1982). Ben-Ner and Estrin (1988) have examined the determinants of wages in Histadrut industry, Rosenstein (1969) and Bar-Haim (1988) are authorities on its workers' participation schemes, and Ben-Porat (1973) has discussed collective bargaining in Histadrut-owned enterprises.

4. In addition to the members and employees of the settlements, and the 'administered economy', Chevrat Ovdim includes a number of corporate-like but more autonomous enterprises originally founded by the settlement movements; and also, some urban producer co-operatives, the most important of which are the two bus services which monopolize public transportation in Israel.
5. Most of the details in this appendix pertaining to the mainstream labour-movement parties are a matter of public record. Perlmutter (1957) and Merhav (1980) have assembled much of the relevant information. In addition, specific sources on the less well-documented radical opposition groups are indicated in the text.

References

Note: All references to 'Falk Institute' are to the Maurice Falk Institute for Economic Research in Israel (Hebrew University of Jerusalem).

Abraham, David (1981), *The Collapse of The Weimar Republic: Political Economy and Crisis* (Princeton, NJ: Princeton University Press).

Achdut, Lea and Carmi, Menachem (1981), *Twenty Five Years of National Insurance in Israel* (in Hebrew) (Jerusalem: Research and Planning Department of the National Insurance Institute).

—— and Tamir, Yossi (1985), 'The Economic Wellbeing of the Retired and Non-retired Elderly: A Study of Seven Countries', unpublished paper, Luxembourg Income Study (LIS).

Aharoni, Yair (1976), *Structure and Performance in the Israeli Economy* (in Hebrew) (Tel Aviv: Cherikover).

—— (1984), 'Managers in the State, Histadrut and Private Sectors in Israel: A Comparative Study', Israel Institute of Business Research, Tel Aviv University, Research Report No. 53/84, Sept.

Ahlen, Kristina (1989), 'Swedish Collective Bargaining under Pressure: Inter-union Rivalry and Incomes Policies, *British Journal of Industrial Relations*, 27(3), 330–46.

Alford, Robert and Friedland, Roger (1985), *Powers of Theory: Capitalism, The State, and Democracy* (Cambridge: Cambridge University Press).

Almogi, Yosef (1980), *Total Commitment* (in Hebrew) (Jerusalem: Eidanim).

Antonovsky, Aaron (1963*a*), 'Socio-Political Attitudes in Israel' (in Hebrew), *Amot*, 6, 11–22.

—— (1963*b*), 'Ideology and Class in Israel' *(in Hebrew), Amot*, 7, 21–8.

—— (1966), 'Classification of Forms, Political Ideologies, and the Man in the Street', *Public Opinion Quarterly*, 30(1), 109–19.

Apple, Nixon (1980), 'The Rise and Fall of Full Employment Capitalism', *Studies in Political Economy*, 4, 5–39.

Arian, Alan (1968), *Ideological Change in Israel* (Cleveland: Case Western Reserve University Press).

—— and Barnes, Samuel H. (1974), 'The Dominant Party System: A Neglected Model of Democratic Stability', *Journal of Politics*, 36(3), 592–614.

Arian, Asher (1973), *The Choosing People: Voting Behavior in Israel* (Cleveland: Case Western Reserve University Press).

—— (1978), 'Political and Administrative Aspects of Welfare Policy in

Israel', research report submitted to the Ford Foundation (Israel Trustees), Tel Aviv University.
—— (1980), 'Introduction', in Arian (ed.), *The Elections in Israel, 1977* (Jerusalem: Jerusalem Academic Press), 9–19.
—— (1981), 'Health Care in Israel: Political and Administrative Aspects', *International Political Science Review*, 2(1); 43–56.
—— (1989), *Politics in Israel: The Second Generation* (2nd edn.) (Chatham, NJ: Chatham House).
—— (ed.) (1980), *The Elections in Israel, 1977* (Jerusalem: Jerusalem Academic Press).
—— and Shamir, Michal (1983), 'The Primarily Political Functions of the Left–Right Continuum', *Comparative Politics*, 15(2), 139–58.
Armingeon, Klaus (1986) 'Formation and Stability of Neo-Corporatist Incomes Policies: A Comparative Analysis', *European Sociological Review*, 2(2), 138–47.
Arnon, Arie (1986*a*), 'Israel–U.S. Relations, 1967–1985: The Economic Aspect and Beyond', unpublished paper, Department of Economics, Ben-Gurion University of the Negev (Beersheba).
—— (1986*b*) 'A Look Beyond the Beijsky Report' (in Hebrew), unpublished) paper, Department of Economics, Ben-Gurion University of the Negev (Beersheba).
Aronoff, Myron J. (1977), *Power and Ritual in the Israeli Labor Party: A Study in Political Anthropology* (Amsterdam: van Gorcum).
Artstein, Yael (1980), 'The Influence of Elections and Differentials on Wages in Israel' (in Hebrew), *Iyunim Bekalkala 1979* (Jerusalem: Israeli Economic Association), 122–7.
—— and Sussman, Zvi (1977), 'Wage and Price Controls and the Effectiveness of Devaluations: The Israeli Experience', unpublished paper, International Monetary Fund and Bank of Israel, Dec.
—— (1989), 'Wage Policy in a High-Inflation Economy: The Israeli Experience', in V. L. Urquidi (ed.), *Incomes Policies*: Papers Prepared for a Conference of the International Economic Association (London: Macmillan), 150–70.
Avizohar, Meir (1978), *Money for All: The Development of Social Insurance in Israel* (in Hebrew) (Tel Aviv: Yariv and Hadar).
—— (1982), 'Money for All', *Jerusalem Quarterly*, 22, 1–63.
—— (1988), 'Ben Gurion and Mapai—From an Organization of Fulfillment to a Political Party, 1930–1947' (in Hebrew), in Shlomo Avineri (ed.), *David Ben-Gurion as a Labour Leader* (in Hebrew) (Tel Aviv: Am Oved), 91–107.
Avniel, Benjamin (1943), *Problems of Labour Relations in Palestine* (Jerusalem: Reuben Mass).
Avrech, Isaiah and Giladi, Dan (eds.) (1973), *Labor and Society in Israel* (Tel Aviv: Tel Aviv University and the Histadrut).

Azmon, Yael (1985), 'Urban Patronage in Israel', in Erik Cohen, Moshe Lissak, and Uri Almagor (eds.), *Comparative Social Dynamics: Essays in Honor of S. N. Eisenstadt* (Boulder, Colo.: Westview Press), 284–94.

Bahat, Shmuel (1979), 'Structural Relations Between Trade Unions and Labour Parties—A Comparative Study' (in Hebrew), unpublished MA thesis, Department of Labour Studies, Tel Aviv University.

Bahral, Uri (1965), *The Effect of Mass Immigration on Wages in Israel* (Jerusalem: Falk Project for Economic Research in Israel).

Bar, Chaviva (1983), 'Arabs from Judea, Samaria and Gaza in Organized Employment in Israel—1983' (in Hebrew), report submitted to the Ministry of Labour by the Israel Institute for Applied Social Research (Jerusalem), Dec.

Bar-Haim, Aviad (1972), 'The Industrial Relations System of the Jewish Community in Palestine in the Mandatory Period until the End of World War II' (in Hebrew), unpublished MA thesis, Department of Sociology, Hebrew University of Jerusalem.

—— (1988),'Workers' Participation and Personnel Policies in Israel', *International Labour Review*, 127(3), 381–97.

Barkai, Haim (1964), 'The Public, Histadrut, and Private Sectors in the Israeli Economy', in *Falk Project for Economic Research in Israel: Sixth Report 1961–1963* (Jerusalem: Falk Project), 15–77.

—— (1980), 'The Cost of Defence in a Retrospective View' (in Hebrew), Falk Institute Research Paper No. 115.

—— (1982), 'Theory and Practice of the Histadrut Industrial Sector', *Jerusalem Quarterly*, 26, 96–108.

—— (1983), *The First Days of the Israeli Economy* (in Hebrew) (Jerusalem: Falk Institute).

—— (1984*a*), 'Israel's Energy Sector in the 1960's and 1970's', Falk Institute Discussion Paper No. 84.03.

—— (1984*b*), 'The Israeli Economy in the Past Decade', *Jerusalem Quarterly*, 32, 3–15.

—— (1987*a*), 'The Defence Industries at a Crossroads' (in Hebrew), Falk Institute Research Paper No. 197.

—— (1987*b*), 'The Cost and Allocation of Social Services, and Priorities in Social Policy', in Yaakov Kop (ed.), *Israel's Social Services 1986–87* (Jerusalem: Center for Social Policy Studies in Israel), 123–137.

—— (1988), 'Economic Patterns in Israel since the Six Day War', Falk Institute Discussion Paper No. 88.04.

Bar-Natan, Moshe (1984), 'Productivity and Factors of Production in the Construction Industry, 1960–1981' (in Hebrew), *Seker Bank Yisrael*, 58, 63–74.

Barkin, Solomon (ed.) (1975), *Worker Militancy and its Consequences, 1965–75: New Directions in Western Industrial Relations* (New York: Praeger).

Bartal, Gabriel (1989), *The Histadrut: Structure and Activities* (10th ed.) (in Hebrew) (Tel Aviv: Histadrut Executive Committee).

Bar-Tsuri, Roni and Batsri, Tikvah (1985), *Strikes in Israel in the Years 1974–1984* (in Hebrew) (Tel Aviv: Histadrut Institute for Economic and Social Research).

Bauboeck, Rainer and Wimmer, Hannes (1988), 'Social Partnership and "Foreigners Policy": on Special Features of Austria's Guest-worker System', *European Journal of Political Research*, 16(6), 659–81.

Beham, Miriam and Kleiman, Ephraim (1968), 'The Price of Recession' (in Hebrew), *Rivon Lebankaut*, 29, 31–42.

Beilin, Yossi (1987), *The Roots of Jewish Industry* (in Hebrew) (Jerusalem: Keter).

Beinin, Joel (1990), *Was the Red Flag Flying There? Marxist Politics and the Arab–Israeli Conflict in Egypt and Israel, 1948–1965* (Berkeley: University of California Press).

Ben-Aharon, Yitzchak (1972), *Struggle for Change* (in Hebrew) (Tel Aviv: Am Oved).

Ben-Avram, Baruch (1978), *Parties and Political Trends in the National Home Period, 1918–1948* (in Hebrew) (Jerusalem: Zalman Shazar Center and the Israeli Historical Society).

Ben-David, Joseph (1965), 'Professionals and Unions in Israel', *Industrial Relations*, 5(1), 48–66.

Ben-Gurion, David (1964), *The Jewish Worker and his Histadrut* (in Hebrew) (Tel Aviv: Histadrut Executive Committee).

Ben-Hanan, Uriel and Temkin, Benny (1986), 'The "Overloaded Juggler": The Electoral–Economic Cycle in Israel, 1951–1984', in Asher Arian and Michal Shamir (eds.), *The Elections in Israel—1984* (Tel Aviv: Ramot), 15–35.

Ben-Meir, Dov (1980), *The Histadrut Lexicon* (in Hebrew) (Tel Aviv: Am Oved).

Ben-Ner, Avner and Estrin, Saul (1988), 'Union Bargaining with Firms and Union Management of Firms: The Impact on Wages, Employment and Productivity', Working Paper 88–02, Industrial Relations Center, University of Minnesota.

Ben-Porat, Amir (1973), 'Industrial Relations: The Productivity Council in Israel', unpublished Ph.D. dissertation, University of Strathclyde, Department of Sociology.

—— (1986), *Between Class and Nation: The Formation of the Jewish Working Class in the Period before Israel's Statehood* (New York: Greenwood Press).

Ben-Porat, Yeshayahu (1963–4), 'Control of the Labour Economy—the Key to Control of the State' (in Hebrew), *Yediot Acharonot*, a series of six articles published Dec. 1963–Jan. 1964.

Ben-Porath, Yoram (1966), *The Arab Labor Force in Israel* (Jerusalem: Falk Institute).

—— (1975), 'The Years of Plenty and the Years of Famine—A Political Business Cycle?', *Kyklos*, 28(2), 400–3.

—— (1983), 'The Conservative Turnabout that Never Was', *Jerusalem Quarterly*, 29, 3–10.

—— (1984), 'Israeli Dilemmas: Economic Relations Between Arabs and Jews', *Dissent*, Fall, 459–67.

—— (1986*a*), 'Public Sector Employment and Wages in the Process of Adjustment', paper presented at the Conference on Economic Issues and Policy in Israel 1985–86, Falk Institute, 15–16 June.

—— (1986*b*), 'Introduction', in Ben-Porath (ed.), *The Economy of Israel: Maturing through Crisis* (Cambridge, Mass.: Harvard University Press), 1–23.

—— (ed.) (1986), *The Economy of Israel: Maturing through Crisis* (Cambridge, Mass.: Harvard University Press).

Ben-Shoham, Yehuda (1985), 'Elections in the Histadrut Trade Unions' (in Hebrew), seminar paper, Department of Sociology, Hebrew University of Jerusalem, Oct.

Berglas, Eitan (1983), 'Defense and the Economy: The Israeli Experience', Falk Institute, Discussion Paper No. 83.01.

—— (1986), 'Taxes and Transfer Payments, 1975–1985' (in Hebrew), Discussion Paper No. 86–12, Sapir Center for Development, Tel Aviv University.

Bernstein, Deborah (1976), 'Contradictions and Protest in the Process of Nation-Building: The Black Panthers of Israel, 1971–1972', unpublished Ph.D. dissertation, University of Sussex.

—— (1980), 'Immigrants and Society—A Critical View of the Dominant School of Israeli Sociology', *British Journal of Sociology*, 31(2), 246–64.

—— (1981), 'Immigrant Transit Camps—The Formation of Dependent Relations in Israeli Society', *Ethnic and Racial Studies*, 1(4), 26–43.

—— (1983*a*), 'The Plough Woman who Cried into the Pots: The Position of Women in the Labor Force in Pre-State Israeli Society', *Jewish Social Studies*, 45(1), 43–56.

—— (1983*b*), 'Economic Growth and Female Labour: The Case of Israel', *The Sociological Review*, 31(2), 263–92.

—— (1984), 'Political Participation: New Immigrants and Veteran Parties in Israeli Society', *Plural Societies*, 15(1), 13–32.

—— and Swirski, Shlomo (1982), 'The Rapid Economic Development of Israel and the Emergence of the Ethnic Division of Labour', *British Journal of Sociology*, 33(1), 64–85.

Bichler, Shimshon (1985), 'Insights into the *Tsena* [Austerity] Period' (in Hebrew), unpublished seminar paper, Department of Economics, Hebrew University of Jerusalem.

—— (1986), 'The Political Economy of National Security in Israel: Some Aspects of the Activities of the Dominant Blocs of Capital' (in Hebrew), unpublished MA thesis, Department of Political Science, Hebrew University of Jerusalem.

Biger, Gideon (1983), *Crown Colony or National Home? The Influence of the British Administration on Palestine 1917–1930* (in Hebrew) (Jerusalem: Yad Ben-Zvi).

Block, Fred (1985), 'Postindustrial Development and the Obsolescence of Economic Categories', *Politics and Society*, 14(1), 71–104.

——(1986), 'Political Choice and the Multiple "Logics" of Capital', *Theory and Society*, 15, 175–92.

——(1987), *Revising State Theory: Essays in Politics and Postindustrialism* (Philadelphia: Temple University Press).

Bober, Arie (ed.) (1972), *The Other Israel: The Radical Case Against Zionism* (Garden City, NY: Doubleday).

Boddy, Raford and Crotty, James (1975), 'Class Conflict and Macro-Policy: The Political Business Cycle', *Review of Radical Political Economics*, 7(1), 1–19.

Bonacich, Edna (1972), 'A Theory Of Ethnic Antagonism: The Split Labor Market', *American Sociological Review*, 37(5), 547–59.

——(1976), 'Advanced Capitalism and Black/White Race Relations in the United States: A Split Labor Market Interpretation', *American Sociological Review*, 41(1), 34–51.

——(1979), 'The Past, Present, and Future of Split Labor Market Theory', *Research in Race and Ethnic Relations*, 1, 17–64.

——(1980), 'The Creation of Dual Labor Markets', paper presented at the Conference on the Structure of Labor Markets and Socio-Economic Stratification, Athens, Ga., 3–5 March.

Bordogna, Lorenzo (1981), 'The Political Business Cycle and the Crisis of Keynesian Politics', paper presented at the Annual Meetings of the American Sociological Association, Toronto, Aug.

Boyer, Robert (1979), 'Wage Formation in Historical Perspective: The French Experience', *Cambridge Journal of Economics*, 3(3), 99–118.

Brauer, David Avrum (1987), 'Histadrut in the Israeli Economy: Centralized Collective Bargaining and Wage Restraint', unpublished Ph.D. dissertation, University of California at Berkeley.

Bregman, Aryeh (1986), *Industry and Industrialization Policy in Israel: Central Issues (1965 to 1985)* (in Hebrew) (Jerusalem: Bank of Israel Research Department).

Brenner, Menachem and Ruthenberg, David (1987), 'The Banks' Intervention in the Capital Market, 1978–83' (in Hebrew), *Sugiyot Bebankaut*, 6, 40–52.

Bruno, Michael (1984), 'External Shocks and Domestic Response: Israel's Macroeconomic Performance 1965–1982', Falk Institute Discussion Paper No. 84.01.

——and Piterman, Sylvia (1987), 'Israel's Stabilization: A Two-Year

Review', Discussion Paper No. 87.05, Bank of Israel Research Department.

Brym, Robert R. (1978), *The Jewish Intelligentsia and Russian Marxism: A Sociological Study of Intellectual Radicalism and Ideological Divergence* (New York: Schocken).

Burstein, Paul (1973), 'Social Structure and Politics in Israel: Voting in the 1969 Israeli Elections', unpublished Ph.D. dissertation, Harvard University.

Cahane, Reuven and Canaan, Shulamit (1973), 'The Behaviour of the Press in Situations of Security Pressure and its Influence on Public Support for the Government' (in Hebrew), Research Report submitted to the Eshkol Institute, Hebrew University of Jerusalem.

Cameron, David (1984), 'The Politics and Economics of the Business Cycle', in Thomas Ferguson and Joel Rogers (eds.), *The Political Economy* (Armonk, NY: M. E. Sharpe), 237–62.

Carmi, Shulamit and Rosenfeld, Henry (1971), 'Immigration, Urbanization and Crisis: The Process of Jewish Colonization in Palestine during the 1920s', *International Journal of Comparative Sociology*, 12(1), 41–57.

—— (1989), 'The Emergence of Militaristic Nationalism in Israel', *International Journal of Politics, Culture and Society*, 3(1), 5–49.

Carnoy, Martin (1984), *The State and Political Theory* (Princeton, NJ: Princeton University Press).

Castles, Francis G. (1978), *The Social Democratic Image of Society* (London: Routledge).

—— (1988), 'Comparative Public Policy Analysis: Problems, Progress and Prospects', in Castles, Franz Lehner and Manfred G. Schmidt (eds.), *Managing Mixed Economies* (Berlin: de Gruyter), 197–223.

—— (1989), 'Introduction: Puzzles of Political Economy', in Castles (ed.), *The Comparative History of Public Policy* (Cambridge: Polity Press), 1–15.

—— (ed.) (1982), *The Impact of Parties: Politics and Policies in Democratic Capitalist States* (London: Sage).

—— (ed.) (1989), *The Comparative History of Public Policy* (Cambridge: Polity Press).

—— Lehner, Franz and Schmidt, Manfred G. (eds.) (1988), *Managing Mixed Economies* (Berlin: de Gruyter).

Chermesh, Ran, Bar-Tsuri, Roni and Barzilai, Yoram (1972), 'Unemployment Grant or Public Works' (in Hebrew), *Bitachon Soziali*, 3, 76–81.

Cnaan, Ram (1985), 'Racial Differences in Social Service Delivery: Jews and Non-Jews in Israel', *Social Development Issues*, 9(2), 56–74.

Cohen, Abraham (1980), 'The Economy of the Arab Sector in Mandatory Palestine (Part 2)' (in Hebrew), *Rivon Lekalkala*, 104, 66–79.

—— (1986), *The Economy of the [Occupied] Territories: The West Bank and the Gaza Strip* (in Hebrew) (Givat Chaviva: Institute for Arab Studies).

Cohen, Aharon (1976), *Israel and the Arab World* (abridged edn.) (Boston: Beacon Press).

Cohen, Mitchell (1987), *Zion and State: Nation, Class and the Shaping of Modern Israel* (Oxford: Basil Blackwell).

Cohen, Raanan (1983), 'The Arab Member's Participation in Histadrut Activities should be Strengthened' (in Hebrew), *Davar*, 8 May.

—— (1985), 'Processes of Political Unification and Voting Patterns of Israeli Arabs' (in Hebrew), unpublished MA thesis, Department of Middle Eastern History, Tel Aviv University.

Commission of Inquiry into the Regulation of Bank Shares (1986), *Final Report* (in Hebrew) (Jerusalem: Ministry of Justice).

Cox, Andrew (1988), 'The Old and New Testaments of Corporatism: Is it Political Form or a Method of Policy-making?', *Political Studies*, 36, 294–308.

Crouch, Colin (1977), *Class Conflict and the Industrial Relations Crisis: Compromise and Corporatism in the Policies of the British State* (London: Heinemann).

—— (1979), 'The State, Capital and Liberal Democracy', in Crouch (ed.), *State and Economy in Contemporary Capitalism* (New York: St Martin's Press), 13–54.

—— (1982*a*), *Trade Unions: The Logic of Collective Action* (London: Fontana).

—— (1982*b*), *The Politics of Industrial Relations* (2nd edn.) (London: Fontana).

—— (1983), 'Pluralism and the New Corporatism: A Rejoinder', *Political Studies*, 31(3), 452–60.

—— (1985), 'Conditions for Trade Union Wage Restraint', in Leon N. Lindberg and Charles S. Maier (eds.), *The Politics of Inflation and Economic Stagnation* (Washington, DC: Brookings Institution), 105–39.

—— (1988), 'Trade Unions in the Exposed Sector: Their Influence on Neo-Corporatist Behaviour', paper prepared for the Conference on Markets, Institutions and Co-operation in Memory of Enzio Tarantelli, Venice, Oct.

—— (ed.) (1979), *State and Economy in Contemporary Capitalism* (New York: St Martin's Press).

—— and Pizzorno, Alessandro (eds.) (1978), *The Resurgence of Class Conflict in Western Europe Since 1968* (two vols.) (London: Macmillan).

Czudnowski, Moshe M. (1970), 'Legislative Recruitment under Proportional Representation in Israel: A Model and a Case Study', *Midwest Journal of Political Science*, 14(2), 216–48.

—— (1972), 'Sociocultural Variables and Legislative Recruitment: Some Theoretical Observations and a Case Study', *Comparative Politics*, 4(4), 561–87.

Danelius, Eva (1944), 'The Industrial Workers in Jewish Palestine 1943–1944', mimeo, (Tel Aviv), Dec.

Daniel, Abraham (1976), *Labor Enterprises in Israel* (Jerusalem: Jerusalem Academic Press).

Derber, Milton (1963), 'Israel's Wage Differential: A Persisting Problem', *Midstream*, 9(1), 60–72.

Diskin, Avraham (1980), 'The 1977 Interparty Distances: A Three-level Analysis', in Asher Arian (ed.), *The Elections in Israel 1977* (Jerusalem: Jerusalem Academic Press), 213–29.

Doeringer, Peter B. and Piore, Michael J. (1971), *Internal Labor Markets and Manpower Analysis* (Lexington, Mass.: Lexington Books).

Doron, Abraham (1967), 'Development of National Insurance in Israel, 1948–1965', unpublished Ph.D. dissertation, London School of Economics.

—— (1984), 'Welfare Policy and Equality' (in Hebrew) in Asher Maniv (ed.), *The Challenge: A Social Movement* (in Hebrew) (Efal: Yad Tabenkin), 83–94.

—— and Kramer, Ralph (1991), *The Welfare State in Israel: The Evolution of Social Security Policy and Practice* (Boulder, Colo.: Westview Press).

Dubin, Robert and Aharoni, Yair (1981), 'Ideology and Reality: Work and Pay in Israel', *Industrial Relations*, 20(1), 18–35.

Dunlop, John T. (1958), *Industrial Relations Systems* (New York: Holt).

Duverger, Maurice (1964), *Political Parties: Their Organization and Activity in the Modern State* (London: Methuen).

Edwards, Richard C., Reich, Michael and Gordon, David M. (eds.) (1973), *Labor Market Segmentation* (Lexington, Mass.: D. C. Heath).

Ehrlich, Avishai (1978), 'The Crisis in Israel—Danger of Fascism', *Khamsin*, 5, 81–113.

—— (1987), 'Israel: Conflict, War and Social Change' in Colin Creighton and Martin Shaw (eds.), *The Sociology of War and Peace* (London: Macmillan), 121–42.

Eisenstadt, Shmuel N. (1967), *Israeli Society* (London: Weidenfeld and Nicolson).

—— (1985), *The Transformation of Israeli Society: An Essay in Interpretation* (Boulder, Colo.: Westview Press).

Enloe, Cynthia (1980), *Ethnic Soldiers: State Security in Divided Societies* (Athens, Ga.: University of Georgia Press).

Esping-Andersen, Gøsta (1985*a*), *Politics Against Markets: The Social Democratic Road to Power* (Princeton, NJ: Princeton University Press).

—— (1985*b*), 'Power and Distributional Regimes', *Politics and Society*, 14(2), 223–56.

—— (1987), 'Institutional Accomodation to Full Employment: A Comparison of Policy Regimes' in Hans Keman, Heikki Paloheimo and Paul F. Whiteley (ed.), *Coping with the Economic Crisis: Alternative Responses to Economic Recession in Advanced Industrial Societies* (London: Sage), 83–110.

——(1989), 'The Three Political Economies of the Welfare State', *Canadian Review of Sociology and Anthropology*, 26(1), 10–36.

——(1990*a*), 'Single-Party Dominance in Sweden: The Saga of Social Democracy', in T. J. Pempel (ed.), *Uncommon Democracies: The One Party Dominant Regimes* (Ithaca, NY: Cornell University Press), 33–57.

——(1990*b*), *The Three Worlds of Welfare Capitalism* (Cambridge: Polity Press).

——and Korpi, Walter (1984), 'Social Policy as Class Politics in Post-War Capitalism: Scandinavia, Austria and Germany', in John H. Goldthorpe (ed.), *Order and Conflict in Contemporary Capitalism* (Oxford: Oxford University Press), 179–208.

Etkin, Yeshayahu (1982), 'Sixty Years of Strikes in Israel' (in Hebrew), unpublished MA thesis, Department of Labour Studies, Tel Aviv University.

Etzioni, Amitai (1959), 'Alternative Ways to Democracy: The Example of Israel', *Political Science Quarterly*, 74(2), 196–214.

Etzioni-Halevy, Eva (1975*a*) 'Protest Politics in the Israeli Democracy', *Political Science Quarterly*, 90(3), 497–520.

——(1975*b*), 'Patterns of Conflict Generation and Conflict "Absorption": The Case of Israeli Labor and Ethnic Politics', *Journal of Conflict Resolution*, 19(2), 286–309.

——and Shapira, Rina (1977), *Political Culture in Israel: Cleavage and Integration among Israeli Jews* (New York: Praeger).

Evans, Peter, Rueschemeyer, Dietrich and Skocpol, Theda (eds.) (1985), *Bringing the State Back In* (Cambridge: Cambridge University Press).

Farjoun, Emanuel (1980), 'Palestinian Workers in Israel—a Reserve Army of Labour', *Khamsin* (London), 7, 107–43. (Originally published May 1978 in Hebrew in *Dapim Adumim* 5 (Matzpen, Jerusalem).)

——(1983), 'Class Divisions in Israeli Society', *Khamsin* (London), 10, 29–39.

Finegold, Julian L. (1978), 'British Economic Policy in Palestine 1920–1948', unpublished Ph.D. dissertation, London School of Economics.

Fishelson, Gideon (1983), 'Dynamics of Income Distribution, in Israel 1970–1979' (in Hebrew), Discussion Paper 83.09, Institute for Social and Labour Research, Tel Aviv University.

Flanagan, Robert J., Soskice, David W. and Ulman, Lloyd (1983), *Unionism, Economic Stabilization, and Incomes Policies: European Experience* (Washington DC: Brookings Institution).

Flapan, Simha (1979), *Zionism and the Palestinians* (London: Croom Helm).

——(1987), *The Birth of Israel: Myths and Realities* (New York: Pantheon).

Frankel, Jonathan (1981), *Prophecy and Politics: Socialism, Nationalism, and the Russian Jews, 1862–1917* (Cambridge: Cambridge University Press).

Frenkel, Shlomo (1982), 'Profiteers of War: A Series of Articles' (in Hebrew), *Haolam Hazeh*, 25 Aug.; 1,8,22 Sept.; 13 Oct; 10 Nov.

——and Bichler, Shimshon (1984), *The Rich Families* (in Hebrew) (Tel Aviv: Cadim).

Friedlander, Dov and Goldscheider, Calvin (1979), *The Population of Israel* (New York: Columbia University Press).

Friedman, Arbraham (1963), *Research on Workers' Committees* (in Hebrew) (Tel Aviv: Histadrut Institute for Economic and Social Research).

——(1974), 'Workers' Committees and the Trade Union: Partners or Rivals?' (in Hebrew) in Rivka-Bar Yosef and Eliezer Leshem (eds.), *Labour Investigations in Israel* (in Hebrew) (Jerusalem: Hebrew University Institute for the Study of Work and Welfare), 126–42.

——(1976), 'Union Structure and Rank and File Revolt: The Israeli Experience', *Relations Industrielles*, 31(2), 261–83.

——*et al.* (1966), 'Public Opinion on the Histadrut' (in Hebrew) in Yosef Olitsky (ed.), *The Histadrut Yearbook 5726* (in Hebrew) (Tel Aviv: Histadrut Executive Committee), 350–60.

Fulcher, James (1987), 'Labour Movement Theory versus Corporatism: Social Democracy in Sweden', *Sociology*, 21(2), 232–52.

——(1988), 'On the Explanation of Industrial Relations Diversity: Labour Movements, Employers and the State in Britain and Sweden', *British Journal of Industrial Relations*, 26(2), 246–74.

Gaathon, A. L. (1971*a*), *Economic Productivity in Israel* (New York: Praeger).

——(1971*b*), 'Wage and Incomes Policy' (in Hebrew), *Rivon Lekalkala*, 69–70, 11–19.

Galai, Dan and Brenner, Menachem (1984), 'The Bank Share Crisis From a Microeconomic Perspective' (in Hebrew), *Rivon Lekalkala*, 119, 909–14.

Galin, A. and Tabb, J. Y. (1971), '1970—A Turning Point in Israel's Industrial Relations System', *Institute for Labour Relations (University of Leuven) Bulletin*, 2, 177–88.

Galin, Amira and Harel, Aharon (1978), *Developments and Trends in the Labour Relations System of Israel* (in Hebrew) (Tel Aviv: Massada).

Giladi, Bina (1980), *Strikes in Israel and the World* (in Hebrew) (Tel Aviv: Institute for the Advancement of Industrial Relations).

Giladi, Dan (1965), 'Private Enterprise, National Capital and the Political Formation of the Right' (in Hebrew), *Avanim*, 5, 90–102.

——(1973), *The Yishuv in the Period of the Fourth Aliyah* (in Hebrew) (Tel Aviv: Am Oved).

Ginzberg, Eli (1968), *Fifth Report on Manpower in Israel* (Jerusalem: Ministry of Labour, Manpower Planning Authority).

Glatt, Joseph (1973), 'The Historical Development of the Histadrut: an Evaluation of Its Post-State Wages Policy, 1948–1967 and its Impact on the Economic Independence of Israel', unpublished Ph.D. dissertation, Columbia University.

Goell, Yosef (1987), 'Histadrut Failure in the Arab Sector', *Jerusalem Post*, 30 Jan.

Goldberg, Giora (1975), 'Labour Exchanges as a Political Instrument in a Developing Society' (in Hebrew), unpublished MA thesis, Department of Political Science, Tel Aviv University.

——(1986), 'The Struggle for Legitimacy: Herut's Road from Opposition to Power', in Stuart Cohen and Eliezer Don-Yehiya (eds.), *Conflict and Consensus in Jewish Political Life* (Ramat Gan: Bar-Ilan University Press), 146–69.

Goldthorpe, John H. (1984), 'The End of Convergence: Corporatist and Dualist Tendencies in Modern Western Societies', in Goldthorpe (ed.), *Order and Conflict in Contemporary Capitalism* (Oxford: Oxford University Press), 315–43.

——(ed.) (1984), *Order and Conflict in Contemporary Capitalism* (Oxford: Oxford University Press).

Gonen, Amiram (1984), 'A Geographical Analysis of the Elections in Jewish Urban Communities', in Dan Caspi, Abraham Diskin and Emanuel Gutmann (eds.), *The Roots of Begin's Success: The 1981 Israeli Elections* (New York: St Martin's Press), 59–87.

——and Hasson, Shlomo (1983), 'The Use of Housing as a Spatio-political Measure: The Israeli Case', *Geoforum*, 14(1), 103–9.

——Gordon, David M. (1972), *Theories of Poverty and Underemployment: Orthodox, Radical and Dual Labor Market Theories* (Lexington, Mass.: DC Heath).

——Edwards, Richard and Reich, Michael (1982), *Segmented Work, Divided Workers: The Historical Transformation of Labor in the United States* (Cambridge: Cambridge University Press).

Greenberg, Stanley (1980), *Race and State in Capitalist Development: South Africa in Comparative Perspective* (New Haven, Conn: Yale University Press).

——(1985) 'The Indifferent Hegemony: Israel and the Palestinians', unpublished paper, Truman Institute, Hebrew University of Jerusalem.

Greenberg, Yitzhak (1983), 'From Workers' Society to Workers' Economy: Evolution of the Idea of Chevrat Ovdim in the Years 1920–1929' (in Hebrew), unpublished Ph.D. dissertation, Department of History, Tel Aviv University.

——(1986), 'Hevrat Ovdim: The Process of Deco-operatization in the Workers' Credit Co-operative' (in Hebrew), *Rivon Lekalkalah*, 130, 757–71.

Greenwald, Carol Schwartz (1972), *Recession as a Policy Instrument: Israel 1965–1969* (London: C. Hurst).

Griffin, Larry J., O'Connell, Philip J. and McCammon, Holly J. (1989), 'National Variation in the Context of Struggle: post-war Class Conflict and Market Distribution in the Capitalist Democracies', *Canadian Review of Sociology and Anthropology*, 26(1), 37–68.

Grinberg, Lev (Luis) (1985), 'The Revolt that Never Was: The "Forum of Thirteen Workers Committees"; A Test Case for Israeli Corporatism' (in Hebrew), unpublished MA thesis, Department of Political Science, Hebrew University of Jerusalem.

—— (1986), 'The Jewish-Arab Drivers' Association Strike of 1931' (in Hebrew), unpublished paper, Department of Sociology, Tel Aviv University.

—— (1991*a*), *Split Corporatism in Israel* (Albany, NY: State University of New York Press).

—— (1991*b*), 'The Crisis of the Israeli Labour Movement 1967–1970: The Political Economy of the Relations between Mapai, the Histadrut, and the State', unpublished Ph.D. dessertation, Department of Sociology, Tel Aviv University.

Gross, Nachum (1979), 'The 1923 Recession and Public Sector Finance in Palestine', Falk Institute Discussion Paper No. 79.4 (revised).

—— (1982), 'The Economic Policy of the Mandatory Government in Palestine', Falk Institute Discussion Paper No. 81.6 (revised).

—— (1988), 'Laying the Foundations of Israel's Economic System: 1948–1951', Falk Institute Discussion Paper No. 88.07.

—— and Metzer, Jacob (1978), 'Public Finance in the Jewish Economy in Interwar Palestine', *Research in Economic History*, 3, 87–159.

Hadar, Shmuel (1988), 'Blurring of the Boundaries between Public and Private in Relations between State and Industry' (in Hebrew), unpublished Ph.D. dissertation, Department of Political Science, Hebrew University of Jerusalem, Israel.

Haidar, Aziz (1985), 'Forms of Economic Entrepreneurship in the Arab Village in Israel' (in Hebrew), unpublished Ph.D. dissertation, Department of Sociology, Hebrew University of Jerusalem.

—— (1987), 'Social Welfare Services for Israel's Arab Population' (Tel Aviv: International Center for Peace in the Middle East).

Halabi, Rafik (1981), *The West Bank Story* (New York: Harcourt, Brace, Jovanovich).

Halevi, H. S. (1980), 'The Bumpy Road to National Health Insurance: The Case of Israel', Discussion Paper D–51–80, Joint Israel (Jerusalem).

Halevi, Nadav (1979), 'The Economic Development of the Jewish Community in Palestine 1917–1947' (in Hebrew), Falk Institute Discussion Paper No. 79.14.

—— (1983*a*), 'Economic Growth and Economic Cycles in the Jewish Economy of Mandatory Palestine' (in Hebrew), *Iyunim Bekalkala 1981*, (Jerusalem: Israeli Economic Association), 313–21.

—— (1983*b*), 'The Structure and Development of Israel's Balance of Payments', Falk Institute Discussion Paper No. 83.02.

—— and Klinov-Malul, Ruth (1968), *The Economic Development of Israel* (New York: Praeger).

Halperin, A. (1968), 'The "Mitun" and Economic Recovery' (in Hebrew), *Rivon Lekalkala*, 56, 287–97.

Halperin, Ariel (1986), 'Military Buildup and Economic Growth in Israel', paper presented at the Conference on Economic Issues and Policy in Israel 1985–1986, Falk Institute, 15–16 June.

Hanoch, Giora (1961), 'Income Differentials in Israel', in *Falk Project for Economic Research in Israel: Fifth Report 1959 and 1960* (Jerusalem: Falk Project), 37–130.

Harel, Gedaliahu (1976), 'Job Evaluation and Wage Setting in the Public Sector of Israel', *Relations Industrielles*, 31(2), 284–99.

Harrison, Bennet (1974), 'The Theory of the Dual Economy', in Bertram Silverman and M. Yanowitch (eds.), *The Worker in 'Post-Industrial' Capitalism* (New York: Free Press), 269–87.

Hasson, Shlomo (1981), 'Social and Spatial Conflicts: The Settlement Process in Israel during the 1950s and the 1960s', *L'Espace Geographique*, 3, 169–79.

Headey, Bruce (1970), 'Trade Unions and National Wages Policy', *Journal of Politics*, 32, 407–39.

Hertzberg, Arthur (ed.) (1966), *The Zionist Idea: A Historical Analysis and Reader* (New York: Harper and Row).

Hicks, Alexander (1988), 'Social Democratic Corporatism and Economic Growth', *Journal of Politics*, 50(3), 677–704.

Higgins, Winton and Apple, Nixon (1983), 'How Limited is Reformism? A Critique of Przeworski and Panitch', *Theory and Society*, 12(5), 603–30.

Hirsch, Fred and Goldthorpe, John H. (eds.) (1978), *The Political Economy of Inflation* (Cambridge, Mass.: Harvard University Press).

Histadrut (1945), 'Social Conditions of Work in Jewish Industry in Palestine in the Year 1945' (in Hebrew), special publication, Histadrut, Department of Statistics and Information.

Hodson, Randy (1983) *Workers' Earnings and Corporate Economic Structure* (New York: Academic Press).

Hoffnung, Menahem (1982), 'Social Protest and the Public Budgeting Process: The Effect of the "Black Panther" Demonstrations on Allocations to Social and Welfare Needs' (in Hebrew), unpublished MA thesis, Department of Political Science, Hebrew University of Jerusalem.

Horowitz, Dan and Lissak, Moshe (1971), 'Authority Without Sovereignty' in Moshe Lissak and Emanuel Gutmann (eds.), *Political Institutions and Processes in Israel* (Jerusalem: Akademon), 1–39.

—— (1978), *Origins of the Israeli Polity: Palestine under the Mandate* (Chicago and London: University of Chicago Press).

—— (1989), *Trouble in Utopia: The Overburdened Polity of Israel* (Albany, NY: State University of New York Press).

Horowitz, David (1936), *Aspects of Economic Policy in Palestine* (Tel Aviv: Jewish Agency, Economic Research Institute).

—— (1948), *The Palestinian Economy in Development* (2nd edn.) (in Hebrew) (Tel Aviv: Dvir for Mossad Bialik).

—— and Hinden, Rita (1938), *Economic Survey of Palestine* (Tel Aviv: Jewish Agency, Economic Research Institute).

Hyman, Richard (1989), *Political Economy of Industrial Relations* (London: Macmillan).

Ishai, Yael (1977), 'Welfare Policy: The Parties' Manifestoes in Elections to the Ninth Knesset' (in Hebrew), *Bitachon Soziali*, 14–15, 17–31.

—— (1978), *Factionalism in the Labour Movement: Faction B in Mapai* (in Hebrew) (Tel Aviv: Am Oved).

—— (1987), *Interest Groups in Israel* (in Hebrew) (Tel Aviv: Am Oved).

Israel Labour Party (1983), 'Histadrut Activities in Arab Settlements: Facts and Conclusions', unpublished report, Minorities Division, May.

Izraeli, Dafna Nundi (1983), 'Israeli Women in the Work Force', *Jerusalem Quarterly*, 27, 59–80.

Jerusalem Institute of Management (1987), *Export-Led Growth Strategy for Israel: Final Report* (Tel Aviv: J. I. M).

Jessop, Bob (1983), 'The Capitalist State and the Rule of Capital: Problems in the Analysis of Business Associations', *West European Politics*, 6(2), 139–62.

—— (1990), 'Regulation Theories in Retrospect and Prospect', *Economy and Society*, 19(2), 153–216.

Jewish Agency (1942), 'Agreements on Cost of Living Allowances in Jewish Industry in Palestine', *Bulletin of the Economic Research Institute of the Jewish Agency*, 6(4–6), 77–83.

—— (1946), *The Economic War Effort of Jewish Palestine* (Jerusalem: Jewish Agency, Department for Trade and Industry).

—— (1947), *Statistical Handbook of Jewish Palestine 1947* (prepared by D. Gurevitch, A. Gertz, and A. Zankner) (Jerusalem: Jewish Agency, Department of Statistics).

Jiryis, Sabri (1976), *The Arabs in Israel* (New York: Monthly Review Press).

Kalecki, Michal (1943), 'Political Aspects of Full Employment', *Political Quarterly*, 14(4), 322–31.

—— (1950), 'Report on Main Current Economic Problems of Israel', mimeo, (Tel Aviv), Sept.

Kalleberg, Arne L. and Sorensen, Aage B. (1979), 'The Sociology of Labor Markets', *Annual Review of Sociology*, 5, 351–79.

Kamen, Charles S. (1987), 'After the Catastrophe: The Arabs in Israel, 1948–51' (in two parts), *Middle Eastern Studies*, 23(4), 453–95 and 24(1), 68–109.

Kaminka, Shlomit (1974), 'The Workers' Committee as a Focus of Tension in Labour Relations in Israeli Industry' (in Hebrew), in Rivka Bar-Yosef and Eliezer Leshem (eds.), *Labour Investigations in Israel* (in Hebrew) (Jerusalem: Hebrew University Institute for the Study of Work and Welfare), 143–55.

Kanovsky, Eliyahu (1970), *The Economic Impact of the Six-Day War: Israel, The Occupied Territories, Egypt, Jordan* (New York: Praeger).

Kantor, Levi (1966), *The Trade Union Arm* (in Hebrew) (Tel Aviv: Aleph).

—— (1977), *'Lelo Masso Panim': The Development of Labour Relations in Israel* (in Hebrew) (Tel Aviv: Yahad).

Kassalow, Everett M. (1969), *Trade Unions and Industrial Relations: An International Comparison* (New York: Random House).

Katzenstein, Peter (1980), 'Capitalism in One Country? Switzerland in the International Economy', Occasional Paper No. 13, Western Societies Program, Cornell University.

—— (1985), *Small States in World Markets: Industrial Policy in Europe* (Ithaca, NY: Cornell University Press).

Katznelson, Berl (1948), *Writings of Berl Katznelson*, vol. vii (in Hebrew) (Tel Aviv: Mapai Party Press).

Kaufman, Roger (1978), 'Why the US Unemployment Rate is So High', *Challenge*, 21(2), 40–9.

Kellner, Yaakov (1976), 'Immigration, Ideology and Social Policy from a Historical Perspective' (in Hebrew), *Bitachon Soziali*, 11, 117–32.

Keman, Hans, Paloheimo, Heikki, and Whiteley, Paul F. (eds.) (1987), *Coping with the Economic Crisis: Alternative Responses to Economic Recession in Advanced Industrial Societies* (London, Sage).

Kerr, Clark *et al.* (1960), *Industrialism and Industrial Man* (Cambridge, Mass.: Harvard University Press).

Kimmerling, Baruch (1974), 'Anomie and Integration in Israeli Society and the Salience of the Israeli-Arab Conflict', *Studies in Comparative International Development*, 9(3), 64–89.

—— (1983*a*), *Zionism and Economy* (Cambridge, Mass.: Schenkman).

—— (1983*b*), *Zionism and Territory: The Socio-Territorial Dimensions of Zionist Politics* (Berkeley: Institute of International Studies, University of California).

—— (1985), *The Interrupted System: Israeli Civilians in War and Routine Times* (with Irit Backer) (New Brunswick, NJ: Transaction).

Kleiman, Ephraim (1964*a*), 'From Cooperative to Industrial Empire: The Story of Solel Boneh', *Midstream*, 10(1), March, 15–26.

—— (1964*b*) 'The Structure of Israel [sic] Manufacturing Industries 1952–1962', unpublished research report, Falk Project for Economic Research in Israel, Jerusalem, Dec.

—— (1987), 'The Histadrut Economy of Israel: In Search of Criteria', *Jerusalem Quarterly*, 41, 77–94.

Klein, Philip (1959), 'The Ministry of Social Welfare in Israel: Proposals on Program and Administration Prepared for the Government of Israel', mimeo, March.

Kolatt, Israel (1973), 'The Concept of the Histadrut: Experience and Change 1920–1948' in Isaiah Avrech and Dan Giladi (eds.), *Labor and*

Society in Israel: A Selection of Studies (Tel Aviv: Tel Aviv University and the Histadrut), 204–27.

Kondor, Yaakov (1986), 'The Underground Economy in Israel: Its Damage to the National Accounts' (in Hebrew), *Rivon Lekalkala*, 129, 692–3.

Kop, Yaakov (ed.) (1983), *Allocation of Resources to the Social Services* (in Hebrew) (Jerusalem: Centre for Social Policy Studies).

—— (1987), *Israel's Social Services, 1986–7* (Jerusalem: Center for Social Policy Studies).

—— (1988), *Socioeconomic Indicators: Israel 1988* (Jerusalem: The Centre for Social Policy Studies).

Kornhauser, Arthur W., Dubin, Robert and Ross, Arthur M. (eds.) (1959), *Industrial Conflict* (New York: McGraw-Hill).

Korpi, Walter (1978), *The Working Class in Welfare Capitalism: Work, Unions and Politics in Sweden* (London: Routledge and Kegan Paul).

—— (1983), *The Democratic Class Struggle* (London: Routledge and Kegan Paul).

—— and Shalev, Michael (1980), 'Strikes, Power and Politics in the Western Nations, 1900–1976', *Political Power and Social Theory*, 1, 301–34.

Kut, Sule Ayse (1987), Corporatism and Political-Economic Performance in Advanced Capitalist Countries: A Comparative Study, unpublished Ph.D. dissertation, State University of New York at Binghamton.

Landau, Jacob M. (1976), *The Arabs and the Histadrut* (Tel Aviv: Ramot).

Landau, Pinhas (1989), *Israeli Banking Today: Dinosaur or Phoenix*? (Jerusalem: Jerusalem Post).

Landau, Simha F. and Pfeffermann, Danny (1988), 'A Time Series Analysis of Violent Crime and its Relation to Prolonged States of Warfare: The Israeli Case', *Criminology*, 26(3), 489–504.

Lange, Peter (1981), 'Consenting to Restraint: The Political Economy of Union Wage Regulation—Some Hypotheses and Data', revised version of paper presented at the Annual Meeting of the American Political Science Association, New York, Sept.

—— (1984), 'Union Democracy and Liberal Corporatism', Occasional Paper No. 16, Western Societies Program, Cornell University.

Laqueur, Walter (1972), *A History of Zionism* (New York: Schocken).

Lash, Scott and Urry, John (1987), *The End of Organized Capitalism* (Cambridge: Polity Press).

Laufer, Leopold Y. (1987), 'U.S. Aid to Israel: Problems and Perspectives', in Gabriel Sheffer (ed.), *Dynamics of Dependence: U.S.–Israeli Relations* (Boulder, Colo.: Westview), 125–63.

Lehman-Wilzig, Sam N. (1981), 'Public Protest and Systemic Stability in Israel: 1960–1979', in Lehman-Wilzig and Bernard Susser (eds.), *Comparative Jewish Politics: Public Life in Israel and the Diaspora* (Ramat Gan: Bar-Ilan University Press), 171–210.

Lehmbruch, Gerhard (1984), 'Concertation and the Structure of Corporatist Networks' in John H. Goldthorpe (ed.), *Order and Conflict in Contemporary Capitalism* (Oxford: Oxford University Press), 60–80.

—— and Schmitter, Philippe C. (eds.) (1982), *Patterns of Corporatist Policy Making* (London: Sage).

Lerner, Abba P. (1957) 'The Histadrut and the Israeli Economy', *Midstream*, Autumn, 74–9.

—— and Ben-Shahar, Haim (1975), *The Economics of Efficiency and Growth: Lessons from Israel and the West Bank* (Cambridge, Mass.: Ballinger).

Leventhal-Shartal, Sara (1985), The Development of the Social Structure of the Labor Market in Palestine and Israel, unpublished MA thesis, Department of Sociology, Hebrew University of Jerusalem.

Lever-Tracy, Constance (1984), 'The Paradigm Crisis of Dualism: Decay or Regeneration?', *Politics and Society*, 13(1), 59–89.

Levine, Chana (1985), 'Confrontation in Principle and Co-operation in Practice: Relations between the Mandatory Government and the Histadrut 1939–47' (in Hebrew), unpublished seminar paper, Department of Sociology, Hebrew University of Jerusalem.

Levite, Ariel and Tarrow, Sidney (1983), 'The Legitimation of Excluded Parties in Dominant Party Systems: The Cases of Israel and Italy', *Comparative Politics*, 15(3), 295–327.

Levy, Haim and Lerman, Zvi (1984), 'Estimates of Capital Costs in Israeli Industry, 1971–1980' (in Hebrew), Falk Institute Discussion Paper No. 84.05.

Lindberg, Leon, Crouch, Colin and Offe, Claus (eds.) (1975), *Stress and Contradiction in Contemporary Capitalism: Public Policy and the Theory of the State* (Lexington, Mass.: DC Heath).

—— and Maier, Charles S. (eds.), (1985), *The Politics of Inflation and Economic Stagnation: Theoretical Approaches and International Case Studies* (Washington, DC: Brookings Institution).

Lindblom, Charles E. (1977), *Politics and Markets: The World's Political-Economic Systems* (New York: Basic Books).

—— (1982), 'The Market As Prison', *Journal of Politics*, 44(2), 324–36.

Lipset, Seymour Martin (1981), *Political Man: The Social Bases of Politics* (Baltimore: Johns Hopkins University Press).

Lissak, Moshe (1969), *Social Mobility in Israel [sic] Society* (Jerusalem: Israel Universities Press).

—— (1985), 'Strategies of Class Formation: The Case of the Labor Movement in the Jewish Community of Palestine, 1918–1948' in Erik Cohen, Moshe Lissak, and Uri Almagor (eds.), *Comparative Social Dynamics: Essays in Honor of S. N. Eisenstadt* (Boulder, Colo.: Westview Press), 245–61.

Lotan, Michael (1966), 'Public Opinion Studies Prior to the Histadrut and Knesset Elections of 1965' (in Hebrew), *Avanim*, 6, 141–60.

Lucas, Noah (1974), *The Modern History of Israel* (London: Weidenfeld and Nicolson).

Lucatz, Noah (1961), 'Histadrut (The Israeli Labor Movement) as a Nationalist and Socialist Movement, 1882–1948: A Study in Ideologies and Political Behavior', unpublished Ph.D. dissertation, Washington University.

Lustick, Ian (1980), *Arabs in the Jewish State: Israel's Control of a National Minority* (Austin, Tex.: University of Texas Press).

Maier, Charles S. (1984), 'Preconditions for Corporatism', in John H. Goldthorpe (ed.), *Order and Conflict in Contemporary Capitalism* (Oxford: Oxford University Press), 39–59.

Makhoul, Najwa (1982), 'Changes in the Employment Structure of Arabs in Israel', *Journal of Palestine Studies*, 11(3), 77–102.

Malkosh, Noah (1961), *Histadrut in Israel: Its Aims and Achievements* (Tel Aviv and New York: Histadrut and US National Committee for Labor Israel).

Margalit, Elkana (1970), *'Hashomer Hatsair'—from Youth Community to Revolutionary Marxism (1913–1936)* (in Hebrew) (Tel Aviv: Tel Aviv University and Hakibbutz Hameuchad).

—— (1976), *Anatomy of a Left [Movement]: Left Poalei Tsiyon in Palestine (1919–1946)* (in Hebrew) (Jerusalem: The Hebrew University).

Marin, Bernd (1985), 'Austria—the Paradigm Case of Liberal Corporatism?' in Wyn Grant (ed.), *The Political Economy of Corporatism* (New York: Macmillan), 89–125.

—— (1986), 'Generalized Political Exchange: Preliminary Considerations', paper prepared for the Workshop on 'Political Exchange: Between Governance and Ideology', European University Institute, Florence, 15–18 Dec.

Marks, Gary (1986), 'Neocorporatism and Incomes Policy in Western Europe and North America', *Comparative Politics*, 18(3), 253–77.

Marom, Arie (1988), 'Inflation and Israel's Banking Industry', *Bank of Israel Economic Review*, 62, 30–41.

Mars, Leonard (1980), 'Leadership and Power among Ashdod Port Workers', in E. Marx (ed.), *A Composite Portrait of Israel* (London: Academic Press).

Martin, Andrew (1973), 'The Politics of Economic Policy in the United States: A Tentative View from a Comparative Perspective', Sage Professional Papers in Comparative Politics, No. 01–040. (Beverly Hills: Sage).

—— (1975), 'Is Democratic Control of Capitalist Economies Possible?', in Leon Lindberg, Colin Crouch, and Claus Offe (eds.), *Stress and Contradiction in Modern Capitalism: Public Policy and the Theory of the State* (Lexington, Mass.: D.C. Heath), 13–56.

Martin, Ross (1983), 'Pluralism and the New Corporatism', *Political Studies*, 31(1), 86–102.

Matras, Judah (1965), *Social Change in Israel* (Chicago: Aldine).
——and Dov Weintraub (1977), 'Ethnic and other Primordial Differentials in Intergenerational Mobility in Israel', Discussion Paper No. 25–177, Brookdale Institute (Jerusalem).
Mayshar, Joram (1984), 'Investment Patterns in Israel', Falk Institute Discussion Paper No. 84.07.
Medding, Peter Y. (1972), *Mapai in Israel: Political Organisation and Government in a New Society* (Cambridge: Cambridge University Press).
——(1990), *The Founding of Israeli Democracy: Parties, Politics and Government* (New York: Oxford University Press).
Merhav, Peretz (1980), *The Israeli Left: History, Problems, Documents* (San Diego, Calif.: A. S. Barnes and Co.).
Meridor (Rubin), Leora (1987), 'The Financing of Government Expenditures in Israel, 1960 to 1983' (in Hebrew), *Seker Bank Yisrael*, 62, 3–31.
——(1988), 'The Role of the Public Sector in the Israeli Economy 1960–1986: Facts, Causes and Implications', Working Paper No. 1–88, MIT Program for the Study of the Israeli Economy.
Messere, Kenneth and Owens, Jeffrey (1979), 'The Treatment of Dependent Children under Income Tax and Social Welfare Systems', *International Social Security Review*, 32(1), 50–9.
Metzer, Jacob (1979), *National Capital for a National Home 1919–1921* (in Hebrew) (Jerusalem: Yad Yitzchak Ben-Zvi).
——(1982), 'Fiscal Incidence and Resource Transfer between Jews and Arabs in Mandatory Palestine', *Research in Economic History*, 7, 87–132.
Meunzner, G. (1942), *The Economic Structure of the Histadrut* (in Hebrew) (Jerusalem: Jewish Agency, Economic Research Institute).
Michael, Avraham and Bar-El, Rafael (1967), *Strikes in Israel, 1960–69* (in Hebrew) (Tel Aviv: Bar-Ilan University).
Michaely, Michael (1963), *Foreign Trade and Capital Import in Israel* (in Hebrew) (Tel Aviv: Am Oved).
Miller-Rubenstein, Sondra (1985), *The Communist Movement in Palestine and Israel, 1919–1984* (Boulder, Colo.: Westview Press).
Ministry of Industry and Commerce (Israel) (1987), *Industry in Israel 1986* (in Hebrew) (Jerusalem: Centre for Industrial Planning, Ministry of Industry and Commerce).
Mintz, Alex (1983), 'The Military-industrial Complex: The Israeli Case', *Journal of Strategic Studies*, 6(3), 103–28.
Mironi, Mordhai and Flagler, John J. (1975), *The Histadrut: A Bibliography* (Minneapolis: Industrial Relations Center, University of Minnesota).
Moab, Yitzhak (1982), 'The Social Security System in Israel, 1976–1980', Survey No. 35, National Insurance Institute (Jerusalem).
Morris, Benny (1988), 'The New Historiography: Israel Confronts its Past', *Tikkun*, 3(6), 19–23 and 99–102.
Nahon, Yaakov (1987), *Patterns of Educational Expansion and the Structure of*

Occupational Opportunities—the Ethnic Dimension (in Hebrew) (Jerusalem: Jerusalem Institute for Israel Studies).

—— (1989), *Self-Employed Workers: The Ethnic Dimension* (in Hebrew) (Jerusalem: Jerusalem Institute for Israel Studies).

Namirovsky, M. (1933), 'The Truth about the Strikes and their Causes' (in Hebrew), *Davar*, 9 and 12 Jan.

—— (1935), 'Industrial Relations and Labour Conditions in Jewish Industry in Palestine, 1935' (in Hebrew), *Davar*, 11 Oct.

O'Connor, James (1973), *The Fiscal Crisis of the State* (New York: St Martin's Press).

Ofer, Gur (1967), *The Service Industries in a Developing Economy: Israel as a Case Study* (New York: Praeger and the Bank of Israel).

Offe, Claus (1975), 'The Theory of the Capitalist State and the Problem of Policy Formation', in Leon N. Lindberg, Robert Alford, and Colin Crouch (eds.), *Stress and Contradiction in Modern Capitalism: Public Policy and the Theory of the State* (Lexington, Mass.: D.C. Heath).

Olson, Mancur (1982), *The Rise and Decline of Nations* (New Haven, Conn.: Yale University Press).

Pack, Howard (1971), *Structural Change and Economic Policy in Israel* (New Haven, Conn.: Yale University Press).

Palestine Government (1943), *Report of the Wages Committee* (Jerusalem: Government Printer).

Panitch, Leo (1976), *Social Democracy and Industrial Militancy* (Cambridge: Cambridge University Press).

—— (1981), 'Trade Unions and the Capitalist State', *New Left Review*, 125, 21–43.

—— (1986), *Working-Class Politics in Crisis: Essays on Labour and the State* (London: Verso).

Paterson, William E. and Thomas, Alastair H. (eds.) (1977), *Social Democratic Parties in Western Europe* (London: Croom Helm).

Patinkin, Don (1960), *The Israel Economy: The First Decade* (Jerusalem: Falk Project for Economic Research in Israel).

Peled, Yoav (1989*a*), 'Labor Market Segmentation and Ethnic Conflict: The Social Bases of Right Wing Politics in Israel', paper presented at the 1989 Annual Meeting of the American Political Science Association, Atlanta, 31 Aug.–3 Sept.

—— (1989*b*), *Class and Ethnicity in the Pale: The Political Economy of Workers' Nationalism in Late Imperial Russia* (New York: St Martin's Press).

—— and Shafir, Gershon (1987), 'Split Labor Market and the State: The Effect of Modernization on Jewish Industrial Workers in Tsarist Russia', *American Journal of Sociology*, 92(6), 1435–1460.

Pempel, T. J. (1989), 'Japan's Creative Conservatism: Continuity Under Challenge', in Francis G. Castles (ed.), *The Comparative History of Public Policy* (Cambridge: Polity Press), 149–91.

——(1990), *Uncommon Democracies: The One Party Dominant Regimes* (Ithaca, NY: Cornell University Press).

Peres, Yochanan and Shemer, Sara (1984), 'The Ethnic Factor in Elections', in Dan Caspi, Abraham Diskin, and Emanuel Gutmann (eds.), *The Roots of Begin's Success: The 1981 Israeli Elections* (London: Croom Helm), 89–111.

Peri, Yoram (1983), *Between Battles and Ballots: Israeli Military in Politics* (Cambridge: Cambridge University Press).

——and Neubach, Amnon (1985), 'The Military-Industrial Complex in Israel: A Pilot Study' (Tel Aviv: International Center For Peace in the Middle East).

Perlmutter, Amos (1957), 'Ideology and Organization: The Politics of Socialistic Parties in Israel, 1897–1957', unpublished Ph.D. dissertation, University of California at Berkeley.

Piore, Michael (1979), *Birds of Passage: Migrant Labor and Industrial Societies* (Cambridge: Cambridge University Press).

Pizzorno, Alessandro (1978), 'Political Exchange and Collective Identity in Industrial Relations', in Colin Crouch and Alessandro Pizzorno (eds.), *The Resurgence of Class Conflict in Western Europe since 1968* vol. ii (London: Macmillan), 277–98.

Plunkett, Margaret L. (1958), 'The Histadrut: The General Federation of Jewish Labor in Israel', *Industrial and Labor Relations Review*, 11(2), 155–82.

Pontusson, Jonas (1983), 'Comparative Political Economy of Advanced Capitalist States: Sweden and France', *Kapitalistate*, 10–11, 43–73.

——(1987), 'Radicalization and Retreat in Swedish Social Democracy', *New Left Review*, 165, 5–33.

——(1990), 'Conditions of Labor-Party Dominance: Sweden and Britain Compared', in T. J. Pempel (ed.), *Uncommon Democracies: The One-Party Dominant Regimes* (Ithaca, NY: Cornell University Press), 58–82.

Portugali, Juval (1986), 'Arab Labour in Tel-Aviv: A Preliminary Study', *International Journal of Urban and Regional Research*, 10(3), 351–75.

Preuss, W. (1935), 'Conditions of Work in Palestinian Industry in 1935' (in Hebrew), *Hameshek Hashitufi*, Aug., 218–24.

——(1953), *Social Policy in Israel and Abroad* (in Hebrew) (Tel Aviv: Am Oved).

——(1965), *The Labour Movement in Israel: Past and Present* (Jerusalem: Rubin Mass).

——and Namirovsky, M. (1931), 'A Statistical Survey of Jewish Workers in Palestine', *International Labour Review*, 23(1), 227–39.

Przeworksi, Adam (1985), *Capitalism and Social Democracy* (Cambridge: Cambridge University Press).

——and Sprague, John (1986), *Paper Stones: A History of Electoral Socialism* (Chicago and London: University of Chicago Press).

—— and Wallerstein, Michael (1982*a*), 'The Structure of Class Conflict in Democratic Capitalist Societies', *American Political Science Review*, 76(2), 215–40.

—— (1982*b*), 'Democracy at the Crossroads', *Democracy*, 2, 52–68.

—— (1988), 'Structural Dependence of the State on Capital', *American Political Science Review*, 82(1), 11–29.

Rabinowitz, Aharon (1962), *In the Service of the Jewish Worker* (in Hebrew; originally published in 1929) (Tel Aviv: Histadrut—Tarbut Vechinuch).

Ragin, Charles C. (1987), *The Comparative Method: Moving Beyond Qualitative and Quantitative Strategies* (Berkeley: University of California Press).

Razin, Assaf (1983), 'US Foreign Aid to Israel', *Jerusalem Quarterly*, 29, 11–19.

Reches, Eli (1976), 'Histadrut Activity in the Arab Sector' (in Hebrew), unpublished paper, Shiloach Institute, Tel Aviv University.

Regev, Ariella (1985), 'The Histadrut and the Arab Sector in Israel: Declared Policy and Reality' (in Hebrew), unpublished MA thesis, Department of Labour Studies, Tel Aviv University.

Regini, Marino (1982), 'Changing Relationships between Labour and the State in Italy', in Philippe C. Schmitter and Gerhard Lehmbruch (eds.), *Trends Towards Corporatist Intermediation* (London: Sage), 109–32.

—— (1984), 'The Conditions for Political Exchange: How Concertation Emerged and Collapsed in Italy and Great Britain', in John H. Goldthorpe (ed.), *Order and Conflict in Contemporary Capitalism* (Oxford: Oxford University Press), 124–42.

Reichman, Shalom and Hasson, Shlomo (1984), 'A Cross-Cultural Diffusion of Colonization: From Posen to Palestine', *Annals of the Association of American Geographers*, 74(1), 57–70.

Rein, Martin and Shalev, Michael (1985), 'The Social Service Labor Market in Israel: Past Experience and Future Options', Final Report to the Jerusalem Institute for Israel Studies, Dec.

Reiss, Nira (1988), *Health Services to the Arab Population in Israel* (Tel Aviv: International Center for Peace in the Middle East).

Remba, Oded (1969), 'The Dilemmas of Israel's Economy', *Midstream*, 15(2), 50–62.

Reshef, Yoni (Yonatan) (1981), 'The Impact of Governmental Change in Israel on the Pattern of Political Exchange between Government, Histadrut and Workers: An Inter-period Comparison, October 1973–June 1981' (in Hebrew), unpublished MA thesis, Department of Labour Studies, Tel Aviv University.

—— (1986), 'Political Exchange in Israel: Histadrut–State Relations', *Industrial Relations*, 25(3), 303–19.

—— and Bemmels, Brian (1989), 'Political and Economic Determinants of Strikes in Israel: A Sectorial Comparison', *Economic and Industrial Democracy*, 10(1), 35–57.

——and Fried, Yitzhak (1986), 'Strikes in Israel: The Histadrut in a Sectorial Perspective, 1965–1982', *Relations Industrielles*, 41(2), 329–46.

Reuveni, Jacob (1974), *The Israeli Civil Service, 1948–1973* (in Hebrew) (Ramat Gan: Massada).

——(1980), 'Currents in Political Economy' (in Hebrew), *Rivon Lekalkala*, 106, 3–10.

——(1985), 'The Political Economy of the Likud 1977–1984: A Diagnostic Examination' (in Hebrew), *Rivon Lekalkala*, 126, 237–47.

Riemer, S. (1960), 'Israel: Ten Years of Economic Dependence', *Oxford Economic Papers (New Series)*, 12(2), 141–69.

Robinson, Donna (1966), 'The Histadrut: An Organization of Resource Allocation', *Yavneh Review*, Spring, 185–204.

Rokkan, Stein (1970), 'Nation-Building, Cleavage Formation and the Structuring of Mass Politics', in Rokkan, *Citizens, Elections, Parties: Approaches to the Comparative Study of the Processes of Development* (Oslo: Universitetsforlaget), 72–144.

Rosen, Giora (1974), 'The Trade Union of the Histadrut in the Period of the Second World War' (in Hebrew), unpublished MA thesis, Department of General History, Tel Aviv University.

Rosenberg, Samuel (ed.) (1989), *The State and the Labor Market* (New York: Plenum Press).

Rosenfeld, Henry (1978), 'The Class Situation of the Arab National Minority in Israel', *Comparative Studies in Society and History*, 20(3), 374–407.

——and Carmi, Shulamit (1976), 'The Privatization of Public Means, the State-Made Middle Class, and the Realization of Family Value in Israel', in J. G. Peristiany (ed.), *Kinship and Modernization in Mediterranean Society* (Rome: Center for Mediterranean Studies), 131–59.

Rosenstein, Eliezer (1969), 'Ideology and Practice of Worker Participation in Management: Experiences in Israel, Yugoslavia and England', unpublished Ph.D. dissertation, University of California at Berkeley.

Ross, Arthur M. and Hartman, Paul T. (1960), *Changing Patterns of Industrial Conflict* (New York: John Wiley and Sons).

Roter, Raphael and Shamai, Nira (1971), 'Patterns of Poverty in Israel: Preliminary Findings' (in Hebrew), *Bitachon Soziali*, 1, 17–28.

Rouhana, Nadim (1986), 'Collective Identity and Arab Voting Patterns', in Asher Arian and Michal Shamir (eds.), *The Elections in Israel—1984* (Tel Aviv: Ramot), 121–49.

Rowley, Robin, Bichler, Shimshon, and Nitzan, Jonathan (1988), 'Some Aspects of Aggregate Concentration in the Israeli Economy 1964–1986', Working Paper No. 7/88, Department of Economics, McGill University.

——, ——, and ——(1989), 'The Armadollar–Petrodollar Coalition and the Middle East', Working Paper No. 10/89, Department of Economics, McGill University.

Rubner, Alex (1960), *The Economy of Israel: A Critical Account of the First Ten Years* (London: Frank Cass).

Sabel, Charles F. (1981), 'The Internal Politics of Trade Unions', in Suzanne Berger (ed.), *Organized Interests in Western Europe: Pluralism, Corporatism and the Transformation of Politics* (Cambridge: Cambridge University Press), 209–44.

Sachar, Howard M. (1979), 'Ingathering and the Struggle for Economic Survival', in Sachar, *A History of Israel, i: From the Rise of Zionism to our Time* (New York: Knopf), 395–428.

Salvati, Michele and Brosio, Giorgio (1979), 'The Rise of Market Politics: Industrial Relations in the Seventies', *Daedalus*, 108(2), 43–71.

Sarnat, Marshall (1966), *Saving and Investment Through Retirement Funds in Israel* (Jerusalem: Falk Institute).

Schatz, Ronald W. (1984), 'Review Essay: Labor Historians, Labor Economics, and the Question of Synthesis', *Journal of American History*, 71(1), 93–100.

Schecter, Stephen B. (1972), 'Israeli Political and Economic Elites and Some Aspects of their Relations', unpublished Ph.D dissertation, London University (LSE).

Schindler, Ruben (1976), 'The Pioneering Ideology and the Roots of Social Welfare in the Pre-State Period of Israel', *Journal of Jewish Community Service*, 52(4), 384–92.

Schmidt, Manfred G. (1982), 'The Role of Parties in Shaping Economic Policy', in Francis G. Castles (ed.), *The Impact of Parties* (London: Sage), 97–176.

—— (1988), 'The Politics of Labour Market Policy: Structural and Political Determinants of Rates of Unemployment in Industrial Nations', in Francis G. Castles, Franz Lehner and Manfred G. Schmidt (eds.), *Managing Mixed Economies* (Berlin: de Gruyter), 4–53.

Schmitter, Philippe C. (1974), 'Still the Century of Corporatism?', *The Review of Politics*, 36(1), 85–131.

—— (1981), 'Interest Intermediation and Regime Governability in Contemporary Western Europe and North America', in Suzanne Berger (ed.), *Organizing Interests in Western Europe* (Cambridge: Cambridge University Press), 285–327.

—— (1985),'Neo-corporatism and the State', in Wyn Grant (ed.), *The Political Economy of Corporatism* (London: Macmillan), 32–62.

—— and Lehmbruch, Gerhard (eds.) (1979), *Trends Towards Corporatist Intermediation* (London: Sage).

Schuldiner, Zvi (1982), 'Dependency Theory or Situations of Dependency?' (in Hebrew), unpublished MA thesis, Department of Political Science, Hebrew University of Jerusalem.

—— (1983), 'Military Power in the International Context: Some Reflections on the Israeli Case', paper presented to the Basso Foundation seminar on 'Military Power in Contemporary Society', Turin, 12–16 Dec.

Segal, Zvi (1976), 'The Seamens' Union 1935–1953: From Local to National Union' (in Hebrew), unpublished MA thesis, Department of Labour Studies, Tel Aviv University.

Segev, Tom (1986), *1949: The First Israelis* (New York: The Free Press).

Semyonov, Moshe (1988), 'Bi-Ethnic Labor Markets, Mono-Ethnic Labor Markets, and Socioeconomic Inequality', *American Sociological Review*, 53, 256–66.

—— and Lewin-Epstein, Noah (1987), *Hewers of Wood and Drawers of Water: Noncitizen Arabs in the Israeli Labor Market* (Ithaca, NY: ILR Press).

Shafir, Gershon (1984), 'Changing Nationalism and Israel's "Open Frontier" on the West Bank', *Theory and Society*, 13(6), 803–27.

—— (1989), *Land, Labor and the Origins of the Israeli-Palestinian Conflict 1882–1914* (Cambridge: Cambridge University Press).

—— and Peled, Yoav (1986), '"Thorns in Your Eyes": The Socio-economic Basis of the Kahane Vote', in Asher Arian and Michal Shamir (eds.), *The Elections in Israel—1984* (Tel Aviv: Ramot), 189–206.

Shalev, Michael (1983*a*), 'The Social Democratic Model and Beyond: Two "Generations" of Comparative Research on the Welfare State', *Comparative Social Research*, 6, 315–51.

—— (1983*b*), 'Class Politics and the Western Welfare State', in S. E. Spiro and E. Yuchtman-Yaar (eds.), *Social Policy Evaluation: Social and Political Perspectives* (New York: Academic Press), 27–50.

—— (1983*c*), 'Social Protection, the Labor Movement, and the State in Israel', paper presented at the ECPR Joint Sessions, Freiburg, 20–5 March.

—— (1984), 'The Mid-sixties Recession: A Political-Economic Analysis of Unemployment in Israel' (in Hebrew), *Machbarot Lemechkar Ulebikoret*, 9, 3–54.

—— (1986), 'Winking an Eye at Cheap Arab Labour', *Jerusalem Post*, 7 Jan.

—— (1989*a*), 'Jewish Organized Labor and the Palestinians: A Study in State/Society Relations in Israel', in Baruch Kimmerling (ed.), *The Israeli State and Society: Boundaries and Frontiers* (Albany NY: State University of New York Press), 96–136.

—— (1989*b*), 'Israel's Domestic Policy Regime: Zionism, Dualism, and the Rise of Capital', in Francis G. Castles (ed.), *The Comparative History of Public Policy* (Cambridge: Polity Press), 100–48.

—— (1990*a*), 'Class Conflict, Corporatism and Comparison: The Japanese Enigma', in S. N. Eisenstadt and E. Ben-Ari (eds.), *Japanese Models of Conflict Resolution* (London: Kegan Paul International), 60–93.

—— (1990*b*), 'The Political Economy of Labor Party Dominance and Decline in Israel', in T. J. Pempel (ed.), *Uncommon Democracies: the One Party Dominant Regimes* (Ithaca, NY: Cornell University Press), 83–127.

——and Grinberg, Lev (1989), 'Histadrut–Government Relations and the Transition from a Likud to a National Unity Government: Continuity and Change in Israel's Economic Crisis', Discussion Paper 19–89, Pinhas Sapir Center for Development, Tel Aviv University.

——and Korpi, Walter (1980), 'Working Class Mobilization and American Exceptionalism', *Economic and Industrial Democracy*, 1(1), 31–61.

Shaliv, A. (1981), 'Industry in Israel', Ministry of Industry and Trade, Centre of Industrial Planning (Jerusalem), Sept.

Shamir, Michal (1986), 'Realignment in the Israeli Party System', in Asher Arian and Michal Shamir (eds.), *The Elections in Israel—1984* (Tel Aviv: Ramot), 267–96.

——and Arian, Asher (1982), 'The Ethnic Vote in Israel's 1981 Elections', *Electoral Studies*, 1(3), 315–31.

Shapira, Anita (1977), *Futile Struggle: Hebrew Labour, 1929–1939* (in Hebrew) (Tel Aviv: Tel Aviv University and Kibbutz Meuhad).

——(1984), 'Gedud ha-Avodah: a Dream that Failed', *Jerusalem Quarterly*, 30, 62–76.

Shapiro, Yonathan (1976), *The Formative Years of the Israeli Labour Party* (London: Sage).

——(1978), 'The Party System and Democracy in Israel', unpublished English version of the author's *Democracy in Israel* (publ. in Hebrew by Massada, 1977).

——(1980), 'The End of a Dominant Party System', in Asher Arian (ed.), *The Elections in Israel, 1977* (Jerusalem: Jerusalem Academic Press), 23–38.

——(1984), *An Elite Without Successors: Generations of Political Leaders in Israel* (in Hebrew) (Tel Aviv: Sifriat Hapoalim).

——and Grinberg, Lev (1988), 'The Crisis of Full Employment, 1957–1965: A Chapter in the Political Economy of Israel' (in Hebrew), Discussion Paper No. 45, Golda Meir Institute, Tel Aviv University.

Sharkansky, Ira (1979), *Wither the State? Politics and Public Enterprise in Three Countries* (Chatham, NJ: Chatham House).

——(1987), *The Political Economy of Israel* (New Brunswick, NJ: Transaction Books).

——and Radian, Alex (1982), 'Changing Domestic Policy 1977–1981', in Robert O. Freedman (ed.), *Israel in the Begin Era* (New York: Praeger), 56–75.

Shavit, Yossi (1984), 'Tracking and Ethnicity in Israeli Secondary Education', *American Sociological Review*, 49(2), 210–20.

——(1988), 'Arabs in the Israeli Economy: A Study of the Enclave Hypothesis', paper prepared for the Meeting of the ISA Research Committee on Social Stratification, Madison, Wis., Aug.

Sherman, A. V. (1958), 'Power Politics in Israel's Economy', *The New Leader*, 22, Sept. 14–16.

Shimshoni, Daniel (1982), *Israeli Democracy: The Middle of the Journey* (New York: Free Press).

Shirom, Arie (1969), 'The Implementation of General Collective Agreements in Enterprises in the Metal Industry' (in Hebrew), *Avodah Ubituach Leumi*, 21(12), 471–4.

——(1971), 'Workers' Committees in the Israeli Labour Relations System: an Appraisal', *Industrial Relations Journal*, 2(1), 66–74.

——(1974), 'Towards the Establishment of a Trilateral Power Structure in Industrial Relations—Lessons of the Strike at "Elite"' (in Hebrew), *Netivei Irgun Uminhal*, 10(3–4), 72–86.

——(1975), 'Union Use of Staff Experts: The Case of the Histadrut', *Industrial and Labor Relations Review*, 29(1), 107–20.

——(1977), 'The Collective Agreement for Production Workers, 1976–1977' (in Hebrew), *Rivon Lekalkala*, 95, 358–67.

——(1980), 'Comment on "Political Parties and Democracy in the Histadrut"', *Industrial Relations*, 19(2), 231–7.

——(1983), *Introduction to Labour Relations in Israel* (in Hebrew) (Tel Aviv: Am Oved).

——(1984), 'Employers' Associations in Israel', in John Windmuller and Alan Gladstone (eds.), *Employers' Associations and Industrial Relations* (Oxford: Clarendon Press), 294–317.

——and Jacobson, Dan (1976), 'The Structure and Function of Israeli Employers' Associations', *Relations Industrielles*, 30(3), 452–75.

Shlonsky, Hagith (1971), 'Welfare in Israel in a Comparative Perspective', Working Paper, Center for the Study of Welfare Policy, University of Chicago, Nov.

Shorter, Edward T. and Tilly, Charles (1974), *Strikes in France 1830–1968* (Cambridge: Cambridge University Press).

Sicron, Moshe (1957), *Immigration to Israel: 1948–1953*, CBS Special Series No. 60 (Jerusalem: Falk Project and Central Bureau of Statistics).

Silver, Beverly (1990), 'The Contradictions of Semiperipheral "Success": The Case of Israel', in William G. Martin (ed.), *Semiperipheral States in the World-Economy* (New York: Greenwood Press), 161–81.

Skocpol, Theda (1984), 'Emerging Agendas and Recurrent Strategies in Historical Sociology', in Skocpol (ed.), *Vision and Method in Historical Sociology* (Cambridge: Cambridge University Press), 356–91.

——(1985), 'Bringing the State Back In: Strategies of Analysis in Current Research', in Peter B. Evans, Dietrich Rueschemeyer, and Theda Skocpol (eds.), *Bringing the State Back In* (Cambridge: Cambridge University Press), 3–37.

Slutsky, Shlomo (1985), '"Hebrew Labour": A Slogan for a Time of Unemployment. The Attitude of the Histadrut to the Entry of Workers from the Territories into the Israeli Labour Market' (in Hebrew), unpublished seminar paper, Department of Sociology, Tel Aviv University, Oct.

Smith, Barbara (1978), 'British Economic Policy in Palestine Towards the Development of the Jewish National Home: 1920–1929', unpublished D.Phil. dissertation, Oxford University.

Smooha, Sammy (1978), *Israel: Pluralism and Conflict* (Berkeley: University of California Press).

—— (1980), *The Orientation and Politicization of the Arab Minority in Israel* (Haifa: Jewish–Arab Centre, Haifa University).

—— (1982), 'Existing and Alternative Policy Towards Arabs in Israel', *Ethnic and Racial Studies*, 5(1), 71–98.

—— (1986), 'Three Approaches to the Sociology of Ethnic Relations in Israel', *Jerusalem Quarterly*, 40, 31–61.

Sokoler, Meir (1984), 'The Inflationary Tax on the Monetary Base, the Inflationary Subsidy Implicit in Cheap Credit, and their Influence on the Inflationary Process in Israel' (in Hebrew), Discussion Paper No. 84.05, Bank of Israel Research Department.

Spilerman, Seymour and Habib, Jack (1976), 'Development Towns in Israel: The Role of Community in Creating Ethnic Disparities in Labor Force Characteristics', *American Journal of Sociology*, 81(4), 781–812.

Sprinzak, Ehud (1977), 'Extreme Politics in Israel', *Jerusalem Quarterly*, 5, 33–47.

Stephens, John D. (1979), *The Transition from Capitalism to Socialism* (London: Macmillan).

Stier, Chaya and Lewin-Epstein, Noah (1988), 'The Sectoral Structure of the Labour Market in Israel' (in Hebrew), *Megamot*, 31(2), 111–32.

Streeck, Wolfgang (1981), 'Qualitative Demands and the Neo-corporatist Manageability of Industrial Relations', *British Journal of Industrial Relations*, 14, 149–69.

—— (1984), 'Neo-Corporatist Industrial Relations and the Economic Crisis in West Germany', Working Paper No. 97, European University Institute (Florence).

—— Schmitter, Philippe, and Martinelli, Alberto (1979), 'The Organization of Business Interests', Discussion Paper No. 80–23, International Institute of Management (Berlin).

Studni, Zeev (1974), 'The Strike of "Nesher" Workers' (in Hebrew), *Meassef*, 6, 166–75.

Sussman, Zvi (1969*a*), 'The Policy of the Histadrut with regard to Wage Differentials: A Study of the Impact of Egalitarian Ideology and Arab Labour on Jewish Wages in Palestine', unpublished Ph.D. dissertation, Hebrew University of Jerusalem.

—— (1969*b*), 'From a National to a Branch-level Wage Policy' (in Hebrew), *Rivon Lekalkala*, 64, 331–41.

—— (1973*a*), 'The Wage Policy of the Histadrut: Its Effect on Israel's Economy', in Isaiah Avrech and Dan Giladi (eds.), *Labor and Society in Israel: a Selection of Studies* (Tel Aviv: Tel Aviv University and the Histadrut), 56–78.

——(1973*b*), 'The Determination of Wages for Unskilled Labor in the Advanced Sector of the Dual Economy of Mandatory Palestine', *Economic Development and Cultural Change*, 22(1), 95–113.

——(1974),'National Wage Restraint Policy' (in Hebrew), *Rivon Lekalkala*, 80–1, 39–52.

——and Zakai, Dan (1985), *Changes in the Wage Structure of the Civil Service and Rising Inflation—Israel: 1974–81* (Jerusalem: Bank of Israel Research Department).

Swirski, Shlomo (1979), 'Remarks on the Historical Sociology of the Yishuv Period' (in Hebrew), *Machbarot Lemechkar Ulebikoret*, 2, 5–41.

——(1984), 'The Oriental Jews in Israel', *Dissent*, Winter, 77–91.

Szereszewski, Robert (1968), *Essays on the Structure of the Jewish Economy in Palestine and Israel* (Jerusalem: Israel Universities' Press for the Falk Institute).

Tabb, Jay Yanai (1964), 'Israel's Socio-Economic Planning and the Role of Its Interest Groups', paper presented at the Research Conference on Industrial Relations and Economic Development, Geneva, 24 Aug.–4 Sept.

——(1966), 'Israel's Socio-Economic Planning and the Role of Its Interest Groups', in Arthur M. Ross (ed.), *Industrial Relations and Economic Development* (London: Macmillan), 273–95.

——Ami, Yosef, and Shaal, Gil (1961), *Labour Relations in Israel* (in Hebrew) (Tel Aviv: Dvir).

Tamari, Salim (1980), 'The Palestinians in the West Bank and Gaza: The Sociology of Dependency', in Khalil Nakhleh and Elia Zureik (eds.), *The Sociology of the Palestinians* (London: Croom Helm), 84–110.

Teveth, Shabbtai (1988), 'Ben-Gurion the Histadrut Secretary' (in Hebrew), in Shlomo Avineri (ed.), *David Ben-Gurion as a Labour Leader* (in Hebrew) (Tel Aviv: Am Oved), 12–45.

Therborn, Göran (1985), 'The Coming of Swedish Social Democracy', in Enzo Collotti (ed.), *L'Internazionale Operaia e Socialista tra le due guerre* (Milan: Fondazione Giancomo Feltrinelli), 527–93.

——(1986), *Why some Peoples are More Unemployed than Others* (London: Verso).

——(1988), 'Does Corporatism Really Matter? The Economic Crisis and Issues of Political Theory', *Journal of Public Policy*, 7(3), 259–84.

——(1989), '"Pillarization" and "Popular Movements", Two Variants of Welfare State Capitalism: the Netherlands and Sweden', in Francis G. Castles (ed.), *The Comparative History of Public Policy* (Cambridge: Polity Press), 192–241.

Titmuss, Richard Morris (1974), *Social Policy* (London: George Allen and Unwin).

Tokatli, Rachel (1979), 'Political Patterns in Labour Relations in Israel' (in Hebrew), unpublished Ph.D. dissertation, Tel Aviv University.

Tov, Imri (1988), 'The Economic Upheaval of 1977—Implementation of Operational Goals' (in Hebrew), *Rivon Lekalkala*, 135–6, 33–47.

Tsaban, Yair (1978), 'The Strike: Analysis' (in Hebrew), *Emda*, 3(8), 16–43.

Tsachor, Zeev (1979), 'The Histadrut—The Formative Period' (in Hebrew), unpublished Ph.D. dissertation, Department of History of the Jewish People, Hebrew University of Jerusalem.

Tufte, Edward R. (1978), *Political Control of the Economy* (Princeton, NJ: Princeton University Press).

Urieli, Nachman and Barzilai, Amnon (1982), *The Rise and Fall of the Democratic Movement for Change* (in Hebrew) (Tel Aviv: Reshefim).

Uusitalo, Hannu (1989), 'Income Distribution in a Comparative Perspective', in Uusitalo, *Income Distribution in Finland* (Helsinki: Central Statistical Office of Finland), 77–83.

Viteles, Harry (1966), *A History of the Co-operative Movement in Israel* (London: Valentine Mitchell).

Vogel, David (1987), 'The New Political Science of Corporate Power', *The Public Interest*, 87, 63–79.

Wasserman, Shlomo *et al.* (1961), 'The Formation of Annual Wage Policy' (in Hebrew), in Yaakov Simons (ed.), *Anthology of Publications and Lectures on Industrial Relations* (in Hebrew) (Jerusalem: Hebrew University, Department of Business Administration), 234–43.

Wasserstein, Bernard (1974), 'British Officials and the Arab–Jewish Conflict in Palestine 1917–1929', unpublished D.Phil. dissertation, Nuffield College, Oxford.

Watad, Muhammad (1966), 'Unemployment Haunts the Arab Village', *New Outlook*, Sept., 29–32.

Weinshall, Theodore (1976), 'The Industrialization of a Rapidly Developing Country—Israel', in Robert Dubin (ed.), *Handbook of Work, Organization and Society* (Chicago: Rand McNally), 949–89.

Weissbrod, Lilly (1983), 'Economic Factors and Political Strategies: The Defeat of the Revisionists in Mandatory Palestine', *Middle Eastern Studies*, 19(3), 326–44.

—— (1984), 'The Rise and Fall of the Revisionist Party, 1928–1935', *Jerusalem Quarterly*, 30, 80–93.

Wilensky, Harold L. (1975), *The Welfare State and Equality: Structural and Ideological Roots of Public Expenditure* (Berkeley University of California Press).

—— (1981), 'Leftism, Catholicism, and Democratic Corporatism: The Role of Political Parties in Recent Welfare State Development', in Peter Flora and Arnold J. Heidenheimer (eds.), *The Development of Welfare States in Europe and America* (New Brunswick, NJ: Transaction), 345–82.

—— and Lebeaux, Charles N. (1965), *Industrial Society and Social Welfare* (New York: Free Press).

Wolfe, Alan (1978), 'Has Social Democracy a Future?', *Comparative Politics*, 11(1), 100–25.

Wolfsfeld, Gadi (1988), *The Politics of Provocation: Participation and Protest in Israel* (Albany, NY: State University of New York Press).

Yadlin, Asher (1980), *Testimony* (in Hebrew) (Jerusalem: Eidanim).

Yago, Glenn (1977), 'Whatever Happened to the Promised Land? Capital Flows and the Israeli State', *Berkeley Journal of Sociology*, 21, 117–46.

Yanai, Nathan (1981), *Party Leadership in Israel: Maintenance and Change* (Ramat Gan and London: Turtledove).

Yatziv, Gadi (1979), 'The Class Basis of Party Affiliation—the Israeli Case' (in Hebrew), Papers in Sociology, Hebrew University of Jerusalem.

Yitzchaki, Aharon (1974), '"Achdut Avodah", a Zionist Socialist Association of Eretz Yisrael Workers, as a Trade Union and in "Chevrat Ovdim" (1919–1926)' (in Hebrew), unpublished Ph.D. dissertation, Department of History of the Jewish People, Hebrew University of Jerusalem.

Yitzchaki, Ilan (1970), 'The Histadrut Pension Funds' (in Hebrew), unpublished seminar paper, Department of Labour Studies, Tel Aviv University.

Yoran, Yosef (1987), 'An Economy in Structural Crisis: Israel since the Oil Crisis and the Yom Kippur War' (in Hebrew), *Rivon Lekalkala*, 131, 827–54.

Zalmanovitch, Yair (1981), 'Histadrut, Kupat Cholim, Government' (in Hebrew), unpublished MA thesis, Department of Political Science, Haifa University.

Zloczower, Avraham (1972), 'Occupation, Mobility and Social Class', *Social Science Information*, 11(5), 329–58.

Zureik, Elia T. (1979), *The Palestinians in Israel: A Study in Internal Colonialism* (London: Routledge and Kegan Paul).

Zweig, Ferdynand (1959), 'The Jewish Trade Union Movement in Israel', *Jewish Journal of Sociology*, 1(1), 23–42.

Author Index

Subject Index